POLITIQUE

The Conway Lectures in Medieval Studies
Delivered in the Medieval Institute of the University of Notre Dame
September 2003

POLITIQUE

Languages of Statecraft between Chaucer and Shakespeare

PAUL STROHM

University of Notre Dame Press
Notre Dame, Indiana

Manufactured in the United States of America

Library of Congress Cataloging-in-Publication Data
Strohm, Paul, 1938–
Politique : languages of statecraft between Chaucer and Shakespeare / Paul Strohm.
p.   cm.—(The Conway lectures in medieval studies)
Includes bibliographical references and index.
ISBN 0-268-04113-x (cloth : alk. paper)
ISBN 0-268-04114-8 (pbk. : alk. paper)
1. English literature—Middle English, 1100–1500—History and criticism.
2. Politics and literature—Great Britain—History—To 1500.
3. Great Britain—Politics and government—1399–1485.   4. Political poetry,
English—History and criticism.   I. Title.   II. Series.
PR275.P63S77   2005
820.9'358'0902—dc22

2005004934

Edward IV on Fortune's Wheel.
Courtesy of British Library. MS Harl 7353.

To Claire Harman

contents

POLITIQUE

introduction

Fifteenth-century England experienced its own 'pre-Machiavellian moment,' climaxing in the tumultuous decades roughly bounded by Richard duke of York's return to England in 1450 and the end of the Yorkist dynasty in 1485.[1] These unruly decades sponsored pragmatic political discussion of a sort not previously seen in England and not to be seen again before the middle of the sixteenth century. Writers of these decades had no need to wait for Machiavelli to find their voice in matters of practical statecraft and political calculation. In corroboration of this point, I read a number of mainly vernacular English political texts of the fifteenth and, occasionally, sixteenth centuries, together with lateral looks at several contemporary writings from Burgundy, France, and Italy. In these texts, I discover a broad contemporary confluence of shrewdly informed, unsentimental writings, keenly concerned with political practice in the world. When compared with these canny precursors, Machiavelli, for all his brilliance, looks less like an inaugurator and more like a participant in a general tendency.

Intricately connected with this activated discussion of worldly politics is a revised, more hopeful view of the individual's relation to Fortune and her operations. Fortune herself had always enjoyed some operative discretion in the mundane world but was always, as it were, divinely deputized as executress of God's decrees. This combination of local discretion and ultimate divine authorization meant that, before the fifteenth century, Fortune would prevail one way or the other. Her decrees could be evaded, but only through strategies of self-curtailment, in which personal expectations and demands were reduced beneath any threshold of recognizably political action. Machiavelli himself stopped short of arguing that Fortune could be trumped or wholly avoided, suggesting only that, at best, one might forestall her ravages by exercising ingenuity in 'leaping from wheel to wheel.'[2] Emergent in fifteenth-century England is, however, an alternative possibility, in which the prudent prince can effectively Fortune-proof himself by exercise of foresight and qualities of *vertue*—this trait remarkably anticipatory of its Italian and Machiavellian counterpart, *virtù*. This view is introduced to England by a poet not known for his innovativeness, John Lydgate, and flourishes in the second half of the fifteenth century.

This emergent view, in which reason can turn the astute prince from Fortune's inevitable victim into her beneficiary or even her master, is illustrated for the later fifteenth century in the frontispiece to this volume. This illustration of the early 1460s, taken from British Library (BL) MS Harley 7353, appears at first glance as a rather conventional rendition of that moment when Edward IV, poised at the top of Fortune's wheel, enjoys his turn at majesty prior to his inevitable descent. This iconography is reinforced by the fact that his Lancastrian predecessors are portrayed, labeled by name, as having already tumbled from the wheel. Its reception as a dour commentary on kingship's limited prospects is encouraged by a whole analytical and representational tradition, stretching back to Boccaccio and Jean de Meun and, behind them, to the rise of the goddess Fortuna and the imagery of her wheel.[3]

This image nevertheless introduces several departures from tradition. One departure is a counterattempt to secure Edward from time and change by situating his accomplishments as something of a terminus, as a fulfillment of past prophecy. Quotations from the Psalms emphasize Edward's kingship as a providential inheritance (Ps. 2:8) and Edward as conqueror (Ps. 2:1–2), as appointed by God (Ps. 2:6), as a liberator from oppression (Ps. 2:3), as an ally of the Lord (Ps. 2:4), and as a beneficiary of God's ire against his adversaries (Ps. 2:5). Rather than haplessly subject to time and change, Edward is shown by images elsewhere in the scroll to enjoy God's protection, his successes divinely ordained. We are shown Edward's genealogy in the form of a Joshua tree; his providential deliverance in the flight to Calais, compared with Christ's deliverance from the Slaughter of the Innocents; his mercy to Henry VI at Northampton, with David's unction for Saul; his vision of the three crowns, to the trinity appearing to Moses in a bush; his own conquest at Towton, compared typologically to the victories of Joshua.

Another of this image's mild surprises involves a new direction for its own exemplarity. Depictions and descriptions of Fortune's wheel invariably possess an exemplary aspect, of an essentially homiletic sort, but this image offers an alternate imagining of its own reception by inscribing an audience consisting of the parliamentary classes of the realm. The wheel is flanked, on the viewer's left, by the clerical hierarchy of the realm and, on the right, by the nobility. These parties are the audience, not just of a moral, but of a political process—and, were it not otherwise political, their adjudicatory presence would make it so. Moreover, this illustration introduces another reallocation of responsibility, in that its crucial actor is not the king himself but rather *Ratio*, or Reason. Although Reason may be partially allegorized as an exemplification of Edward's own inner reason, this image of Reason on public view and arrayed in the robes of an English judge accents a new and more general role of Reason as an arbiter of secular conduct. In this respect, Reason may be thought to exemplify the highest statutory principles on which these parliamentary classes operate.[4] Earlier iconographic traditions had placed Fortune on her own wheel, and later medieval representations increased her centrality (and the world's variousness) by making her responsible for turning the wheel, often with a hand-crank.[5] Henceforth, this illustration suggests, other principles will guide the rotation of her wheel.

The most significant of this image's departures, and the most indicative of a new fifteenth-century climate, involves the nature of *Ratio*'s activities. For *Ratio* is not implementing the process, or even just overseeing it, but *intervening* in a new and unprecedented way, by 'spiking' the wheel to arrest its course. The suggestion is, in other words, that the worldly minded prince who consults properly within the realm and who allies himself to Reason can defeat arbitrary Fortune and can secure himself in the world. Armed with the right qualities and the right associates, Edward may hope to stop, or at least substantially to forestall, the unwelcome rotation of fortunes to which his less well counseled predecessors have been subjected. This is, I want to suggest, a very new and even audacious mind-set, a mind-set that both sponsors and relies upon new assumptions and a new language for the conduct of worldly affairs. Within Fortune's own traditional ambit, other forces now prevail. In this evacuation of Fortune from her own representational abode, she is scandalously revealed as supernumerary, as inessential to a description of alterations in the political process. In one of his revealing asides, the mid-fifteenth-century Burgundian and French statesman

Commynes refers to 'so-called fortune'—to 'la fortune ou ce qu'on y appelle.'[6] Similarly, a Milanese ambassador, predicting that Edward IV will rashly overstep and thus fall prey to Queen Margaret, expects him to provide a remarkable example of what prudent men, in excuse for human errors, have called Fortune ('uno singulo exemplo de quella che li prudenti homini in excusa de li errori humani han nominato fortuna').[7] In each case, the implication, widely shared in the middle decades of the fifteenth century, is that 'Fortune' really stands in for causes that, more fully understood, might be neutralized or even mastered altogether.[8]

The idea that Fortune might be mastered, her wheel arrested in its course, opens a space for the practice of statecraft, for a conception of the state as a conscious creation and a product of human exertion. Burckhardt's characterization of the quattrocento Italian state as *Kunstwerk,* as work of art, has long since fallen by the wayside of historical discussion, and I am unready to court anachronism by declaring myself an uncritical follower.[9] Yet, as the author of a bold and oversimplifying generalization, Burckhardt might at least receive some credit for the discussion he helped to inspire. I mean to suggest that he was not all wrong in his announcement of a 'new fact' about the Italian state 'as the outcome of reflection and calculation.' New kinds of 'reflection' and, especially, 'calculation' about politics and the state are fully on view in fifteenth-century England, and appear often in my study— although more in relation to particular linguistic contexts than to political philosophy writ large.

The depiction of Edward IV on Fortune's wheel requires accompanying writing for its effects, both in its citation of prophecy and in labeling the figure by the wheel as *Ratio* or *Resoun.* Like every other development that interests me in this study, this check to Fortune's wheel is signaled by, and requires, the resignification of an older terminology and the emergence of a newer one. For the artistry of statecraft, as I describe it, relies crucially upon new language and revised linguistic deployments. A general reluctance to view the fifteenth century as innovative in any significant respect lingers as our unfortunate legacy from all those bold theories of 'Early Modern' revolution and departure. The time is right to revise this view of the fifteenth century as a time of stasis, or even decline, in the linguistic as well as coordinate political spheres. One rallying point for such reconsideration is a coterie volume, *Revolution Reassessed,* published by Christopher Coleman and David Starkey, in which G. R. Elton's account of Tudor 'Revolution' is revised by an account of Yorkist England as an age of significant governmental reform;

and, moveover, 'an age in which the need for reform was widely recognized and was justified in language that prefigured the sixteenth-century usage.'[10]

Discovering in the mid-fifteenth century the rise of a 'new and still unfinalized English political language,' Starkey centers his own analysis on the origins in the 1450s of *commonwealth/commonweal.*[11] I am much concerned here with an emphasis on *politique* behavior, a term no longer referring only to those who make generous arrangements for the good of all but also to those who make the best possible arrangements for themselves. Stretched far from its earlier, optimistic shape, *politique* behavior now extends to those who employ lies, deceptions, and even falsely sworn oaths as possible elements of good political practice. The arts of *pollecie* are considered, especially the extension of its aegis to include not only those acts beneficial to the common good but also those that suggest circumspection and thoughtful self-interest. I am interested in the concept of *parcyalle* behavior, not just as an aberration or abrogation of good conduct, but as a potential accompaniment of normal legal and political practice. Rather than devastating to one's good repute, *dowblenesse,* as a derivative of partiality, comes to be seen as an allowable or even inevitable tendency, as at worst an acceptable downside and at best a sign of worldly good practice. Writers of this period will give a novel and unprecedented turn to existing ideas of *perjury,* in which the capacity for tactical untruth or even blasphemous misuse of the sacraments is recognized not just as a criminal flaw but as a possible element of astute leadership. Several of the traditional Cardinal Virtues—especially those designated as moral or secular rather than theological—are given new application. New valuations are placed upon such established traits as *prudence* and *vertue* itself for the magistrate or secular ruler, with the advantage of such qualities to policy making underpinning their revalorization in political discourse. *Resoun* is assigned a new role in their implementation; no longer simply counseling the avoidance of earthly ambitions and objectives, new-style reason is redeployed as an antidote to Fortune's snares. The workhorse terms are long-standing, with one combination or other of fortitude, temperance, justice, and prudence stretching back to Aristotle's *Ethics,* and available to the Middle Ages in writings by Cicero, Macrobius, Vincent of Beauvais, and others. But they are increasingly put to new work in a burgeoning discussion of statecraft, practical strategy, and the art of personal advancement and political survival.

My conceptual interest in this topic is partially adumbrated in Quentin Skinner's remark, 'The clearest sign that a society has entered into the selfconscious possession of a new concept is . . . that a new vocabulary comes to be generated, in terms of which the concept is then articulated and discussed.'[12] I find much in this formulation to admire, including Skinner's emphasis on the inextricable connection between language and politics. Yet, even as he captures much of the impetus behind my own work, my experience in writing this study argues for necessary modification of his terms and assumptions. Undoubtedly aware that in raising the matter of linguistic innovation he is tackling one of the most perplexing of issues, he seems inclined to take refuge in a partial obfuscation, suggesting that a new vocabulary 'comes to be generated,' without suggesting why or how. But, even as he discreetly veils his presuppositions on the one hand, so does he reveal them on the other. For his central assumption is that linguistic change proceeds from settled resolve: from conscious purpose or intent. As implied in this short quotation, his model presupposes a rational and purposeful world, in which actors always know what they are doing, and why, and do not plunge ahead into a maelstrom of words and deeds without a cogent consideration of means and ends, costs and benefits. This presupposition is, in turn, revealed in the temporal decorum that he postulates for the unfolding of a linguistic event. In the statement quoted above, (1) concepts precede language, and (2) as a result of them language comes to be 'generated,' and (3) new language enables retroactive discussion of the concepts that have sponsored its introduction.

Despite a professed interest in wholly new language, most of Skinner's imagined situations then skirt the issue of innovation by imagining a purposeful or intending actor who sets out to explain and justify a set of actions in existing terms. This 'political actor' becomes an 'agent' by selecting among descriptive terms already in existence and already possessed of distinctive criteria for their application. Such agents are not wholly sovereign, though, since their self-justifying activity requires them to choose within 'the normative vocabulary which any society employs for description and appraisal of its political life' (p. xii). Language, in other words, asserts itself as a guard rail, by requiring an agent to justify his prior choices by apt choice among preexisting linguistic terms. Thus, '[t]o recover the nature of the normative vocabulary available to an agent for the description and appraisal of his conduct is at the same time to indicate one of the constraints on his conduct itself.'[13] Regarding language as an external constraint, this model devalues its more active importance as a crucible of new perceptions and actions.

By imagining that social change occurs prior to, and hence independently of, language, this system leaves crucial areas of linguistic and social activity under- or unacknowledged. Language is permitted an impact upon conduct, in the sense that our agent must elect behaviors consistent with this or that term's protective umbrella. But the ghost in this machine is, at every point, the prelinguistic intention that governs choice within the aegis of 'prevailing language.' Certainly, I applaud Skinner's contextual treatment of language and linguistic choice, and I would not be dwelling on his theories if I did not find them provocative and illuminating. But the ordinary relation of text and context, language and social reality, seem to me far less purposeful, and far more vitally reciprocal, than his system allows.[14] In my view, full engagement with the complexities of linguistic situations can only be hindered, or even prevented, by a determination to regard all linguistic phenomena as issuing from the settled intentions of fully self-aware actors. My own view is that we come closer to the dynamics of linguistic process when we look first to see how language is deployed in actual situations, taking as an analytical starting point what a text is and *does,* rather than what it was intended to do.[15]

I propose to retain Skinner's interest in linguistic innovation and in larger linguistic and social matrices in which utterances are formed, while jettisoning his insistence on clearly defined intentions and orderly causal sequences. This step enables a sense of language as actively and immediately implicated in the formulation of new social possibilities—not just available for after-the-fact rationalizations, but rather present at the creation. In this regard I might mention a second, and more enduring, allegiance to the political linguistics of J. G. A. Pocock, especially as expressed in 'The Concept of a Language and the *Métier d' Historien.*'[16] Pocock's particular contribution to the discussion is his perception that 'language determines what can be said in it, but is capable of being modified by what is said in it' (p. 20). His explanation hinges on the interaction of *langue,* or language-system, on the one hand and *parole,* or individual utterance, on the other. Pressured by the exigencies of its context or circumstances of articulation, the individual utterance may be itself innovative, reinstating a superseded usage, resignifying an inherited term, proposing a new application. This is not to suggest an absence of constraint by the existence of a language system and the formation of an utterance within that system. As Pocock rather awkwardly but importantly formulates it: 'We may think—it is important to be able to think—of [an individual's] *parole* as a response to pressures imposed upon him by the *paroles* of others; but if we are to write history in terms of the interactions of *parole* and *langue,* it is important to see his *parole* as a response to the conventions of *langue* which he is using and of which he is more or less aware' (p. 33). Fair enough. But the thing I value most in Pocock's system is his awareness that the individual speech-act, considered as an event in its own right, possesses a dynamic capacity, a capacity not only for selective reiteration but also for innovation.[17] I do not mean to canonize Pocock. He seems to me unnecessarily skittish, and perhaps even a bit phobic, in his need to protect his concept of *langue* from contamination by unprecedented applications of *parole* ('if we allow the boundaries between *parole* and *langue* to become too fluid, any utterance which long sustains an individual style may be mistaken for the language in which it was uttered'—p. 21). An ultimately more serious problem—surprising for a historian—is that, granting the importance of context in the determination of utterance, he opts for a rather depleted sense in which the context of an utterance is merely other utterances, solely linguistic rather than linguistic *and* material. But these are merely cavils, and the responsibility for finding my own voice on such matters as the singularity of the utterance and the materiality of context rests with me in the course of this study. In the meantime, I embrace Pocock's salutary awareness of a possible synergy between altered situations and novel utterances, in the production of new political descriptions and—just possibly—new political actions as well.

All this comes down finally to words—to what they mean or are taken to mean, to who uses them or gets to use them. Old words freshly employed, imported words borrowed from adjacent languages or contexts, new coinages—words will, in a sense, jostle with speakers *of* words as protagonists of this study. For words possess their own capacity to underwrite or undermine, inspire or disable, political initiatives. This view of words is the basis of my common cause with John Watts, who has provocatively argued that, rather than conform to preexisting political ideas, words might contain within themselves not only corroborative but also innovative possibilities— or, at the very least, the capacity to underwrite new courses of action. 'Following this line of thought,' he says, 'it might be argued that the "political ideas" that really shape politics are soundbites, buzz-words, strings of interrelated terms and pre-packaged sections of argument: they exist, and flourish, and propagate themselves principally in the words which constitute them.'[18] Language—that is, words and phrases—may, in this sense, be regarded as possessing its own capacity for incitement, a corroborative or even initiatory or 'action-seeking' dimension, prior to any settled resolve on the part of the person who wields it.[19] What I want to suggest is a heady creative brew in which performative or action-seeking languages—in close association with symbolic deeds and events—create something new.[20] I speak of a matrix, predominantly linguistic but also symbolic in a more general sense, that 'structures' action, along the lines of the theories of regulated improvisation and structuration originally proposed by Bourdieu and Giddens.[21]

In their task of producing new social possibilities, the writings considered in this study invariably possess a highly activated sense of audience, an assumption that attentive reception is not theirs automatically or by right but must be sought and won. Their aspirational 'audience' is less a constant than a moving variable. Because these writings often set out to create their own constituency as an element of their performance, the formation of an 'audience' becomes one of the text's goals, and a matter for the analyst's inquiry and conjecture, rather than a settled point of reference. Most of the works under consideration are contextualized in ways that allow us to know one thing or another about their audience: that Lydgate's *Fall of Princes* is a sponsored production for Duke Humfrey, that Fortescue's 'Declaration' readdresses the public of his letters from Scotland, that the 1460 'Verses Posted on the Gates of Canterbury' are broadly aimed at the populace of that city, that the earlier versions of the *Arrivall* of Edward IV were written to reassure princes of Europe, and the like. Yet each of these works is also audience-seeking in less explicit ways, oriented partway toward an unspecified shadow audience, the engagement of which is one of its unstated goals. Closely associated with these works' search for their own audience is their reliance upon new possibilities for circulation. New or enhanced technologies of address include the production of elaborate texts for time- and site-specific bill posting; the preparation of sponsored history in the form of pamphlets, newsletters, and sponsored chronicles; and, although represented here by only one instance, the preparation of illustrated rolls for public display.[22] Perhaps most dramatically of all, the stimulating interface between manuscript and print culture will come into play, especially in the circumstances surrounding the mid-sixteenth-century composition of the *Mirror for Magistrates*.

A further expression of these works' interest in audience is their sensitivity to what may be considered apt sites and forums of public persuasion. Such a forum might have a parliamentary flavor, but I am equally interested in a range of other, unofficial or nonparliamentary occasions. These might include a crowd gathered for purposes of acclamation, as in the first stages of Edward IV's move to the crown; or the wary citizens of York who first resisted and then acquiesced in Edward's 1471 effort to regain his crown; or the London populace who debunked Henry VI's last, failed, public procession, purportedly dressed in his old blue gown and preceded by an elderly retainer carrying a foxtail on a staff (as a result of which, we are told, 'he lost many and wan noon or Rygth ffewe').[23]

The processes by which audiences are composed and addressed are fluid and provisional, varying with the situations in which they are employed. Rather than win over a monolithic 'audience' all at once, these texts must content themselves with partial or provisional gains in a fluid or indeterminate situation. In fact, with respect to such simplifying labels as 'Lancastrian' or 'Yorkist,' there was quite simply no monolithic audience to be won.[24] I hope I may be permitted to use these terms from time to time, simply as a matter of convenience in delineating a general or relative position, but always with a sense of how unrevealing they are, with respect to the political cross-currents at any particular moment in time. Militating against confident use of these terms is the presence of opportunists, crossovers, turncoats, and the genuinely uncommitted; the ebb and flow of temporary interests; and also the distinctive interests of regions and localities.[25] Even the most dedicated partisans often changed positions in the course of their careers. One case to be considered is that of Chief Justice Fortescue, the leading jurist of the century, who endured the most extraordinary travails throughout his later life in support of the Lancastrian cause, only to change sides in the end. Similarly, in the religious sphere, writings often traverse the fuzzy boundary between 'orthodox' and 'heterodox.' A case in point is that of Bishop Pecock, who perceived himself as an ardent defender of orthodoxy and clerical privilege, yet whose various imprudences led to the banning of his work and the requirement that he attend the burning of his own books. In the turbulent conditions of the fifteenth century, and in the competitive linguistic situation I am describing, the fault lines between different camps and positions often lie disguised. The lack of any unitary or secure enunciative position enjoins new styles and tactics of advocacy, as well as a certain tentativeness on the part of most expositors. John Watts observes that in midcentury 'it seems that the poetic/polemical ambivalences . . . are more multi-faceted and complex than those of the early Lancastrian period. Perhaps that's a result of the relative fragmentariness and inarticulateness of so much mid-century public writing, as if the alternative applicability of almost everything that can be said politically has become more obvious to writers and undermined some of their expressive confidence.'[26]

Unlike the detached or decontexted utterances of early speech-act theory, these writings aim to constitute and to address actual audiences in determinate, contested situations. But in one very important sense they retain what speech-act theory used to call a 'performative' or self-performing element.[27] One activity common to all these texts is their interest in establishing their rights of coinage, access, and fair use with respect to the very language they employ. Thus, simply by successfully employing an exciting or sought-after political concept or term, the text has, in effect, already 'done' something, has demonstrated its entitlement to that language and its sought-after benefits. The language of which I speak may be considered 'ideological,' in the sense of possessing ideological interest, marking itself out as an object of desire by virtue of its enriched symbolic potentiality. Such language is ideological, not in the old-fashioned sense that it practices upon unwary people, but rather in the different sense of being *itself* practiced upon, treated as an object of possible appropriation. Far from determining the contours of the text in which it appears, such language is itself the goal of the text's largest strategic designs. Effectively up for grabs, charged terms and buzzwords are available for appropriation and use—that is, to be 'performed'—by the program or policy whose advocates are able to claim them, thus gaining the right to their latent or accumulated symbolic capital.

Implicit in my remarks thus far is the fact that the audience of these texts is often an audience that has not yet quite solidified, and has, moreover, not yet made up its mind. Surprisingly often, writings on opposite sides of an issue will find themselves in competition for what is effectively the same audience. Moreover, texts on different sides of an issue will court acceptance or approval via the use of similar or even identical words, and will even exhibit considerable tactical similarity in their deployment. Borne out here is another of Pocock's contentions about language—that in the case of any genuine *langue* we discover not a single or idiosyncratic user but a group of users, all enjoying access. As he puts it, 'the more institutionalized a language and the more public it becomes, the more it becomes available for the purposes of a diversity of utterants articulating a diversity of concerns' (p. 24).[28] In my view, the diversity of what he terms this 'multiplex' community of discourse (p. 25) sets a stage for possible competition—competition for singular or sectional possession of what might seem a common linguistic resource. Behind what might otherwise seem a bland facade of apparent sameness or repetitiveness, a struggle is often being waged, with different parties attempting capture and possession of a finite set of key political terms.

The texts of this study may generally be viewed as competitors for, rather than secure possessors of, an emergent political language. An illustrative example may be appropriate here. Because (partly from political realities of textual preservation) so many of the texts considered circulated around the claims of Richard duke of York and his son Edward IV, I might commence with a text issued in defense of Henry VI's prerogative, and supportive of the recent proscription of York and his followers in 1459. This is the text called the *Somnium Vigilantis,* or the Dream of the Watchful (One).[29] Surviving is a fairly full fragment of this piece, executed with accompanying Latin and French commentary, but mainly in rather ambitiously conceived and floridly couched English. This text's own complicated insertion in the contentions of its day is well borne out by the manuscript—British Library Royal MS 17 D.xv—in which it appears. Bound with it are a *Canterbury Tales* of separate provenance (but nonetheless a work that, in my reading, may be understood as dealing with the founding and formation of a model state, with a 'governor,' consent of the governed, consultation, mechanisms of dispute resolution, and the like).[30] Also present in this mainly vernacular compilation are works of both 'Yorkist' and 'Lancastrian' persuasion. The former is represented by Fortescue's 'Declaration,' a work belatedly rejecting the author's own previous arguments in defense of Lancastrian legitimacy (and discussed in some detail in chapter 3 of the present study), together with a balade on the return of Edward IV in 1471 and a 1475 printed document illustrative of Yorkist diplomacy. The latter is represented by the *Somnium* itself. My point, of course, is that this collection illustrates an apparent interest in gathering a group of political texts illustrative of a larger field of contention, each fighting its particular corner as best it can.

The dialogic nature of this collection is, in turn, borne out in the dialogism of the *Somnium* itself. The aim of the text is to uphold the parliamentary accusation of treason, and consequent attainder, against the duke of York following his rout at Ludlow in 1459. But, as part of the staging of its argument, this text devotes unusual space and detail to an enumeration of the very Yorkist positions it intends to refute. First, a rather glib Yorkist argues for clemency for the duke of York and his followers. Then, in rejoinder, a spokesman of the king, or Regius Orator, rebuts his arguments in detail, with confidence, and with a security in his vantage point that even permits a certain amount of well-placed sarcasm. Certainly this text retains a relatively 'bounded' or distinct sense of two different rhetorical positions and communities of opinion. Yet, for all the difference between the two argu-

mentative positions outlined in this text, an extensive network of shared terminologies and common assumptions undergirds both positions. In the operations of this network we may begin to discern the beginnings of a new
language of politics, and even a new cast of mind toward politics and political process.

This exchange is structured according to certain conventions of formal
debate and occurs, if not in a parliamentary setting, at least in a 'noble place'
with its own rules of courteous behavior. This unnamed venue may, in my understanding, be taken as a figure for what might be called the 'public sphere,'
an arena in which public opinion is shaped by the apt use of language. The
centrality of language in deliberation and the implicit rules of linguistic
contestation are emphasized from the outset. The Lancastrian Regius Orator, for example, immediately faults his adversary for use of 'such langage
that longeth more for a soverain [in address to] his subget than unto you.'
A contest for possession of certain terms of good political conduct ensues.
The Yorkist speaker, proposing to correct 'a rumour that is oones take in
the wlgare voice,' proposes a norm of 'prudent direccioun' by which a ruler
or party should be obliged to attack the most pressing of evils—in this case,
the external enemies of the realm, rather than its disloyal subjects. Acknowledging, in effect, his concern over terms and their possession, he complains
about the way in which terminology has been wielded against his party,
with the duke of York's actions ascribed to 'rebellyoun or such other odious
names.' He proposes the substitution of an alternate and more favorable
nomenclature, according to which the recent rising might 'be ascrybed rather
to vertue and magnanymite.' The Regius Orator responds with his own bat-
tery of terms, countering the Yorkist standard of *prudence* with a Lancastrian respect for *reison*, arrogating it to his position while denying his adversary any 'grounde of reysone.' Bandying such terms, these adversaries begin
to sound like a worldly version of the debate of the Four Daughters of God,
in which Mercy and Peace are at strife with Truth and Justice over the implications of Christ's sacrifice. Here *vertue* and *reison* are offered in exemplification of regal conduct, and a contention over dynastic legitimacy is recast as a struggle for the right to possess and wield the key terms of a political
vocabulary.

Prominent among these terms is Starkey's *commen welthe*, that emergent
term of political art so prominent in the 1450s. Both sides represent themselves as champions of the common good. York's follower argues for exon-
eration based on public-spirited motives of inclusion: that the proscribed

Yorkists 'entende the commen welthe of alle the royame, for the which it is reasonable and worshipfull to expose himselfe to grete jeoperde of goodis and lyfe.' Henry's defender retorts that 'amonge many thinges by the whiche the commone welthe of a royame stondyth the most principall is this, a due subjeccion with fayithfuyll and voluntarie honoure and thair appertenaunce to be yolden to the soverain in the sayd royame and that none incompatible astat be usurped by ony personne'—that the rightful king is the best judge of the people's needs and that an intending usurper can hardly 'be called withoute lesynge protectoure or procuroure of the commen welth.' Similarly, both adversaries evoke the standards of public good and well-managed polity and political necessity. A rudimentary vocabulary of public good and common profit was, of course, available in the fourteenth century as well; but this text reveals a considerable proliferation in the vocabulary of responsible statecraft, and the extent of reliance upon it. The Regius Orator presumes that all parties will agree to a common goal of *polytique operacioun*. And he also presumes that his king will meet that standard well, that 'the kynge and . . . his tru lordes' may be trusted to exhibit 'grete regitive prudennce and pollitique provisioun' against their enemies. *Regitive prudennce* is his riposte to the Yorkist attempt to cloak their arguments in that virtue. And the crucial category of the *pollitique*—a term in rapid mutation throughout this period—here appears in each of its crucial fifteenth-century senses: referring both to something like 'thrifty or efficient management' and simultaneously to 'shrewd provision for one's own self-interest.' Self-interest is, of course, a matter of contention here, since the thrust of the loyalist argument is that York's followers falsely cloak themselves in the language of the common good, while actually defrauding the realm: 'in alle thaire worchinge thar entent was righe noght as it apered evermore. And so thoghe thay dyd many glorius and bostynge dedes with a colorable semblant and pretens of the commen welth and sayd that they entended but goode yet evermore thaire conclusioun was infecte with reprefe, how so be it that the peple in many places was desayved and blyndede by the subtile and coverte malice and colorable frauds that they used in all thinges.' Henry's supporter takes the high road, characterizing obedience to the crowned king as natural, due, and grounded in the king's own exercise of reason, describing the king's power 'to the whiche euery subjecte oght naturaly due subjectioun and obeyssaunce and promtytude of jeopard of his body and goodes for the fulfyllynge of his highe and dredefull commaundements made by reason.' Behind such naturalization of (temporarily) vested authority and defamation of the motives of those (temporarily) out of power, a deeper and more tacit assumption unites the two parties of this debate: both deploy the language of public good, even as both seek to instate their own sectional or special aims as expression of the general interest.

Both participants in the ongoing debate that comprises the *Somnium* take for granted the fact of an ongoing contest, in the course of which a consequential and not yet fully committed public is making up its mind about things. Both assume that points under contention will be resolved not providentially or in heaven, or even by standards of right and wrong, but rather in the arena of public opinion. Describing missteps by the Yorkists after St. Albans, the author says that their behavior 'withdrue the hartes of many of the kinges peple enclyning [to] thaim by cavyllous persuasions to thar entent'— that is, that their intentions were revealed in so negative a light that people who might otherwise have deserted the king remained loyal to him. Describing a Yorkist assault upon the king at Kenilworth Castle, the author is less interested in the act itself than in its negative implications for the Yorkist public relations offensive. The behavior in question, the Regius Orator sarcastically observes, is unlikely to win converts, constituting 'no point of persuacion of the good publique.' Referring to the duke of York's own previous titles, he argues that nomenclature must be applied with more care. One who gives way to his own sensual affection has violated a point 'be longyng to the preservacion and encres of every policie' and cannot 'be called withoute lesynge protectoure or procuroure of the commen welth.' He charges the Yorkists with insincerity and misrepresentation in their courtship of public opinion: 'Thoghe thay dyd many glorius and bostynge dedes with a colorable semblant and pretens of the commen welth and sayd that they entended but goode . . . how so be it that the peple in many places was desayved and blyndede by the subtile and coverte malice and colorable fraudes that they used in all thinges.' Having raised the issue of 'persuacion,' he views the Yorkists' actions from the standpoint of their power to attract allegiance or conviction, and finds them wanting: 'Trow ye thay will have procured the commone welth? Certenly I hold him not very tru that thynketh other wyse but that thaire intent was so subverted to commone welthe as it may be provyd expressely by thairgument of thar demeynynge towardis the kynges peple.' Understanding that the contest is one of persuasion and proof, he debunks his adversary's position, finding it off the mark, in that it contains 'more derisions thann letters' and employs 'wordes of blasphemie rether thann of persuasioun.'

Additional recognition of this text's role in a contest of public persuasion is present in the legal summation, or *narracio,* with which it concludes. There, complaint is made against those who devise rumors and lies ('cez controueurs de nouelles et mansongues') whose inventions stir trouble among the commons and are the cause of many malicious assemblies ('forment trouble le commyng et sont causes de plusseurs mauuailx conuenticles'). Even as this text expresses abhorrence of public debate and political process, though, it engages in exactly such an attempt to win hearts and minds by deployment of persuasive speech. This text participates with evident relish in marshaling a newly enhanced language of political responsibility. Not only is this language the medium by which the debate is conducted, but the right to its employment is the prize awarded to the ultimate winner.

I might return, in brief conclusion, to the *Somnium*'s comment about *blasphemie* as inimical to true political persuasion. True persuasion, the Lancastrian speaker seems to suggest, should occur within a framework of respect for constituted authority. Disrespect of the Yorkists for Henry VI as seated king comprises a form of political blasphemy, in which the sacred elements of kingship are derided, and by which the implicit rules of political debate are transgressed. Blasphemy, the *Somnium* author seems to suggest, is an impropriety in the political sphere, an inappropriate mingling of the sacred and the secular. Suggested here is a tendency of which we will see the barest beginnings in the works of this study, a separation of the political and the religious realms. While composing this study I found myself wrestling constantly with a temptation to spout generalizations about the rise of 'secular' politics. Yet, by its very nature, no political writing of the fifteenth or even the sixteenth century is ever really and truly secular right down to its core. The political discussion I seek to describe is itself double-minded on these matters: ostensibly secular recitals are permeated with religious language and vice versa. Even when isolated, ironized, banished, or otherwise discouraged, religious concepts constantly either linger or return; either outstay their apparent welcome or repropagate when least expected. Machiavelli himself is amply providential in much of his thinking, and even Fortune as he represents and deploys it cannot completely be stripped of its implicit theism and acknowledgment of divine rebuke. What may be asserted is not that God, and divine justice, cease altogether to matter but that their citation becomes more gestural than ever before, and that—once cited—divine factors are likely to be moved to the back burner so that a more purely practical discussion can ensue. In my occasional uses of the word 'secular' I am speaking, in other words, about a matter of relative autonomy, a temporary analytical construct that functions as an effective 'secular sphere.' In this situation, practical (versus providential or divinely ordained) activity is brought to the fore, and providential determination is not so much actively denied as infinitely postponed. In such abeyance or postponement, divine determination functions more or less as the material basis functions in the theories of late and post-Marxists like Althusser: as determinative, but only in the 'last instance,' and with a tacitly agreed upon understanding that (as E. P. Thompson observed)[31] the 'last instance' never comes.

I have chosen the *Somnium* as a representative, rather than an exceptional, text. Political controversialists of the fifteenth century customarily addressed themselves in similar ways to adherents and to the unpersuaded, employing a burgeoning language of political persuasion in a quest for favorable judgments. This language is to be found in all kinds of places: imaginary and practical, literary and without literary pretension, in prose and poetry. It is also found in several different categories and genres: newsletters, histories, memoirs, epistles, statutes, devotional writings, exempla, plays, mirrors, poems, and more. It is, preeminently, what Janet Coleman has called a 'mixed' language and reflects what David Rundle has called a 'varied heritage.'[32] It comes into English from multiple sources—classical, humanistic, continental—and from several different languages, and it occurs within an English vernacular itself engaged in rapid mutation from its 'middle' to its 'early modern' form.

Had I set out to construct a diachronic history of this language's emergence, the fifteenth century would have been displaced from this book's center and assimilated to a much more synoptic narrative. In this more synoptic narrative, key roles would have been assigned to a number of actors and texts only glancingly represented here. William of Moerbeke's translation of Aristotle's *Politics* would have occupied a central role, with its emphasis on the *politicum,* or political regime, as would such derivative texts as Giles of Rome's *De Regimine Principum* with its discussions of the *regimen politicum.*[33] Equally important is the medieval Ciceronian/Senecan tradition, as transmitted by such intermediate writers as Brunetto Latini with his reliance upon republican Roman sources to define politics as rule according to reason and justice.[34] No less important is Latini's solidification of the same traditions in his discussion of Prudence and the other moral or secular virtues.[35] Closer to home, I might well have begun this study in the fourteenth century, especially with the writings of John Gower since his writings on *policie* in book 7 of the *Confessio Amantis* possess particular pertinence to my interests here.[36] Gower also anticipates key aspects of Lydgate's suggestion that men, rather than Fortune, create worldly destinies. In a colophon to MS Bodley 902 of the *Confessio,* he describes the *Vox Clamantis* as treating evils, as a result of which, and not because of Fortune, such crimes (as the rising of 1381) occur among men ('culpas . . . , ex quibus et non a fortuna talia inter homines contingunt enormia').[37] I have sought not to neglect his contribution altogether, or the contribution of James Simpson's fine analysis of his political texts, through local citations in my notes.[38]

Another ancillary subject that might well have found a place within a more comprehensive conception of my subject is the influence of fifteenth-century English humanism, and its introduction of pertinent and freshly employed terms of secular statecraft. Important work on humanistic backgrounds to fifteenth-century English literature was pioneered by R. Weiss in *Humanism in England in the Fifteenth Century,*[39] although Weiss is disappointingly dismissive of the labors of fifteenth-century Latinate humanists and protohumanists.[40] Very important background studies of vernacular humanism in the fifteenth and sixteenth centuries, introducing a wealth of new and arresting detail, have recently been completed by, respectively, Daniel Wakelin, "Vernacular Humanism in England c. 1440–1485" (for the fifteenth century)[41] and Cathy Shrank, *Writing the Nation in Reformation England* (for the mid-sixteenth century).[42]

Finally, though, my decision has been to concentrate on mainly vernacular, fifteenth-century writings, together with some of their sixteenth-century ramifications. This delimitation arises partly in my desire to institute a feasible, or perhaps I should say 'achievable,' research design. It also seeks to avoid repetition of excellent and available work on the tradition of Aristotle's *Politics* in the later Middle Ages on the one hand and early modern humanism on the other. But the main reason for my decision to concentrate on developments in fifteenth-century England is my conviction that the imaginative accomplishments of Lydgate, Fortescue, Pecock, Whethamstede, Warkworth, and other writers of that period remain seriously undercredited. As do the writings of the unnamed authors who composed the *Somnium Vigilantis,* the Yorkist poems of the early 1460s, the *Arrivall of Edward IV,* and the later years of the so-called *Great Chronicle of London,* to mention a few. All contributed to an indispensable linguistic resource, which is the refinement of a language of practical politics (and accompanying symbolic gesture) in a period insufficiently recognized for innovation.

A political language is a work of many hands. Even while admiring individual authorial accomplishment, I wish also to solicit admiration for a collective linguistic and symbolic endeavor. The mid-fifteenth century is a moment of such common activity, often abetted by practitioners and controversialists more likely to have considered themselves enemies than friends. In their writings we glimpse the contours of an emerging fifteenth-century public sphere. This sphere was marked not so much by concord and agreement as by contention among competing interests. All its contestatory parties nevertheless participate in what might be considered a common discussion. Unlike some of the more academic and Latinate discussions of earlier centuries, this was one that claimants to political authority, or simply to participation in the public life of the realm, had little choice but to join. Some joined it personally, and others by proxy in texts addressed to them or written on their behalf. But all would have acknowledged the existence of a realm of written controversy too important to ignore.

I am grateful to a number of scholars who have assisted me with their conversation, correction, and encouragement. These include David Aers, Caroline Barron, Richard Beadle, Sarah Beckwith, Mishtooni Bose, Mereal Connor, Susan Crane, Margretta DeGrazia, A. S. G. Edwards, Thomas Freeman, Alexandra Gillespie, Kantik Ghosh, Robert Hanning, Jean Howard, Matthew Leigh, Margaret Meserve, Phyllis Rackin, Larry Scanlon, James Simpson, James Shapiro, Peter Stallybrass, and Nancy Warren. Maura Nolan and David Wallace each read and helpfully commented on two chapters. Miri Rubin proved herself, as always, a true and generous friend by reading and commenting on the whole. In addition, I wish to mention several vital occasions. I am particularly indebted to Thomas Noble, head of the Medieval Institute at the University of Notre Dame, for inviting me to give the core sections of this volume as the 2003 Collins Lectures at that institution, and to Jill Mann and Michael Lapidge for their hospitality. Another is a session arranged by David Wallace for the Medieval-Renaissance group of the University of Pennsylvania, at which I gave the lecture (now chapter 5) that launched this volume, and experienced the generosity and forbearance of that institution's early modernists. Another is a lively workout on the first draft of my introduction with the New York City medieval work-in-progress group (METS). Another is a happy month at the University of Melbourne, arranged by Stephanie Trigg, allowing me to write my Fortescue section. Another is a session at the University of Miami arranged by Tom Goodmann and Michelle Warren, at which I was encouraged to amplify my thoughts on Commynes and the Milanese ambassadors. Finally, I wish to conclude by mentioning (with special emphasis) the unrivaled collegiality of John Watts, who consented to share with me the challenges of organizing and chairing a 2000–2002 Oxford University interdisciplinary research seminar on textuality and history. His receptivity to scholarly exchange—an exchange continuing into the proof stage of this volume—has been a constant inspiration in the investigation of these topics.

one

Politique Perjury in the *Arrivall* of Edward IV

I. REPETITION 'PUTS A PATTERN ON VIEW'[1]

Pattern is essential to the production of historical events. Although newly evident patterns have their occasional uses, established or repeated patterns are the real motors of late-medieval public process. Political claimants rely constantly upon repeated pattern as a support to imagination, as a cloak of motive, or as a guarantee of public intelligibility for their choices and actions. Contemporary participants and subsequent chroniclers rely equally upon pattern and for similar reasons: to make sense of disparate evidence, to organize narrative accounts, to build meaning-making consensus. Working from the written record, we can hardly know which party to credit for a pattern's emergence. Known pattern may be introduced by protagonists who produce actions within its contours; by onlookers who interpret events with reference to the familiar; by the chronicler or other *reporteur* who adopts the implicit patterning proper to a known narrative genre. The subsequent analyst has little choice but to accept a principle of multiple or even diffuse determination, with all parties to an event reliant upon the seductions and advantages of preexistent pattern.

Although patterns assist in the production and promulgation of historical events, they do not necessarily determine these events' precise character. A given pattern may operate differently for the various people within its ambit, or for those responsible for its iteration. Consider the murders of Richard II and Henry VI, which unfold as if from a single script. Preexisting pattern may be supposed to play a part in each event's production, especially in the subsequent case of Henry VI. Both monarchs were imprisoned by their opponents. Both died under muffled circumstances, with their own excessive grief alleged as a cause. Both corpses were displayed publicly in order to terminate rumor and dynastic claim. The patterning of such an event is, in some respects, held in common by all participants, with each, in effect, assigned a role in a patterned process. But the pattern does not constrain each participant to a unitary view of the situation. One perspective for the victims; if Adam of Usk is correct, the extraordinarily self-aware Richard II was fully conscious of his assigned role in the micro-drama of the fallen prince.[2] Another for the murderers, presumably in each case driven by a mixture of dynastic loyalty and personal greed. Another for the architects of the deed, fully aware of the practical problems generated by a predecessor's survival. A plethora of perspectives for the beholding public and for variously situated chroniclers and other subsequent interpreters, who responded with extreme diversity to so unsettling an event. All such parties rely upon pattern, but their interest *in* pattern could hardly be said to be the same.

The supple way in which pattern lends itself to varied uses and effects helps to explain the extent to which the reader of Polydore Vergil or Hall or any narrative historian is so ceaselessly confronted with the familiar: recurring cycles of exiles and returns, attainders and exonerations, sudden elevations and summary executions. Shakespeare's genius in his Henry VI plays consists partly in recognizing and capitalizing upon the prevalence of repeated pattern. Repetition virtually becomes what these plays are *about.* They are constantly energized by a conflict between pattern, as epitomized by a powerful and regressive cyclical undertow, and an ostensibly more progressive narrative of Tudor emergence. Finally, the status of pattern—the extent of pattern's success in imposing its own nightmarish recurrences versus the possibility of capping or terminating an unwholesome sequence—is these plays' unending meditation.

The prevalence of late-medieval repetition was not lost upon contemporary and near-contemporary commentators. Thus Angelo Acciaioli shrewdly suggested in a 1451 ambassadorial dispatch to the duke of Milan that the English might be lapsing into a familiar pattern, thinking of doing villainy to Henry VI, as they had done to other of their kings ('né sta il decto Re sanza pericolo che gl'Inghilesi non gli faccino villania, come hanno facto a degli altri loro Re').[3] And Shakepeare's Richard II, armed with his author's own retrospective knowledge of fifteenth-century events, describes the problems of recurrence that will plague his successors, warning Northumberland that Bolingbroke 'shall think that thou, which know'st the way / To plant unrightful kings, wilt know again' (V.1). The powerful effects of pattern as exemplum and admonitory example were well known to all, not only in the fifteenth century, but also in the century that followed. A recognition of the power of precedent is neatly embodied in Elizabeth's observation about the implications of Essex's sponsorship of performances of *Richard II* on the eve of his rebellion.[4]

The repetition considered here involves the temporarily deposed Edward IV's landing at Ravenspur in March 1471. This occasion was viewed by contemporaries, and by the principal contemporary chroniclers, as a symbolically significant reprise of the temporarily disinherited Henry Bolingbroke's landing at Ravenspur in June 1399. In each case, the protagonist apparently canvassed a landing in Norfolk before putting in at Ravenspur.[5] Each landed with few followers and dubious prospects. Each claimed only to seek his ducal inheritance, and persuaded others of that limited objective. Each, having thus masked his ultimate intentions, was thought by some to have perjured himself. Within a matter of months, each had marched into London and successfully claimed the throne.

Initiating discussion of this coincidence was the author-compiler of the principal source-text for Edward's landing, the anonymous *Historie of the Arrivall of Edward IV*.[6] (For the convenience of the reader, and thanks to the generosity of the University of Notre Dame Press, the body of this text, in its Camden Society edition, is reprinted as an appendix to this chapter.) Precursor versions of his frankly Yorkist account were composed soon after the event, and circulated on the Continent and in England in newsletter formats, and subsequently addressed to an English audience in the augmented format of the *Arrivall*. Having described Edward's inauspicious touchdown at Norfolk, and storms that dispersed his flotilla, the *Arrivall* proceeds:

> The Kynge . . . landed within Humber on holdernes syde at a place cal-
> lyd Raveneresporne, even in the same place where somtime usurpowr
> henrye of derby aftar called Kynge henry the IV landed, aftar his exile
> contrary and to the dissobeysaunce of his sovereigne lord, Kynge Rich-
> ard the II. (32v)

An easy landing place on a geographically inhospitable coast,[7] a discreet place
for disembarcation in a potentially hostile countryside, a convenient place
with respect to the ducal seat of York, an expectation of support from the earl
of Northumberland—Ravenspur may have commended itself to Edward
for innumerable reasons unrelated to Bolingbroke's previous pattern.[8] But,
as corroborated and reinforced by this pro-Yorkist author's acknowledgment
of pattern, Edward's choice of landing place almost certainly had something
to do with this influential precedent and Edward's desire to capitalize on it—
even as Bolingbroke's confident royal trajectory appears to have commanded
Edward's attention all along.

Representational, and ultimately political, capital is to be had from invocation of so influential a precedent. But, as even preliminary and limited
analysis will show, this is 'venture capital'—capital that can be commanded
only with some accompanying risk. The attempt is, of course, to capture the
affirmative upside of Bolingbroke's maneuver, including his own broad initial
appeal, the success of his gesture, and the like. In this respect, Edward can
be seen in the light of his counterparts in Marx's *Eighteenth Brumaire,* who
cloak innovation in the masks and drapery of the near or far past, wielding
'this time-honoured disguise and this borrowed language.'[9] But an adherence
to pattern also carries a downside risk for an imitator who wants to capitalize upon some, but not all, of a pattern's previous implications. Here, the risk
for Edward involves the difficulty of establishing a difference between his
own reassertion of legitimate sovereign claims and the stark fact of Henry's
original usurpation. If he is successfully to enlist some elements and to dis-
card others from Bolingbroke's mixed symbolic inheritance, Edward must
capture the affirmative momentum contained in his predecessor's pattern of
exile and return even as he evades any imputation of Bolingbroke's usurpatious intentions. Whether the intention is Edward's or belongs to those who
subsequently wrote about him, his hope for this pattern would seem clear-cut
enough, as would his strategy for enlisting it. His hope is to enlist his predecessor's successful and indeed inexorable progress to the throne, and the

strategy is to assert that his act of repetition has the paradoxical effect of righting an original wrong and terminating a Lancastrian misadventure.

Falling on Edward as historical actor and, especially, on the *Arrivall* author as subsequent publicist and proponent is a task that may be described narratively as first opening and then closing a sequence. Sought, in other words, is what a modern narratologist might call a 'paradigmatic' closure. Edward's landing evokes a shared paradigm (Edward like Bolingbroke lands at Ravenspur), but must inflect or alter that paradigm in order to close the sequence on terms favorable to Edward's cause. Putting this same point in medieval terms, we may say that Edward's landing offers itself as the successful reversal or 'type,' of which Bolingbroke's landing is the perverse anticipation or 'antitype.' Typologically viewed, an Old Testament event both predicts and requires a subsequent, or New Testament, response—a response that both completes it and, in some cases, sets it right. Thus the Israelites' crossing of the Red Sea is completed by the sacrament of Baptism—a sacrament that not only makes sense of an earlier and inchoate enactment, but that to some extent redresses the trauma of the original Exodus by opening a path to a more lasting form of salvation. Perhaps more relevantly, one common typological interpretation had it that Christ's cross stood on the place of Adam and Eve's tree of the knowledge of good and evil, the crucifixion necessitated by Adam's fall, and also offering a form of redress for that dire event. By analogy, Edward's landing 'even in the same place' as Henry's might be understood as an action necessitated by Henry's original (Lancastrian) usurpation, and also as an opportunity for redress by restoration of a rightful dynasty. It would thus be the 'type' of successfully instituted kingship—both necessitated by and corrective of its negative antetype/antitype in Henry's wrongful seizure.

But the problem with a recognized pattern, and precedent, rests in the difficulty of using it for some things and not for others. In this case the affirmative and negative elements of Henry's previous pattern will finally turn out to be inextricable. Especially once the word *usurprowr* enters the descriptive register, at any level or for any purpose, its negative implications cannot easily be confined, let alone expunged. Rather than conclusively confined to the first instance, the idea of usurpation can hardly help but invade and corrupt the successor event. The readepted Henry VI whom Edward sought to supplant was, after all, an anointed king, and his supplantation could hardly avoid being regarded, even by Yorkist well-wishers, as a form of usurpation.[10] This comparison is, in other words, already tainted, and Edward must pay the tariff exacted of those who pursue a strategy of repetition. Even if ostensibly completed or closed by Edward's resumption of the crown, this repetition cannot escape an inadvertent effect, which is to reveal certain awkward congruences, and to offer them up for evaluation.

2. PATTERN AND PERJURY

One of the congruences that repetition 'puts on view' involves the matter of perjury. If this pattern shows Edward behaving like a king, it also and inevitably shows him, with Bolingbroke, behaving like a perjuror. Like his predecessor, Edward is represented in all accounts as promising that he sought no more than his dukedom, and by some accounts as more explicitly perjuring himself with false oaths, abuse of the Mass, and other forsworn activities. But here a point of comparison arises. Rather than simply hung around Edward's neck, the fact of his apparent perjury turns out to be the beginning, rather than the end, of a meaning-making process. Perjury would appear at first to pose an identical representational challenge for both Bolingbroke and Edward: how can this embarrassment be explained away? Yet, even as perjury arises within each narrative process, it will finally be treated very differently in the latter case. In this difference lies a key to the altered political terrain of the later fifteenth century, and to an attitudinal shift of considerable magnitude that has apparently occurred between these two perjured events.

Like Edward after him, the future Henry IV arrived announcing that he sought only the restoration of his ducal heritage. His early plans undoubtedly underwent modification, resulting from unanticipated support, unexpected defections from Richard's cause, and the like. Yet surely no one—or at least no one benefiting from the reflective vantage point of several years after most chronicle accounts were written—could have been so naive as to take this initial disclaimer at face value. Nevertheless, because their writers are unwilling to concede Bolingbroke to be a perjuror, the prevailing mode of the pro-Lancastrian chronicle is to brazen the whole thing out, to treat his disclaimer of regal ambition with bland evasion as a representation of his true intentions rather than as a tactical lie. Walsingham's *Historia*, for example, has him wronged by his exile and disinheritance ('exilium suum et exhaeredationem'), returning to England in pursuit of his rightful claim ('ad petendum haereditatem suam'), trusting in justice and public favor for its restoration.[11] His claim is itself neutralized or euphemized in this account; the implication is that only his 'ducal' claim is initially at issue, yet Walsingham leaves this matter purposely vague and thus frees Henry from any taint of perjury. As his account continues, so many lords join him from fear of Richard's tyranny that he soon finds himself leading an enormous army. Richard is cornered in Conwy, and then—in a major disavowal of Lancastrian responsibility—is *himself* made to raise the previously unaddressed question of kingship, offering to step down ('indicavit se velle regno cedere'), so long as his personal security and that of eight followers should be guaranteed. We soon have Richard in London, cheerfully ('vultu hilari') absolving his followers of their oaths of allegiance and desiring that Bolingbroke succeed him as king of the realm. In other words, Bolingbroke is presented as essentially passive in a process that inexorably swept him to the throne, abetted by Richard's acquiesence and even tacit allegiance, and driven forward by his fellow subjects' earnest desires. Only a very close reading of the Lancastrian chronicles discovers any deception or wrongdoing on Bolingbroke's part, and only then in the form of fleeting allusion to the solemn assurances, or perhaps sworn oaths to respect Richard's kingship that, 'concessis et firmatis,' secured Richard's surrender at Conwy.

In the few less friendly chronicles that have survived, however, this matter of bad faith is brought to the fore, at least in the slightly displaced form of accusations against Bolingbroke's overzealous followers. The *Dieulacres Chronicle,* for example, underscores this bad faith by having his chief negotiators pledge their faith upon the sacrament: 'Then, as chiefly negotiated by the archbishop of Canterbury and the earl of Northumberland, and sworn upon the sacrament of the body of Christ, they promised that king Richard should retain his regal power and dominion ('Tunc per mediacionem precipue archiepiscopi cantuariensis et comitis Northamhimbrorum et super sacramentum corporis Christi iurati quot rex Ricardus staret in suo regali potestate et dominio promiserunt').[12] Also displacing Bolingbroke's bad faith onto the actions of his deputies, arch-loyalist Creton portrays Northumberland's misfeasance in the most unmistakable terms. Perhaps because he writes in French, in which the term is more common, he is the first to speak of perjury.[13] Having proposed to Richard (still safely situated within the walls of Conwy Castle) that Bolingbroke be permitted to sue on his knees for Richard's mercy and then conduct him honorably to a session of parliament, Northumberland adds:

'Be sure of all this:
I will swear to you upon Christ's body,
Sacered by the priest's hand, that duke Henry
Will loyally keep to all that you have asked
And all I have said.' (p. 356)[14]

Then, Richard agrees (although with a great deal of skeptical reserve), on the express condition of the oath, since:

'I know well that you are honorable,
Nor for robes, jewels, or gifts
Would you perjure yourself: for those men
['. . . je scay bien que vous estes preudons,
Ne pour avoir robes, joyaux ne dons
Ne vous vouldriez *pariurer*']
Who perjure themselves ['Qui *se pariure*']
Exist shamefully. . . .'
Then the earl, without saying more,
Made his oath on the body of our lord.
Alas, his own blood must have mocked him,
For he knew well the contrary. (p. 360)

Moreover, in his account of Northumberland's outrageous deception, Creton comes very close to assigning Bolingbroke a share of responsibility. As Northumberland tells it, assuring Richard of his right to speak in these matters,

. . . for he [Bolingbroke] so promised me
On the body of God ['Sur le corps dieu'] when I last
Parted from him. (p. 357)

So here we have Bolingbroke as an abettor and virtual participant in an act of perjury—though still at a remove.

Closest actually to charging Bolingbroke with perjury were his eventual enemies, including Northumberland and the northern lords, his effective kingmakers. As Harding tells it in his own widely circulated fifteenth-century chronicle, Bolingbroke landed with a mere forty men, and from this position of weakness was faced with the task of securing the support of the northern lords with their formidable military array. His shrewd response was to claim no more than his due: 'There swore the duke vpon the Sacrament, / To cleyme no more but his modir heritage, / His fadir landes and his wifes in good entent.'[15] According to Henry (Hotspur) Percy's statement of his 'quarell' in 1403, appended to Harding's chronicle, Bolingbroke swore at Doncaster upon the holy gospels, touching and kissing them, to proclaim that, with respect to the kingdom or to the status of kings, saving only his inheritance and the inheritance owing to his wife, in England, King Richard should reign for the term of his life ('apud Doncastre tu iurasti nobis supra sacra Evangelia corporaliter per te tacta et osculata numquam clamare coronam [seu] regium statum, nisi solummodo hereditatem tuam propriam et hereditatem uxoris tue in anglia et quod Ricardus dominus noster rex et tunc regnaret ad terminum vite sue'—f. 192v).[16] Harding explains that Bolingbroke betrayed his *oth* despite the pleas of the Percies, but he does not go so far as to claim that the oath was *itself* taken in bad faith.[17] The most extreme accusation made against him is that he took an oath and subsequently, under pressure of unfolding events and tempted by the crown, broke it. One senses that an accusation of having knowingly forsworn himself *at the time*, whether swearing on the consecrated host or the relics of Bridlington, is so dire a conclusion that even the most skeptical analysts skirt it, leaving it a matter of implication, or reassign it to deputies like Northumberland. To conclude with the obvious: even Bolingbroke's foes quailed at so grave an accusation, and no one considering him an oath-breaker could have thought the better of him for it.

The mid-fifteenth-century Lancastrians naturally enough sought to preserve the opprobrium attached to false swearing in their portrayals of Richard duke of York. For, as suggested by the abundant evidence of his oathbreaking supplied by the Bill of Attainder in the Parliament of 1459, York had rendered himself vulnerable on this front. The Bill notes three such instances, beginning with York's 1452 oath of submission to Henry VI, sworn after Dartford in 1452. The Rolls of Parliament quote the oath in full, including the highly performative words in which Richard swears 'by the holy Evangelies conteyned in this Boke that I lay my hande upon, and by the holy Crosse that I here touche, and by the blessed Sacrament of oure Lordes body that I shall nowe with his mercy receyve.'[18] Also noted is an act of allegiance taken at Coventry in 1456, in which 'the seid Duc of York there swore on the holy Evaungelies, and signed the Acte with his hande' (p. 347). Undated is yet one more instance: 'Also to remembre of another Othe and suerte swoure, and signed of the seid Duk of Yorks hands, and sealed, of true and feithfull obeisaunce to You [Henry VI] and youre succession' (pp. 347–48). Copies of all these documents are included or appended. At the same time, York is barraged by accusations of perfidy and untruthfulness: 'fals and traiterous ymaginations . . . and diligent labours born up with colourable lies' (p. 346); 'untrouth, falsenesse and cruelte, subtily coloured, and feyned zelyng' (p. 348).[19]

Even as supporters of the crown sought to hold Richard duke of York to his oaths, so did Richard seek to undermine the oath's solemnity in late medieval culture. At the 1460 Westminster Parliament, seeking to press his claim on the throne following his party's victory at the battle of Northampton, he directly challenged the contention of the anxious lords that they considered themselves bound by their oaths to the king. These former and frequent oath-takers stated to him that 'the Lordes of this lond must nedes calle to their remembrauncez, the grete Othes the which they have made to the Kyng oure Soverayn Lord . . . and that the Lordes may not breke thoo Othes' (*Rolls of Parliament*, 5, p. 376). Richard, in return, argued for several sorts of higher, or at least alternate, considerations: 'man shuld have rather consideration to trouth, right and justice in this mater accordyngly with the wille of the lawe of God, then to any promise or ooth made by hym into the contrarie . . .; that the vertu and nature of an ooth is to conferme trouth, and of noo wise to ympugne it; and over that, that by the ooth of feaute, homage or ligeaunce, noo man is bounded to any inconvenient or unlawfull thyng' (p. 377). Even if *inconvenient* is taken in the sense of 'unfitting,' rather than in some more modern way, it is still a remarkably telling choice. As is Richard's additional assurance that 'for asmuch as the mater of Othes is a mater spirituell,' he stands ready to answer before any judge—so long as he is 'spirituell competent' and the meeting held at a 'place and tyme convenable' (p. 377).

Richard's evasive remarks on the motility of oaths (quickly embraced and endorsed by the lords) capture something of a new, midcentury spirit, and this new ethos flowers fully in the *Arrivall*'s account of Edward's landing at Ravenspur and his accompanying oath that reclamation of his dukedom is the summit of his ambitions. Repeating—in fact, as depicted in the *Arrivall*, almost doggedly repeating—Bolingbroke's perjured claim, Edward cannot fail to expose himself as being, like Bolingbroke before him, a perjuror. But the *Arrivall* takes a different tack, on its face rather surprising for a professedly Yorkist text, presenting Edward as embracing a similar declaration, *in full knowledge of his ultimate objective and with a deliberate attempt to deceive.* In this characterization, Edward is determined to claim the throne but astutely able to bide his time until the proper moment to announce his full objective. The situation as described is that Edward landed with few troops, and gained few immediate adherents from the Yorkshire countryside, finding the people massively organized against him, 'redye to resiste hym in chalenginge of the Royme and the crowne' (32v). His only tactical opening was to limit his claim to the dukedom, since 'the people bare hym right great favowr to be also duke of yorke and to have that of right apartayned unto hym' (32v). Thus Edward determined that, until his strength should grow to the point that he could challenge the crown, 'he and all thos of his felowshipe shuld noyse and say openly where so evar they came that his entent and purpos was only to claime to be duke of yorke and to have and enioy th'enheritaunce that he was borne vnto by the right of the full noble prince his fathar and none othar' (33r). The particular, and rather disingenuous, reasoning by which Edward justified his tactic was that those who supported his limited claim were overlooking an unspoken corollary, which was that according to the succession agreement of 1460 not only Edward's father, Richard duke of York, but also Richard's heirs were to advance to the throne; 'his sayd fathar bisydes that he was rightfully duke of yorke he was also verrey trew and rightwise enheritoure to the roylme and corone of England' (33r). Thus we are offered a willfully, and doubly duplicitous, schemer, whose claim of the throne is 'covertly pretendyd' (34r) or masked under the 'qwarell of his father,' itself divided between an overt claim on the dukedom and a covert claim on the throne.

Have the terms of regal conduct migrated so far that perjury, still a blemish in the fourteenth century, has now become a perverse badge of honor? In a word, yes. The *Arrivall* is a composite text, and cannot be thought to take an absolutely unified view of every representational situation it takes in hand.[20] Nevertheless, the admission of Edward's perjury proposes itself not simply as a lapse into candor resulting from the text's composite nature, but appears to be an integral and active element of its Yorkist program. Consider, for example, a particularly damning sequence the *Arrivall* author appears to have deliberately borrowed from a now-lost source involving Edward's arduous dealings with the Lancastrian-leaning citizens of York. Here he depicts a series of challenges by concerned local citizens to which Edward ambiguously or misleadingly responds. First off, a local vicar and a gentleman identified as Martyn of the Sea oppose his passage to York, but are then mollified by Edward's pretense of claiming only the dukedom: 'he and all his felowshipe pretendyd by any manar langage none othar qwarell but for the right that was his fathars the duke of yorke' (33v). Our author comments with satisfaction that their provisional support was based on an oversight encouraged by Edward, that of 'not discoveringe ne remembringe' (33r) his royal claim. Furthermore, another citizen named Coniers, the recorder of the city, ambiguously warns him to expect a bad reception, and then meets him outside the gates to 'put him in lyke discomforte as afore' (33v). Coniers is, however, overborne by a contingent of well-wishers, who usher Edward within the gates, where Edward 'shewed them th'entent and purpos of his coming in such forme and with such maner langage, that the people contentyd them therwithe' (33v). When evasions and double-talk don't work, money evidently will; other possible opponents are 'some whate enduced to be the more benivolent for money that the Kynge gave them' (33v).[21]

Why, we must ask, has the *Arrivall* retained enough of this potentially defamatory account that its outlines can still be ascertained? The answer is not that the *Arrivall* has drifted off into an unconsidered anti-Yorkist eddy but rather that its whole understanding of perjury, and its potential for defamation, has changed. Rather than a matter for displacement or evasion, as it was in the accounts of Bolingbroke's machinations, it has now become something different, an affirmative element of a claimant's, as it were, c.v. The *Arrivall* carries forward its Yorkist argument by imagining and portraying an environment in which deception, temporization, and sharp dealing are understood not as disqualifications but as positive entitlements to the throne. Needful, that is, in a world in which practical calculation is registered as a sovereign virtue, trumping claims of divine election or tests of divine will. The *Arrivall* author rises to this task with an unreserved endorsement of politically astute behavior and a hardheaded analysis of situations.[22]

3. EDWARD AND THE 'CHRISTIAN SYSTEM'

If Edward is so serviceable in his own behalf, what remains for the sacred? What, in particular, is the status of his frequent professions of devotion to God's ultimate arbitration? How are we to read his words before Barnet, as reported in the *Arrivall*, to the effect that 'he commytted his cawse and qwarell to Allmyghty God'? Or how are we to read the author's own profession, closely echoing that of the *memoire* or original newsletter, that Edward's recovery of the throne was accomplished 'with the helpe of Almighty God, the moaste glorious Virigin Mary his mothar, and of Seint George, and of the Saynts of heven'? Despite the apparently unrestricted nature of such avowals, a careful balance—including a syntactic balance—is maintained between accounts of Edward's exertions on the one hand and God's endorsement on the other. Back in the *memoire* such balance was already apparent, when Harpisfeld wrote of the rapid reconquest of the kingdom 'par laide et grace de Dieu, il a par son grant sens et bonne pollicie passe et eschape pluseurs grans perilz'[23]—'by the aid and grace of God, he by his considerable sense and good policy has passed and escaped many great perils.' And now we read, in close translation, that 'moienaunt [by means of] the helpe and grace of all myghty God by his wysdome and polyqwe he escaped and passyd many great perills and daungars and dificulties' (48v). In each case, two causes—God's favor and shrewd politics—are crowded together without syntactic preference and with deliberate ambiguity. In the first, *pollicie*—not in its traditional sense of 'polity' but in its emergent fifteenth-century sense of 'apt choice'—is balanced against God's aid and grace. In the second, *polyqwe*—not in its traditional sense of 'public-spirited' but in its emergent fifteenth-century sense of 'enlightened self-interest'—is balanced against God's help and grace.[24] Yet a resolution does, I think, emerge in the body of each narration. As between God as the mover of actions, or as their approving cosponsor and welcome endorser, I have little hesitation in concluding upon the latter. Without Edward's exercise of *pollicie* and *polyqwe*, events might have taken another turn. Paradoxically, the subsidiary relation of providence to individual initiative is most clear at this narrative's most apparently fervent moment, that of Edward's 'miracle' at Daventre.

This brilliantly engineered miracle poaches upon and colonizes an existing occasion, the ritual procession prescribed for Palm Sunday.[25] Among the several brilliances of this imaginative choice for a miracle are its highly public nature, a participatory character that already shapes the congregation into a polity devoted to the welcome of a monarch, and, especially, the inevitable symbolic overflow in which the Aves hailing Christ's entry into Jerusalem redound to the benefit of Edward as returning monarch. This latter association is underscored by the precise timing of the miracle:

> The same Palme Sonday, the Kynge went in procession, and all the people aftar . . . and, whan the processyon was comen into the churche and, by ordar of the service were comen to that place where the vale

shulbe drawne vp afore the Roode, that all the people shall honor the Roode with the anthem Ave three tymes begon, in a pillar of the churche directly aforne the place where Kynge knelyd and devowtly honoryd the Roode was a lytle ymage of Seint Anne . . . And even sodaynly at that season of the service the bords compassynge the ymage about, gave a great crak and a little openyd, whiche the Kynge well perceyved and all the people about hym. (37r−v)

Wendy Scase has perceptively analyzed this moment, as a counterpart of the ingenious and device-driven stagings of divine favor that customarily mark the processional entries and other occasions by which late-medieval monarchy performs itself.[26] Such stagings are usually accompanied by bits of official interpretation: either sung anthems, or prophetic/interpretative recitations, or written scripts or legible placards, or a combination of these devices. Here, no such devices are employed, but rather Edward himself acts as his own interpreter: 'The Kynge this seinge thanked and honoryd God and Seint Anne takynge it for a good signe and token of good and prosperous aventure that God wold send hym, in that he had to do' (37v). With Edward at the interpretative fulcrum, God obliges by providing a 'signe and token' of his good favor. Yet there is little question in this text, I think, about where the initiative ultimately lies.

We have in this scene a co-optation, in which the established liturgical and devotional processes of parish worship are bent towards the legitimation of an effectively worldly course of action.[27] Already evident at this moment is a mature example of that process which Michel de Certeau would attribute to the seventeenth century, in which the Christian system 'is transformed into a sacred theater of the system which will take its place.'[28] De Certeau imagines this transformation of the sacred to occur as a consequence of weakness, of a weakened Christian system. Here we encounter it, if Eamon Duffy is correct, at a moment of vitality and strength;[29] yet at a moment when its co-optation is no less possible, and the greater symbolic prize is to be won.

4. PRE-MACHIAVELLIAN *POLITIQUE*

Professing trust in God but cultivating his own *polyqwe*, Edward is portrayed within a discourse of practical political calculation emerging to view in the second half of the fifteenth century. Embodied in newsletters, dispatches, memoirs, and short chronicles, this discourse pays occasional lip service to providential and other divine influences but effectively brackets them, in favor of more immediate and pragmatic forms of political assessment.[30] By virtue of such writings, the mid-fifteenth century may be described as a pre-Machiavellian moment, a moment when the arts of worldly political practice enjoyed temporary sway. My aim here is to draw brief examples of this moment from three texts—from the dispatches of the Milanese ambassadors to the king of France in 1450–60, the diplomatic *Mémoires* of Philippe de Commynes, and, of course, the *Arrivall* itself.[31]

The Milanese Ambassadors

The dispatches of the Milanese ambassadors are purpose-written: shaped within situations of practical exigency, often sent in cypher, and constantly expressive of a very new technology of statecraft. Thus, with a certain realism of assessment as their very rationale, they possess a functionality that need hardly surprise us. Instructed by the duke himself to proceed *aptamente* and to privilege the useful, or *utile,* these ambassadors not only focus on the substance of conversations, but on the attitudes and expressions of those with whom they speak and other practical indicators by which political intention might be construed. This does not mean that God and the operations of providence are absent from the conversation. The divine and divine business are, however, moved to the periphery of the decision-making process, to be dealt with when the time is right. The precedence of the worldly is neatly captured by Angelo Acciaioli's discussion of the king of France's response to the duke of Burgundy's proposal that they go on crusade: '[T]he Duke, through his envoys, informed the King that he wished to go on crusade in order to win back the Holy Sepulcher, and asked aid of him. The King replied that this was a worthy idea ['Risposegli che questo era buono pensiero'] but that first he wanted to see what was going to have to be done in regard to war with the English.'[32]

   This kind of balancing act issues in a bemused or easygoing lightness of tone in which religion and religious matters are taken as a common frame of reference, but not necessarily as active determinants of the situations under analysis. Duke Francesco Sforza of Milan comments in exasperation, of a temperamental ally, that 'from the first day he entered our territories until the day he finally took his departure, we have paid the honors we would have paid to God had he come to this world' ('gli havimo facto fare quello honore che haveressimo facto a Dio se fosse venuto in terra'—pp. 134–35). And an ambassador who has just written a particularly long letter comments to his duke, 'Lord, I have narrated to you the old and new testament both' ('Signore, io ve ho narrato il Testamento Vechio e Novo'—pp. 245, 248). (A similarly bemused note will be struck by Commynes; speaking of the vagaries of counsel, he observes that 'we are all human, and who seeks to find those who would never fail to speak wisely . . . must seek in heaven, since such persons are not to be found among mankind' ('qui les vouldroit chercher telz que jamais ne faillissent à parler saigement . . . il les fauldroit chercher au ciel, car on ne les trouveroit pas entre les hommes).'[33] At the same time, deference to divine determination, while certainly present in these dispatches, has compacted itself mainly into pious ejaculations or turns of phrase. *Piaque a Dio* and *per la gratia di Dio* are peppered throughout; but, in the meantime, practical calculation appears to rule events.

As in the subsequent writings of Machiavelli, Fortune intrudes from time to time, but in a considerably altered aspect. No longer designed to turn beholders from the vicissitudes of the world to the security of faith, these references urge a prudent self-protection and an astute response to her caprice. Angelo Acciaioli, writing to his duke in 1451, concedes the possible intervention of Fortune but bets on his own powers of prediction: 'although fortune can indeed dispose of these matters as she pleases ['benchè la fortuna possi disporre assai di queste cose'], nevertheless I hope in God to be able to say that you can have confidence that what I write to you will come about' (pp. 43–44). And the same ambassador, writing again to the duke in 1451–52 about news of a secret clause in a treaty with the Genoese, insists upon his respect for Fortune but indicates situations in which she may be kept at bay: 'Although in all matters fortune can do much ['Benchè in tucte le cose la fortuna possi assai . . .'], nevertheless I did not think that in this matter she was going to exert her power' (pp. 52–53).

In these fifteenth-century communications, dissimulation and disenchanted description need not await the coming of the sixteenth century or Machiavellian master articulation. Found in the Milanese archives is a letter of 1460, evidently intercepted or gotten by intrigue, and translated into Italian, sent by French operative Ragnault de Dresnay to the king of France. In his opinion, the duke of Milan is not to be trusted but rather to be suspected of dissimulation. God is nowhere in sight when our duke takes the stage, under suspicion that 'he seeks only to dissimulate ['dissimulare'] in order the better to arrange his affairs; that, in addition, he has secret understandings . . . to which he trusts; and that, if he should find things going well for him or could move to the accomplishment of his design, neither his honor nor his love for you would prevent him from putting his plans into execution' (pp. 284–85). From the evidence of the duke's own archives, de Dresnay has it right. Pious utterance aside, the good fifteenth-century prince will seek to orchestrate effects by terms under his own control.

So what has changed here, in comparison with the earlier medieval situation? The strategic deployment of a false exterior self is a staple of medieval moralizing discussion, as manifested in personified characters like 'false-seeming' and hypocrisy, dressed in their friars' copes in order to deceive the world. But revealed in the cases of such staples of moral allegory are permanent 'traits'; unalterable dispositions that may be read off as moral flaws. Whereas something different seems to be at stake in the French observer's view of the duke of Milan. Assessment of the duke's conduct is less moral than strategic. His is an improvisatory way of meeting the world, in which the means employed are directed toward, and judged in relation to, the end they serve. In the earlier medieval case the means are the object of evaluation, to be assessed according to what they reveal about the moral disposition of the character under observation. Now, rather than an object of assessment in their own right, means are judged according to the practical results they achieve.

Commynes

If the Milanese exhort each other to conduct themselves skillfully or *aptamente,* the retired diplomat Philippe de Commynes shows an equally keen interest in identifying a quality of *habilité,* or artful trickery, in the conduct of affairs.[34] Here is his comment, for example, on the connivances employed by Lord Wenlock who as captain of Calais in 1470 deceived his nominal patrons Edward IV and the duke of Burgundy, to advance the interests of the earl of Warwick:

> Because it is necessary to be well informed of the deceptions and evils of this world, and equally the good deeds, not at all so as to use them but to guard against them, I will declare a deception or artful trick—whatever one would wish to call it, but it was shrewdly conducted ['vueil declarer une tromperie ou habilité, ainsi qu'on la vouldra nommer, care

elle fut saigement conduicte'—III, chap. 4, p. 187]—for I also wish that one should hear the deceptions of our neighbors, and our own.

To the extent that they are branded as *tromperies,* these connivances are presented under a screen of mild disapproval. Yet this disapproval is no more than the residual effect of a Freudian disavowal: that process by which we license those proscribed thoughts that attract us the most. The reader easily understands and accepts the true nature of Commynes's attraction. This is, he says in effect, the way of the world, and you must know it—with respect both to our neighbors' actions and our own.

The particular situation is that, Warwick having fled England in one of the several abrupt reversals of that year, Wenlock as lord of Calais lent him surreptitious advice and comfort and furthered his scheme to reinstate Henry VI on the throne—despite, as Commynes goes on to emphasize, his continued enjoyment of a Yorkist appointment to his post and his receipt of a pension from the duke of Burgundy. The plot now thickens, as does Commynes' obvious pleasure in recounting it. For Commynes has a certain pride in his own ability to penetrate and describe ruses and plots; as he says to his reader:

> With respect to these secrets, artful deceptions or deceptions ['De ses secretz, habilités ou tromperies'—III, chap. 5, p. 190], that have been accomplished in our part of the world, you won't hear a truer account from anyone, at least with respect to those which have occurred during the last twenty years or more.

With this proven guide at our elbow, we are ready to be shown the secret of Wenlock's undoing.

Wenlock happens to have been acquainted with a certain English lady, whom he hoped to employ in the cause of making peace between Warwick and the French king, to Warwick's, and his own, ultimate advantage. Yet, Commynes informs us, 'as he beguiled others, he was himself deceived by this lady, for her mission was to conduct a large deal ['ung grand marché'] of her own, which she finally accomplished to the prejudice of the earl of Warwick and all his following' (III, chap. 5, pp. 189–90). This lady's 'secret' enterprise was to convince the duke of Clarence to desert the cause of Warwick and the French and return to the Yorkist and Burgundian fold—a step he was ultimately to take with disastrous consequences for himself and his new Lancastrian allies. Her rhetorical ploy—perhaps no ploy at all but simply a bit of realism—was to persuade Clarence that Warwick had no intention of preferring his claim as successor of Henry VI over that of the prince of Wales, to whom Warwick had already married his daughter. And so Wenlock turns out to be a 'guiler guiled,' a half-smart player over-matched by a smarter adversary: 'And although Lord Wenlock was an adroit [*habile*] man in his own right, this lady deceived him, and executed this scheme which led to the death of the duke of Warwick and all his followers' (p. 190). Commynes describes her dealings with the ill-fated Wenlock as 'ceste marchandise' (III, chap. 7, p. 200). And what a wonderful term indeed, with its simultaneous blend of 'negotiation' and 'commerce'! What better term for an undercover transaction, in which every attachment has a price and loyalties are bought and sold.

But where is God, and how does divine providence operate, in so calculating a world? Commynes' disposition is certainly not to deny God's action in the world, yet the form of God's introduction is telling, with respect to his actual state of mind. Most typically, God is introduced at the end of a long and detailed and highly circumstantial analysis of human motives, the import of which is to render God unnecessary in any explanatory sense. Thus, pinpointing the problems of the English as internal division and usurpation, he declares that such matters are decided in heaven: 'de telles choses le partaige s'en faict au ciel' (I, chap. 3, p. 62). Detailing the lapses and miscalculations leading to defeat for the count of Charolais in the battle of Montlhéry, he irrelevantly adds that God holds such outcomes in his hand: 'en cela monstra Dieu que les batailles sont en sa main' (I, chap. 3, p. 63). Minutely particularizing the 'expedians et habilitez' which won the seige of Liege for the lord of Humbercourt, all of which 'procedent de grand sens,' he nevertheless concludes that all this depends upon God alone: 'procede de la grace de Dieu seullement' (II, chap. 3, p. 127). After a masterful survey of the devastating effects of misjudgment in going to war, and recommending circumspection, he adds that God trumps human enterprise: 'quant Dieu y veult mectre la main, rien n'y vault' (II, chap. 5. p. 132). Such examples could be multiplied indefinitely; the point is that, both syntactically and logically, God is rendered extrinsic to Commynes' actual explanatory systems.

Although Commynes has a place for God in his scheme, this place is a rather estranged and belated one, with God emerging as something like a 'cyclical principle.' Commenting on the political instability of the English in the decades before the accession of Henry VII, he attributes this lamentable situation to a certain 'disposition divine':

> [T]o my mind, this results from nothing less than a divine disposition ['mon advis est qu'il ne se faict pas que par disposition divine'], since when princes or realms have long enjoyed prosperity and riches and have begun to misrecognize the source of their grace, God prepares an enemy or enmity of which they had no inkling, as you can see from the kings named in the Bible. (I, chap. 7, pp. 81–82)

As I have said, God here sounds suspiciously like a principle of reciprocity or equilibrium, somewhat more concerned with long durations and successions than with the justice of individual outcomes. God sounds, in other words, a good deal like Fortune herself, and not significantly less capricious with respect to personal fates. This, then, is the sense in which I partially agree with the frequent suggestion that Commynes is committed to the secularization of political discourse.[35] God lingers as an object of deference, and so a concept of outright 'secularization' cannot quite be made to apply in this case. Still, we are offered a form of de facto secularization, in which God is effectively excluded from a political sphere converted in its turn to an arena for the exercise of natural politics.[36]

As we might suppose, Commynes and his peers entertained a rather condescending attitude to the English and their powers of political analysis. Finding the English enmeshed in murky providential and predestinarian thinking, the French doubt their capacity to develop a language or capacity for practical political analysis. Consider, in this respect, Commynes' extended and devastating account of the utter prevalence of Louis XI's machinations against Edward IV's fumbling incursion of 1475. As Commynes puts it: 'King Edward and his advisers had no experience of the practices of the French, and merely went about their business in a fatheaded sort of way; resulting in their inability to grasp the dissimulations routinely employed over here' ('Ce roy Edouard ne ses gens n'avoient point fort praticqué les faictz de ce royaulme, et alloient grossement en besongne; par quoy ne peurent si tost entendre les dissimulations dont on use deça et ailleurs') (IV, chap. 6, pp. 250–51). The English, in fact, permit themselves to be gulled in multiple ways, but Commynes is particularly amused by their susceptibility in believing themselves a providential nation, succored by prophecy and bolstered by divine intervention. The disadvantageous peace once made, the English array it in the terms of prophetic discourse—in which, as Commynes observes, they are never lacking ('dont les Angloys ne sont jamais despourveuz'—IV, chap. 10, p. 267). Their greatest folly is in believing the Holy Ghost to be their collaborator, as evidenced by the fact of a white pigeon landing on their king's tent: 'they base everything on prophecies' ('car tous se fondent en prophecies'—IV, chap. 10, p. 270). And their evidence was that a white pigeon was discovered on the tent of the king of England the day of the meeting and, however much noise the soldiers made, it was unwilling to fly away' ('Ce qui leur faisoit dire, c'estoit que ung pijon blanc s'estoit trouvé sur la tante du roy d'Angleterre le jour de la veue, et, pour quelque bruit qu'il y eust en l'ost, il ne s'estoit voulu bouger'). The French, of course, had a less credulous explanation: 'But, in the opinion of some, it was a bit wet, and the sun came out, and the pigeon came to rest on this tent, which was the highest one, in order to dry itself' ('mais, à l'oppinion d'aulcuns, il avoit ung peu pleu, et puis vint ung grand souleil, et ce pijon se vint mettre sur ceste tante, qui estoit la plus haulte, pour s'essuyer'). This latter, more practical explanation, was that of a Gascon gentleman in the service of the English, commenting aside to Commynes that he was aware that the English were an object of mockery to the French ('que nous nous mocquerions fort du roy d'Angleterre et d'eulx').[37]

The *Arrivall*

Had the French any basis for their mirth? Perhaps. But the English were also well on their way to setting aside their reliance on providential thinking in favor of a practical language of political calculation. Despite the annoyance of Commynes in dealing with Wenlock on behalf of the duke of Burgundy, he nevertheless appears to regard Wenlock's manuevers as standard enough, or even estimable, within the parameters of the time. A similar flexibility in assessment is revealed in the *Arrivall*'s treatment of the earl of Northumberland, who snookered the marquis of Montague out of a chance to oppose Edward IV in battle when the latter emerged in weakened condition from the city of York (33v–34r). Warwick's brother Montague, holding Pontefract Castle with a force superior to Edward's own, allowed him to pass towards the midlands without contest: 'in no wyse trowbled hym, no none of the fellowshipe, but sufferyd him to passe in peasceable wyse were it with good will or noo men may iuge at theyr pleaswre.' Our author then pauses to assess this outcome, in a fashion dear to him and importantly contributory to building up his own style of pragmatic political assessment, by listing four main explanatory considerations: (1) that some of Montague's troops were actually covertly loyal to Edward; (2) that his troops were primarily in the service of the earl of Northumberland and awaited his command; (3) that Northumberland actually favored Edward but was not certain that this favor extended to all his followers; (4) that animosities lingered from the earlier battle of Towton, in which Edward's forces had slain many local kinsmen. Pausing in his analysis, the *Arrivall* author awards the earl of Northumberland an accolade, for thus succeeding in neutralizing the Marquis:

> And so it may be resonably iudged that this was a notable good service *and politiqwely done,* by th'erle. For his sittynge still caused the citie of Yorke to do as they dyd and no werse and every man in all thos northe partes to sit still also, and suffre the Kynge to passe as he dyd. (34r)

Returning to his list of reasons, our author adds (5) the heartiness of Edward's small band and (6) the cumulative effect of Edward's own success at York, as a result of which successive opponents reckoned that he had received more encouragement than was actually the case.

To return, however, to the earl of Northumberland's accolade, bestowed for his prudent and carefully calculated inactivity. Here *politiqwely* is — like *polyqwe* above — employed in a rather new way. What might loosely be called the dominant 'high medieval' sense of the term — solidified in the late thirteenth century via translations of Aristotle's *Ethics* and, especially, *Politics,* and also through concurrent Ciceronian sources — is affirmative in nature, revolving around enlightened concepts of rule in the common interest.[38] A locus classicus for this sense of *le politique,* derived in the first instance from Aristotle's *Ethics,* is found in Brunetto Latini's *Tresor,* in which he defines the *politique* as central among the sciences that enable governance of 'un people et une comune' according to reason and justice: 'selonc raison et selonc justice.'[39] This definition remained continually available, but in time was accompanied by such generalized derivatives as 'pertaining to governance' or 'dominated by fixed laws,' or else, when used as a term of approbation, something along the lines of 'consensual' or 'respectful of settled arrangements' or 'thrifty' or 'efficient.'[40] All these senses are rather opposite to, or at least remote from, the sense in which the word is used here, which is something like 'shrewd,' 'diplomatic,' 'holding something in reserve,' 'knowing more than one tells.' This is a new usage and a new kind of accolade — peculiar,

I am arguing, to the fifteenth century. The earl deserves it all the more, given that one of the kinsmen slain by the Yorkists at Towton was Northumberland's predecessor, his father, the third earl. Northumberland thus plays what might be considered a very cool hand. In the process, both he and Edward, profiting from their rather scrupulous calculations of self-interest and doing whatever it takes to realize their goals, come out looking to me for all the world like a couple of Renaissance princes, worthy of their own North Italian city-states!

The genius of the *Arrivall* author is analytical. He gives us a cast of characters who are all masters of calculation, and he takes delight in the constant, and minute, dissection of the different considerations weighed when decisions were taken. Thus, in addition to these reflections on Montague's dilemma and Northumberland's adept evasions, he goes on to perform a series of such analyses: Clarence's six considerations in deserting Warwick for Edward; Warwick's four reasons for refusing reconciliation with Edward; London's five reasons for opening its gates to Edward; the three reasons why the armies of the North decided not to oppose Edward; the three reasons why Falconbridge made inroads in London; the four reasons why his forces besieged the city from the south. For short summary, consider the case of Clarence, with which we are already partly acquainted through Commynes. Clarence, having yielded to 'the sybtyle compassynge of th'Erle of Warwike' in the first place, already began to reconsider his allegiance during Edward's brief exile in Holland. Among his considerations: the exclusion of his family from succession; the likelihood of war with his own brother; the elusiveness of security in such a state of division; the coolness of his own reception by the Lancastrians (who had been breaking their appointments!); the unlikelihood that his own claims to succession would be heeded; the unnaturalness of strife between brothers. We are told that, even before Edward's expedition, a blizzard of covert mediations had occurred. We already know about the dissimulative *damoiselle* who 'shopped' Clarence under Wenlock's nose, and now the list is greatly augmented: 'By right covert wayes and meanes were good mediators and mediatricis[:] the highe and myghty princis my lady theyr mothar[,] my lady of Exceter, my lady of Southfolke[,] theyre systars, my Lord Cardinall of Cantorbery, my lord of bathe[,] my lord of Essex[,] and most specially my lady of Bourgoigne' (35v). Interestingly, the *Arrivall* author's list has a great deal in common with Commynes' own shrewd recital of the *damoiselle*'s probable suasions: that he should not destroy his own lineage by collaborating with the house of Lancaster; that they been long-standing enemies; and, especially, that he might consider well that Warwick had espoused his daughter to the prince of Wales, and intended to make him king of England and had sworn homage to him—in other words, that Clarence's own hopes for reward from Warwick were deluded in the extreme. Here we are shown Clarence making a practical judgment, the covert stitch-up occurring, and then Clarence concealing his own intentions until his dramatic switch back to Edward at Banbury—in an elaborately stage-managed pageant of reconcilation, the results of which had been concealed until the last instant although agreed long before. The relish with which the *Arrivall* author conducts such analyses (akin to those of the master statesman Commynes, and no less elegant) is evident throughout his text. Whether he has in fact actually captured Clarence's reasoning is beside the point for this discussion; the point is that the *Arrivall* author creates and inhabits a universe in which calculation and naked self-interest are at the forefront, and subjects of consuming interest for author and audience alike.

Facilitating events in the *Arrivall* are not only covert embassies but also *espial* or spycraft, infiltration, rumor-mongering, bribery, assassination, staged processionals, dumbshows of clemency followed by wholesale political executions, public relations blitzes (after Tewkesbury, Edward 'forgate not to send from thens his messengars with writyngs all abowte'—45r), and the like. All this is to the end, not of providential kingship or the announcement of Edward as the recipient of God's election, but rather of demonstrating his capacity better to control the sources and agents of power.

In this sense, the *Arrivall* constitutes a brilliant early anticipation of the conditions of Shakespeare's histories, as David Kastan describes them: they 'expose the idealizations of political power . . . by revealing that power passes to him who can best control and manipulate the visual and verbal symbols of authority.'[41] In Kastan's view, such a display of the assumptions and resources of power constitutes an exposure of its 'mystifications' (p. 115), and leads to a derogation of authority. Nor do I disagree, especially when such representations revealed kingship to be 'strategic rather than sacramental' (p. 121), even in that late-sixteenth-century apogee of sacramental kingship.[42] A difference remains, though, from the Shakespearean situation described by Kastan, in that the third quarter of the fifteenth century appears to have been a time when a tradeoff seemed more fully acceptable: the relinquishment of some sacramental authority (a pretty threadbare raiment by the time we get to Edward anyway) in return for an acknowledgment that power deserves to pass 'to him who can best control and manipulate the . . . symbols of authority.' Something remarkably unabashed seems to be happening here. The *Arrivall* takes what might be called a 'gamble,' initiated by its willingness to display unsacral or even unkingly aspects of Edward's conduct. But it then seeks to win its gamble and to collect all bets by recapturing a sense of Edward's qualification for office within a revised, effectively nonsacral, description of astute kingship. Its double stratagem is to risk demystification by exposing with unusual candor the actual mechanisms of power, even as it remystifies the king as secular overlord by displaying him as a master tactician and manipulator of power.

Edward's behavior, like that of all fourteenth- and fifteenth-century claimants and kings, is profoundly theatrical. It need not await the development of the Elizabethan stage to discover its own obsession with costume, procession, and symbolic staging.[43] In addition, as Kastan observes of kingship on the Elizabethan stage, theatricality has the effect of constituting subjects as spectators, as an audience with an opportunity to judge. Ultimately locating 'sovereignty in the common will of subjects,'[44] this process could only unnerve an enthroned monarch, in the course of her rule. Yet the situation may differ in the mid-fifteenth century, when no monarch was securely enthroned and when the constant necessity to solicit the will of subjects was well understood by all. An illustrative juncture in Henry VI's kingship occurred in April 1471, when, just prior to Edward's arrival in the city, his minders sent him on a much-derided procession along the traditional route from Paul's through Cheap and Cornhill, ignominiously accompanied, in a fashion which won him no applause: 'the progresse . . . was more lyker a play then the shewyng of a prynce to wynne mennys hertys, ffor by this mean he lost many & wan noon or Rygth ffewe, and evyr he was shewid In a long blew goune of velvet as thowth he hadd noo moo to change wt.'[45] The cost of this failed procession to Henry is also noted in the *Arrivall*, which observes that his power was 'litle and feble as there and then was shewyd.' By contrast, upon his arrival in London Edward processed the same route well accompanied, adding diversions to the bishop's palace (where he was presented with Henry as prisoner) and thence to Westminster, thus anchoring the results and consequences of his more successful overture. The theatricality of Edward's power was taken for granted, as was the theatricality of all fifteenth-century power, and his ability to command a public response was an acknowledged element of his success.[46]

Even at its most apparently devout, the *Arrivall* thus presents a practical arena of power in which the symbolic is at the mercy of tactical aims and the sacred is everywhere available for enlistment in statecraft's opportunistic objectives. Within the coming narratives of Tudor ascendancy, a form of backlash will ensue, in which the suborned and partially neglected apparatus of divine providence is refreshed and reenlisted in a new dynastic cause.

5. PERJURY AGAIN: TUDOR RECASTINGS

Perjury—here understood as the deliberate violation of a sworn, and hence sacred, oath—percolates through these narratives. The question is less whether perjury has implicitly or overtly occurred than how it is to be judged. Although certain fluctuations of opinion can be seen, the Tudor tendency is clear: perjury is not, in the final analysis, to be excused, nor is a definition of *politique* behavior that embraces perjury as one of its affirmative tactics to be condoned. We encounter in the transition to the Tudor era what Quentin Skinner describes as a moment of failed ideological initiative, in which a term briefly attains a new sense, but then, 'after a period of confusion about the criteria for applying a disputed term, the final outcome may not be polysemy, but rather a reversion to the employment of the original criteria, together with a corresponding obsolescence of the newer usages.'[47]

John Stow occupies a halfway position in the general Tudor drift toward condemnation of Edward's double-dealing. He stops short of a full-blown perjury accusation, but dismisses Edward as a shallow opportunist. Stow had access to a copy of the *Arrivall,* and eventually copied it in his own hand, but did not use it in his *Annales.*[48] Indeed, in selecting his other sources, Stow shows an interest in building up the weaker Lancastrian side of the account, embracing details that display Edward in not only a duplicitous but also a starkly ignoble light. For this purpose, he draws upon an alternate Lancastrian source. This is the chronicle of or by John Warkworth, completed (or left off) soon after Edward's readeption. Warkworth takes a consistently anti-Edwardian line, emphasizing his duplicitous cruelty, including the murder of prisoners after Tewkesbury. Perhaps the most damning of his representations is that of Edward's charade in the aftermath of the 'Ravenys-spore' landing, when he went about masquerading as a supporter of Henry and the Prince: 'And thereto afore alle pepl, he cryed "A! Kinge Herry! A! Kynge and Prynce Edwarde!" and wered ane estryche feder, Prynce Edwardes lyvery.'[49] The satiric possibilities of Edward, festooned with the livery of the prince whose death he was about to engineer, do not escape Stow, who offers the following account of Edward's 'wether beaten' landing:

> King Edward . . . would have landed in Essex, but there the Earle of Oxfords brother put them off, and after hee landed sore wether beaten at Rauensporne. . . . As king Edward passed the countery, he shewed the earle of Northumberlands letters and seales, that sent for him, saying, that he came to clayme no title of the crowne, but only his dukedome of Yorke, nor would not haue done afore, but at the exciting of the Earle of Warwicke, and cryed in euery place, king Henry and Prince Edward, wearing an Estrich feather prince Edwards liuery.[50]

Warkworth's and Stow's chronicles are both, in their respective ways, a bit off the beaten track. The main Tudor tradition derives from Polydore Vergil and proceeds through Hall to Holinshed and thence to Shakespeare. This tradition takes a less satiric but more severe line about Edward's perjury—a line that finally all but closes the door on the brief moment of unapologetic *politique*.

The inaugural Tudor account is Polydore Vergil's *Anglica Historia,* begun around 1506, completed in manuscript by 1513, and then successively revised for printed publication in 1534, 1546, and 1555.[51] Vergil treats Edward's duplicitous promise as a pivotal moment in the vicissitudes of fifteenth-century English succession. Rather than extracting Edward from his predecessor's perfidy, however, it puts him deeper in the mire, no closer at all to a resolution and able only to reiterate the deed. As always, Edward is understood to have duplicitously misstated his claim. In the English of the anonymous Tudor translation of Vergil's 1546 edition, 'he causyd yt to be blowen abrode that he sowght only for his dukedom of Yorke ['tantummodo suum principatum Eboracensem, quaerere divulgat'], to thintent that by this reasonable and rightewouse request he might get more favor at all handes.'[52] Vergil goes on to represent Edward's maneuver in a much more critical light than did the *Arrivall*. Perhaps under the influence of the fifteenth-century chronicler Harding, who had impugned Henry IV's motives by pointing out that he touched and kissed the holy gospels in support of his lie, Vergil emphasizes the aspect of perjury in Edward's promise. In fact, his promise to be faithful to Henry VI becomes, like Henry IV's parallel promise, a sworn 'othe': 'the next day very early in the morning, *whyle a pryest sayd masse* at the gate wherby he was to enter the towne, he *emong the holy mysteryes* promysyd by othe, devoutly and reverently, to observe' courtesy to York and the prerogative of Henry VI (p. 139; emphasis added).

Having portrayed Edward lying in the company of the Host, Vergil pauses to point the matter by reflecting upon a situation in which men perjure themselves before God by making a sworn promise they already intend to break: 'Thus oftentimes as well men of highe as of low cawling blyndyd with covetousnes, and forgetting all religyon and honesty, ar woont to make promyse in swearing the thimmortal God, which promyse neverthelesse they ar already determynyd to breake before they make yt' (p. 139). Vergil here adopts the voice of the moralist, but at least the moralist with a full grasp of the perfidies he is moralizing about. Vergil's *Historia* was actually finished in the same year (1516) as Machiavelli's *Prince*. Yet he needed to know nothing of this new and scandalous analysis of machination in quest of political ends, since he already could have learned everything he needed to know about such deceits from the unflustered appraisals of the *Arrivall*. Edward IV indeed has much in common with Machiavelli's Alexander VI, about whom Machiavelli will later say: 'there never was a man with greater efficacy in asserting a thing, and in affirming it with greater oaths, who observed it less; nonetheless, his deceits succeeded at his will, because he well knew this aspect of the world.'[53]

Vergil walks a fine line. He seems able to grasp, and in fact to take explicit note of, a new standard of *politique* behavior. But this is a development he is obliged to deplore. His own enterprise is bent away from an emerging science of early modern political behavior and toward the reassertion of a providential scheme. His characters get away with nothing, invariably paying what they owe. In his 1534 edition, he observes that Henry IV's false oath and ensuing usurpation ultimately caught up with the otherwise innocent Henry VI (pp. 514–15), and he also makes Edward's heirs pay for his transgression. Describing Richard III's murder of Edward's sons and the intervention of God as 'revenger of falshed and treason,' he locates the cause in Edward's *perjury*, pausing even to define the term: 'That fortunyd peradventure to thse two innocent impes because Edward ther fathyr commytted the offence of perjury, by reason of that most solemne othe which . . . he tooke at the gates of the cytie of York, meaning one thing inwardly and promysyng an other in expresse woordes outwardly' (p. 190).

Edward Hall, composing his 'Vnion of the two noble and illustre fame-lies,' offers a free but generally faithful rendering of Vergil (noted among his enumerated sources as 'Polidorus'). If anything, his reading of Edward's false promise is even more severe than Vergil's: 'in the next mornyng, at the gate where he should enter, a priest beyng redy to say masse, in the masse tyme, receyung the body of our blessed Sauior, solemply swearyng to kepe and ob-serue the two Articles aboue mencioned, and agreed upon, when it was far vnlike, tht he either entended or purposed to obserue any of them.'[54] Hall ac-tually sharpens Vergil's indictment. Vergil only placed him '*among the holy mysteryes,*' whereas Hall has him taking communion. Then, like Vergil, he moves *periurie* to the forefront, and agrees in tracing the death of the princes at the hands of Richard III to the anger of an offended God. Hall, like Ver-gil, is interested in the parallel between Henry IV's falsity as 'first aucthor of deuision' and Edward's own perjury, and the punishments meted to each. The point made by these Tudor historians is that Edward's false promise can lead only to retribution and more betrayal. His landing at Ravenspur can end nothing, 'complete' nothing, but only continue a sterile sequence; until, that is, for Hall and the Tudor historians, the advent of Henry VII, the event that will put an end to senseless repetition.

As regards the *Arrivall*'s experiment with *politique,* the door is closing in several different ways. One form of closure runs from Warkworth through Stow, and may be considered generally 'Lancastrian' in sentiment, empha-sizing Edward's shallow opportunism. A second runs from Vergil to Hall, and, aiming at a union of the two houses, clears the ground for this claim by disallowing Edward's claim to have set anything right by perjured tactics after Ravenspur. The third, and culminating, tradition is that of Holinshed. In Holinshed, we reencounter the *Arrivall,* in a racy and effective adapta-tion, drawn rather closely from 'Mastar Flyghtwod's' manuscript.[55] Thus in Holinshed we read a familiar passage: 'The king . . . landed within Humber on Holdernesse side, at a place called Rauenspurgh, euen in the same place where Henrie erle of Derbie, after called king Henrie the fourth landed, when he came to depriue king Richard the second of the crowne, and to vssurpe it to himselfe' (p. 303). Indeed, Holinshed takes us up to the gates of York, in very much the terms of the *Arrivall.* Yet the unique thing about the Holinshed text is that it immediately follows his extract from the *Arrivall* with a passage based upon the Vergil-Hall tradition, in which Edward in-vites reprisal by falsely swearing upon the sacrament of communion: 'And (as some write) there was a priest readie to saie masse, in which masse time the king receiued the sacrament of the communion, and there solemnlie sware to kéepe and obserue two speciall articles.' This fusion of the *Arrivall* with the Vergil-Hall tradition is sealed by a further homiletic moment, peculiar to Holinshed's 1587 edition, and thus probably contributed by Abraham Fleming.[56] Noting that, in the Vergil-Hall tradition, the perjured prince courts reprisal, Holinshed rather primly concludes, 'And suerlie, if an oth among priuate men is religiouslie to be kept . . . doubtlesse of princes it is verie nicelie and preciselie to be observed.' Thus, with a rather tame sentiment attached, the once-formidable *Arrivall,* with its unabashed Yorkism and its frank respect for a new kind of *politique,* assumes its place within a compromise formation.[57]

Departing from such prim moralization, Shakespeare's *True Tragedie of Richarde Duke of Yorke* sponsors what amounts to a partial return of the political repressed.[58] Shakespeare's text, that is, retrieves the possibility of practical calculation, although now split into stronger and weaker variants. The stronger is embodied in Richard duke of Gloucester, who is able to cite Machiavelli by reputation, if not by chapter and verse, with his intention to 'set the murderous Machiavel to school' (3.2.192).[59] The weaker variant is assigned to Edward IV before the walls of York: 'When we grow stronger, then we'll make our claim. / Till then 'tis wisdom to conceal our meaning' (4.8.59–60).[60] Edward is now hesitant, now seeks a 'safe' way to the crown. In order to propel him to the throne, Shakespeare must introduce the character of Montgomery, mentioned only fleetingly in Hall and Holinshed, to force his hand, by offering to fight in Edward's behalf only if he proclaims himself king. Meantime, it is Gloucester—already present and already hotheaded in Wavrin's account—who now carries the momentum of Edward's claim, wryly glossing his brother's intentions, seconding Montgomery, pressing for proclamation. The search for practical and nonprovidential statecraft lives on, but grotesquely, in Gloucester's flawed example, awaiting a more favorable hearing during the 'Machiavellian moment' of the seventeenth century.

APPENDIX.

THE HISTORIE OF THE ARRIVALL OF KING EDWARD IV

Edited from Stow's transcript (BL MS Harley 543, ff. 32–49) by John Bruce, Camden Society, ser. 1, no. 1 (London, 1838).

A.D. 1471

Here aftar folowethe the mannar how the moaste noble and right victorious prince Edwarde, by the grace of God, Kinge of England and of Fraunce, and Lord of Irland, in the yere of grace 1471, in the monethe of Marche, departed out of Zeland; toke the sea; aryved in England; and, by his force and valliannes, of newe redewced and reconqueryd the sayde realme, upon and agaynst th'Erle of Warwicke, his traytor and rebell, calling himselfe Lievetenaunte of England, by pretensed auctoritie of the usurpowre Henry, and his complices; and, also, upon and agains Edward, callynge hymselfe prince of Wales, sonne to the sayde Henry than wrongfully occupienge the Royme and Crowne of England; and, upon many othur greate and myghty Lords, noble men, and othar, beinge mightily accompaigned. Compiled and put in this forme suinge, by a servaunt of the Kyngs, that presently saw in effect a great parte of his exploytes, and the resydewe knewe by true relation of them that were present at every tyme.

IN the yere of grace 1471, aftar the comptinge of the church of England, the ij. day of Marche, endynge the x. yere of the reigne of our soveraign Lord Kynge Edwarde the IV. by the grace of God Kynge of England and of Fraunce, and Lord of Irland, the sayde moaste noble kynge accompanied with ij thowsand Englyshe men, well chosen, entendynge to passe the sea, and to reentar and recovar his realme of England, at that tyme usurpyd and occupied by Henry, callyd Henry the VI., by the traytorous meanes of his greate rebell Richard, Erle of Warwicke, and his complices, entred into his shipe, afore the haven of Flisshinge, in Zeland, the sayde ij. day of Marche; and, forasmoche as aftar he was in the shippe, and the felowshipe also, with all that to them appertayned, the wynd fell not good for hym, he therefore wold not retorne agayne to the land, but abode in his shipe, and all his felowshipe in lyke wyse, by the space of ix dayes, abydynge good wynde and wether; whiche had the xj. day of Marche, he made saile, and so did all the shipps that awayted upon hym, takyng theyr cowrse streyght over [towards] the coste of Norfolke, and came before Crowmere, the Tusedaye, agayne even, the xij. day of Marche; withar the Kynge sent on land Ser Robart Chambarlayne, Syr Gilbert Debenham, Knyghts, and othar, trustinge by them to have some knowledge how the land inward was disposed towards hym, and, specially, the countries there nere adioyninge, as in party so they browght hym knowledge from suche as for that caws wer sent into thos parties, from his trew servaunts and partakars within the land, whiche tolde them, for certayne, that thos parties wer right sore beset by th'Erle of War-wyke, and his adherents, and, in especiall, by th'Erle of Oxenforde, in such wyse that, of lyklyhood, it might not be for his wele to lande in that con-trye; and a great cawse was, for the Duke of Norfolke was had owt of the contrye, and all the gentlemen to whom th'Erle of Warwyke bare any sus-picion ware, afore that, sent for by letars of privie seale, and put in warde about London, or els found suerty; natheles, the sayd ij Knyghts, and they that came on land with them, had right good chere, and turned agayne to the sea. Whos report herd, the Kynge garte make course towards the north partyes. The same night followinge, upon the morne, Wenesday, and Thurs-day the xiiij. daye of Marche, fell great stormes, wynds and tempests upon the sea, so that the sayde xiiij. day, in great torment, he came to Humbrehede, where the othar shipps were dissevered from hym, and every from other, so that, of necessitye, they were dryven to land, every fere from other. The Kynge, with his shippe aloone, wherein was the Lord Hastings, his Cham-barlayne, and other to the nombar of v^c well chosen men, landed within Humber, on Holdernes syde, at a place called Ravenersporne, even in the same place where somtime the Usurpowr Henry of Derby, aftar called Kynge Henry the IV. landed, aftar his exile, contrary and to the dissobey-sance of his sovereigne lord, Kynge Richard the II. whome, aftar that, he wrongfully distressed, and put from his reigne and regalie, and usurped it falsely to hymselfe and to his isswe, from whome was linially descended Kynge Henry, at this tyme usinge and usurpinge the corone, as sonne to his eldest sonne, somtyme callyd Kynge Henry the V. The Kyng's brothar Rich-ard, Duke of Glowcestar, and, in his company, iij^c men, landyd at an othar place iiij myle from thens. The Earle Rivers, and the felowshipe beinge in his companye, to the nombar of ij^c, landyd at a place called Powle, xiiij myle from there the Kynge landyd, and the reminaunt of the felowshipe wher they myght best get land. That night the Kynge was lodgyd at a power vil-lage, ij myle from his landynge, with a few with hym; but that nyght, and in the morninge, the resydewe that were comen in his shipe, the rage of the tempest somewhate appeasyd, landyd and alwaye drewe towards the Kynge. And on the morne, the xv. day of Marche, from every landynge place the felowshipe came hoole toward hym. As to the folks of the countrye there came but right few to hym, or almost none, for, by the scuringe of suche persons as for that cawse were, by his said rebells, sent afore into thos partes for to move them to be agains his highnes, the people were sore endwsed to be contrary to hym, and not to receyve, ne accepe hym, as for theyr Kynge; natwithstondynge, for the love and favour that before they had borne to the prince of fulnoble memorye, his father, Duke of Yorke, the people bare hym right great favowr to be also Duke of Yorke, and to have that of right apartayned unto hym, by the right of the sayde noble prince his fathar. And, upon this opinion, the people of the countrie, whiche in greate nombar, and in dyvars placis, were gatheryd, and in harnes, redye to resiste hym in chalenginge of the Royme and the crowne, were disposyd to content them selfe, and in noo wyse to annoy hym, ne his felowshipe, they affirmynge that to such entent were [they] comen, and none othar. Whereupon, the hoole felowshipe of the Kyngs comen and assembled togethar, he toke advise what was best to doo, and concludyd brifely, that, albe it his enemies and chefe rebells were in the sowthe partes, at London and ther about, and that the next way towards them had be by Lyncolneshire, yet, in asmooche as, yf they shulde have taken that waye, they must have gon eft sones to the watar agayne, and passyd ovar Humbar, whiche they abhoryd for to doo; and also, for that, yf they so dyd it would have be thowght that they had withdrawe them for feare, which note of sklaundar they wer right lothe to suffar; for thes, and othar goode considerations, they determined in themselves not to goo agayne to the watar, but to holde the right waye to his City of Yorke. The Kynge determined also, that, for as longe as he shuld be in passynge thrughe and by the contrye, and to the tyme that he myght, by th'assistaunce of his trew servaunts, subiects and lovars, whiche he trustyd veryly in his progres shuld come unto hym, be of suche myght and puissaunce as that were lykly to make a sufficient party, he, and all thos of his felowshipe, shuld noyse, and say openly, where so evar they came, that his entent and purpos was only to claime to be Duke of Yorke, and to have and enioy th'enheritaunce that he was borne unto, by the right of the full noble prince his fathar, and none othar. Thrwghe whiche noysynge the people of the contrye that were gatheryd and assembled in dyvars placis, to the number of vi or vij thowsand men, by the ledinge and gwydynge of a priste the vycar of   , in one place, and a gentleman of the same contrye, callyd, Martyn of the See, to th'entent to have resisted and lettyd hym his passage, by the stiringe of his rebells, theyr complices, and adherents, toke occasyon to owe and beare hym favowre in that qwarell, not discoveringe, ne remembringe, that his sayd fathar, bisydes that he was rightfully Duke of Yorke, he was also verrey trew and rightwise enheritoure to the roylme and corone of England &c. and so he was declared by [the] iij astates of the land, at a parliament holden at Westmynster, unto this day never repelled, ne revoked. And, under this manar, he kepinge furthe his purpos with all his felowshipe, toke the right way to a gode towne called Beverley, being in his high way towards Yorke. He sent to an othar gode towne, walled, but vj myle thens, called Kyngstown upon Hull, desyringe th'enhabitants to have openyd it unto hym, but they refused so to doo, by the meanes and stirings of his rebells, whiche aforne had sent thethar, and to all the contrye, strict commandements willing, and also charginge, them, at all their powers, to withstonde the Kinge, in caase he there aryved. And, therefore, levinge that towne, he kept his way forthe streight to Yorke. And nere this way were also assembled great compaignies in divars places, muche people of the contrie, as it was reported, but they cam not in syght, but all they suffred hym to pas forthe by the contrye; eythar, for that he and all his felowshipe pretendyd by any manar langage none other qwarell but for the right that was his fathars, the Duke of Yorke; or ells, for that, thowghe they were in nombar mo than he, yet they durst not take upon them to make hym any manifest warre, knowynge well the great curage and hardiness that he was of, with the parfete asswrance of the felowshipe that was with hym; or ells, paradventure, for that certayne of theyr capitaines and gadrers were some whate enduced to be the more benivolent for money that the Kynge gave them; wherfore the Kynge, keping furthe his way, cam beforn Yorke, Monday the xviij. day of the same monithe. Trewthe it is that aforne the Kynge came at the citie, by iij myles, came unto him one callyd Thomas Coniers, Recordar of the citie, whiche had not bene afore that named trwe to the Kyngs partie. He tolde hym that it was not good for hym to come to the citie, for eyther he shuld not be suffred to enter, or els, in caas he enteryd, he was lost, and undone, and all his. The Kynge, seeing so ferforthly he was in his iorney that in no wyse he might goo backe with that he had begone, and that no good myght folowe but only of hardies, decreed in hymselfe constantly to purswe that he had begon, and rathar to abyde what God and good fortune woulde gyve hym, thowghe it were to hym uncertayne, rathar than by laches, or defaulte of curage, to susteyne reprooche, that of lyklihode therby shulde have ensued; And so, therfore, notwithstondynge the discorag-

inge words of the Recordar, which had be afore suspecte to hym and his partie, he kept boldely forthe his iorney, streyght towards the citie. And, within
a while, came to hym, owt of the citie, Robart Clifford and Richard Burghe,
whiche gave hym and his felowshipe bettar comforte, affirmyng, that in the
qwarell aforesayde of his father the Duke of Yorke, he shuld be receyvyde and
sufferyd to passe; whereby, better somewhate encoragyd, he kepte his waye;
natheles efte sonnes cam the sayde Coniers, and put hym in lyke discomforte
as afore. And so, sometyme comfortyd and sometyme discomfortyd, he came
to the gates afore the citie, where his felashipe made a stoppe, and himself
and xvj or xvij persons, in the ledinge of the sayde Clifford and Richard
Burgh, passed even in at the gates, and came to the worshipfull folks whiche
were assembled a little within the gates, and shewed them th'entent and purpos of his comming, in suche forme, and with such maner langage, that the
people contentyd them therwithe, and so receyvyd him, and all his felawshipe, that night, when he and all his feloshipe abode and were refreshed
well to they had dyned on the morne, and than departed out of the cite to
Tadcastar, a towne of th'Erls of Northumbarland, x mile sowthwards. And,
on the morow after that, he toke his waye towards Wakefielde and Sendall,
a grete lordshipe appartayninge to the Duke of Yorke, leving the Castell of
Pomfrete on his lefte hand, wher abode, and was, the Marqwes Montagwe,
that in no wyse trowbled hym, ne none of his fellowshipe, but sufferyd hym
to passe in peasceable wyse, were it with good will, or noo, men may iuge at
theyr pleaswre; I deme ye; but, trouth it is, that he ne had nat, ne cowthe
not have gatheryd, ne made, a felashipe of nombar sufficient to have openly
resistyd hym in hys qwarell, ne in Kyng Henries qwarell; and one great caws
was, for great partie of the people in thos partis lovyd the Kyngs person well,
and cowthe nat be encoragyd directly to doo agayne hym in that qwarell of
the Duke of Yorke, which in almannar langage of all his fellawshipe was covertly pretendyd, and none othar. An othar grete cawse was, for grete partye of [the] noble men and comons in thos parties were towards th'Erle of
Northumbarland, and would not stire with any lorde or noble man other
than with the sayde Earle, or at leaste by his commandement. And, for soo
muche as he sat still, in suche wise that yf the Marques wolde have done his
besines to have assembled them in any manier qwarell, neithar for his love,
whiche they bare hym non, ne for any commandement of higher auctoritie,
they ne wolde in no cawse, ne qwarell, have assisted hym. Wherein it may
right well appere, that the said Erle, in this behalfe, dyd the Kynge right
gode and notable service, and, as it is deemed in the conceipts of many men,

he cowthe nat hav done hym any beter service, ne not thowghe he had openly declared hym selfe extremly parte-takar with the Kynge in his rightwys qwar-ell, and, for that entent, have gatheryd and assemblyd all the people that he might have made; for, how be it he loved the Kynge trewly and parfectly, as the Kynge thereof had certayne knowledge, and wolde, as of himselfe and all his power, have served hym trwely, yet was it demyd, and lykly it was to be trewe, that many gentlemen, and othar, whiche would have be araysed by him, woulde not so fully and extremly have determyned them selfe in the Kyng's right and qwarell as th'Erle wolde have done hymselfe; havynge in theyr freshe remembraunce, how that the Kynge at the first entrie-winning of his right to the Royme and Crowne of England, had and won a great bat-taile in those same parties, where theyr Maistar, th'Erlls fathar, was slayne, many of theyr fathars, theyr sonns, theyr britherne, and kynsemen, and othar many of theyr neighbowrs; wherefore, and nat without cawse, it was thowght that they cowthe nat have borne verrey good will, and done theyr best service, to the Kynge, at this tyme, and in this quarell. And so it may be resonably judged that this was a notable good service, and politiquely done, by th'Erle. For his sittynge still caused the citie of Yorke to do so as they dyd, and no werse, and every man in all thos northe partes to sit still also, and suffre the Kynge to passe as he dyd, nat with standynge many were right evill disposed of them selfe agaynes the Kynge, and , in especiall, in his qwarell. Where-fore the Kynge may say as Julius Cesar sayde, he that is nat agaynst me is with me. And othar right greate cause why the Marqwes made nat a felawshippe agaynst hym for to have trowbled hym [was], for thowghe all the Kynges [felowshipe] at that season were nat many in nombar, yet they were so habiled, and so well piked men, and, in theyr werke they hadd on hand, so willed, that it had bene right hard to right-a-great felashipe, moche greatar than they, or gretar than that the Marques, or his frends, at that tyme, cowthe have made, or assembled, to have put the Kynge and his sayde felawshipe to any distresse. And othar cawse [was,] where as he cam thrwghe the cuntre there, the people toke an opinion, that yf the people of the contries where-thrwghe he had passed aforne, had owght him any mannar of malice, or evill will, they would some what have shewed it whan he was amongs them, but, inasmoche as no man had so don aforne, it was a declaration and evidence to all thos by whome he passyd after, that in all the othar contries wer none but his goode lovars; and greate foly it had bene to the lattar cuntries to have at-tempted that the former cuntries would not, thinkynge verilie that, in suche case, they, as his lovars, would rathar have ayded hym thann he shulde have bene distressed; wherefore he passed with moche bettar will.

Abowte Wakefylde, and in thos parties, came some folks unto hym, but not so many as he supposed wolde have comen; nevarthelesse his nombar was encreasyd. And so from thens he passyd forthe to Doncastar, and so forthe to Notyngham. And to that towne came unto hym two good Knyghts, Syr William Parre, and Ser James Harington, with two good bands of men, well arrayed, and habled for warr, the nombar of vi^c men.

The Kynge, beinge at Notyngham, and or he came there, sent the scorers alabowte the contries adioynynge, to aspie and serche yf any gaderyngs were in any place agaynst hym; some of whome came to Newerke, and undarstode well that there was, within the towne, the Duke of Excestar, th'Erle of Oxforde, the Lord Bardolf, and othar, with great felowshipe, which th'Erle and they had gatheryd in Essex, in Northfolke, Sowthfolke, Cambridgeshire, Huntyngdonshire, and Lyncolneshire, to the nombar of iiij^M men. The sayde Duke and Erll, havynge knowledge that the sayde forrydars of the Kyngs had bene aforne the towne in the evenynge, thinkynge verily that the Kynge, and his hole hoste, were approchinge nere, and would have come upon them, determyned shortly within themselfe that [they] might not abyde his comynge. Wherefore, erly, abowte two of the cloke in the mornynge, they flede out of the towne, and ther they lost parte of the people that they had gatheryd and browght with them thethar. Trewthe it was, that, whan the Kynges aforne-ridars had thus espyed theyr beinge, they acertaynyd the Kynge therof, at Notyngham, which, incontinent, assembled all his felowshipe, and toke the streyght waye to-them-wards, within three myle of the towne. And, there, came to hym certayne tydings that they were fledd owt of Newerke, gonn, and disperpled; wherefore he returnyd agayne to Notyngham, determyned to kepe the next and right way towards his sayd great Rebell, th'Erle of Warwike, the which he knew well was departyd out of London, and comen into Warwikeshire, where he besterd hym, and in the countries nere adioynynge, t'assemble all that he myght, to th'entent to have made a myghty filde agaynst the Kynge, and to have distressyd hym. Wherefore, from Notyngham, the Kynge toke the streyght way towards hym, by Leicestre; but, as sonne as he hard of the Kyngs comyng onwards, and approchinge nere, eythar for that hym thowght not to be of swfficient powere to gyve hym batayle in that playne filde, or els, for that he lacked hardines and cowrage soo to doo, albe it he had assembled greatar nombar than the Kynge had at that tyme;

for by the pretensed auctoritie of Henry, than callyd Kynge, he was constitute Lievetenaunt of England, and, whereas he cowthe nat arrayse the people
with good will, he streyghtly charged them to come forthe upon payne of
deathe; he withdrew hymselfe, and all his fellowshipe, into a strong wallyd
towne there nere by hym, callyd Coventrye.

At Leycestar came to the Kynge ryght-a-fayre felawshipe of folks, to
the nombar of iij^M men, well habyled for the wers, suche as were veryly to
be trustyd, as thos that wowlde uttarly inparte with hym at beste and worste
in his qwarell, withe all theyr force and myght to do hym theyr trew service.
And, in substaunce, they were suche as were towards the Lord Hastings, the
Kyngs Chambarlayne, and, for that entent above sayd, came to hym, stiryd by
his messages sent unto them, and by his servaunts, frinds, and lovars, suche
as were in the contrie.

And so, bettar accompanyed than he had bene at any tyme aforne, he departyd from Leycestar, and cam before the towne of Coventrie, the xxix. day
of Marche. And when he undarstode the sayde Earle within the towne [was]
closyd, and with hym great people, to the nombar of vj or vij^M men, the Kynge
desyred hym to come owte, with all his people, into the filde, to determyne
his qwarell in playne fielde, which the same Earle refused to do at that tyme,
and so he dyd iij dayes aftar-ensuinge continually. The Kynge, seinge this,
drwe hym and all his hooste streght to Warwike, viij small myles from thens,
where he was receyvyd as Kynge, and so made his proclamations from that
tyme forthe wards; where he toke his lodgyngs, wenynge thereby to have
gyven the sayde Earle gretar cowrage to have yssyed owte of the towne of
Coventyre, and to have taken the field, but he ne would so doo. Nathelesse
dayly came certayne personns on the sayde Erlls behalve to the Kinge, and
made greate moynes, and desired him to treate withe hym, for some gode
and expedient appoyntment. And, how be it the Kynge, by the advise of his
Counseylors, grauntyd the sayd Erle his lyfe, and all his people beinge there
at that tyme, and dyvers othar fayre offers made hym, consythar his great and
haynows offenses; which semyd resonable, and that for the wele of peax and
tranquilitie of the Realme of England, and for ther-by to avoyde th'effusyon
of Christen bloode, yet he ne woulde accepte the sayde offars, ne accorde
thereunto, but yf he myght have had suche apoyntment unreasonable as
myght nat in eny wyse stande with the Kynges honowr and swretye.

Here is to be remembride how that, at suche season aforne, as whan the
Kynge was in Holand, the Duke of Clarence, the Kyngs second brothar, consyderinge the great inconveniences whereunto as well his brother the Kynge,

he, and his brother the Duke of Glocestar, were fallen unto, thrwghe and by
the devisyon that was betwixt them, whereunto, by the subtyle compassynge
of th'Erle of Warwike, and his complices, they were browght, and enduced;
as, first to be remembred, the disheritinge of them all from the Royme and
Crowne of England, and that therto apperteynyd; and, besyds that, the mortall warre and detestable, lykely to falle betwixt them; and, ovar this, that yt
was evident that to what party so evar God woulde graunte the victorye,
that, notwithstandynge, the wynner shuld nat be in eny bettar suerty therefore of his owne estate and parson, but abyde in as greate, or greatar, dangar
than they wer in at that tyme. And, in especiall, he considred well, that
hymselfe was had in great suspicion, despite, disdeigne, and hatered, with
all the lordes, noblemen, and othar, that were adherents and full partakers
with Henry, the Usurpar, Margaret his wyfe, and his sonne Edward, called
Prince; he sawe also, that they dayly laboryd amongs them, brekynge theyr
appoyntments made with hym, and of lyklihed, aftar that, shuld continually more and more fervently entend, conspire, and procure the distruction
of hym, and of all his blode, wherethrwghe it apperyd also, that the Roylme
and Regalie shuld remaygne to suche as thereunto myght nat in eny wyse
have eny rightwyse title. And, for that it was unnaturall, and agaynes God,
to suffar any suche werre to continew and endure betwixt them, yf it myght
otharwyse be, and, for othar many and great considerations, that by right
wyse men and virtuex were layed afore hym, in many behalfs, he was agreed
to entend to some good apointment for this pacification. By right covert wayes
and meanes were goode mediators, and mediatricis, the highe and myghty
princis my Lady, theyr mothar; my lady of Exceter, my lady of Southfolke,
theyre systars; my Lord Cardinall of Cantorbery; my Lord of Bathe; my
Lord of Essex; and, moste specially, my Lady of Bourgoigne; and othar, by
mediacions of certayne priests, and othar well disposyd parsouns. Abowte
the Kyngs beinge in Holland, and in other partes beyond the sea, great and
diligent labowre, with all effect, was continually made by the high and mighty
princesse, the Duches of Bowrgine, which at no season ceasyd to send hir
sarvaunts, and messengars, to the Kynge, wher he was, and to my sayd Lorde
of Clarence, into England; and so dyd his verrey good devowre in that behalfe my Lord of Hastings, the Kyng's Chambarlayne, so that a parfecte accord was appoyntyd, accordyd, concludyd, and assured, betwixt them; wherein
the sayde Duke of Clarence full honorably and trwly acquited hym; for, as
sune as he was acertaygned of the Kyngs arivall in the north parties, he
assembled anon suche as would do for hym, and, assone as he godly myght,

drew towards the Kynge, hym to ayde and assyste agaynste all his enemyes, accompanied with mo than iiij^M.

The Kynge, that tyme beinge at Warwyke, and undarstondynge his neere approchinge, upon an aftarnone isswyd out of Warwike, with all his felowshipe, by the space of three myles, into a fayre fylde towards Banbery, where he saw the Duke, his brothar, in faire array, come towards hym, with a greate felashipe. And, whan they were togedars, within lesse than an halfe myle, the Kynge set his people in aray, the bannars [displayed] and lefte them standynge still, takynge with hym his brothar of Glocestar, the Lord Rivers, Lord Hastings, and fewe othar, and went towarde his brothar of Clarence. And, in lyke wyse, the Duke, for his partye takynge with hym a fewe noble men, and levinge his hoost in good order, departyd from them towards the Kynge. And so they mett betwixt both hostes, where was right kynde and lovynge langwage betwixt them twoo, with parfite accord knyt togethars for evar here aftar, with as hartyly lovynge chere and countenaunce, as might be betwix two bretherne of so grete nobley and astate. And than, in lyke wyse, spake togethar the two Dukes of Clarence and Glocestar, and, aftar, the othar noble men beinge there with them, whereof all the people there that lovyd them, and awght them theyr trew service, were right glade and ioyows, and thanked God highly of that ioyows metynge, unitie, and accorde, hopynge that, therby, shuld growe unto them prosperows fortune, in all that they shuld aftar that have a doo. And than the trompetts and minstrels blew uppe, and, with that, the Kynge browght his brothar Clarence, and suche as were there with hym, to his felowshipe, whom the sayd Duke welcomyd into the land in his best manner, and they thanked God, and hym, and honoryd hym as it apparteygned.

Aftar this, the Kynge, yet levinge his hooste standynge still, with the sayd few persons went with his brothar of Clarence to his hoste, whome he hertily welcomyd, and promised hym largely of his grace and good love, and, from thens, they all came hoole togethars to the Kyngs hooste, when ethar party welcomyd and jocundly receyvyd othar, with perfect frindlynes; and, so, with greate gladnes, bothe hostes, with theyr princes, togethars went to Warwyke, with the Kynge, and ther lodged, and in the countrie nere adioyninge.

Sone aftar this the Duke of Clarence, beinge right desyrows to have procuryd a goode accorde betwyxt the Kynge and th'Erle of Warwyke; not only for th'Erle, but also for to reconsyle therby unto the Kyngs good grace many lordes and noble men of his land, of whom many had largly taken parte with th'Erle; and this for the weale of peax and tranquilitie in the land, and in advoydynge of cruell and mortall were, that, of the contrary, was lykly, in shortyme, to enswe; he made, therefore, his mocions, as well to the Kynge as to th'Erle, by messagis sendynge to and fro, bothe for the well above sayde, as to acquite hym trwly and kyndly in the love he bare unto hym, and his blood, whereunto he was allied by the marriage of his dowghtar. The Kynge, at th'ynstaunce of his sayd brothar, the Duke, was content to shew hym largly his grace, with dyvars good condicions, and profitable for th'Erle yf that he woulde have acceptyd them. But th'Erle, whether he in maner dispaired of any good pardurable continuaunce of good accord betwixt the Kynge and hym, for tyme to come, consyderinge so great attemptes by hym comytted agaynst the Kynge; or els, for that willinge to enterteigne the greate promises, pacts, and othes, to the contrary, made solempnily, and also priuately sworne, to the Frenche Kynge, Qwene Margarete, and hir sonne Edward, in the qwarell of them, and of his owne sechinge, wherefrom he ne couthe departe, without grete desklaundar; or els, for that he had afore thowght, and therefore purveyed, that, in caase he myght nat get to have the ovar-hand of the Kynge, his meanes were founden of sure and certayne escape by the sea to Calais, whiche was enswryd to hym selfe in every caas that myght hape hym, so that it myght fortwne hym for to come thethar; or els, for that certayne parsons beinge with hym in companye, as th'Erle of Oxenforde, and othar, beinge desposed in extrem malice agaynst the Kynge, wolde not suffre hym t'accepte any mannar of appoyntment, were it resonable or unresonable, but causyd hym to refuse almannar of appointements; whiche as many men deme was the verray cawse of none acceptinge of the Kynges [grace]; wherefore all suche treaty brake and toke none effecte.

In this meane season of the Kyngs beinge at Warwyke, cam to the Erle of Warwyke, to Coventrye, the Duke of Excestar, the Marques Mountagwe, th'Erle of Oxenforde, with the many othar in great nombar, by whos than commynge dayly grew and encreasyd the felowshipe of that partye. The Kynge, with his brithern, this consyderinge, and that in no wyse he cowthe provoke hym to come owt of the towne, ne thinkynge it behoffoll to assayll, ne to tary for the asseginge therof; as well for avoydaunce of greate slaghtars that shuld therby enswe, and for that it was thowght more expedient to them to draw towards London, and there, with helpe of God, and th'assystaunce of his trwe lords, lovars, and servaunts, whiche were there, in thos partes, in great nombar; knowynge also, that his principall advarsarye, Henry, with many his partakers, were at London, ther usurpynge and usynge the authoritie royall, which barred and letted the Kyng of many aydes and assystaunces, that he shuld and mowght hav had, in divars parties, yf he myght ones shew hymselffe of powere to breke their auctoritie; wherefore, by th'advyse of his sayd brithern, and othar of his cownsell, he toke his purpose to London wards, and so departyd fro Warwicke; yet, efte sones, shewinge him, and his hoste, before Coventrie, and desyringe the sayd Erle, and his felashipe, to come owte, and for to determyne his qwarell by battayle, whiche he and they utterly refused, wherefore the Kynge and his brethern kept forthe theyr purpos sowthewardes. And this was the v. day of Aprell the Friday.

On the Satarday, the Kynge, with all his hooste, cam to a towne called Daventre, where the Kynge, with greate devocion, hard all divine service upon the morne, Palme-Sonday, in the parishe churche, wher God, and Seint Anne, shewyd a fayre miracle; a goode pronostique of good aventure that aftar shuld befall unto the Kynge by the hand of God, and mediation, of that holy matron Seynt Anne. For, so it was, that, afore that tyme, the Kynge, beinge out of his realme, in great trowble, thowght, and hevines, for the infortwne and adversitie that was fallen hym, full often, and, specially upon the sea, he prayed to God, owr Lady, and Seint George, and, amonges othar saynts, he specially prayed Seint Anne to helpe hym, where that he promysed, that, at the next tyme that it shuld hape hym to se any ymage of Seint Anne, he shuld therto make his prayers, and gyve his offeringe, in the honor and worshipe of that blessyd Saynte. So it fell, that, the same Palme Sonday, the Kynge went in procession, and all the people aftar, in goode devotion, as the service of that daye askethe, and, whan the processyon was comen into the curche, and, by ordar of the service, were comen to that place where the vale shulbe drawne up afore the Roode, that all the people shall honor the Roode, with the anthem, *Ave*, three tymes begon, in a pillar of the churche, directly aforne the place where Kynge knelyd, and devowtly honoryd the Roode, was a lytle ymage of Seint Anne, made of alleblastar, standynge fixed to the piller, closed and claspyd togethars with four bordes, small, payntyd, and gowynge rownd abowt the image, in a manar of a compas, lyke as it is to see comonly, and all abowt, where as suche ymages be wont to be made for to be solde and set up in churches, chapells, crosses, and oratories, in many placis. And this ymage was thus shett, closed, and claspyd, accordynge to the rulles that, in all the churchis of England, be observyd, all ymages to be hid from Ashe Wednesday to Estarday in the mornynge. And so the sayd ymage had bene from Ashwensday to that tyme. And even sodaynly, at that season of the service, the bords compassynge the ymage about gave a great crak, and a little openyd, whiche the Kynge well perceyveyd and all the people about hym. And anon, aftar, the bords drewe and closed togethars agayne, withowt any mans hand, or touchinge, and, as thowghe it had bene a thinge done with a violence, with a greter might it openyd all abrod, and so the ymage stode, open and discovert, in syght of all the people there beynge. The Kynge, this seinge, thanked and honoryd God, and Seint Anne, takynge it for a good signe, and token of good and prosperous aventure that God wold send hym in that he had to do, and, remembringe his promyse, he honoryd God, and Seint Anne, in that same place, and gave his offrings. All thos, also, that were present and sawe this worshippyd and thanked God and Seint Anne, there, and many offeryd; takyng of this signe, shewed by the power of God, good hope of theyr good spede for to come.

The Kynge from that towne went to a good towne callyd Northampton, wher he was well receyved, and, from thens toke the next way towardes London, levynge always behynd hym in his jowrney a good bande of speres and archars, his behynd-rydars, to countar, yf it had neded, suche of th'Erls partye as, peradventure, he shuld have sent t ha ve trowbled hym on the bakhalfe, yf he so had done.

Here it is to be remembered, that, in this season of the Kyngs comynge towards and beinge at Warwyke, and of the comynge to hym of his brothar the Duke of Clarence, Edmond callynge himselfe Duke of Somarset, John of Somarset his brothar, callyd Marqwes Dorset, Thomas Courtney, callynge hym self th'Erle of Devonshire, beinge at London, had knowledge owt of Fraunce, that Qwene Margaret, and hir sonne, callyd Prince of Wales, the Countes of Warwyke, the Prior of Seint Johns, the Lord Wenloke, with othar many, theyr adherents and parte-takers, with all that evar they myght make, were ready at the sea-syde commynge, puposynge to arive in the West Contrie; wherefore they departyd owt of London, and went into the west parties, and ther bestyrd them right greatly to make an assemblye of asmoche people for to receyve them at theyr comynge, them to accompany, fortyfy, and assyst, agaynst the Kynge, and all his partakars, in the qwarels of Henry, callyd Kynge, and occupinge the regalie for that tym. And trew it was that she, hir sonne, the Countes of Warwike, the Lords, and othar of theyr fellowshipe, entryd theyr ships for that entent the xxiiij. of Marche, and so continuyd theyr abode in theyr ships, or they myght land in England, to the xiij. day of Aprell, for defawlt of good wynd, and for grete tempests upon the sea, that time, as who saythe, continuynge by the space of xx dayes. But leve we this, and retorne agayne to the Kyngs progrese in his jowrney towards

London, tellynge how that he came upon the Twesday, the ix. day of Aprill, from whens he sent comfortable messagis to the Qwene to Westminstar, and to his trew Lords, servaunts, and lovars, beynge at London; whereupon, by the moste covert meanes that they cowthe, [they] avised and practysed how that he myght be receyved and welcomyd at his sayde city of London. Th'Erle of Warwike, knowenge this his iowrneynge, and approchinge to London, sent his lettars to them of the citie, willinge and chargynge them to resyste him, and let the receyvynge of hym and of his. He wrote also to his brothar, th'Archbysshope of Yorke, desyrynge hym to put hym in the uttarmoste de-vowr he cowthe, to provoke the citie agayns hym, and kepe hym owt, for two or three dayes; promisynge that he wolde not fayle to come with great pui-sance on the bakhalfe, trustinge utterly to dystrese and distroye hym and his, as to the same he had, by his othar writyngs, encharged the maior, and the aldermen, and the comons of the citie.

Hereupon, the ix. day of Aprell, th'Archbyshope callyd unto hym to-gethars, at Seint Powles, within the sayde Citie of London, suche lords, gentlemen, and othar, as were of that partye, [with] as many men in har-neys of theyr servaunts and othar as they cowthe make, which, in all, passed nat in nombar vj or vij^M men, and, thereupon, cawsed Henry, callyd Kynge, to take an horse and ryde from Powles thrwghe Chepe, and so made a circute abowte to Walbroke, as the generall processyon of London hathe bene accustomyd, and so returned agayne to Powles, to the Bysshops Palays, where he sayd Henry at that tyme was lodged, supposynge, that whan he had shewyd hym in this arraye, they shuld have provokyd the citizens, and th'enhabitants of the citie, to have stonde and comen to them, and fortified that partye; but, trewthe it is, that the rewlars of the citie were at the coun-sell, and hadd set men at all the gates and wardes, and they, seynge by this manner of doinge, that the power of the sayde Henry, and his adherents, was so litle and feble as there and then was shewyd, they cowld thereby take no corage to draw to them, ne to fortefye theyr partye, and, for that they fearyd, but rathar the contrary, for so moche as they sawe well that, yf they wolde so have done, ther myght was so lytle that it was nat for them to have ones attemptyd to have resystid the Kynge in this comynge, whiche approched nere unto the citie, and was that nyght at Seint Albons. They also of the citie in great nombar, and, namly, of the moaste worshipfull, were fully disposed to favowr the Kynge, and to have the citie opne unto hym at his comynge. They of the citie also consideryd, that he was notably well accompanied with many good, hable, and well-willed men, whiche, for no power, nor no re-

sistence that myght be made, would spare to attempt, and suporte, the takynge the citie, by all wayes possible; whereof they ne shuld have failled, con-
sideringe that the Kynge at that tyme had many greate and myghty frinds, lovars, and servitors, within the sayd citie, whiche would not have fayled by
dryvers enterprises have made the citie open unto hym; as this myght nat be
unknowne unto right many of the sayde citie; and, also, as might appere
by that was don aftar in that behalfe and to that entent. Thus, what for love
that many bare to the Kynge, and what for drade that many men had, how
that, in caas the citie shuld have bene wonne upon them by foarce, the citie-
sens shuld therefore have susteygned harmes and damagis irreparable, and for
many othar great consyderations, the maior, aldarmen, and othar worshipfull of the citie, determined clerly amongs them selfe to kepe the citie for the
Kynge, and to opne it to hym, at his comynge; as so they sent to hym that
therein they would be gwydyd to his pleaswre. Th'Archbyshope of Yorke, undarstondynge the Kyngs commyng, and approchinge nere to the citie, sent
secretly unto hym desyringe to be admittyd to his grace, and to be undar
good appoyntement, promittynge therefore to do unto hym great pleaswre
for his well and swertye; whereunto the Kynge, for good cawses and considerations, agreed so to take hym to his grace. Th'Archbyshope, therof assuryd,
was ryght well pleasyd, and therefore wele and trwlye acquite hym, in ob-
servynge the promyse that he had made to the Kynge in that behalfe.

The same nyght followynge the towre of London was taken for the
Kyngs beholfe; whereby he had a playne entrie into the citie thowghe all
they had not bene determyned to have receyvyd hym in, as they were. And
on the morow, the Thursday, the xj. day of Aprell, the Kynge came, and had
playne overture of the sayd citie, and rode streight to Powles churche, and
from thens went into the Byshops paleis, where th'Archbyshope of Yorke
presentyd hym selfe to the Kyngs good grace, and, in his hand, the usurpowr,
Kynge Henry; and there was the Kynge seasyd of hym and dyvars rebels.
From Powles the Kynge went to Westmynstar, there honoryd, made his devout prayers, and gave thankyngs to God, Saint Petre, and Saint Edward, and
than went the Qwene, and comfortyd hir; that had a longe tyme abyden and
soiourned at Westmynstar, asswringe hir parson only by the great fraunchis
of that holy place, in right great trowble, sorow, and hevines, whiche she sus-
tayned with all mannar pacience that belonged to eny creature, and as constantly as hathe bene sene at any tyme any of so highe estate to endure; in
the whiche season natheles she had browght into this worlde, to the Kyngs
greatyste joy, a fayre sonn, a prince, where with she presentyd hym at his

comynge, to his herts synguler comforte and gladnes, and to all them that hym trewly loved and wolde serve. From thens, that nyght, the Kynge retornyd to London, and the Qwene with hym, and lodged at the lodgynge of my lady his mothar; where they harde devyne service that nyght, and upon the morne, Good Fryeday; where also, on the morn, the Kynge tooke advise of the great lords of his blood, and othar of his counsell, for the adventures that were lykly for to come.

Th'Erle of Warrewike, callynge hymselfe lievetenaunt of England, and so constitute by the pretensed auctoritie of Kynge Henry, beynge at Coventrie, and undrestandinge well that the Kinge wolde moche doo to be received in at London, and wist nat, in certeyne, ye or no, isshued owt of Coventrie with a great puissance, the lords, and all that he might make with hym, and, by Northampton, tooke theire way aftar the Kynge, supposinge verrely to have had right great advantage upon hym by one of the two waies; eithar, that the citie shuld have kepte the Kynge owte, whiche failed; or els, in caas he were received in, he shulde there [have] kepte and observyd the solempnitie of Estar, and, yf he so dyd, he thowght sodaynly to come upon hym, take hym, and distroy hym, and his people [to have] disceaveyed, but the Kyng, well advertised of this yvell and malicious purpos, dyd grate diligence to recountre hym, or he might come nere to the citie, as ferre from it as he goodly myght; and, therfore, with a great armye, he departyd out of the citie of London towards hym, upon the Saturdaye, Ester's even the xiij. day of Aprell. And so he toke in his companye to the felde, Kynge Henrye; and soo, that aftar none, he roode to Barnete, x myles owte of London, where his aforne-riders had founden the afore-riders of th'Erles of Warwikes hooste, and bet them, and chaced them out of the towne, more some what than an halfe myle; when, undre an hedge-syde, were redy assembled a great people, in array, of th'Erls of Warwike. The Kynge, comynge aftar to the sayde towne, and undarstanding all this, wolde [ne] suffre one man to abyde in the same towne, but had them all to the field with hym, and drewe towards his enemies, without the towne. And, for it was right derke, and he myght not well se where his enemyes were enbataylled afore hym, he lodged hym, and all his hoste, afore them, moche nere[r] then he had supposed, but he toke nat his ground so even in the front afore them as he wold have don yf he might bettar have sene them, butt somewhate a-syden-hande, where he disposed all his people, in good arraye, all that nyght; and so they kept them still, without any mannar langwage, or noyse, but as lytle as they well myght. Bothe parties had goons, and ordinaunce, but th'Erle of Warwike had many moo then the Kynge, and therefore, on the nyght, weninge gretly to have anoyed the Kinge, and his hooste, with shot of gonnes, th'Erls fielde shotte gunes almoste all the nyght. But, thanked be God! It so fortuned that they alway ovarshote the Kyngs hoste, and hurtyd them nothinge, and the cawse was the Kyngs hoste lay muche nerrar them than they demyd. And, with that also, the Kyng, and his hoste, kept passinge greate silence alnyght, and made, as who saythe, no noyse, whereby they might nat know the very place where they lay. And, for that they should not know it, the Kynge suffred no gonns to be shote on his syd, al that nyght, or els right fewe, whiche was to hym great advauntage, for, therby, they myght have estemed the ground that he lay in, and have leveled their gunns nere.

On the morow, betymes, The Kynge, undarstandinge that the day approched nere, betwyxt four and five of the cloke, natwithstandynge there was a greate myste and letted the syght of eithar othar, yet he commytted his cawse and qwarell to Allmyghty God, avancyd bannars, dyd blowe up trumpets, and set upon them, firste with shotte, and, than and sone, they joyned and came to hand-strokes, wherein his enemies manly and coragiously receyved them, as well in shotte as in hand-stroks what they ioyned; whiche ioynynge of theyr bothe batteyls was nat directly frount to frount, as they so shulde have ioyned ne had be the myste, whiche suffred neythar party to se othar, but for a litle space, and that of lyklyhod cawsed the bataile to be the more crewell and mortall; for, so it was, that the one ende of theyr batayle ovarrechyd th'end of the Kyngs battayle, and so, at that end, they were myche myghtyar than was the Kyngs bataile at the same [end] that ioyned with them, whiche was the west ende, and, therefore, upon that party of the Kyngs battayle, they had a gretar distress upon the Kyngs party, wherefore many flede towards Barnet, and so forthe to London, or evar they lafte; and they fell in the chace of them, and dyd moche harme. But the other parties, and the residewe of neithar bataile, might se that disrese, ne the fleinge, ne the chace, by cawse of [the] great myste that was, whiche wolde nat suffre no man to se but a litle from hym; and so the Kyngs battayle, which saw none of all that, was therby in nothing discoragyd, for, save only a fewe that were nere unto them, no man wiste thereof; also the othar party by the same distres, flyght, or chace, were therefore nevar the gretlyar coragyd. And, in lykewise, at the est end, the Kyngs batayle, whan they cam to ioninge, ovarrechyd theyr batayle, and so distresyd them theyr gretly, and soo drwe nere towards the

Kynge, who was abowt the myddest of the battayle, and systeygned all the myght and weight thereof. Netheles, upon the same litle distresse at the west end anon ranne to Westmynstar, and to London, and so forthe furthar to othar contries, that the Kynge was distressed, and his fielde loste, but, the lawde be to Almyghty God! it was otharwyse; forthe Kynge, trusting verely in God's helpe, owr blessyd ladyes, and Seynt George, toke to hym great hardies and corage for to supprese the falcehode of all them that so falcely and so traytorowsly had conspired agaynst hym, wherethrwghe, with the faythefull, welbelovyd, and myghty assystaunce of his felawshipe, that in great nombar deseveryd nat from his parson, and were as well asswred unto hym as to them was possyble, he mannly, vigorowsly, and valliantly assayled them, in the mydst and strongest of theyr battaile, where he, with great violence, bett and bare down afore hym all that stode in hys way, and, than, turned to the range, first on that one hand, and than on that othar hand, in lengthe, and so bet and bare them downe, so that nothing myght stande in the syght of hym and the welle asswred felowshipe that attendyd trewly upon hym; so that, blessed be God! he wan the filde there, and the perfite victory remayned unto hym, and to his rebells the discomfiture of xxx^M men, as they nombrid them selves.

In this battayle was slayne the Erle of Warwyke, somewhat fleinge, which was taken and reputed as chefe of the felde, in that he was callyd amongs them lyvetenaunt of England, so constitute by the pretensed aucthoritye of Kynge Henry. Ther was also slayne the Marques Montagwe, in playne battayle, and many othar knyghts, squiers, noble men, and othar. The Duke of Excestar was smytten downe, and sore woundyd, and lafte for dead; but he was not well knowne, and so lafte by a lytle out of the fielde, and so, aftar, he escaped. The Erle of Oxenford fled, and toke into the contrie, and, in his flyenge, fell in company with certayne northen men, that also fled from the same filde, and so went he, in theyr company, northwards, and, aftar that, into Scotland.

This battayle duryd, fightynge and skirmishinge, some tyme in one place and some tyme in an othar, ryght dowbtefully, becawse of the myste, by the space of thre howrs, or it was fully achivyd; and the victory is gyven to hym by God, by the mediacion of the moaste blessyd virgen and modre, owr lady Seint Mary; the glorious martire Seint George, and all the saynts of heven, mayntaynynge his qwarell to be trew and rightwys, with many-fold good and contynuall prayers, whiche many devout persons, religiows and othar, ceasyd not to yelde unto God for his good spede, and, in especiall, that same day and season, whan it pleasyd God t'accepte the prayers of people being confessyd and in clene lyfe, whiche was the Estare mornynge, the tyme of the servyce-doynge of the resurection, comonly, by all the churches of England. And, albe hit the vyctorye remayned to the Kynge, yet was it not without grete danger and hurt, for ther were slayne in the filde the Lorde Cromwell, the Lord Say, the Lord Mountjoies sonne and heyre, and many othar good Knyghts, and squiers, gode yemen, and many othar meniall servaunts of the Kyngs. And it is to wete, that it cowthe not be judged that the Kyngs hoste passyd in nombar ix^M men; but, suche a great and gracious Lorde is Almyghty God, that it plesythe hym gyvythe the victory as well to fewe as to many, wherefore, to hym be the lawde and the thanks. And so the Kynge gave him speciall lovinge, and all that were with hym. This thus done, the Kynge, the same day, aftar that he had a little refresshed hym and his hoste, at Barnette, he gathered his felowshipe togethars, and, with them, returned to his Citie of London, where into he was welcomyd and receyvyd with moche ioy and gladnesse. And so rode he forthe steryght unto Powles at London, and there was receyvyed with my Lorde Cardinall of England, and many othar bysshops, prelates, lords spirituall, and temporall, and othar, in grete nombar, whiche all humbly thanked and lovyd God of his grace, that it plesyd hym that day to gyve to theyr prynce, and soveraygne lord, so prosperous a iowrney, wherby he had supprised them that, of so great malice, had procured and laboryd at theyr powers his uttar destruction, contrary to God, and to theyr faythes and liegeances.

On the morow aftar, the Kynge commandyd that the bodyes of the deade lords, th'Erle of Warwicke, and hys brothar the Marques, shuld be browght to Powles in London, and, in the churche there, openly shewyd to all the people; to th'entent that, aftar that, the people shuld not be abused by feyned seditiows tales, which many of them that were wonnt to be towards th'Erle of Warwyke had bene accustomyd to make, and, paradventure, so would have made aftar that, ne had the deade bodyes there be shewyd, opne, and naked, and well knowne; for, dowbtles ells the rumore shuld have bene sowne abowte, in all contries, that they bothe, or els, at the leaste, th'Erle of Warwyke, was yet on lyve, upon cursed entent therby to have cawsyd newe murmors, insurrections, and rebellyons, amongst indisposed people; suche, namely, as many dayes had bene lad to great inconveniences, and mischevs-doynge, moyenaut the false, faynyd fables, and disclandars, that, by his subtilitie and malicious moyvyng, were wont to be seditiously sowne and blowne abowt all the land, by suche persons as cowthe use, and longe had usyd, that cursed custome; whereof, as it is comonly sayde, right many were towards hym, and, for that entent, returnyd and waged with hym.

Here aftar folowithe how that Qwene Margaret, with her sonne Edward, called Prince of Wales, aftar theyr arryvall in the west contrye, assembled greate people and cam to Tewkesberye, where the Kynge delyveryd theym battayle, distressed theym and theyr felawshipe, [and] the sayd Edward, the Duke of Somarset, and othar, were slayne.

Aftar all thes things thus fallen, the Twseday in Estar weke, the xvj. day of Aprile, came certayn tydyngs to the Kynge how that Qwene Margaret, hir sonne Edward, callyd Prince of Wales, the Countese of Warwyke, the Priowr of Seint Johns, that tyme called Tresorar of England, the Lord Wenloke, and many othere knyghts, squiers, and othar of theyr party, whiche longe had bene owt of the land with them, with suche also as, with the sayde Priowr of Seint Johns, had gon into Fraunce to fet them into England, were arryved, and landed in the west-contrye, upon Estar day, at Waymowthe, aftar longe abydynge passage, and beyng on the sea, and landinge agayne for defawlte of good wynde and wethar. For, trewthe it is, that the Qwene, and Edward hir sonne, with all theyr felowshipe, entendinge to passe out of Normandy into England, toke first the sea, at Humflew, in the monithe of Marche, the xxiiij. day of the same, and, from that tyme forthe wards, they cowlde nat have any stable wethar to passe with; for and it were one day good, anon it chaunged upon them, and was agaynst them, and fayne they were therefor to goo to land agayne. And so, at divars tymes, they toke the sea, and forsoke it agayne, tyll it was the xiij. day of Aprill, Estars Even. That day they passyd. The Countysse of Warwyke had a shippe of avaunctage, and, therefore, landyd afore the othar, at Portsmowthe, and, from thens, she went to Sowthampton, entendynge to have gon towards the Qwene, whiche was landyd at Wemowthe. But, beinge there, she had certayne knowledge that the Kynge had wonne the fielde upon her howsband, at Barnet, and there slayne hym, wherefore she would no farthar goo towards the Qwene, but, secretly, gat ovar Hampton-watar into the new forreste, where she tooke hir to the fraunches of an abbey called Beawlew, whiche, as it is sayde, is ample, and as large as the franchesse of Westmynstar, or of Seint Martins at London.

The Qwene, Margarete, and hir sonne went from there she landyd to an abbey nere by, callyd Seern, and all the lords, and the remenaunt of the fellowshipe with them. Thethar came unto them Edmond, callyd Duke of Somerset, Thomas Courteney, callyd th'Erle of Devonshire, with othar, and welcomyd them into England; comfortyd them, and put them in good hope that, albe it they had lost one felde, whereof the Qwene had knowledge the same day, Monday, the xv. day of Aprell, and was therefore right hevy and sory, yet it was to thinke that they shuld have ryght good spede, and that, for that los, theyr partye was nevar the febler, but rathar strongar, and that they dowted nothinge but that they shuld assemble so great puisaunce of people in dyvars partis of England, trewly asswred unto theyr partye, that it shuld not mowe lye in the Kyngs powere to resyste them; and in that contrye they would begyne. And so, forthewith, they sent alabout in Somarsetshere, Dorsetshire, and parte of Wiltshere, for to arredy and arays the people by a certayne day, suche, algats, as the sayde lords, and theyr partakers, afore that had greatly laboryd to that entent, preparinge the contry by all meanes to them posseble. And, for that they would gather and arrays up the powere of Devonshire and Cornewaile, they drew from thens more west ward to the citie of Excestar, movinge Edward, callyd Prince, and his mothar, the Qwene, to doo the same; trustynge that theyr presence-shewynge in the contrye shuld cawse moche more, and the sonnar, the people to com to theyr helpe and assistaunce.

At Excestar, they sent for Syr John Arundell, Syr Hughe Courteney, and many othar on whom they had any trust, and, in substaunce, they araysed the hoole myghte of Cornwall and Devonshire, and so, with great people, they departyd out of Excestre, and toke the ryght waye to Glastonberye, and, from thens, to the city of Bathe, withar they came the

day of Aprell; and, as they went, they gatheryd the hable men of all thos partes. The cuntrie had bene so longe laboryd afore by th'Erle of Warwike, and such as he for that caws sent thethar to move them to take Kynge Henry's partie, and, now of late, they were also sore laboryd for the same entent, and thereunto the more lyghtly enducyd, by Edmond, callyd Duke of Somarset, and Thomas Courtney, callyd th'Erle of Devonshire, for that they reputyd them old enheritors of that contrie.

The Kynge beynge at London, and havynge knowledge of all this theyr demeanyng from tyme to tyme, anon purveyed for the relevynge of his sycke and hurt men, that had bene with hym at Barnet fielde, which were ryght many in nombar, what left at London, and what in the contrye, and sent to all partes to get hym freshe men, and, incontinent, prepared all things that was thowght behovefull for a new field; whiche he saw was imminent and comyng on. So purveyed he artilary, and ordinaunce, gonns, and othar, for the filde gret plentye. And Fryday, the xix. day of Aprille, he departyd out of London, and went to Wyndsore, ther to thanke and honor God, and Seint George, where he kept also the feaste of Seint George, tarienge somwhat the longar there for that he had commaundyd all the people, and thos that wold serve hym in this iourney, to draw unto hym thithar, and from thens, suche waye as shulde happen hym take towards his enemyes. And, for so moche as they at that season were in an angle of the land, and nedes they must take one of the two wayes, that is to say, eythar to come streight to Salisbery, and so, that way, towards London; or ells, alonge by the sea-coaste into Hampshire, Sussex, and Kent, and so to London, to make in the way theyr people the mo in nombar; or els, they, nat thynkyng themselves to be of puisaunce lykly to have a doo with the Kynge, and, therefore, paradventure, wowlde drawe northwards into Lancasshyre and Cheshere, trustynge also to have in theyr waye th'assystaunce of Walchemen, by the meane of Jasper called Erle of Penbroke, whiche, for that cawse, had bene afore sent into the contrie of Wales, to arays them, and make them redy to assyst that partye at theyr comynge; for whiche consyderations, the Kynge cawsed great diligence to be done by meane of espies, and by them he had knowledge, from tyme to tyme, of theyr purposes in that behalfe. Yf they would have taken estwards theyr way, his entent was to encountar them as sonne as he myght, and the farthar from London that shuld be to hym posseble, for th'entent that they shuld assemble no myght owt of eny contrye but where they then were, but, for so moche as he undarstode well they toke the othar waye, towards northwest, he hastyd hym, with his host, all that he myght, upon the purpos that he had taken to stope them theyr waye and passage into thos parties whereunto their desyre was to goo, and to make them the more myghty, whiche passagis of lykelyhode eythar must be at Glowcestar, or els at Tewkesbery, or farthar of at Worcestar. And, algates, the Kynge lay so that, would they or no, he nedes shuld nowe recountar them, or stope them, and put them bake. They in lyke wyse, thynkynge by theyr wysdomes that suche was, or of convenience muste be, the purpos of the Kyngs party, therefore put them gretly in devowre to abwse the Kyngs party in that behalfe, for which cawse and purpos they sent theyr aforerydars streight from Excestar to Shaftesbery, and aftarwards to Salisbery, and toke them the streight way to Tawnton, and to Glastonberye, to Wells, and there abouts, hovinge in the contrye; from whens, an othar tyme, they sent theyr forrydars to a towne called Yevell, and to a towne callyd Bruton, to make men to undarstond that they would have drawne towards Redynge, and by Barkeshire, and Oxfordshire, have drawne towards London, or ells fallen upon the Kynge at some great advangage. Suche mannar sendynge natheles servyd them of two thyngs; one was, to call and arays the people to make towards them for theyr helpe owt of all thos parties; an othar was, to have abusyd the Kynge in his approchyng towards them but, thanked be God, he was nat hereof unadvertysed, but, by goode and sad advyse, purveyed for every way, as may appere in tellyng furthe his progres from Wyndsowr towards them; from whence he departyd the Wedensday, the morne aftar Saynt Georgis day, the xxiiij. day of Aprell, so kepinge his iorney that he cam to Abyndon the Satarday next, the xxvij. day; where he was the Sonday; and, on the Monday, at Cicestre; where he had certayne tydyngs that they wowld, on Twesday next, [be] at Bathe, as so they were; and that on the morne next, the Wedensday, they wowld com on streight towards the Kyngs battayle. For whiche cawse, and for that he would se and set his people in array, he drove all the people owt of the towne, and lodgyd hym, and his hoste, that nyght in the fielde, iij myle out of the towne, And, on the morow, he, having no certayne tydyngs of theyr comynge forward, went to Malmesbury, sekynge upon them. And there had he knowledge that they, undarstandynge his approchinge and marchinge neare to them, had lefte theyr purpos of gevynge battayle, and turned asyde-hand, and went to Bristowe, a good and stronge wallyd towne, where they were greatly refreshed and relyved, by such as were the Kyngs rebells in that towne, of money, men, and artilarye; wherethrwghe they toke new corage, the Thursday aftar to take the filde, and gyve the Kynge battayll, for which intent they had sent forrydars to a towne ix myle from Bristow, callyd Sudbury, and, a myle towards the Kynge, they apoynted a grownd for theyr fielde at a place callyd Sudbury hill. The Kynge, heringe this, the same Thursday, first day of May, with all his hooste in array and fayre ordinaunce came towards the place by them apoyntyd for theyr fielde. Th'enemyes alsoo avauncyd them forthe, the same day, owt of Bristow, makynge semblaunce as thowghe they would have comen streyght to the place appoyntyd, but, havynge knoledge of the Kyngs approochinge, they lefte that way, albe it theyr herbengars were come afore them as ferre as Sudberye towne; where they distressed certayne of the Kyngs partye, five or six, such as neglygently pressed so ferre forwards, dredynge no dangar, but only entendyng to have purveyed ther theyr masters lodgyngs; and so they changyd theyr sayd purpos, and toke theyr way streyght to Berkley, travelyng all that nyght, and, from thens, towards the towne of Gloucestar. The Kynge, the same Thursday, sonne aftar none, came nere to the same grownd, called Sudbury hill, and, nat havynge eny certaynty of his enemys, sent his scowrers alabowte in the cuntrye, trustynge by them to have wist where they had bene. Aboute that place was a great and a fayre large playne, called a would, and dowbtfull it was for to pas ferther, to he myght here somewhate of them, supposynge that they were right nere, as so they myght well have bene, yf they had kepte forthe the way they toke owt of Bristow. And when he cowthe nat here any certayntye of them, he avauncyd forwards his hoole battayle, and lodgyd his vaward beyonde the hill, in a valley towards the towne of Sudberye, and lodged hymselfe, with the remenaunt of his hooste, at the selfe hill called Sudberry hill. Early in the mornynge, sonne aftar three of the cloke, the Kynge had certayne tydyngs that they had taken theyre way by Barkley toward Goucestar, as so they toke indede. Whereupon he toke advise of his counsell of that he had to doo for the stopynge of theyr wayes, at two passagys afore namyd, by Glocestar, or els by Tewkesberye, and, first, he purvayed for Gloucestar, and sent thethar certayne servaunts of his owne to Richard Bewchamp, sonne and heyr to the Lord Bewchampe, to whom afore he had comyttyd the rule and governaunce of the towne and castell of Gloucestar, commandynge hym to kepe the towne and castle for the Kynge, and that he, with suche helpe as he myght have, shuld defend the same agaynst them, in caas they woulde in any wise assayle them; as it was suppos they so would doo that same aforenone; lettynge them wete that he would have good espye upon them yf they so did. And, yf he myght know that they so dyde, he promised to come theyr rescows, and comforte. With this the Kyngs message they were well receyved at Gloucestar, and the towne and castell put in sure and save kepinge of the sayd Richard, and the sayde Kynges servaunts. Whiche message was sent and done in right good season, for certayne it is the Kyngs enemyes were put in sure hope, and determyned to have enteryd the towne, and ethar have kept it agaynst the Kynge, or, at the leaste, to have passed thrwghe the towne into othar contries, where they thowght [to] have bene myghtely assysted, as well with Welchemen, whiche they demed shuld have fallen to them in thos parties, in the company of Jasper, called Earle of Penbroke, as also for to have goten into theyr companye, by that way-takynge, greate nombar of men of Lancashire, and Chesshere, upon whom they muche trustyd. For whiche cawses they had greatly travayled theyr people all that nyght and mornynge, upon the Fryday, to the about ten of the cloke they were comen afore Goucestar; where there entent was uttarly denyed them by Richard Bewchampe, and othar of the Kyngs servaunts, that, for the cawse, the Kynge had sent thethar. Natwithstandynge, many of the inhabytaunts of that towne were greatly disposed towards them, as they had certayne knowledge. Of this demenynge they toke right great displeasure, and made great manasys, and pretendyd as thowghe they wowlde have assaultyd the towne, and wonne it upon them, but, as well thos that kepte the towne as the sayde enemyes that so pretendyd, knewe well, that the Kynge with a myghty puisawnce was nere to them, and, yf eny affraye had there be made, he myght sone have bene upon them, and taken upon them ryght grete advantage; wherefore they in the towne nothynge dowbtyd, and they withoute durste not for feare begynne any suche werke; and, therefore, they shortly toke theyr conclusyon for to go the next way to Tewkesbery, withar they came the same day, about four aftar none. By whiche tyme they hadd so travaylled theyr hoaste that nyght and daye that they were ryght wery for travaylynge; for by that tyme they had travaylyd xxxvj longe myles, in a fowle contrye, all in lanes and stonny wayes, betwyxt woodes, without any good refresshynge. And, for as mooche as the greatar parte of theyr hooste were fotemen, the othar partye of the hoste, whan they were comen to Tewkesbery, cowthe, ne myght, have laboryd any furthar, but yf they wolde wilfully have forsaken and lefte theyr fotemen behynd them, and therto themselves that were horsemen were ryght werye of that iorwney, as so were theyr horses. So, whethar it were of theyr election and good will, or no, but that they were veryly compelled to byde by two cawses; one was, for werines of theyr people, which they supposed nat theyr people woulde have eny longer endured; an other, for they knew well that the Kynge ever approchyd towards them, nere and nere, evar redy, in good aray and ordinaunce, to have pursuyd and fallen uppon them, yf they wolde any ferther have gon, and, paradventure, to theyr moste dyssavantage. They therefore determyned t'abyde there th'aventure that God would send them in the qwarell they had taken in hand. And, for that entent, the same nyght they pight them in a fielde, in a close even at the townes ende; the towne, and the abbey, at theyr backs; afore them, and upon every hand of them, fowle lanes, and depe dikes, and many hedges, with hylls, and valleys, a ryght evill place to approche, as cowlde well have bene devysed.

The Kynge, the same mornynge, the Fryday, erly, avanced his banners, and devyded his hole hoost in three battayles, and sent afore hym his for-rydars, and scorars, on every syde hym, and so, in fayre arraye and ordinaunce, he toke his way thrwghe the champain contrye, callyd Cotteswolde, trav-aylynge all his people, whereof were moo than iij^M fotemen, that Fryday, which was right-an-hot day, xxx myle and more; whiche his people might nat finde, in all the way, horse-mete, ne mans-meate, ne so moche as drynke for theyr horses, save in one litle broke, where was full letle relefe, it was so sone trowbled with the cariages that had passed it. And all that day was evarmore the Kyngs hoste within v or vj myles of his enemyes; he in playne contry and they amongst woods; havynge allway good espialls upon them. So, continuynge that iourney to he came, with all his hooste, to a village callyd Chiltenham, but five myles from Tewkesberye, where the Kynge had certayn knolege that, but litle afore his comynge thethar, his enemyes were comen to Tewkesbury, and there were takynge a field, wherein they purposed to abyde, and delyver him battayle. Whereupon the Kynge made no longar taryenge, but a litle confortyd hymselfe, and his people, with suche meate and drynke as he had done to be caried with hym, for vitalyge of his hooste; and, incontinent, set forthe towards his enemyes, and toke the fielde, and lodgyd hym selfe, and all his hooste, within three myle of them.

Upon the morow followynge, Saterday, the iiij. day of May, [the Kynge] apparailed hymselfe, and all his hoost set in good array; ordeined three wards; displayed his bannars; dyd blowe up the trompets; commytted his caws and qwarell to Almyghty God, to owr most blessyd lady his mothar, Vyrgyn Mary, the glorious martyr Seint George, and all the saynts; and avaunced, di-rectly upon his enemyes; approchinge to theyr filde, whiche was strongly in a marvaylows strong grownd pyght, full difficult to be assayled. Netheles the Kyngs ordinance was so conveniently layde afore them, and his vawarde so sore oppressyd them, with shott of arrows, that they gave them right-a-sharpe shwre. Also they dyd agayne-ward to them, bothe with shot of ar-rows and gonnes, whereof netheles they ne had not so great plenty as had the Kynge. In the front of theyr field were so evell lanes, and depe dykes, so many hedges, trees, and busshes, that it was right hard to approche them nere, and come to hands; but Edmond, called Duke of Somarset, having that day the vawarde, withar it were for that he and his fellowshipe were sore annoyed in the place where they were, as well with gonnes-shott, as with shot of arrows, whiche they ne wowlde nor durst abyde, or els, of great harte and corage, knyghtly and manly avaunsyd hymselfe, with his fellowshipe, some-what asyde-hand the Kyngs vawarde, and, by certayne pathes and wayes therefore afore purveyed, and to the Kyngs party unknowne, he departyd out of the field, passyd a lane, and came into a fayre place, or cloos, even afore

the Kynge where he was enbatteled, and, from the hill that was in that one of
the closes, he set right fiercely upon th'end of the Kyngs battayle. The Kynge,
full manly, set forthe even upon them, enteryd and wann the dyke, and hedge,
upon them, into the cloose, and, with great vyolence, put them upe towards
the hyll, and, so also, the Kyng's vaward, being in the rule of the Duke of
Gloucestar.

Here it is to be remembred, how that, whan the Kynge was comyn afore
theyr fielde, or he set upon them, he consydered that, upon the right hand of
theyr field, there was a parke, and therein moche wood, and he, thinkynge to
purvey a remedye in caace his sayd enemyes had layed any bushement in
that wood, of horsemen, he chose, out of his fellashyppe, ij^c speres, and set
them in a plomp, togethars, nere a qwartar of a myle from the fielde, gy-
venge them charge to have good eye upon that cornar of the woode, if caas
that eny nede were, and to put them in devowre, and, yf they saw none suche,
as they thowght most behovfull for tyme and space, to employ themselfe in
the best wyse as they cowlde; which provisyon cam as well to poynt at this
tyme of the battayle as cowthe well have been devysed, for the sayd spers of
the Kyngs party, seinge no lyklynes of eny busshement in the sayd woode-
corner, seinge also goode oportunitie t'employ them selfe well, cam and
brake on, all at ones, upon the Duke of Somerset, and his vawarde, asyde-
hand, unadvysed, whereof they, seinge the Kynge gave them ynoughe to
doo afore them, were gretly dismaied and abasshed, and so toke them to
flyght into the parke, and into the medowe that was nere, and into lanes,
and dykes, where they best hopyd to escape the dangar; of whom, netheles, many were distressed, taken, and slayne; and, even at this point of theyr
flyght, the Kynge coragiously set upon that othar felde, were was chefe Edward, called Prince, and, in short while, put hym to discomfiture and flyght;
and so fell in the chase of them that many of them were slayne, and, namely,
at a mylene, in the medowe fast by the towne, were many drownyd; many
rann towards the towne; many to the churche, to the abbey; and els where;
as they best myght.

In the wynnynge of the fielde such as abode hand-stroks were slayne incontinent; Edward, called Prince, was taken, fleinge to the towne wards, and
slayne, in the fielde. Ther was also slayne Thomas, called th'Erle of Devonshire; John of Somarset, called Marqwes Dorset; Lord Wenloke; with many
othar in great nombar.

Thus this done, and with God's myght atchyved, the Kynge toke the
right way to th'abbey there, to gyve unto Almyghty God lawde and thanke

for the vyctorye, that, of his mercy, he had that day grauntyd and gyven unto hym; where he was receyvyd with procession, and so convayed thrwghe the churche, and the qwere, to the hy awtere, with grete devocion praysenge God, and yeldynge unto hym convenient lawde. And, where there were fledd into the sayd churche many of his rebels, in great nombar

or moo, hopynge there to have bene relevyd and savyd from bodyly harme, he gave them all his fre pardon, albe it there ne was, ne had nat at any thyme bene grauntyd, any fraunchise to that place for any offendars agaynst theyr prince havynge recowrse thethar, but that it had bene lefull to the Kynge to have commaundyd them to have bene drawne out of the churche, and had done them to be executyd as his traytors, yf so had bene his pleasure; but, at the reverence of the blessyd Trinitie, the moste holy vyrgyn Mary, and the holy martir Seint George, by whos grace and helpe he had that day attenygned so noble a victory; and, at the same reverence, he grauntyd the corpses of the sayd Edward, and othar so slayne in the field, or ells where, to be buryed there, in churche, or ells where it pleasyd the servaunts, frends, or neighbowrs, without any qwarteryng, or defoulyng theyr bodyes, by settying upe at any opne place.

This battayll thus done and atchived, and the Kyngs grace thus largly shewed, it was so that, in the abbey, and othar places of the towne, were founden Edmond, callyd Duke of Somerset, the prior of Seynt Johns, called Ser John Longstrother, Ser Thomas Tressham, Ser Gervaux of Clyfton, knyghts, squiers, and othar notable parsonnes dyvers, whiche all, dyvers tymes, were browght afore the Kyng's brothar, the Duke of Gloucestar and Constable of England, and the Duke of Norfolke, Marshall of England, theyr iudges; and so were iudged to deathe, in the mydst of the towne, Edmond duke of Somarset, and the sayd Prior of Seint Johns, with many othar gentils that there were taken, and that of longe tyme had provoked and continuyd the great rebellyon that so long had endured in the land agaynst the Kynge, and contrye to the wele of the Realme. The sayd Duke, and othar thus iudged, were executyd, in the mydste of the towne, upon a scaffolde therefore made, behedyd evereche one, and without eny othar dismembringe, or settynge up, licensyd to be buryed.

All these thyngs thus done, the Twesday, the vij. day of May, the Kynge departyd from Tewxbery, towards his citie of Worcestar, and, on the waye, he had certayne knowledge that Qwene Margarete was founden nat fer from thens, in a powre religiows place, where she had hyd hir selfe, for the surty of hir parson, the Satrudaye, erlye in the mornynge, aftar hir sonne Edward, callyd Prince, was gon to the filde, for to withdraw hir selfe from the adventure of the battayle; of whome also he was assured that she shuld be at his commaundement.

The Kynge, beinge at Worcestar, had certayne knowledge also, that certayne his rebells of the northe partyes beganne to make commocions, and assembles of people agaynst hym, in the qwarell of Henry, callyd Kynge; for whiche cawse he kept nat the ryght way to London, as he had purposyd, but, entendyng to prepare a new felashipp agaynst the sayd rebells in the north, and, to be in a good strengthe of people, whatsoevar shuld happe, he determined hym selfe to goo to Coventrye, as he so dyd the xi. day of the sayd monythe; where he refresshed well suche as were laft withe hym of his hoste, by the space of three dayes; and thethar was browght unto hym Qwene Margaret. He forgate not to send from thens his messengars, with writyngs, all abowte the contryes nere adioyninge, to suche in especiall as he trustyd best that they would do hym service. Trewth it is whiles the Kynge, in alwyse, thus preparyd a new armye, came certayne tydyngs unto hym, how they of the northe had herd the certeyntye of his great vyctories, and how that he disposyd hym to come towards them, with a great armye, and they, sore dredyng his good spede, and great fortunes; nat havynge any of the Warewyks, or Nevells, blode, whom unto they myght have restyd, as they had done afore; knowynge also, for certaynty, that th'Erle of Northumbarland was nothinge of theyr partye, but that he wowld resyste and withstand them at his uttarmoste powere, uttarly takynge parte with the Kynge, and his qwarell; the cheftaynes of them that were maliciowsly dysposed, and, for evell entent, as above, have commoned and begone to assemble the people, anon, upon thies knowledge and considerations, they withdrew them from any ferthar proceding to theyr said rebellyon, as folks not lykly to maintayne theire fals qwarell and partye. They lefte theyr bands, and compaignes, and dyvars of them made menes to th'Erle of Northumbarland, besechinge hym to be good meane to the Kynge for his grace and pardone. Some of the scowrars wer taken and put in warde. The citie of Yorke, and othar good townes, and contryes, lowly submittinge them, and [promysinge] than to the Kynge theyr dwe obedyence. And so, by the xiiij. day of May, it was knowne clerly, by suche as were sent unto the Kynge from th'Erle of Northombarland, from the citie of Yorke, and othar dyvars places in the northe, that there was no rebellyon in all the northe begon, but that it was so passyfied that it ne myght ne shwld anoy the Kynge, in any wyse. Wherefore it was to hym thowght, and to all hys counsell, that for to goo

into the northe for eny pacification, or punishement of suche parsons, it was
not nedefull as at that tyme; and so it was most clerly declaryd, the same
daye, by th'Erle of Northombarland, who cam streyght to the Kynge to
Coventrye, out of the northe contrye; as his departynge well asswred that
the contrye was in good and sure tranquilitie, without any comotions, or unlawfull gatheryngs. Whiche Erle cam not accompanied greatly, but with a
fewe folkes, and nat arrayed in manar of warr, for he had no mannar knowledge but that the Kynge, aftar this his great victories acchived, shuld have
good pax, every where in his realme; but it was nat so, for the Kynge had
knowledge, or that he cam to Coventrye, by lettars sent hym by lords of his
blode beinge at London this season, that the bastard Fawcomberge, whiche,
a lytle afore that, had bene sent to the sea by th'Erle of Warwyke, and had
dystressed many marchaunt-shipps of Portyngall, and taken the ships and
goods to hym selfe, in breche of the amitie that of longe tyme had bene betwyxt the realmes of England and Portyngall, he had callyd unto hym, and
to his fellowshipe, grete partyes and nombars of marinars, out of every party
and porte of England, and many othar traytors, and misgoverned men, of
every contrye of England, and also othar contries, that had great corage to
atend to thefte and roberye. It was shewed the Kyng that dayly his nombar
drew gretar and gretar, and that he was gone to Calays, and browght many
men with hym, from thens, into Kent, where he began to gathar his people in
great nombar, entendyng, by lyklyhode, to do some great myschevous dede.

Aftar the Kynge was at Coventrye, he had dayly messages from the
Lords at London, how that the bastard had assembled greate people, and
bothe by lande many thowsands, and, by watar with all his shipps ful of
people, he came afore London, thinkynge to robbe, and spoyle, and do al-
maner of myschefe; and therto many of the contrye of Kent were assentynge,
and cam with theyr good wills, as people redy to be appliable to suche sedi-
tious commocions. Othar of Kentyshe people that wowld righte fayne have
sytten still at home, and nat to have ronne into the dangar of suche rebellyon,
by force and violence of suche riotows people as were of the sayd bastards
company, for feare of deathe, and othar great manasses, and thretynynges,
were compellyd, some to goo with the bastard, in theyr parsons; suche, specially, as were hable in parsons, yf they had aray, and myght not wage to such
as would goo, they were compellyd, by lyke foarce, to lene them theyr araye,
and harnes; and such as were unharnesyd, aged, and unhable, and of honor,
they were compelled to send men waged, or to gyve mony wherewith to wage
men to goo to the sayd bastards company. So that, ryght in a shorte tyme,

the sayd bastard and his felowship had assembled to the nombar of xvj or xvij^M men, as they accomptyd themselves. Whiche came afore London the xij. day of May, in the qwarell of Kynge Henry, whome they sayd they woulde have owte of the Towre of London, as they pretendyd. And, for that cawse, they desyred the citizens of London that they myght have free entrye into the citie where, first, theyr entent was to have with them the sayd Henry, and aftar, to passe pesceably thrwghe the citie, as they sayd, without any grevaunce to be done to eny parson; upon th'entent from thens to goo towards the Kynge, where so evar they myght finde hym, hym to distroy and all his partakars, in qwarell of the sayde Henry, yf they myght have of hym the ovar-hand.

But, so it was, that the Maior, Aldarmen, and othar officers and citizens of London denied them theyr entrye. As this was in doinge ovar came from London freshe tydyngs to the Kynge, from the Lords, and the citizens, which, with right grete instance, moved the Kinge, in all possible haste, to approche and com to the citie, to the defence of the Qwene, than being in the Tower of London, my Lorde Prince, and my Ladies his doghtars, and of the Lords, and of the citie, whiche, as they all wrote, was likly to stand in the grettest ioperdy that evar they stode. In consideration had for that gret nombar of the persones within the citie were rather disposyd to have helped to have suche mischiefe wroght that to defend it; some, for they were maliciowsly disposed, and were, in theyr harts perciall to th'Erle of Warwickes qwarell, and to the party of Henry, wherefore were many; some, for they were powre; some, mens servaunts, mens prentises, which would have bene right glade of a comon robery, to th'entent they might largely have put theyr hands in riche mens coffres.

Thes manar of writings moved the Kynge greatly to haste hym thetharwards; but it was behovefull, or that he came there, he were furnesshyd of as great, or gretar, hooste than he had had at any tyme sithe his comynge into the land; natheles, for that suche armye might nat be prepared so sonne as he woulde, the sayd xiiij. day of May, he apoyntyd a notable, and a well chosen, felawshipe owt of his hooste, and them sent unto the citie of London, afore his comynge, to the nombar of xv^c men, well besene; for the comforte of the Quene, the Lords, and the citizens. And hymselfe departyd out of Coventrie towards London the xvj. day of May.

Here is to be remembred, that, whan the bastard and his felashipe myght not purchace of the maior and citezens of London the overtur of the sayd citie, for theyr passage thrwghe, as above, neythar for theyr promises, ne for great thretenyngs and manassyngs, they made sembland to passe ovar Thames, by Kyngstone Brige, x myles above London, and thethar drewe them the hole hooste, levynge all theyr shipps afore Seint Katheryns, a lytle from the Towre of London; pretendyng that they shuld come and dystroy Westmynstar, and than the subarbs of London, and assay the uttarmoste agaynst the citye, revengynge that theyr entrye was denied them, and theyr passage thrwghe the citie, and so forthe, with theyr hole multitude, have passed thrwghe the contries agaynst the Kynge. But, so it was, as they were onwards in this journey, the bastard had certayne knowledge that the Kynge was greatly assistyd with all the Lords of the Realme in substaunce, great nombar of noble men and othar, in greater nombar than in eny tyme he had had afore; they, greatly fearinge his highe corage and knyghthood, and the great vyctories that God had sent hym, they delayed withe watar wyne (?) and so retowrned agayne, and came before London, and shewyd themselfe in hoole battayle in Seint Georgis filde. And that for dyvers consideracions; for ones, they dowbtyd gretly the recountar of the Kynge; also the multytud of them cam rathar for robbinge than for revengynge by way of battayle; they doubted, also, to assayle the citie on that othar syde of Thamis, for, lykly it was, that, in caas they myght not prevayle, they of London shuld lyghtly stoppe them theyr wayes homeward unto theyr contrye. And for to devide theyr hoost, some upon the one syde of London and some upon the othar syde, they thought it foly, forsomoche as, with fewe folks, they myght have broken the brydges aftar them, and, with right fewe folks, have kepte and stopped theyr passage.

Here folowethe howe the sayd bastard Faucomberge, with his felashippe, assayled the citie of London, and set fyer upon the bridge of London, and brent greate parte thereof, and upon othar two gates of the sayde citie; and how they were honorably recountred, and discomfeted, and dryven to the watar, and soo the citie delyveryd from them.

The bastard and his fellashippe, thus returnyd agayne from Kyngstonn brigge, afore London, purposynge to execute theyr great rancowr and malice agayns the citie of London, and that in all haste, to th'entent they myght have theyr praye afore the Kyngs comynge, whiche they thowght not to abyde, and it to cary awaye in theyr shipps, whiche were ready to attend for the same entent of roberye, but a myle or two from the sayde citie. Wherefore, incontinent, they assayled the citie with greate violence, with shot of goons, suche as they had browght owt of theyr shipps, in great nombar, and layd them on length the watar syde, streight ovar agaynst the citie; where with they prevayled no thinge, for the citizens agayne-warde in dyvars placis layde ordinance, and made so sharp shott agaynst them, that they durst not abyde in eny place alonge the watarsyde, and so were dryven from theyr owne ordinaunce. Wherefore the bastard purveyed an othar mean to annoy and greve the sayde Citie sore, and therefore ordeynyd a great fellowshipe to set fyre upon the bridge, and to brene the howsynge upon the bridge, and, through therby, to make them an open way into sayd citie. An othar greate felashipe he sett ovar the watar with his shipps, mo then iij^M men, whiche were devided into two partes; one partye went to Algate, wenyng to have entred the citie there, by assaulte; an othar partye went to Bysshops-gate, wenynge to have entred there by an othar assaulte; wher they shot goonns and arrows into the citie, and dyd moche harme and hurte. And, at the laste, set fiere upon the gates, for to have brent them, and so trustinge to have entred at large. Theyr brennynge at the bridge profytid them of no thynge; albe they brent many howses to the nombar of iij^{xx}, but the citizens hadd set suche ordenaunce in theyr ways that, thowghe all the way had been open, it had bene to harde for them to have entred by that way, but upon theyr lyves. The maior, aldarmen, and worshipfull citizens of the citie were in good array, and set to every parte, where was behovefull, greate felowshipe, welle ordered, and ordeyned, for to withstand the malice of thes forsayd rebells.

To the citizens, and defence of the citie, came th'Erle of Essex, and many knights, squiers, gentlemen, and yemen, right well arraied, which had right great diligence in orderinge the citizens, and firste to prepare and ordayne for the defence and surtye of the sayd cittie and people thereof where it was necessarye, and preparyd how and where they myght best ysswe owt upon them, and put them from theyr purpos. By which medelinge of gentlemen, and lords servauntes, with the citizens, in every parte, the citizens were greatly encoragyd to set sharply upon them with one hoole entent, where elles it had be lykely they shuld nat have willed to have done so moche therto as was donne. For, as it is aforesayde, greate nombar of the citie were there that with right good wille woulde they have bene sofferyd to have enteryd the citie, to th'entent to have fallen to myscheffe and robberye with them. And so, aftar continuynge of muche shote of gonnes and arrows a greate while, upon bothe parties, th'Erle Ryvers, that was with the Qwene, in the Tower of London, gatheryd unto hym a felashipe right well chosen, and habiled, of iiij or v c men, and ysswyd owt at a posterne upon them, and, even upon a poynt, cam upon the Kentyshe men beinge abowte the assawltynge of Algate, and mightely laied upon them with arrows, and upon them in hands, and so killyd and toke many of them, dryvynge them from the same gate to the watar syde. Yet netheles, three placis wer fiers brennynge all at ones. The Maior, Aldarmen, and many of the sayd citie, were anone in theyr harnes, and parted theyr felashippe into divers partes, as them thowght moste behofefull, but a great parte of the citizens were at Algate, and with them many gentlemen and yemen, which all made the defence that they best myght; and shott many gouns, and arrows, amonge them; but for thy the Kentishemen spared nat to assayle at bothe the gates, so that the sayde lorde and citizens determined in themselve to arredy them in good array, and to ysswe owt upon them, in hands, and put them to flyght and discomfiture. About iiij^M and [mo] fell in the chas of them, and slew mo than vij^c of them. Many were taken, and aftar hanged; the remenaunt went to the watarsyde, and toke theyr boates, and went to theyr shipps, and ovar to that othar syde agayn.

Thes haynows traytowrs and robbers, the bastard and his felawshyppe, seing they cowthe in nowyse profite to theyr entents, by litle and litle withdrewe them to the Blackhethe, to an hill three myle from London the xvj., xvij., and xviij. day of Maye, there abydynge by the space of three dayes; but, theyr abydynge, they had certayne knowledge that the Kynge was comynge with great puisaunce, whereof they greatly adrad, seinge that they myght nat have theyr praye of London, ne havynge hardies to abyde the Kynge and his puisaunce, they disperbled; they of Calais, to Calais, the sonest they cowlde; suche as were of othar contrys, into theyrs; many of Kent, to theyr howses; the mariners, and myschevows robbars, rebells, and riotours with them, to theyr shipps; and drewe downe to the sea coaste with all theyr shipps.

The Kynge this season, well accompanied and mightely with great lordes, and in substaunce all the noblemen of the land, with many othar able men, well arraied for the werre, to the nombar of xxx^M horsemen, cam to the citie of London, sone aftar the disperblynge of the Kentyshe hooste, the xxj. day of Maye, the Twesdaye; where he was honorably receyved of all the people, the maior, aldermen, and many othar worshipfull men, citizens of the sayd citie. At the metyng of them the Kynge dubed Knyghtes the maior, the recordar, dyvars aldarmen, with othar worshipfull of the sayd citie of London, whiche as hadd mannly and honorably acquit them selfe agaynst the bastard, and his crwell hooste; honoringe, and rewardinge them with the ordar, of his good love and grace, for theyr trwe acquitaill, and as they had ryght well and trewly deservyd that tyme.

Here it is to be remembred, that, from the tyme of Tewkesbery fielde, where Edward, called Prince, was slayne, thanne, and sonne aftar, wer taken, and slayne, and at the Kyngs wylle, all the noblemen that came from beyond the see with the sayde Edward, called Prince, and othar also theyr parte-takers as many as were of eny might or puisaunce. Qwene Margaret, hirselfe, taken, and browght to the Kynge; and, in every party of England, where any commotion was begonne for Kynge Henry's party, anone they were rebuked, so that it appered to every mann at eye the sayde partie was extincte and re-pressed for evar, without any mannar hope of agayne quikkening; utterly de-spaired of any maner of hoope or releve. The certaintie of all whiche came to the knowledge of the sayd Henry, late called Kyng, being in the Tower of London; not havynge, afore that, knowledge of the saide matars, he toke it to so great dispite, ire, and indingnation, that, of pure displeasure, and melen-coly, he dyed the xxiij. day of the monithe of May. Whom the Kynge dyd to be browght to the friers prechars at London, and there, his funerall service donne, to be caried, by watar, to an Abbey upon Thamys syd, xvj myles from London, called Chartsey, and there honorably enteryd.

The Kynge, incontinent aftar his comynge to London, taried but one daye, and went with his hole army, aftar his sayd traytors into Kent, them to represse, in caas they were in any place assembled, and for to let them to as-semble by any comocion to be made amongs them, wher unto they, hereto-forne, have often tymes bene accustomyd to doo. But, trewthe it was, that they were disperbled as afore; but the sayd bastard Faucomberge, with great nombar of mariners, and many othar mischevows men, called his sowldiours, or men of were, went streyght to Sandwyche, and there kept the towne with strengthe, and many great and small shipps, abowt xl and vij, in the haven, all undar his rule. And, as sone as they undarstode the Kynge and his hoste aprochid nere unto them, the sayd bastard sent unto hym, suche meanes as best he cowthe, humbly to sew for his grace and pardon, and them of his feloshipe, and, by appoyntement, willed there to be delyveryd to the Kyngs behove all his shipps, and became his trwe liegemen, with as streight prom-yse of trew legiaunce as cowthe be devised for them to be made, whiche, aftar delyberation taken in that parte, for certayn great consyderations, was grauntyd. Wherefore the Kynge sent thethar his brothar Richard, Duke of Gloucestar, to receyve them in his name, and all the shipps; as he so dyd the xxvj. day of the same monithe; the Kynge that tyme beinge at Cantorbery.

And thus, with the helpe of Almighty god, the moaste glorious Virgin Mary his mothar, and of Seint George, and of [all] the Saynts of heven, was begon, finished, and termined, the reentrie and perfecte recover of the iuste title and right of owr sayd soveraygne Lord Kynge Edward the Fowrthe, to his realme and crowne of England, within the space of xj wekes; in the whiche season, moienaunt the helpe and grace of Allmyghty God, by his wysdome, and polyqwe, he escaped and passyd many great perills, and daungars, and dificulties, wherein he had bene; and, by his full noble and knyghtly cowrage, hathe optayned two right-great, crwell, and mortall battayles; put to flight and discomfeture dyvars great assembles of his rebells, and riotows persons, in many partyes of his land; the whiche, thowghe all they were also rygorously and maliciously disposed, as they myght be, they were, netheles, so affrayde and afferyd of the verey asswryd courage and manhod that restethe in the person of our seyd sovereigne lord, that they were, anon, as confused. Whereby it apperithe, and faythfully is belevyd, that with the helpe of Almyghty god, whiche from his begynning hitharto hathe not fayled hym, in short tyme he shall appeas his subgetes thrwghe all his royalme; that peace and tranquillitie shall growe and multiplye in the same, from day to day, to the honour and lovynge of Almyghty God, the encreace of his singuler and famows renoume, and to the greate ioye and consolation of his frinds, alies, and well-willers, and to all his people, and to the great confusion of all his enemys, and evyll wyllars.

Here endethe the arryvaile of Kynge Edward the Fowrthe. Out of Mastar Flyghtwods boke, Recordar of London.

t w o

Lydgate and the Rise of *Pollecie* in the *Mirror* Tradition

THE SIXTEENTH-CENTURY *MIRROR FOR MAGISTRATES* BEARS CERTAIN external similarities to the cautionary accounts of fallen princes that proliferated in the thirteenth and fourteenth centuries, most influentially in Boccaccio's *De Casibus Vivorum Illustrium*. Yet, more than any of its precessors, the *Mirror* proposes a provisional or even unsettled exemplarity, urging that its readers engage in a highly active interpretative exercise. Its complaining princes do not simply bewail their fates, but insist that their readers ponder Fortune's gifts as well as her deceits, their own choices for good as well as ill, their reluctant reliance on unstable textual processes to get their stories told. 'Hearken awhyle,' they say, and 'mark this,' and 'behold my hape,' in the words of an earlier, more 'medieval' style of exemplarity. But the reader is treated as a coadjudicator of their choices and experiences. 'Way the cause,' they say, and 'make thou therefore of my lyfe.' They inveigh against the possible untruthfulness of 'slye wryters'—thus reminding their reader of the necessity for vigilant and revisionary interpretation of received sources. Increasingly, the deposed prince's complaint moves from a univocal and fixed viewpoint on an accomplished past and towards a sense that the meaning of precedent lies open to reconsideration, disagreement, and possible innovation. Although the past has an undeniable claim upon the present, the present-day assessment of its claim involves a good deal more than simple deference or passive rediscovery. The meaning of the past invites active reinvention in relation to emergent situations.

This sense of the past as possible stimulant to present imagination is what kept the tradition of *De Casibus* or the narrative of the fallen prince so long in favor with a succession of European literary avant-gardes. Postulation of an 'avant-garde' identity may seem brash or misplaced in the case of a genre now generally regarded as musty and dull. But this genre's capacity for a provocative fusion of past and present horizons relayed excitement and even a whiff of danger to large numbers of readers over a period of four centuries. It engaged the talents of leading writers in each of those centuries, successively commanding the attention of Jean de Meun, Boccaccio, Chaucer, Laurent de Premierfait, Lydgate, Baldwin, Ferrers, Sackville, and more. Nor was its pertinence as a pattern of human experience unworthy of the younger Shakespeare's attention. This genre's 'danger' rests in the relation it establishes between the past and the present. This relation shifts from case to case and author to author, but the constancy of the genre's appeal rests in the unfixed and highly adaptable nature of its exemplarity. The plaintive prince's lesson might finally land anywhere, affix itself to any contemporary case. The past is, on the one hand, safely over, sealed from the present, and sanitized as 'tradition'; it yet lies, on the other, open to reinterpretation, subject to unruly and unpredictable revival as an affront to settled arrangements of power.

Practitioners in this tradition address its own generic past with an attitude of what might be called 'respectful opportunism.' In William Baldwin's preface to the 1559 edition of the *Mirror for Magistrates* we learn that, when the members of the syndicate first met earlier in that decade to decide upon their charge, Lydgate's predecessor volume was borne into the room and was present as a physical object throughout their deliberations. According to Baldwin, 'Whan certayne of theym to the number of seuen, were throughe a generall assent at an appoynted time and place gathered together . . . I resorted vnto them, bering with me the booke of Bochas, translated by Dan Lidgate.'[1] Their purpose, he says, was 'for better obseruation of his order,' taking 'order' in what I would suppose to be something like *ordinatio*, or general arrangement and strategy. He says that the order was 'lyked well,' but not well enough to persuade the *Mirror* syndicate to resuscitate either Boccaccio or Lydgate to serve as narrator-reporteur: 'seynge that both Bochas and Lidgate were dead, [and] neyther were there any alyue that meddled with lyke argument.' All agreed, instead, that Baldwin should 'vsurpe Bochas rowme.' Nevertheless, Boccaccio and Lydgate are brought respectfully before the meeting, assigned a place at the table, as it were, and acknowledged as precedental in the syndicate's activities. Nor was the original intention that Lydgate's text should fall by the wayside. Had publication difficulties not intervened, Lydgate's volume would have provided literal shelter for the first printing of its own successor. The *Mirror* was, as attested by a surviving title page and an extant sheet of the canceled original, first intended to be published as a 'continuacion' of Wayland's 1555 edition of Lydgate.[2] Once the *Mirror* did go forward, as a freestanding 1559 edition in its own right, it promptly and decisively eclipsed Lydgate's predecessor volume. Nevertheless, Lydgate was provocatively if ambivalently invoked at the moment of the *Mirror*'s creation.

The *Mirror,* like every text in the falls of princes tradition, is effectively Janus-faced, looking back respectfully at the predecessors to whom a debt is owed, and looking for opportunities to resituate its admonitions in a new political context. We have here a particular kind of readeption, in which a narrative is brought back or recovered, but in new and potentially transformative ways. Within such a process, the existence of a source or a prior narrative can offer the shelter of tradition to its successor, even as the new version strains always to 'break shelter,' casting off the comforts of its own approved form in order to comment incisively on its present-time world. I thus see in this often-maligned genre not stasis, but dynamism, resulting from a constant push-and-pull between earlier premises and new applications. This chapter is an attempt to situate this dynamism in two of its 'present' moments, by considering two exemplary textual concentrations: first Lydgate's fifteenth-century reworking of Premerfait's rendering of Boccaccio, and then the 1559 and 1563 editions of the *Mirror for Magistrates.* The dynamism of Lydgate's text has, I believe, been seriously underacknowledged; that of the *Mirror* has been conceded and respected, but not well understood.

I. PREMIERFAIT, LYDGATE, AND THE TURN TO THE WORLD

Accounts of the downfalls of princes and illustrious persons must be understood not only as instructive, but as challenging, gripping, and potentially dangerous for the medieval and early modern audiences. For the reader of conventional taste they were less likely to be found boring, as is sometimes supposed, than disturbing—perhaps even, in some respects, almost 'too hot to handle.' From its earliest instantiations in Jean de Meun in the late thirteenth century and Boccaccio in the mid-fourteenth century on through the *Mirror for Magistrates* in the mid-sixteenth century, the narrative of a prince's fall never ceased to display upstart energies. In the hands of Jean de Meun's Reason, it serves as a schoolman's riposte to softheaded accounts of worldly love. In those of Chaucer's Monk it offers a dolorous protohumanist reflection on the woes that beset earthly enterprises. In the adaptations of Premierfait and Lydgate, it is a vehicle of sage counsel to the worldly prince. In Baldwin and his fellows, it is a new resource for the pursuit of practical statecraft. As a genre it was always making itself anew, testing and stretching its resources and those of its audiences.

Within English literature, this genre's risky potentialities have been consistently underestimated, largely as a result of a single, influential misprision. I refer to Chaucer's Knight's interruption of the Monk's tragic series. This interruption and its rationale have been subject to remarkably literal and credulous interpretation, considering their author's well-recognized propensity to create characters who tell only a portion of the truth about their ostensible motivations. The Monk having told the seventeenth of his promised series of a hundred tragedies, in which we are repeatedly shown the assaults of Fortune upon trusting men and 'regnes that been proude,' the Knight interrupts:

> 'Hoo!' quod the Knyght, 'good sire, namoore of this!
> That ye han seyd is right ynough, ywis,
> And muchel moore; for litel hevynesse
> Is right ynough to muche folk, I gesse.
> I seye for me, it is a greet disese,
> Whereas men han been in greet welthe and ese,
> To heeren of hire sodeyn fal, allas!' (Bk. 2, ll. 3957–73)

Readers have generally concluded that the Knight is bored by the Monk's recital. But that is not really what the Knight says. What he *does* say is that these narratives cause him 'disese,' or make him uneasy; troubling to the generality of people, they are especially disturbing to *him*—that is, to the pilgrimage's representative of aristocratic privilege. Harry Bailly supports him, but rather incoherently, whereas the Knight has a precise theory about his own response, involving a proposed remedy for the situation: rather than seeing privilege overthrown, he wishes it to endure and 'abide' (l. 3967). In keeping with the best contemporary theory, he is prepared to view this privilege as earned rather than just inherited (ll. 3965–66); but *as* privilege it is then invited to naturalize itself and indefinitely abide, securing itself against all that would, operating under the name of 'Fortune,' render it insecure. In a manuscript prepared early in the fifteenth century for French aristocrat Jean of Angoulême, during his long imprisonment in England, we find marginal testimony to contemporary agreement with the Knight's view; the Monk's tragedies are declared 'valde absurda,' and the scribe (probably on Jean's instructions) cuts them off even before the Knight has had his chance.[3]

One aspect of the Knight's response may involve literary taste, and an incapacity for the shock of the new; as Renate Haas has shown, the Monk's narratives represent the precocious introduction into English literature of the most recent, and cutting-edge, Italian humanist thought in their linkage of classical literary forms and precedents with the malign mainspring of Fortune.[4] So seen, as what she calls 'a brilliant response to the most advanced literary and philosophical discussion of the age,' the *Monk's Tale* might be expected to provoke a certain amount of incomprehension, and perhaps even a backlash as well. But the Knight, possibly joined by readers like Jean of Angoulême, entertains an additional, and ideological, complaint besides. He is far from wishing that reading about falls of princes should discourage worldly aspirations; rather, he wants a genre to tell him something about worldly prosperity, its acquisition and good maintenance. In adopting this position, the Knight reveals himself as, paradoxically, something of a forward thinker, with regard to what would become a prevalent fifteenth-century view. In the Chaucerian lexicon, the Knight is thinking superficially here. Within the larger Chaucerian canon, only seriously confused people think they can beat Fortune at her game. This is, for example, Criseyde's position, in her soon-to-be utterly discredited oath to be true to Troilus forever; counseling Troilus's compliance with her plan to desert Troy, she recommends patience and adds,

> '. . . think that lord is he
> Of Fortune ay that naught wole of hire recche,
> And she ne daunteth no wight but a wrecche.' (IV, ll. 1587–89)

Chaucer's Knight is hardly compromised to the extent that Criseyde is soon
to be, but Chaucer—like Boccaccio—would have considered such disrespect for Fortune's authority ill advised.[5]

Boccaccio's chief goal in his *De Casibus* was, as Henry Ansgar Kelly
has observed, that of 'providing object lessons to the wicked,' and most
particularly to 'high-ranking knaves and fools.'[6] As Boccaccio spells it out
in his opening remarks, his intention is to address the conduct of great men
('mores hominum illustrium'), noting that their error is to neglect the operations of Fortune, behaving as if they had drugged Fortune into an eternal
sleep with herbs or incantatory songs, and had anchored their prinicipali-
ties with iron hooks to an adamantine cliff.[7] The aim of all this is that men
might see the insubstantiality of such illusions, gaining thereby a sense of
God's power, their own fraility, and the lubricity of Fortune ('Fortune lu-
bricum noscant')—not, that is, in order to harness these forces for their advantage, since they are inherently ungovernable, but to learn to curtain their
expectations ('letis modum ponere discant'). Boccaccio's intentions in composing this work were presumably multiple: to win fame by displaying himself as adept in the deployment of classical examples (see his discussion with
Petrarch in book 8); to vie with the scope and severity and classical learning
of Petrarch's own *De Remediis utriusque Fortune;* to extend the somber tenets
of his own late-life religious conservatism into the analysis of the real world.
David Wallace has added yet another motive almost diametrically opposed
to that of Petrarch's rather fawning praise of illustrious men in *De Viris Il-
lustribus,* which is to assail contemporary tyranny and to exalt republican
values.[8] The one thing he had *no* intention of doing was to write a cheerful
'self-help' book for ambitious princes, in the form of a book of regiment or
noriture or other guide to worldly success.[9] Boccaccio, who remains profoundly conservative in the matter of earthly advancement, offers an infinity
of ways and means by which earthly aspirations can be undone, and none at
all by which they can be advanced or sustained.

Nevertheless, Boccaccio's rigorously dour and world-denying insistence
on the inevitable collapse of worldly hopes contained contradictory elements
that would contribute ultimately to its own unraveling. Oddly, the principal element of instability within Boccaccio's vision is lodged in an apparently self-consistent claim: the dominion of Fortune in earthly affairs. As
in Dante, when Virgil describes Fortune as a divine appointee and executress
of God's will—as 'general ministra e duce'[10]—Boccaccio treats Fortuna as
coextensive with God's will, or at least insofar as such matters are accessible

to vulgar understanding ('Et quid deus siue [vt eorum more loquar] fortuna'). Yet, even in Dante, Fortune possesses a certain autonomy, ruling her own domain ('suo regno,' l. 88) on earth. The implication of this partial autonomy is that acts dictated by Fortune can never quite be regarded as unequivocal expressions of God's will, and the assimilation of Fortune to God's will can never be complete. Once allowed her own domain and any degree of independence with respect to God's will, Fortune becomes something other than an executress and something more like an emblem of worldly insecurity and the arbitrariry of fates. One might say that she operates as an 'uncertainty principle.' The vital point is that uncertainty invites countermeasures *in the world*. For acknowledgment of uncertainty has the paradoxical potential to redirect attention to the world. Even Machiavelli, after all, was a great believer in Fortune, but not Fortune as chastisement to the worldly. Rather, Machiavelli's Fortune is treated mainly as an incentive for precautionary action and a spur to enterprise—hardly the purpose that Dante, Jean de Meun, Boccaccio, Chaucer (or at least his Monk), and other thirteenth- and fourteenth-century exponents of the *De Casibus* tradition seem originally to have had in mind.[11]

I speak here of an implication that is only latent and unrealized in Boccaccio's writings. For its exemplification and more systematic pursuit, one must turn to his subsequent adaptors. The realization of this newly aggressive and worldly-wise stance towards the ravages of Fortune begins with two authors not normally known for innovation. With Laurent de Premierfait and John Lydgate, the *De Casibus* tradition was turned practically inside out: bent round to serve a set of analytical and political purposes quite distinct from, and diametrically opposed to, its original objectives. Lydgate, in a prologue noting his indebtedness to Laurent, says as much, albeit in language partly so conventionalized (treating of 'old chaff,' 'cleene corn,' and the like) that a jaded reader is likely to miss the revisionary thrust animating his words. His language serves not just as respectful boilerplate but also as a description of what he is actually doing:

> Artificeres hauyng exercise
> May chaunge and turne bi good discrecioun
> Shappis, formys, and newli hem deuyse,
> Make and vnmake in many sondry wyse,
> As potteres, which to that craft entende,
> Breke and renewe ther vesselis to a-mende. (Bk. 1, ll. 9–14)

This dedication to breaking and remaking does not occur in a vacuum. Whatever the exploitable internal disequilibriums of the genre, Premierfait and Lydgate shared an external incentive to 'make it new' around the wishes of powerful aristocratic patrons. Boccaccio wrote for Cavalcanti, a dedicatee and friend, but not a noble patron.[12] Although Chaucer was not indifferent to the attentions of the great, having written at various times for John of Gaunt and Richard II, he seems in the first instance to have compiled his *Canterbury Tales* for the edification and enjoyment of a circle of friends and associates, and also with a partial eye on posterity, but not really as an incentive to patronage or sop to the great.[13] Whereas Laurent de Premierfait's first and second renderings of Boccaccio were completed in the first decade of the fifteenth century for the duc de Berry and Lydgate's rendering of Laurent in the fourth decade of the fifteenth century for Humfrey duke of Gloucester.[14]

One might loosely, but I think not inaccurately, suppose that the reading tastes and expectations of the duc de Berry and Humfrey duke of Gloucester would have more in common with those of Chaucer's Knight and with Jean of Angoulême than with, say, Chaucer's Monk or, in the more secular sphere, a fourteenth-century humanist or man of letters. And, indeed, we find Laurent touting his work with a series of promises already partly estranged from Boccaccio's original purposes, and far better adapted to uptake by a man of the world. To such a reader, he offers 'a proven manner by which each man and woman can emancipate and exempt themselves from adverse circumstance and from the reversals of fortune' ('vne prouuable maniere par quoy chasciun homme et femme puissent eulx affranchir et exempter des cas et des trebuschetz de fortune').[15] In the same vein, he promises to do everybody a good turn by opening the way to an escape from the consequences of mutable and blind fortune ('... en ouura[n]t la voye deschaper les cas de fortune muable et au[e]uglesse').[16] So, too, do we encounter an inclination on Lydgate's part to rethink Boccaccio's dour message in terms of an aristocratic patron's wishes. That Lydgate has his patron much on his mind is constantly evident—even to the extent of inserting highly unlikely words into Petrarch's exhortation to Boccaccio, in his reworking of a passage ultimately derived from *De Casibus*, book 8:

> Yet at the laste, thynk, for thi socour
> Sum roial prince shal quyte thi labour. (Bk. 8, ll. 146–47)

Having aspirationally found such a prince, Lydgate sets out to please him. One necessary preliminary to pleasing Humfrey is, in effect, a rewriting of the entire contract or convention customary to the *De Casibus* tradition, in which the princely reader is expected to take his admonitory knocks at the hands of a severely moralistic author. Now allowed is a much sunnier proposition, according to which, rather than found subject to Fortune, the prince might set himself beyond Fortune and might educate himself in the ways of Fortune's avoidance. As Lydgate introduces him, Humfrey is a self-stabilizing prince, unsubject to change and studious in the arts of fortune-proofing:

> Stable in study alwey he doth continue,
> Settyng a-side alle chaungis of Fortune. (Bk. 1, ll. 389–90)

These lines could be read as a traditional Boethian or Petrarchan compliment, according to which Humfrey achieves stability, and can ignore alterations of Fortune, by curtailing his own ambitions and objectives. The larger context of Lydgate's argument, however, suggests to the contrary that Humfrey's 'stability' will amount to continuance in his princely office. For, Lydgate promises us, the leader who follows God and orders his activities according to the language of civic virtue will be bound by no unwelcome term limit ('God will keepe hym that he shal nat fall, / Longe preserve his domynacioun'— bk. 2, ll. 577–78). Nor is Humfrey reluctant to instruct Lydgate in his business, setting parameters for his task, including even the 'lowly' tone he is expected to assume (bk. 2, l. 153). Humfrey's main point is, in fact, not far from that of the Knight: misfortunes are not simply to be lingered upon but remedies provided. Lydgate summarizes his task in this way:

> That I sholde in eueri tragedie
> Afftir the processe made mencioun,
> At the eende sette a remedie,
> With a lenvoie conueied be resoun,
> And afftir that, with humble affeccioun,
> To noble pryncis lowli it directe,
> Bi otheres fallyng [thei myht] themsilff correcte. (Bk. 2, ll. 148–54)

And, nothing loath, reports that ' I obeied his biddyng and plesaunce / . . . As I coude' (bk. 2, ll. 155, 157).

Humfrey's own interest in the control of malign Fortune by knowledge and foresight is signaled by the presence in his library in the 1420s–30s of Coluccio Salutati's *De Fato ete Fortuna.* This text argues for the minimization of Fortune's powers by the exercise of foresight.[17] As Coluccio expresses it, in the translation of R. J. Lyall, 'ubi plurimum sit sapientie, minimum debeat esse fortune' ('where knowledge is the greatest, the least the power of fortune must be').[18] For his part, Lyall wants to argue for the possible use of this text by James I of Scotland, whose own *Kingis Quair* imagines that Fortune might be superseded. Somewhat chronologically pressured, this argument requires a very early introduction into England of Salutati's text. Viewed from a slightly different and less chronologically constrained perspective, though, this text, and James's poem, and Lydgate's own revision of the *De Casibus* tradition may all be meaningfully coordinated around an emergent interest in the positive political management of Fortune's ravages, in the first decades of the fifteenth century.

In accordance with this emergent interest, Lydgate and Premierfait readdress the problem of Fortune's own erratic activities in the world. Rather than follow their predecessors in recommending caution in the face of erratic Fortune, Premierfait and Lydgate recommend precautionary action. Some of these actions might be considered traditional, in the sense that Petrarch and others had always proposed that a 'remedy' of Fortune might lie in a modification and suppression of worldly aspirations and desires. This is the traditional route of what might be called 'self-exemption' from Fortune's betrayals; the route that Premierfait proposes, and that *sapience,* or wisdom, recommends: 'Se donques homme veult soy affranchir et exempter de mal heur, Il lui convie[n]t auoir la vertu de sapience qui en soy seule contient tous biens sans co[m]mixcon ce mal.' Yet, having made that point, he provides his *sage* man with supplemental assistance, including a cluster of other allies who will support him in the world. These are allies who will support him, not in the rejection of the world, but rather in the struggle to maintain himself in a worldly and pragmatic situation. As introduced in Premierfait's and Lydgate's texts through Seneca's example of Stilbon, these abiding virtues are effectively the Cardinal Virtues of Christian tradition, but with emphasis upon the four 'moral' or 'rational' virtues that precede Christian tradition and then were incorporated in it. These are the virtues appropriate to an active life lived in a worldly and political sphere (prudence, justice, fortitude, temperance), rather than the subsequent and separately derived 'theologi-

cal' virtues (faith, hope, and charity).[19] Threatened with loss of life and property, Stilbon responds that he remains in secure possession of 'Iustice, prudence, magnanimite, attemprance, and the consoling memory of virtuous
deeds.'[20] The virtues in question are not entirely static; for example, Premierfait offers magnanimity in place of the more common fortitude. But they are,
most crucially, operative in the world, and available as a resource in worldly
decision making.[21]

　　Reaching back to Aristotle's *Ethics*, and reiterated in Cicero and Seneca,
the moral or rational virtues were always implicitly political in their application,[22] and this element came progressively to the fore in the course of
the Middle Ages. A particular conduit between antiquity and the Middle
Ages is the influential passage in Macrobius, who cites Plotinus in support
of his claim that all virtues are those of the political man, since man is (by
definition) a social animal: 'sunt politicae hominis qua sociale animal est.'[23]
First among them all, in his reordered version (Prudence, Courage, Temperance, Justice), is political prudence, directed by reason: 'It is the property
of the political man's prudence ['politici prudentiae'] to refer all he intends
or does to the standard of reason, and to seek nothing but what is right.'[24]
Macrobius was widely promulgated by numerous medieval compilers and
commentators, including Vincent of Beauvais in his *Speculum Doctrinale*.[25]
Additional weight to the linkage of politics and the moral virtues was given
by Brunetto Latini in his extensive treatment of Prudence and other virtues
in juxtaposition with *politique* and 'li nobles governemens de la cite.'[26] Likewise influential were the many manuscripts, not only in Latin but in all the
major vernaculars of Europe, of the twelfth-century *Moralium Dogma Philosophorum*. This text not only expounds the virtues in comprehensive detail,
but in a context that treats them as, above all, *politice* or political in nature.[27]

　　Books of ostensible advice to princes, however, remain the primary home
for such materials. In 1411–12, Hoccleve enumerates the virtues and discusses
Prudence in some depth in his *Regiment of Princes*, a work addressed to a
prince but not limited in its interest to princes alone.[28] (His ultimate point
is that the sovereign's prudence will advise him to seek the love of his subjects, including promptly paying pensions to those who, like Hoccleve, deserve them.) So in 1422 does James Yonge's Englishing of a French *Gouernaunce of Prynces* devote considerable space to an exposition of the virtues
of Wysdome, Ryghtfulnes, Streynthe, and Tempure—noting that these are
renderings of Latin Prudencia, Iusticia, Fortitudo, and Temporancia, but that

'a man may sette dyuers Englyshe for euery of ham.'[29] As would normally be the case, these works consist of advice to princes or books of princely nurture, in the broad tradition inaugurated by Aristotle and augmented by Giles of Rome, together with liberal borrowing from John of Salisbury, the Old Testament, Boethius, Cicero, Seneca, and others. The book of advice to princes is, in other words, the Virtues' natural generic home. The important revision of the *De Casibus* tradition undertaken by Premierfait and Lydgate is to offer the Virtues a new generic home—and, in the process, to transform the *fall* of princes into a generic hybrid, one that accommodates significant features of the separate *advice* tradition.[30]

This shift is broadly visible at a number of points in the Premierfait-Lydgate enterprise, as in those moments when they segue to the discourse of political responsibility and enlightened rule. Consider, as an example of this tendency, the extended passage in book 2 when Lydgate revises Boccaccio, and even Premierfait, by eliminating strictures against unjust princes in favor of an extended recital on the interdependencies of the 'body politic,' drawing upon John of Salisbury, from a volume conveniently provided by his patron, as its source (bk. 3, ll. 827 f.). Or the moment in book 7 when, following upon strictures on temperance, Lydgate adopts the language of a book of *noriture* by arguing for the application of temperance to the management of the noble household (bk. 7, ll. 1314–34). This amiable kidnapping of Boccaccio's monitory purposes is embodied in the robust language of Virtue with which Lydgate peppers his text—a language already thoroughly politicized within its own discursive bounds. Thus, although the world is variable, with 'wo' succeeding 'merthe' (conclusion, ll. 3621–28), *vertue* will nevertheless be found to permit a steady ascent of Fortune's wheel, exemplified by the four moral virtues and operating according to *resoun*.

In an addition to his sources (in his reworking of a moment when Boccaccio and Laurent engage in colloquy with boastful Fortune and soberly assess their own writerly resources), Lydgate suddenly and surprisingly blurts out:

A man that is enarmed in vertu . . .
And hath al hool his hertli aduertence
On rihtwisnesse, force & on prudence,
With ther suster callid attemperaunce,
Hath a saufconduit ageyn thi variaunce! (Bk. 6, ll. 253, 256–59)

The centrality assigned to *prudence* by Macrobius and Latini was, as in Albertus Magnus's revision of Aristotle, based on its public and political nature,[31] and Lydgate extends but particularizes this reasoning with respect to the prince's instinct for political self-preservation.[32] Just as Albertus reversed Aristotle's priority by advancing justice and prudence (public virtues) over fortitude and temperance (private ones), so does Lydgate keep all four virtues in play, but effectively finds more for justice and prudence to *do*. At the same time, he puts fortitude in motion, partially transforming it from private to public by renaming it *force* and associating it with new allies (*rihtwisnesse, force, prudence*), even as temperance is set slightly to one side ('with ther suster'). These adjustments might be contrasted to Petrarch's own earlier endorsement of the inner or private virtues of moderation (temperance) and patience (fortitude) as crucial allies in the struggle to subdue one's own ambitions, and thus to render oneself impervious to the buffets of Fortune fair and foul. This means, for example, that Lydgate drops Boccaccio's reflections on God's inscrutability ('O dei secretum investigabile'—lib. 6, lxiii) in favor of a far more upbeat envoy to 'myhti princis':

> Lat resoun medle for you to leyn hostages,—
> Compassioun, merci, partyng of almesse,
> Toward heuene to supporte your feeblesse . . .
> [Your way is perilous] But-yif prudence bi gret auysenesse
> With prouidence preserue your puissaunce
> Geyn worldli chaung & Fortunys variaunce. (Bk. 6, ll. 1746–48, 1755–57)

In Lydgate, *vertu,* and such 'virtuous' allies as righteousness, strength, and prudence are enlisted not against but on behalf of the struggle for earthly renown, and as a line of practical defense against the ravages of 'Fortunys variaunce.'[33]

Another familiar player now seen in a revised role is *resoun*.[34] Dante's Vergil spoke in the voice of reason when he advised the Pilgrim on 'the short-lived mockery / of all the wealth that is in Fortune's keep' (*Inferno*, canto 7, ll. 61–62). Reason was a presiding figure of Alan of Lille's *Anticlaudianus*, sponsoring practical action in the world. It was Reason who vainly advised the Lover to despise Fortune and give no value to her favors in Jean de Meun's *Roman de la Rose* (ll. 6343–45); or, as the ME *Romaunt* renders Reason's words,

> ... she is Fortune verely,
> In whom no man shulde affy,
> Nor in hir yeftis have fiaunce. (ll. 5479–81)

So, too, was Reason the spokesperson of Petrarch's *De Remediis,* marshaling the resources of the classical virtues against the human passions, borne forward by Fortune's emissaries, Prosperity and Adversity. *Raisoun,* in derivation from Seneca, was portrayed as a steadying influence in Gower's *Mirour:* 'Senec t'enseigne que tu fras; / Si tout le mond veintre voldras, / Lors a raisoun te fai soubgit.'[35] But Lydgate introduces Reason in different way, less as a source of contempt for the world and more as an ally in worldly endeavors. In her earlier incarnations—and in avatars such as Lady Philosophy in Boethius (bk. 2, par. 8)—reason stood outside any system of worldly reward or punishment, and argued only for contempt of the world. Here, reason is brought *into* the world, and becomes an active asset for the magnate or other protagonist who would judge worldly situations for his own advantage. She is, as it were, deputized; brought in, suited up, and made ready to play.

Similarly, just as *resoun* now becomes a vital ally in the struggle for worldly self-aggrandizement, so *prouidence* is chosen over ME *purveiance* as a characterization of the apt foresight or prudent arrangement that will permit mighty princes to perpetuate their rule. The coexistence of these two terms in the fourteenth and fifteenth centuries permitted a diversification of function in which God's foreknowing and beneficent arrangement of events became *purveiaunce.* Consider in this regard Lydgate's own preference for the term 'heuenly purueaunce' when God's activity is in question,[36] and Chaucer makes the same choice in his Boethius, *Knight's Tale,* and elsewhere in his works. By contrast, *prouidence* is far more often applied to worldly affairs. (Only with the seventh century would Providence come into common use in a sense more common today, as a predestinarian expression of God's will.) Thus with Lydgate's *prouidence* we are once again returned to the ambit of human activity, and all that human ingenuity can accomplish in opposition to 'worldli chaung & Fortynys variaunce.'

A cast of characters dominated by the secular Virtues operates to similar effect in Lydgate's 'Mumming at London,' a small production piece apparently written for a prominent secular audience described by its headnote as 'the gret estates of this lande.'[37] This mumming brings out an elaborately costumed Fortune as a kind of empress of the world, constantly altering her 'transmutacyouns' (l. 8). In specific reference to the tradition of the falls of princes, she cites Alexander, Caesar, Gyges, and Cresus as leading victims who, having tasted her tun of sweetness, had no choice but to drink from her alternate tun of bitterness. The Virtues are then introduced with emphasis on their capacity to 'overgo' and 'oppress' the power of this blind goddess:

> Foure ladyes shall come heer anoon,
> Which shal hir power ouergoone,
> And the malys eeke oppresse
> Of this blynde, fals goddesse. (ll. 133–36)

The first of them is Prudence, who is herself said (with a nod to Seneca) to possess the gift of foresight or *prouydence*. Aided by Lady Prudence, the prince or magistrate will be proof against reversal:

> Thane this lady is his guyde,
> Him to defende on euery side
> Ageyns Fortune goode and peruerse
> And al hir power for to reuerse. (ll. 164–67)

So will Righteousness arm him against 'Fortune's doublenesse' (l. 217), even as Fortitude or Magnificence will 'Alle hir changes . . . sette at nought' (l. 242). The aid of these three enabled Henry V 'To putte Fortune under foote' (l. 276), even as Attempraunce will set all vices 'in stabulnesse' (l. 287). Collectively, these virtues will enable the prudent person to avoid Fortune's snares and to neutralize her powers; the commentator promises that, under their purview, 'Frome Fortune yee may thane go free' (l. 326). In fact, so armed, his audience has earned the right even to command the virtues: the mumming ends with an invitation for the audience to request that the four virtues (Fortune having been expelled) sing whatever 'nuwe songe' it wishes (l. 340). Wishful thinking indeed, but the imaginary enchainments of Fortune's powers are very much of a piece with progressive fifteenth-century thinking on such matters.

Of particular pertinence is the fact that—in addition to being headnoted to the 'gret estates'—this appears to be a household mumming. At its end, a gracious invitation is extended:

> And yee foure susters, gladde of cheer,
> Shoule abyde here al this yeer
> In this housholde at libertee. (ll. 333–35)

The audience invited to dwell with the virtues presumably consists of something other than early humanists or learned scholars. Here familiarized for prosperous urban society are the Ciceronian and Senecan Virtues, gathered around the fireside, singing 'request numbers' for their new patrons. This text thus marks a moment of cultural diffusion, from the study to the zone of the active political life, expressed in the vernacular and lived out in the cultural milieu of a capital-mercantile city, circa 1422–30.[38]

The penetration of the Virtues into the active political culture of the realm has been well marked by Caroline Barron in 'The Political Culture of Medieval London.' A key example of the growth of such a culture is the decoration of the main facade of the London Guildhall, circa 1430. There were depicted the four moral virtues of 'Discipline (Prudence), Justice, Fortitude and Temperance, each trampling a conquered vice.'[39] These conclusions are based on William Edgerton's verses, looking back to a period before the destruction of the facade in the iconoclasm of the sixteenth century:

> . . . Iesu Christ aloft doth stand,
> Law and learning on eyther hand,
> Discipline in the Deuils necke,
> And hard by her are three direct,
> There iustice, Fortitude and Temperaunce stand,
> Where find ye the like in all this land?[40]

Edgerton notes that his readers all know they have seen these subjects, although they may have forgotten exactly where. His point is that such statuary is fast disappearing in the face of a new politics of representation; but that familiarity with these subjects can nevertheless be considered widespread. Barron goes on to amplify this suggestion about the ubiquity of this representational tradition by assigning responsibility for the statues to the city's common clerk John Carpenter, himself possessed of related writings. She notes that 'When he drew up his will in 1442 Carpenter owned a remarkably extensive collection of books which included two copies of the *Secreta Secretorum*, a French book entitled *De Corpore Pollecie* and a treatise on the Four Cardinal Virtues, attributed to Seneca.'[41]

Such general discussions of virtue as a political asset allowed Lydgate and his audience a more optimistic purchase on the prince's career trajectory. In book 9, finishing with the sobering instance of Andronicus's tyranny, Lydgate adopts this upbeat tone:

Noble princis, ye that be desirous
To perseuere in your domynacioun . . .
Cherissheth trouthe, put falsnesse doun,
Beth merciable, mesurid be resoun . . .
That ye bi grace may haue a good eending. (Bk. 9, ll. 1506 – 7,
   1509 – 10, 1512).

A telling ambiguity arises in Lydgate's concluding line. The prince, having ordered his affairs by good covenants, *resoun,* and other proven means, is to enjoy a good ending—a conclusion that would, in a conventionally Christian text, refer to a well-composed death and an ultimate heavenly reward. Yet here the context of Lydgate's remark, emphasizing the prince's prospects for perseverance in his 'domynacioun,' suggests that the 'good eending' will involve a successful prosecution of a protracted period of secular rule. In a similar vein, Lydgate urges princes to seek a reputation for 'prudent policie' by observing such principles as 'Oppressith no man; doth no tirannye' (bk. 9, ll. 2047, 2045). A mid-sixteenth-century reader of Lydgate's Bodley 263, one Iohannes Godsaluus, captures this shift exactly right, and even pinpoints one of Lydgate's own crucial sources when in 1549 he adds as a summative comment on the whole work this excerpt from Chaucer's 'Lack of Steadfastness':

Prince desire to be honorable
Cherishe thy folke & hate extorcion
Suffre nothing tht may be reprouable
To thyne estate doon in thy region
Shewe forth the yerde of castigac[i]on
Drede god / do lawe / loue trouth and worthines
And wedd thy folke againe to stedfastnes.[42]

These robust strictures, hailed in from a more explicit discussion of good worldly practice, propose a new convenant that will wed the prince and his people to 'steadfastness' in the face of worldly variance.[43]

Lydgate's popularity—with, as documented by A. S. G. Edwards,[44] some thirty-nine extant complete manuscripts and forty excerpts, as well as large printed editions[45]—must be considered as plural and irreducible to a single cause. Undoubtedly, as Edwards observes, some of Lydgate's popularity must be related to his sheer sententiousness.[46] This observation may be borne out with respect to the passages most frequently copied out from the manuscript for separate publication; they tend to be drawn from Lydgate's Envoys, and thus to be naturally rather separable from the whole, and to deal with matters of sentence. Nonetheless, the most frequently copied passage of all, a stanza from the conclusion of book 2, is at once sententious and consistent with the possibility that the work's massive popularity may derive in part from its worldly vocabulary and prescriptions. Existing in eleven freestanding copies is this stanza, on the linkage between deceit and treason (bk. 2, l. 4431) and the assurance that fraud and deceit will rebound against the perpetrator:

> Deceit deceyueth and shal be deceyued,
> For be deceit[e] who is deceyuable,
> Thouh his deceitis be nat out parceyued,
> To a decyuour deceit is retournable;
> Fraude quit with fraude is guerdon couenable:
> For who with fraude fraudulent is founde,
> To a diffraudere fraude will ay rebounde. (Bk. 2, ll. 4432–38)

This may be viewed as a 'medieval' passage, to the extent that deceit and fraud, in such guises as false-seeming and hypocrisy, are defects familiar to that period. A different conclusion emerges, however, according to the distinction proposed in the previous chapter, between hypocrisy as a 'trait' and hypocrisy as a 'behavior,' with the former regarded as more characteristically medieval and the latter as effectively postmedieval. By this standard, the present passage falls on the 'behavioral' side of the divide. Although a closed system leading to inevitable punishment is sententiously proposed, the system is itself very much of this world. Deceit and fraud are condemned as courses of action likely to prove unprofitable, rather than as sins in a spiritually based view of the world.

2. UNEVEN DEVELOPMENTS: CALVERLEY AND CAVENDISH

Lydgate's co-optation of the *De Casibus* tradition in the cause of an affirmative prolongation of princely power was part of his legacy to the late fifteenth and early sixteenth century. A particularly apposite example is provided by William Calverley's sixteenth-century *Dyalogue*, in which Lydgate's praise of Henry V in terms of his good *gouernaunce* and *discrecioun* and his *hih prudence* are reworked in praise of Henry VIII, for his *noble polycie* and *discrecyon* and *prudence.*[47] Calverley is very much in the spirit of Lydgate when he has his Defendant advise his Plaintiff (who has complained against Fortune and her 'double whele') that everybody blames Fortune but that the Plaintiff must inspect his own faults and review his own self-governance. The Defendant recommends in favor of foresight, including his own intention to rely upon

> . . . descrecion sure
> And vpon prudence founde my workes all
> Than to counsel Attempraunce I do call
> Warely prouydinge in my selfe within
> The ende of thinges before that I begynne. (ll. 253–59)

In the case of both Lydgate and Calverley, providence is introduced as an exclusively secular form of foresight, under the dominion of the prince. As Lydgate says of Henry V,

> He hath conserued in this regioun,
>
> Duryng his tyme, off ful hih prudence,
> Pes and quiete and sustened riht,
> Yit nathwithstandyng his noble prouidence,
> He is in deede proued a goode knyht,
> Eied as Argus with resoun and forsiht. (I, ll. 378–83)

Or, as Calverley says of Henry VIII,

> Conserued is this most noble region
>
> Duringe his tyme longe by his prudence
> Pease and quiete he sustayneth by right
> That natwithstanding his noble prouydence
> In this worlde lyueth nat a better knight
> Eyed as Argus with reason and foresyth. (ll. 496–501)

In each case (reading 'notwithstanding' as something like 'even beyond'), the monarch first exercises prudent foresight and then proves himself by valiant deeds. The immediate point is that *prouidence*—or foresight—remains for Calverley as for Lydgate a feature of rational statecraft. Like

Humfrey and Henry V, Henry VIII need not seek for divine assistance, either in the future or in the past; properly armed with worldly virtues, he can look out for himself.

Any development as transformative as the one I am describing here must occur unevenly, and over a period of time, rather than consistently or all at once. Several mid-sixteenth-century examples suggest that the Premierfait-Lydgate view of the 'fortune-proof' prince enjoyed an uneven Tudor reception. One notable holdout was George Cavendish. Before, or during, 1554, retired retinue man Cavendish began a Lydgatean series of narratives of fickle fortune and her operations against near-contemporary princes, magistrates (see l. 1476), and highly placed servants.[48] His work made halting process, including several contemplated stopping points within its own bounds, and he then returned to it at least once, after November 1558, to add an epitaph for Queen Mary. His startup date is significant, both for its proximity to the two printings of Lydgate's *Fall* in 1554 and for its probable compositional overlap with the first, postponed draft of the *Mirror for Magistrates.* Cavendish was a generation—or really two generations—older than most members of the *Mirror* syndicate, and he worked in isolation from them. His work was carried on in detachment, was little circulated (with only two manuscript copies and one fragment extant), and remains conceptually distinct. Hungry as was the syndicate for usable tragedies—finding room, for example, for Skelton's tragedy of Edward IV—I am in some doubt that they would have accommodated Cavendish's work, even had they known of it. For, although in some respects a kindred spirit, this failed and disillusioned former servant and ally of Wolsey lacked altogether the implicit or underlying commitment of Baldwin and the first *Mirror* authors to the line of civic thinking that imagined the operations of Fortune as preventable by reason, prudent foresight, and other virtuous initiatives.

Again and again, he insists that nothing prevents Fortune's ultimate sway; even characters disposed to sobriety and virtue are finally overwhelmed. As the virtuous countess of Salisbury tells it,

> Yet at the last / for all my sober lyfe
> The chaunce of ffortune / I cowld no wyse resist. (ll. 1084–85)

Cavendish is, in short, a cultural conservative, whose main bugbears were social mobility of any sort and indulgence in any kind of lustful pleasures but most especially those of a fleshly sort. When Cavendish associates himself with 'Thes Clarkes old / that wrott wofull tragedies' (l. 1985), he may well be thinking of Lydgate, but, despite his frequent Lydgate borrowings, his heart is more with the genre's austere founders, whose socially pessimistic applications more nearly correspond with his own.

In describing Cavendish as a cultural conservative, I do not mean to deny him any social purchase at all. His writings, for example, effect a bold assimilation of the malign interventions of Fortune to the capricious workings of an erratic preferment system. Himself a disappointed courtier, he views Fortune as an untrustworthy source of advancement. Thus Anne Boleyn's brother, George Bulleyn, enjoyed temporary favor 'when ffortune preferred me / to highe dignytes' (l. 285). Norris, recipient of Henry VIII's favor and then disfavor, is precariously preferred by that lord, acting, in effect, as Fortune's deputy:

> My souerayn lord / extendyd his benygnytie.
> To be Grome of his stoole / he dyd highly avaunce
> Of all his prevye chamber / I had the souerayntie. (ll. 352–54)

So is Weston similarly tempted into trouble, forgetting to 'serue' God but choosing an earthly lord instead:

> I was dayntely norysshed / vnder the kynges wyng
> Who highly fauored me / and loved me so well. (ll. 415–16)

Breerton, too, enjoyed *ffauor* to his destruction:

> But late / I was in welthe / the world cn it record
> Fflorysshyng in ffauor / ffreshely besen
> Gentilman of the Chamber / with myt souerayn lord
> Tyll fortune onwares / hathe disseyved me clen. (ll. 449–52)

So too did Smeton, son of a carpenter, live humbly,

> Tyll that Gentill prynce / kyng ofthis realme
> Toke me / de stercore / et erigens pauperem
> And beyng but a boy / clame vppe the hyghe stage. (ll. 496–98)

Advancement is, in all these cases, the ultimate source of woe, even as in the case of others like Anne Boleyn's father, advanced to an earldom on Anne's behalf. Her mistaken reasoning was:

> . . . ffortune / wold me neuer faylle
> She was so redy / to auance all to my comfort. (ll. 556–57)

Sometimes the advancement is proferred by the prince, sometimes by Fortune without intermediary—as in the case of Katherine Howard, to whose queenship 'ffortune dyd me preferre' (l. 869). The point is that the Court (see ll. 945, 976) is the arena or 'stage' upon which these victims enact a drama of Fortune's falsity, and the furnishings and trappings of this drama are the imagined rewards of power and the courtier's or magistrate's successful life.

Satiric analyses of court politics are common enough in other early modern writers from Skelton to Wyatt. But, by introducing contemporary images of fickle courtly favor to the fall of princes, Cavendish plays his own part in the conversion of the genre to one of practical political analysis. Even so, Cavendish stops well short of suggesting that a career can be 'fortune-proofed,' or that the exercise of virtue or moderation might in any way avail the secular practitioner. If Fortune is identified with capricious preferment, Fortune's own master remains God himself, and this God is unopen to appeal, an agent of stern correction at best and at worst a force of malicious caprice.[49] Even as this God sternly corrects 'with his dyvyn Rod' (l. 957; see also l. 1209), so does he mock mankind's follies:

> Trust in hyme therfore / whiche eternally above dothe sytt
> Beholdyng your madenes / whiche ye so myche esteme!
> Laughyng thereat / and for ffoly dothe it deme (ll. 1214–16)

And, in a more ambiguous but quite disturbing passage, Thomas Arundel describes the favor he enjoyed from Katherine Howard (now 'dekayd') and explains that God now plagues him from privy malice—the malice probably being Arundel's own, but nevertheless ambiguously assigned: 'Se of prevye malice / how God nowe plagethe me' (l. 1783). This God is hardly interested in rewarding reason, virtue, or much of anything else, for that matter, save a possible preference for those who stay completely out of harm's, and

Fortune's, way. 'Yf Reason had rewled me . . .' (l. 1677) ponders the duke of Somerset. But the fact is that, in Cavendish's verses, reason *never* rules *anybody*.

3. THE *MIRROR* AND WHAT IT REFRACTS

Despite Cavendish and other conservative exceptions, the mid-sixteenth century enjoyed a set of new circumstances favorable to continuing generic overhaul. One was the emergence of the print medium, with its encouragement of new printer-writer-reader relations. Also in play were new forms of careerism, in which a Calvinist-inflected theory of the state empowered a stratum of civil servants. Audience demand increased for a language of statecraft and civic virtue that would, while nominally coexisting with a superseded language of providence and theocracy, seize the active foreground with its capacity to enhance worldly and mobilize practical power.

Within this world of new possibilities, Lydgate offered two different interpretative trajectories. The occasions of his mid-sixteenth-century republication and uptake suggest that each was activated to some degree. On the one hand, his appearance on a publisher's list spelled order, traditionality, and continuity. One can, after all, hardly mistake the fact that the two midcentury reprints of *Fall of Princes*—by Tottel and Wayland (probably both in 1554)—occurred during the Marian retrenchment, as did editions of the *Daunce of Macabree* and, more substantially, the *Troy Book*. On the other hand, I have argued for Lydgate's approach to a language of worldly politics as inherently progressive and transformative, and evidence developed by scholars of the early printed book suggests that this aspect of his work might also have been recognized. John Thompson and Alexandra Gillespie, following independent lines of analysis, have agreed that the printer who initially approached Baldwin was not the Catholic Wayland who sought unsuccessfully to bring forward the *Mirror* as a continuation to his 1554 edition of Lydgate's *Fall* but rather his predecessor, the Protestant Whitchurch, from whom Wayland appears to have received prepared copies of some texts, including Lydgate's *Fall*.[50] When the impetus for reprinting Lydgate is reassigned to the end of the reign of Edward VI rather than the beginning of the reign of Mary, his republication seems an altogether more progressive venture. Thus we find Lydgate, as Gillespie puts it, 'at the juncture of seemingly antithetical

Edwardian and Marian interest in his text,' and she concludes that 'no single meaning for the books associated with him can be determined' (ms. p. 22). Precisely so. A Marian audience might perceive Lydgate as a pillar of reaction, even as an Edwardian audience, and then an Elizabethan one, might see him as a force for innovation. Baldwin and his fellows might likewise have viewed Lydgate in two respects: as a traditionalist shelter for their radical enterprise, and simultaneously, in their initial Edwardian moment, as an incentive to bold political-textual intervention. As vehicles of political self-reliance, the sixteenth-century republications of Lydgate—and especially those of Tottel in 1554 and Wayland in 1554–55—may thus be seen not only as nostalgic or backward-looking but also as progressive with respect to an emergent language and practice of secular politics.

Having given both shelter and impetus to the new *Mirror*, and having also served as a template for some of its constituent verses,[51] Lydgate falls away, not unlike the first or 'booster' stage of those more recent 'moon rockets.' Once the *Mirror* appeared, Lydgate was not to be reprinted again until the scholarly editions of the modern era. But his venture—one strand of which remained undeniably progressive—had been deemed worthy of association with a publishing project imbued with every aspect of the insurgent and the new. Furthermore, the very title page of the first *Mirror for Magistrates* reiterates the affirmative turn to which Lydgate earlier committed himself: 'wherin may be seen what vices bring menne to destruccion, *wyth notable warniges howe the like may be auoyded*.' Thus Lydgate's presence there at Baldwin's organizational meeting is consistent with all the other respects in which the *Mirror* announces itself as a bold departure: in its origin as a collaboration between printers and writers, in the collective nature and broad ideological base of the syndicate that produced it, in its scandalous suppression during the reign of Mary, in the enlivened present-time compositional scene imagined and depicted in its endnotes and addresses to the reader, in the urgency of the first-person voice in which the fallen princes address their readers. But let me attempt to disaggregate some of these elements.

Print Culture

According to Baldwin, the plan of affixing English and more modern instances to a reedition of Lydgate originated with a printer and his circle— whether Wayland, or, following Thompson and Gillespie, Whitchurch— although the idea of forming a publishing syndicate was evidently his own:

Whan the Printer had purposed with hym selfe to printe Lidgates bok
of the fall of Princes . . . he was counsailed by dyuers . . . to procure to
haue the storye contynewed from where as Bochas lefte, vnto this pre-
sente time. . . . Whiche aduyse lyked him so well, that he required me
to take paynes therin: but because it was a matter passyng my wyt and
skyll, and more thankles than gaineful to meddle in, I refused vtterly to
vndertake it, excepte I might haue the helpe of such, as in wyt were apte.
('Baldwin to the Reader,' p. 68)

Baldwin recruited followers 'to the numbre of seuen,' who met at an appointed time and place for the furtherance of their plan. Their primary
inspiration was to be Hall's *Union of the Two Noble . . . Families,* with sec-
ondary influence from Fabyan and others (see Prose Links 4, 24; Tragedy
15, ll. 15–35). The links suggest that contributors pressed forward eagerly,
engaging even, according to a polite presentational fiction, in on-the-spot
composition (as at the end of Prose 6). In fact, Baldwin separately suggests
that some of his contributors were rather dilatory, to the extent that he had
to modify his plan ('Whan I first took it in hand, I had the helpe of many
graunted, & offred of sum, but of few perfourmed, skarce of any'—'To the
nobilitye and all other in office'—p. 63). Yet, even granting organizational
problems that no editor will fail to recognize, the prevailing impression is
one of very constructive symbiosis, initially involving Whitchurch and his
circle, and successor Wayland, and the diverse hands comprising Baldwin's
original syndicate and its successors. We are told that when the syndicate
regathered for its 'second meeting' their new printer (Thomas Marsh) was
among those present: 'There founde I the prynter and all the rest of our
frendes and furderers assembled & tarying for vs, Save Maister Ferrers, who
shortly after according to hys promys came thyther' (p. 243, ll. 5–7).

The excitement of such collaboration, and the centrality of printers'
agendas to the enterprise, may be glimpsed in eventual contributor John Hig-
gins's account of the background of his 1574 prequel to the *Mirror,* with the
culture and procedures of printed production explicitly credited as a source of
artistic inspiration. Finding himself in autumnal season and spirit, he imagines himself reading 'some booke, of mourning theame' ('Parts Added,'
Induction, l. 15). He therefore betakes himself to a printing establishment
('Wherfore I went to Printers straight vnto, / To seeke some worke of price
I surely mente—ll. 19–20) and, finding there the *Mirror,* is so enflamed
that he stands and reads it twice through (ll. 26–28). This leads to his own

imitative and usurpatious prequel, which, by dint of chronology, he arranges to have known as 'THE FIRST parte of the Mirour,' arranging to have the 1574 reissue of the original retitled as 'THE LAST parte of the Mirour.' This copycat endeavor is, like the original, hatched in and around a printing establishment; is, in effect, 'printer driven,' with commerce and a persistent need for ready copy as partial determinants.[52] Yet the chequered history of that first edition suggests that more factors than commerce were relevant here.

Careerism and Readership

The *intended* audience of the *Mirror*, as defined by the 'you' addressed by Baldwin in his Preface, consists of 'the nobilitye and all other in office'—the latter variously addressed as officers, rulers, magistrates, and justices—an influential body by no means limited to the king and the aristocracy, but rather engaged in what might loosely be called 'nonhereditary' service. At the same time, the parameters of this influential group remained unclear. As Foster has observed, ideas of community prevalent in the sixteenth century, especially in London, militated against any hard-and-fast distinction between rulers and ruled. Nevertheless, a rough-and-ready sense of a ruling elite would have been available; in London, for example, Foster specifies the important officials who stood for elective office, including 'common councilmen, hospital officers, auditors of the Bridgehouse and Chamber, bridgemasters, chamberlains, aldermen, sheriffs, and mayors.'[53] Similarly, the intended audience of the *Mirror* would seem to consist of what might loosely be called a 'bureaucratic elite.' This supposition receives support from a suggestion made by Annabel Patterson in the case of another collective or syndicated production, Holinshed's *Chronicles*—that the diverse persons enlisted in the enterprise give some sense of the range of its audience appeal.[54] In this case, pursuit of the identities of those responsible for the 1559 and 1563 editions by Lily Bess Campbell and others yields a group of moderate diversity, well situated in what might be called the 'middle strata' of the nation, but decidedly in forms of literate service characteristic of a professional bureaucracy that had been in formation throughout the fifteenth and sixteenth centuries.[55] Campbell's composite portraits of Baldwin, Ferrers, Chaloner, and Phaer, augmented by later contributors Sackville, Churchyard, Dolman, Seager, and Cavyl, and possible contributor Holinshed, represent these men as active, accomplished, and, above all else, politically adroit, with most of them (even though the majority were Protestant throughout) active and in many cases actively serving, across the reigns of Edward, Mary, and Elizabeth. Just to give the flavor of some of their activities: Baldwin was not only employed with Whitchurch and other printers, but was already a distinguished poet and a familiar of the court of Edward VI; George Ferrers was servant, successively, of Henry VIII, Edward VI, whom he served as Master of Revels, and a loyalist collaborator with the Privy Council during the reign of Queen Mary; Chaloner, likewise, served across four reigns, ultimately as an ambassador under Elizabeth; Phaer served as MP and translated the first seven books of the Aeneid, and so on. Arnold Hauser long ago associated the emergence of new literary forms (and, by extension, in this case, modified ones) with the concurrent emergence of supportive classes of interested persons;[56] and the mixture of sameness and diversity of this group, supplemented by evidence of personal friendships (see Campbell, *Mirror*, pp. 32–33), strongly argue for the existence of such a class. It is appropriate in its civic interests, and more than adequate in numbers, to support the several editions of the *Mirror*.[57]

One aspect of the work's production and dissemination remains unexplained. In 1555, despite the protective coloration offered by the unoffending Lydgate, distribution of the *Mirror* was 'hyndred,' according to Baldwin, 'by the lord Chauncellour that then was.' Then, in his preface to the 1563 edition, he adds that the first part was 'licenced, and imprynted in the fyrst yeare of the rayne of this our most noble and vertuous Queene.' Despite this apparent chronological 'smoking gun,' Campbell is at great pains to argue that the predominantly Protestant affiliations of most members of the syndicate had little to do with this proscription, and that 'the authors were more conspicuous as opportunists than as Protestants' (*Mirror*, p. 7). Yet one may sympathize with the conclusion of W. F. Trench (however faulty his particulars) that Protestantism had *something* to do with the chancellor's intervention.[58]

Given the close association of the *Mirror* with Hall's *Union*, the hindrance of the former and the proscription of the latter would seem to be linked. Campbell herself admits that chronicles like Hall's were enlisted during the reign of Edward VI 'as part of the new Protestant propaganda.'[59] Certainly, even a cursory look at the relevant Marian proclamation—in which 'Halles Cronycles' keep company with a list otherwise comprised entirely by religious-controversialist works by Luther, Calvin, Zwingli, Erasmus, Bale, Tyndale, Cranmer, Fryth, and the 'Common Prayer Book of

Edward VI'[60]—suggests that Hall's *Chronicle* was seen to endorse an effectively 'Protestant' and providential view of English history. Meanwhile, the *Mirror* itself is in some ways even more explicitly Protestant than Hall, in the basis of its theory of the prerogatives of the 'magistrate' class. This basis is nowhere more evident than in Baldwin's introduction, where, as even Campbell acknowledges, the influence of Calvin's *Institutes* is paramont. As she first pointed out, Calvin's 'whosoeuer be in place of magistrates are named gods', in Thomas Norton's 1561 and 1562 translations,[61] is closely paralleled in Baldwin's 'Ye be all Gods, as many as have in your charge any ministracion of Iustice'—and, as in *Gorboduc,* also published in 1561, many of Baldwin's remarks may be read as virtual glosses on the sentiments of Calvin. Presumably, the *Mirror*'s involvement with Hall got it in trouble with the Marian authorities; but, just possibly, the causal chain ran the other way round, with Hall in trouble as a result of its role in the production of the Calvinist-tainted *Mirror,* the latter work remaining unmentioned in the proclamation since its publication had already been successfully derailed.

Proving the *Mirror* 'Protestant' in sentiment is very far from my concern, because I can easily enough agree with Campbell that its appeal ultimately lay in other, less sectarian concerns. Yet I *am* interested in the issue of Protestantism as it helps to elicit the *Mirror*'s contemporaneous controversiality and exciting topicality. The *Mirror* is brought forward with all the excitement that accompanies the furtherance of a *cause,* and, although I think the cause not to be 'Protestantism' per se, I would argue that the urgent discussion of philosophies of the secular state by Calvinists and others is a contributory component of the *Mirror*'s excitement. Other, related excitements of this text nevertheless divorce themselves from the particularities of Calvin's rather deterministic view of divine right, and enter territories less charted still. I refer here to my central interest in this study: in the extent to which, without ever disavowing Calvin's larger providential frame, the *Mirror* extends and refines its inheritance from Premierfait and Lydgate, an inheritance centered upon the transmission and refinement of a new language for the pursuit of practical statecraft.

The New Language of the Secular State

The decisive move of the fifteenth and sixteenth centuries is to detach Fortune from its reliance upon God's Providence, treating it as an autonomous locus of unpredictability in human affairs . . . and thus as an apt incentive to human precaution. In the fourteenth century, Boccaccio treated Fortune as tantamont to, and as a vulgar synonmym for, God's will ('quid Deus, siue [ut eorum more loquar] fortuna, . . .possit'),[62] and Chaucer, in at least one of his chosen narrative voices, viewed it as 'executrice of wierdes,' joining with heavenly influences as determinant of human behaviors 'under God' (*Troilus*, III, ll. 617–19).[63] By contrast, a flood of fifteenth- and sixteenth-century commentaries and treatises—many prior to or independent of the influence of Machiavelli, who in this sense may be seen less as an innovator and more as an exemplar of a general tendency—effect a severance of God's purveiaunce on the one hand and the exercise of practical and worldly decision making on the other.[64]

The effect of this severance is not to deny the pervasiveness of Fortune—Machiavelli is, for example, an enormous respecter of its sway in human affairs—but to treat its omnipresence as an incentive to strategic improvisation and countermeasure, based on good judgment, canny foresight, and reliance upon reason. In other words, as compared to the prevalent earlier view, in which Fortune is immune to defensive action (*Inferno*, 7.81–84) or can be forestalled only by a calculated curtailment of worldly hopes along the lines advocated by Petrarch and Boccaccio, the emergent position rewards activity and enterprise. An extension of this notion might indeed be Machiavelli's imagining that Fortune may be checked or baffled by one able to leap 'from wheel to wheel.'[65] As in other respects, though, one need not await Machiavelli for such a possibility to arise. In his study of the *Prince* and its forerunners, Allan H. Gilbert cites a range of pertinent prior commentaries, including Patricius's late-fifteenth-century *De Regno*, with its argument that 'As the good pilot surveys all quarters of the sky that he may be prepared against all the violence of the winds, so the prince fortifies himself against all adverse circumstances.' Another is Guicciardini's early-sixteenth-century advice: 'Fortune sometimes does miracles for him who tempts her, but much more rarely for him who does not make any move. . . . Therefore I should praise him who would decide, when there comes an occasion which offers hope at least equal to its peril, to take it.'[66] Or, closer to home, we may take the example of Thomas Blundeville's 1574 treatise, 'The true order and Methode of wryting and reading Hystories,' written under decided Italian influence, but re-presenting these concepts for an English audience. Blundeville distinguishes between outward causes, including Fortune, and inward causes, which belong within the sphere and control of human volition. Inward causes spring from reason and appetite, and are located within precise circumstances of time, place, means, and instrument; above all, they depend upon calculation of 'possibilitie, occasion, and successe.'[67] The effect of all such analyses is to treat Fortune not as a truly independent variable but simply as the unassimilated explanatory fraction that has not yet yielded (but which could probably be made to yield) to hardheaded political analysis. This is the view, after all, of Commynes, with his urbane reference to 'la fortune, ou ce que on y appelle' (I, chap. 12, p. 99). Commynes speaks here of the count of Charolois, who as duke of Burgundy allowed himself to be deceived by the extent of his apparent success; the model of an infatuated duke, raised to glory and then brought low, is the very pattern of Fortune and her wheel, but the duke's mistakes—minutely detailed by Commynes—are completely his own.

I refrain from describing this development as a pure-and-simple 'secularization.' As with Commynes, the Milanese ambassadors, the *Arrivall* author, and many other exponents of hardheaded analysis I am discussing in the course of these chapters, Blundeville displays no intention of denying God's ultimate sway. Following upon his careful analysis of the 'meanes' by which human actions are effected, he attributes all to God's system of 'iuste rewardes' to the virtuous and 'euill successes' to the wicked. At the same time, this is a *deferred* attribution, subsequent to the delineation of a worldly and practical sphere for the analysis of human conduct. This kind of reverential, but also highly 'enabling,' deferral or displacement of God's sway prevails in sixteenth-century discourse. For a codification, one might think of Jean Bodin's influential separation of the divine, the natural, and the human— with the latter concerning 'the acts of man while leading his life in the midst of society.'[68]

4. A *POLITIKE* WORLD

The *Mirror of Magistrates* is no more disposed than Blundeville to deny God's ultimate sway. Yet the *Mirror* also embraces the operational distinction between God's sphere and the more secular sphere of Fortune's operations. Even as pious claims are made for God's total control and powers of moral rebuke on the one hand, assertions are made of Fortune's amoral and arbitrary sway on the other. Willard Farnham notes this tension in his classic study of the passages from medieval to Renaissance tragedy, and argues for its resolution via a growing late-Tudor attachment to 'tragic justice' and vice's rebuke.[69] Such a shift can indeed be observed in the *Mirror*'s subsequent development, from the relative indeterminacy of the 1559 edition's intent 'to shewe the slipery deceytes of the wauering lady' to the 1571 edition's intent to show 'with howe greueous plagues, vices are punished.' But, in the *Mirror*'s 1559 and 1563 editions, emphasis falls squarely on an effectively autonomous and worldly sphere, and an opportunistic analysis of political activity in the world. God's purveiaunce remains gesturally present, but only as a pious distraction from what I would presume to call the 'real' business of the tragedies: to imagine the terms of a political life beneath, between, or in spite of the prepossessing scaffold of professed Tudor belief.

The radicalism of the *Mirror* consists not in a pretension of holding a mirror 'up to nature'—that most traditional and most bogus of representational claims—but rather in presenting a speculative world of realpolitik in which the magistrate is offered imaginative participation. 'Mirrored' is not an external reality of apparent causes, but a set of more nebulous possibilities that the magistrate is invited to explore on the basis of his own predispositions. As Baldwin puts it, 'here as in a loking glas, you shall see (if any vice be in you) how the like hath bene punished in other heretofore' ('Dedication,' p. 65). A pious enough sentiment on its surface, but Baldwin ultimately proposes a complicated interaction. For this mirror does not simply show 'reality' back to itself, but shows reality awry, in terms of the proclivities of the tainted viewer. What the reader will see in this mirror is what Guillaume's dreamer sees in Narcissus's Well: not himself and not a faithful reproduction of the whole garden, but rather the object of his actual desire.[70] Offered to the reader of this *Mirror*, under an alibi of admonition and self-improvement, is actually an indulgence in a world he, as magistrate, already knows something about: an unstable world of manipulation, concealment, intrigue, and false-seeming—a world he might, and in fact must, engage if he seeks the 'preseruacion' of his 'Estate.' In short: the realm of guilty enjoyment is nothing other than worldly politics, and the price of admission is a curiosity about the 'vice' in question.

At the same time, the *Mirror* positions itself to address and channel its readers' refracted desires by adopting a complicated, and ultimately (in an artistic sense) liberatory, attitude towards the histories it recounts. The syndicate members seem at first to pay a great deal of deferential attention to the accuracy of the histories they employ as source materials, painstakingly sorting out small contradictions and deviances. For example, one of the reported conversations among the syndicate concerns Edward IV's in-laws:

> An other moued a question about a great matter, and that is the vary-
> aunce of the cronycles about the lord Thomas Graye Marquis Dorcet:
> whome Fabian every where calleth the Queenes brother. Syr Thomas
> More and Hall call hym the Queenes sonne. . . . This disagreying of
> wryters is a great hinderaunce of the truthe, & no small cumbrauns to
> such as be diligent readers. (Prose 20, p. 267)

All such disagreements can, they say, create confusion in the matter of noble
titles, and they wish for 'a true and perfecte cronicle . . . to be wrytten' to decide such controversies. Yet, they observe, such matters of detail are not the
ultimate objective at all:

> For the onlye thynge which is purposed herin, is by example of others
> miseries, to diswade all men from all sinnes and vices. If by the way we
> touche any thing concernyng titles, we folow therin Halles cronicle.
> And where we seme to swarve from hys reasons and causes of dyuers
> doynges, there we gather vpon coniecture such thinges as seem most
> probable, or at the least most convenient for the furderaunce of our
> purpose. (Prose 20, p. 267)

Thus what seems an extreme deference to the claims of history turns out
merely to be a convenience, so long as it does not interfere with other goals.
'Most probable' is good enough, so long as it serves the syndicate's 'purpose.' That this 'purpose' transcends the stated objective of dissuading men
from vice is implicit in my argument; the *Mirror*'s persistent determination
is to provide a forum for reimagining the terms and conditions of practical
statecraft.

How does the *Mirror* wield its newfound freedom? Even allowing for
the 'diversitie' of its authorial voices, as acknowledged in the preface to the
1563 edition, the 1559 and 1563 editions display certain consistencies. Situating their readers, like the audience of a play, in a position of partial security,[71]
they expose them to a world of consternated values. This world offers least
certainty in the places of greatest presumed trust: 'That where most cause is
of affyaunce, / Euen there is founde moste weake assurance' (Gloucester,
p. 92, ll. 33–34). Law, rather than provide a secure framework, is subject
to interested interpretation: 'The lawes we interpreted and statutes of the
lande, / Not trulye by the texte, but nuly by a glose' (Tresilian, p. 77, ll. 71–72).
A 'crafty compas' cloaks harsh rigor in a 'habyte of reason' (Gloucester, p. 98,

ll. 184–85). Deceptive stratagems abound, as when Thomas earl of Salisbury describes broken oaths, the deployment of false information, and unpredictable shifts and lapses of loyalty (pp. 148–49, ll. 157, 171–72). Clarence tells us how Warwick used his own daughter for bait (p. 223, ll. 90–91), and 'with forged tales' Richard induces Edward IV to murder his own brother. So is James the First victimized by his uncle's crafty deceits ('But he . . . / To get the crowne, began to fetch a fetch'—p. 155, ll. 20–21), and this same uncle, a 'trusted traytour,' effects the destruction of other innocents through his 'craftes' (p. 158, ll. 96, 92). This is a world in which virtue is 'with infamy opprest' and 'yll attemptes' are achieved (Salisbury, p. 144, ll. 23, 25). We learn in the complaint of Jack Cade that lying 'shift' and 'false perswasions,' no matter how transparent, are likely to make at least temporary headway (p. 173, ll. 50, 59). This is also a world of paradoxical and unintended consequences; confessing that his accusations against Bolingbroke were inspired by sly 'shyftes,' Mowbray is himself surprised to learn that 'spyte and enuy causeth glory sprout' (p. 105, ll. 92, 96). In such a world, Clarence has learned, persons who attempt to fly their fate are likely to bring it on: 'When men suppose by fetches of their owne, / To flye theyr fate, they further on the same' (p. 234, ll. 384–85). This is, further, as Clarence ruefully explains, a world in which false prophecies are preferred over true:

> True prophecies have fowly been reiect:
> The false which brede both murder, warre & strife,
> Belyved to the losse of many a goodmans life. (P. 229, ll. 250–52)

And, in this world upside down, as Rivers complains, 'false practises' are often praised for 'prudent pollicie' (p. 261, ll. 442–43).

Such conditions are wholly consistent with a traditional stance of *contemptus mundi* and rejection of the world. What marks the difference in the case of the *Mirror* is its implication that useful lessons are here to be learned, not so much tending towards the world's rejection as towards a preventative response to worldly vicissitudes. Describing his father's downfall, Richard duke of York explains that he was driven to plot against Henry VI by Lancastrian misdeeds, embracing a path of 'politik procurance' (p. 184, l. 47)—not, in his case, a successful course of action, but certainly, in the world of these narratives, a comprehensible one. Thomas earl of Salisbury speaks in bitter condemnation when he says that 'The ende in dede, is iudge of euery thing' (p. 144, l. 29), but he also speaks with undeniable truth about the actual conditions of action in this world. He may mean that 'ends' or intentions need to be taken into account when actions are judged, or that first conclusions about guilt or innocence may be supplanted in the long run, or that, for better or worse, practical outcomes are what matter most. His words linger beyond the immediate circumstances of their utterance, opening a practical vantage upon questions of means and ends.

Resulting from this embrace of uncertainty is a flood of practical advice about conduct, advice with a decidedly more 'worldly' cast than that customarily encountered in older 'regiments' of princes. Admitting himself an ultimate loser, Suffolk is, for example, nevertheless a font of advice about how to best play one's cards. Speaking of winning French towns soon to be lost, he observes:

> Wherby I see there is more glory in
> The keping thinges than is in their attayne:
> To get and kepe not is but losse of payne.
> Therfore ought men prouide to saue their winnings
> In al attemptes, els lose they their beginninges. (P. 164, ll. 52–56).

Suffolk dies wretchedly in the end, accusing himself of vice and oppression of others . . . but only after having had his 'day in court.' Besides, by his own exertions he has prolonged his own period of success; as an alternative ending to the 1571 text has it, 'God is iust, whose stroke delayed long' (p. 169). So, too, does Warwick, although unsuccessful in the end, have a great deal to say about the foundations of his own partial success. Speaking, albeit somewhat defensively, in his own behalf, he offers his conduct as prescription for best practice in an uncertain world:

> Perchaunce thou thinkest my doinges were not such
> As I and other do affirme they were.
> And in thy minde I see thou musest much
> What meanes I vsed, that should me so prefer:
> Where because I wil thou shalt not erre,
> The truth of all I wil at large recite,
> The short is this: I was no hippocrite.
> I never did nor sayd, save what I mente,
> The common weale was still my chiefest care. (Pp. 208–9, ll. 85–93)

Interestingly, though Warwick might lie open to just critique for his self-exonerations, the syndicate seems to think otherwise. Baldwin tells us in his address to the reader, 'As soone as the Erle had ended his admonicion, sure (quoth one) I thinke the Erle of Warwicke although he wer a glorious man, hath sayd no more of him selfe than what is true' (p. 211). And this judgment is allowed to stand.

Another 'mixed case,' and even more interestingly so, is Lord Hastings, added to the 1563 edition. Regarded by one member of the syndicate as 'very darke, and hard to be vnderstood,' and prized by another for the same reason, this complicated and verbally knotty exposition displays its speaker's constant resistance to assimilation by any kind of convenient moral exemplarity. It is precisely as a mixed, and even contradictory, case that Hastings presents himself: 'even amyds my vyce,' he says, 'my vertue shoane' (p. 271, l. 82). His insistence throughout is on the impossibility of any simple judgment in his case, and on the need to assess opportunity and circumstance. Early on, he considers, but then rejects, the temptation to array himself with the mantle of martyrdom, viewing himself as too fortunately arrayed to be considered within that frame (p. 269, ll. 21–24). All patterns, in fact, weary him ('stale is the paterne'—p. 277, l. 253), and he deliberates extensively on his own stubborn refusal to accept the portents of his own downfall ('What should we thinke of sygnes? They are but happs'—p. 287, l. 489). The ultimate point, he argues, is not that signs determine destiny, or that 'twyncklyng sterres flyng downe the fixed fate' (p. 287, l. 501). God's providence, is, in his view, operative, but allows free choice ('And hath he erst restraynd his provydence? / Or is he nygard of his free dispence?—p. 288, ll. 521–22); only weaklings plead Fortune as the source of their earthly woes ('Whoe fortune fayne to father theyr abuse'—p. 288, l. 528). Hastings settles finally upon a kind of stoic refusal to embroider or excuse his downfall; words register nothing but 'the speakers stynkyng breath' (p. 292, l. 646). In the end of it all, Hastings rejects one kind of exemplarity—the simple narrative curvature of a proud life undone by Fortune—in favor of the more diffuse lesson giving we might expect to encounter in a rather disenchanted book of good conduct or sage counsel. In this sense, he bears out a revisionary motive animating this collection: rather than dissuade us from the world, he returns us to the world, with sharpened judgment and a heightened instinct of self-preservation.

Pitching in enthusiastically on Hastings' behalf, the poet-narrator continues in a similar vein: no fame or report goes untouched by the operations of subsequent revisionary report or 'after fame' (p. 295, l. 715), and the lesson to be learned by readers of Hastings' downfall is that they might as well keep their motives and stratagems to themselves ('Your polytyke secretes gard'— p. 295, l. 713). The offshoot of all this is not, however, simple resignation. Rather, the reader is repeatedly admonished to read circumstances correctly, not to repeat Hastings' blind errors, to cultivate the art of apt choice. In pursuance of this philosophy, this narrative buries us in a blizzard of apothegms and maxims, such as: 'Beware to ryse by serving princely lust' (p. 271, l. 71); 'Oft hangeth he hym selfe, whoe others weenth to snare' (p. 280, l. 306); 'Trust not to sone, ne all to lyght mistrust' (p. 281, l. 339); 'The pleasyngst meanes boade not the luckiest endes' (p. 285, l. 441); 'Beware of flaterers, frends in outward showe' (p. 292, l. 629), and much more.

Finally, rather than yield itself to the exemplarity of a standard *De Casibus* rendition, the Hastings narrative claims a realm of inscrutability for its protagonist. Hastings has his own 'polytyke secretes,' and these secrets are vulnerable to betrayal by false friends and misinterpretation by subsequent commentators. These 'secrets' issue in a range of choices for good and ill, for merited public esteem and for rash misjudgement, for civic responsibility and for personal mismanagment. They give us, in the end, a mixed case, a case from which no unitary or summative lesson is to be learned. The acknowledgment, however, of a mixed and perplexing insertion in a world that demands complicated choices among problematic alternatives is *itself* innovative, in relation to a tradition normally possessed of more predictable exemplarity.

In my view, the excitement of the *Mirror* lies less in its larger assertions about God's providential plan, or even in its enactment of what Campbell has described as accepted Tudor principles of history's educative function,[72] than in a less obtrusive set of assertions about the inevitable political valences of everyday life. As in the case of Lydgate, though with some alteration of terms, these assertions are conveyed through the introduction and deployment of new kinds of language, or accepted language newly used. Coursing through the different recitals of the early *Mirror* is a new language of civic virtue. Echoing through the different tragedies (in forms I have taken the liberty of italicizing in the several paragraphs that follow) is a language conducive to the establishment of a responsible and well-regulated public sphere.

Thus we encounter early, and frequent, reference to the public good, on the part of the very persons who have violated its trust. Tresilian, describing the Appellants' attempt to restrain the excesses of Richard II (of which Tresilian was, of course, himself a beneficiary), says that

> . . . they called a parlyament
> Francke and free for all men witout checke to debate
> As well for *weale publyke,* as for the princes state. (P. 78, ll. 103–5)

Deploring his own conduct, he wishes for procedures respectful of 'the pathes of *equitie in iudgement*' (p. 79, l. 128). And, speaking from the other side of that particular divide, Appellant Thomas duke of Gloucester regrets that at Radcot Bridge he and his associates employed armor rather than judicial robes 'to parle of the *Publyke weale*' (p. 96, l. 121). Yet Lord Mowbray nevertheless considers Thomas to have been an exemplary 'warder of the *common weale*' (p. 104, l. 78). The public interest is best served through virtue, and this term is used throughout, always in its sense as a 'moral' or 'rational' (rather than a theological) virtue. Richard II has learned too late that the happy prince follows *vertue* and restrains his personal will by the exercise of wisdom (p. 111, ll. 2–3). What he now wishes is that he had chosen a course not disrespectful of 'Good *counsayle, lawe,* or *vertue*' (p. 112, l. 26). Confessing that he inappropriately connived against Humfrey duke of Gloucester in the matter of Henry VI's marriage, William duke of Suffolk laments that '*vertue* starves, but lustfoode must be larded' (p. 166, l. 103). Hastings, speaking of the struggle for worldly advancement, says that 'Some *vertue* rayseth, some clyme by sluttyshe sortes' (p. 270, l. 58). Thomas earl of Salisbury argues that princely regiment is best marked by mildness, justice, and *vertuous* life (p. 147, l. 125).

As in Lydgate, a key to virtuous avoidance of Fortune's snares is the exercise of reason. Thomas duke of Gloucester, arguing for careful analysis of situations and interrogation of superficial loyalties, concludes: 'Let none trust Fortune, but folowe *Reason*' (p. 92, l. 34). The problem with Radcot Bridge, he says, is that the Appellants came with drawn swords, 'In stede of *Reason* declaryng our Zeale' (p. 96, l. 124). Reason's unlikely apostle turns out, however, to be Jack Cade, who believes even the planets tributary to its power:

> But such is *Reason,* that they brynge to fine
> No worke, vnayded of our lust and wyl:
> For heauen and earth are subiect both to skyl. (P. 171, ll. 10–12)

Unsurprisingly, he seems prepared to assign the exercise of *skyl* principally to God ('The skyl of God ruleth al'—l. 13). Yet, this due concession being made, Cade switches and assigns generous scope for human reason and human responsibility for worldly affairs:

> Yet through the *skyl* God hath in *Reason* wrought
> And geuen man, no lust nor wyl so course
> But may be stayed or swaged of the sourse
> So that it shall in nothing force the mynde
> To worke our wo. (p. 171, ll. 17–21)

Cade thus joins the ranks of those who believe Fortune merely an alibi for defective human behavior and failure to exercise right reason:

> Now if this happe wherby we yelde our mynde
> To lust and wyll, be fortune, as we name her,
> Than is she iustly called false and blynde. (p. 172, ll. 29–31)

'By saint mary,' exclaims a member of the syndicate upon hearing this, 'yf Iacke wer as well learned, as you haue made his oracion, What so ever he was by byrth, I warraunt hym a gentylman by his learning. Howe notably and Philosopher like hath he discrybed Fortune and the causes of worldly cumbraunce?' (p. 178, ll. 1–5). Indeed. And how very 'worldly' his explanation, which pays due deference to God, but opens a more practical perspective on the exercise of human judgment in the world.

Given this drift of things, no wonder that attributions and assessments of human *pollicy* resound through these narrations. As with other words central to this study, *policy*'s range of possible implications, and adaptability to the demands now placed upon it, had been several centuries in the making. In the fourteenth century, *policy/pollecie* normally meant something along the lines of a broadly constructive or enlightened course of action, one that serves the common good as well as or even instead of one's own singular interest. An example is John Gower's previously mentioned five points of *Policie*— broad principles of good rule to which all public-spirited rulers subscribe. A related sense, prevalent throughout the fourteenth and fifteenth centuries, would simply have 'policy' as equivalent to 'polity'—the total social body, especially viewed with respect to actions that will promote harmony and well-being. This is the sense of Christine de Pisan's *Livre de Corps de Policie*, which treats the 'body of policy' as the universal social body and details actions appropriate to its good maintenance, and the same sense carries over into the fifteenth-century English translation, the *Body of Polycye*, possibly datable to the later years of the reign of Edward IV.[73]

Entering the fifteenth century, the sense of 'policy' diversifies. Together with its earlier emphasis on practice beneficent for the common weal, one of its emergent senses veered toward the more neutral sense of a settled or adopted 'policy' in today's sense of a chosen or settled course of action; consider in this regard Fortescue's expectation that the king's counselors will advise him 'vppon the materes off the pollycye of the reaume.'[74] John Watts has taken note of this generalization of the word's sense: 'Government *is* "policie," a word whose connotations of representation and participation were strong, but which could also be used to mean "policy," "politics," "prudence," and the institutions and structures which existed to promote them all.'[75] Latent in such categories as 'politics' and 'prudence' is an emergent sense in which *policie* began to tilt towards conduct we might label 'self-interested' or 'shrewd.' Note, in this regard, the usage of George Ashby, whose 'De actiua pollecia principis' (popularly entitled *Active Policy of a Prince*) probably composed in the 1450s and addressed to Edward prince of Wales, is a compendium of lore bearing on the prince's self-maintenance in office.[76] There, speaking to the same problem of the 'over-mighty subject' that would concern Fortescue in *Governance,* he proposes that the prince allow no subject to equal his wealth:

> . . . to youre richesse make neuer man liche,
> If ye wol stande in peas and be set by.
> So wol god and polleci sykerly,
> Lyke as ye in estate other excelle,
> In proper richesse ye sholde bere the belle. (ll. 641–45)

Presumably God, in endorsing this precept, occupies a higher ground of principle. But the element of *'polleci'* at stake is much less ethical in nature than it is expedient. The prince committed to active pursuit of his own interests will have reason to heed Ashby's advice, for practical reasons that Fortescue's ninth chapter fully details. At a more vernacular level, the word also accrues senses of astuteness and self-interest. The Vitellius A.xvi chronicle of London uses the term in the former sense, when it praises the duke of Gloucester for appeasing rebellious currents in Wales by the exercise of 'his *pollecy.*'[77] John Paston II definitely uses the word in the context of self-interest, in a letter of 1477 where he declines to enter a transaction involving one of his manors: 'it weer noo convenient long to exchange for suche a thing, more it were not *polesy* for me to sett that maner jn suche case, for alle maner off happis.'[78]

Thus we need hardly be surprised that in the mid-sixteenth-century *Mirror* the term is at least potentially tainted by imputations of self-interest. These imputations certainly underpinned the disapproval expressed in its account of Edward IV's efforts to advance his interests by *pollicy* (p. 204, l. 31). Of course, the term's ambit remains highly varied. More affirmatively, George duke of Clarence commends Warwick and his brother for 'marciall *pollicy*' (p. 225, l. 123), together with other crucial virtues. Anthony lord Rivers is exercised against 'Such pollyng heades as prayse for prudent *pollicie* / False practises' (p. 261, ll. 442–43), and Humfrey duke of Gloucester describes his honorable responsibility as encompassing 'ciuil *pollicie*' (p. 451, l. 200). Another positive reading of this disposition is advanced by Hastings, who lists 'Pallas *pollecie*' as one of his areas of accomplishment (p. 296, l. 750).

Inherent in policy's exercise is the character of the *politique*.[79] Even as the former term migrated from public interest to self interest, so was the latter term in a process of movement from public-spirited to self-serving behavior. This trajectory has been noted and well described by Nicolai Rubinstein, who comments that 'In Elizabethan England, "policy" and "politic" came to be generally used as denoting cunning, and altogether amoral conduct based on expediency.'[80] Although agreeing completely with this arc of meaning as Rubinstein describes it, I maintain that crucial shifts in the meaning of these words occurred in the fifteenth century, and did not await, as in his explanatory system, 'the impact of Machiavelli, and of anti-Machiavellianism, on political thought' (p. 54). Thus, already in the fifteenth century, we may observe this closely coordinate shift. In the very letter in which he weighs matters of personal *polesy*, John Paston II's thoughts drift to matters of *poletyk* procedure. Complaining about certain impediments in a marriage negotiation conducted on behalf of John III, he offers a general precept: 'I thynke notte a mater happy, more well handelyd, nore poletykly dalte with, when jt can neuer be fynysshyd with-owte an inconvenience, and to any suche bargayne I kepe neuer to be condescentyng nere of cowncell' (p. 503). As quoted in chapter 1 of this study, Harpisfeld's French *memoire* evoked this sense in praising Edward IV for 'grant sens et bonne pollicie,' even as the *Arrivall* commended him for his shrewdness or *polyqwe*.[81] This new sense of the *politique* was well instated in the fifteenth century, and its transformative impact on the *De Casibus* tradition was well recognized, even in the writings of

George Ashby, the advocate of princely *polleci*. In his *Active Policy of a Prince*, Ashby argues that the prince should read *De Casibus* narratives as found in chronicles, to gain instruction in *polletike* procedures: 'to guyde hym in siche cases lyke / As other men dude that were polletike' (ll. 209–10). As in Lydgate and Premierfait, the motive is less to avoid vice for its own sake than to maintain oneself in power. For, we learn, it is not 'vices' alone but also 'negligence' (l. 163) that can drive the inadvertent from office.

As in the case of *pollecie*, the *Mirror* draws on various senses of the *politique*, including its practitioner's interest in his own strategies of survival. Richard duke of York describes his father Richard earl of Cambridge's ill-judged but comprehensible decision to oppose the Lancastrians as a matter of '*politik* procurance' (p. 184, l. 47); his plot's biggest problem is simply that it didn't succeed. Using the term in a more affirmative and thus traditional sense is Humfrey duke of Gloucester, who, disdaining an unjust interpretation of the law, thinks 'the same no order *politike* (p. 452, l. 222)—that is, inconsistent with the public weal. And we recall the murkier zone of Hastings' own '*polytyke* secrets,' that area in which civil problems are addressed and resolutions privately made.

The point is that exercise of *pollicie* and promotion of the *politique* need be neither all good nor all bad, but, within the world of the *Mirror*, these terms are available for condemnation and praise, along a spectrum of actions ranging from civic-minded and 'indifferent' in the highest fifteenth- and sixteenth-century sense of the term through self-interested and 'partial' in the most dubious of its early senses.[82] Moreover, the use of these terms indicates the elaboration of a recognized area in which worldly thinking is done and worldly decisions made, both by political protagonists and by subsequent analysts of their choices. I believe this quiet, but persistent, act of delineation the *Mirror*'s most charged activity, the central source of the contemporary excitement it clearly aroused, but the specifics of which have never been satisfactorily explained.

5. RICHARD DUKE OF YORK'S 'TRUE TRAGEDIE' AS SHAKESPEARE'S MIRROR

Extending over centuries and expressed in a variety of languages and registers, the ongoing discussion of Fortune is so mixed in character that no text conceived within its ambit is likely, or even able, to sustain a unitary view of its subject. Rather, as in most speculative conversations of long antecedence, different ways of talking jostle together within the confined space of the new text, each bearing traces of its own temporal origins. Such a text is Shakespeare's early *Henry VI, Part 3*, or, as it was originally called, *The True Tragedie of Richard Duke of York*.

I do not care to enter the debate about whether, or in what fashion, Shakespeare read the *Mirror for Magistrates*.[83] Yet, whether or not Shakespeare encountered the *Mirror* itself, the *Mirror* tradition reached him as a rich and internally varied confluence of propositions about the ravages of Fortune, the perils of eminence, and the instability of earthly affairs — some in the larger *Mirror* tradition and others embodied in chronicles, sermons, and other writings. Adam of Usk, for example, attributes to the imprisoned Richard II a thorough knowledge of the tradition, in his lamentation over the ruination of so many precessor-kings. This wide-ranging and well-informed lamentation includes 'the names and the histories of those who had suffered such fates, from the time when the realm was first inhabited.' Adam is, in turn, moved by the recital and knows how to respond to it: 'reflecting to myself on the glories of his former state and on the fickle fortune of this world.'[84] If Adam and his imagined Richard can so extraordinarily extemporize within a diffusely received philosophical and argumentative structure, why should we expect less of Shakespeare, who had his own separate access to many of the same sources on which the *Mirror* authors originally drew? Shakespeare's history plays are richly steeped in the *kinds* of observations about personal destiny associated with the *Mirror*, and whether he found such observations within the covers of that particular volume seems to me an unnecessary speculation. More pertinent is the way in which his dramatic text opens itself to a world of varied pronouncement on the role of Fortune in magisterial careers, offering itself as a kind of *carrefour*, or place of convergence, among and between them, allowing each perspective on Fortune to retain and even to broadcast the marks and assumptions of its own time and place of origin.

My examples are drawn from the *True Tragedie*. Here the lamentative Henry VI possesses his own very developed view of Fortune and the ebb and flow of magnate fortunes, epitomized in his soliloquizing, 'Let me embrace thee, sour adversity, / For wise men say it is the wisest course' (3.1.24–25). He has earlier elaborated this view with a pronounced bucolic turn. Observing the ebb and flow of battlefield fortunes, he seeks a hillside seat and imagines himself a 'homely swain,' exclaiming:

> Ah, what a life were this! How sweet! How lovely!
> Gives not the hawthorn bush a sweeter shade
> To shepherds looking on their seely sheep
> Than doth a rich embroidered canopy
> To kings that fear their subjects' treachery? (2.5.22; 41–45)

Given the opportunity, he enacts his own wish for withdrawal from the world, resigning the day-to-day operations of the kingdom to his restorer Warwick, whose own cynical ends are well served by this resignation, and who praises it in terms we have previously encountered:

> Your grace hath still been famed for virtuous,
> And may now seem as wise as virtuous
> By spying and avoiding fortune's malice. (4.7.26–28)

Contemporaries like John Blacman more often cast Henry's unworldliness in a frame of Christian-anchoritic withdrawal from the world.[85] But Shakespeare's Henry (with Warwick's cynical approval) seems more in the vein of those early humanists, who, Virgilian and classically influenced, proposed the evasion of Fortune by a tempering of ambitions and a policy of retreat from active engagement with the world. Henry's virtue, by long habit regarded as saintly in its character, is also the classical virtue advocated, for example, by Petrarch, whose influential work on the remedy or avoidance of Fortune (*De Remediis Utriusque Fortune*) was an important precedent for Boccaccio's own *De Casibus*. Thus it is, as Petrarch admonishes his dedicatee, that only virtue can deliver us from the perils of Fortune—good no less than ill—and that the exercise of virtue requires him to cultivate a state of mind undistracted by the pursuits of the world.[86]

That Henry's disposition is pitiable is revealed clearly enough by the condescension of the men of action who surround him and determine his ultimate fate. These men nevertheless find other ways to refer their own successes and failures to the operations of Fortune. Thus, Edward IV, returning from exile in France, employs Fortune as a synonym for something like 'luck' or 'happenstance,' when he notes the reversal of which he is beneficiary:

> . . . thus far fortune maketh us amends,
> And says that once more I shall interchange
> My wanèd state for Henry's regal crown. (4.8.2–4)

Elsewhere, he reduces Fortune to a virtual figure of speech: 'If ffortune serve me I'll requite this kindness' (4.8.77). Likewise, Somerset seems to use 'fortune' merely as a synonym for 'outcome,' when, bowing to the inevitable, he declares his intention to stoop with patience to my fortune' (5.5.6), having fallen into his adversaries' hands after the final Lancastrian defeat. All agree, in one way or another, that Fortune is variable; thus Edward notices at his moment of triumph, 'Thus far our fortune keeps an upward course' (5.3.51)—with his 'Thus far' as necessary qualification. Among those noticing, and reinforcing, Fortune's variability is the earl of Warwick, who, brought low at the end, discourses upon his 'fall':

> Lo now my glory smeared in dust and blood.
> My parks, my walks, my manors that I had,
> Even now forsake me, and of all my lands
> Is nothing left me but my body's length.
> Why, what is pomp, rule, reign, but earth and dust?
> And, live we how we can, yet die we must. (5.2.23–28)

Here Shakespeare, whether knowingly or unknowingly, delivers a form of direct riposte to the *Mirror* tradition. For Warwick's *Mirror* narrative is one of the most un- or antigeneric of the 1559 edition, marked by the cavils and attempted self-justifications on which I have already commented, and altogether eschewing the traditional exemplification of the world's betrayal in favor of prudent political admonitions and terms of 'good conduct' ('Such as covet peoples love to get / . . . Live liberally, and kepe them out of det'— p. 210, ll. 121, 123). Whereas Shakespeare, fully conversant with the less progressive norms of the larger tradition in which the *Mirror* was situated, effectively restores to the Warwick narrative the kind of ending it might have enjoyed in more conventional rendition—rewriting it as, from the conservative viewpoint of medieval tradition, it 'should have been.'

All this for received or medieval tradition. An alternate view of Fortune also walks at large in this play, sketched out—however broadly—in its rendition of Richard duke of Gloucester (and future Richard III) as a 'Machiavellian' of the first stripe. Machiavelli enters, of course, in the guise of the 'stage Machiavel.' But, as Victoria Kahn has shown, the stage Machiavel may have embodied a higher quality of actual perception about the real writer's practices and arguments than is usually allowed to be the case. In Richard's embodiment of the rhetorical and the theatrical, he promises a variety of aspirational and temporary control over Fortune and events not altogether different from that which Machiavelli enacted in his style of argumentation.[87] Thus, in his rhapsodic account of his own objectives, Richard not only emphasizes his unscrupulousness but also the sheer theatricality of the means by which his goals are to be attained:

> Why, I can smile, and murder whiles I smile,
> And cry 'Content!' to that which grieves my heart,
> And wet my cheeks with artificial tears,
> And frame my face to all occasions. . . .
> I'll play the orator as well as Nestor,
> Deceive more slyly than Ulysses could,
> And, like a Sinon, take another Troy.
> I can add colours to the chameleon,
> Change shapes with Proteus for advantages,
> And set the murderous Machiavel to school. (3.2.182 – 85, 188 – 93)[88]

With respect to sheer bloody-mindedness, Richard simplifies and vulgarizes his Machiavellian allegiance. But, in stressing his ability to adjust to external occasions, Richard grasps something essential about the Machiavellian mode, and, as in Kahn's formulation of the matter, the dissimulative possibilities inherent in his rhetorical tradition.

Simultaneously, the same Shakespeare play also offers us a more indigenous version of Machiavellianism than Richard's. At a moment of dire reversal, this Edward summons the lessons and possibilities of the prototypical 'political science' immanent in the fifteenth- and sixteenth-century *De Casibus* tradition, declaring:

> Though fortune's malice overthrow my state,
> My mind exceeds the compass of her wheel. (4.4.19 – 20)

One might argue that Edward here simply places himself in the mainstream of Boethian tradition, in which the production of an outlook inured to reversal and the blows of Fortune is the ultimate defense against her wiles. Yet the Boethian—and the Petrarchan and Boccaccian—view of Fortune does not expect the possessor of so developed a philosophical position to remain in the arena of contestation for worldly rewards.[89] Edward's view of a mind 'exceeding the compass' of Fortune's wheel is not that of a person who has rejected the world, but rather that of an active competitor for worldly success who takes full strategic advantage of his enlarged perspective in order to hatch counterstrategies and ingenious new proposals. Among the welter of commentary present in this play, Edward's view seems most fully to embrace the new insights progressively emerging in Premierfait, Lydgate, and the *Mirror*. Edward here acknowledges Fortune's capricious malice, but—in keeping with the emergent tradition I am seeking to limn—as a force that can be thought about, and, if not forestalled, at least considered, rejoined, comprehended. Edward's elsewhere embraces something of the resignation recommended by Petrarch and Boccaccio ('It boots not to resist both wind and tide'—4.4.32). This same resignation predominates in the quarto version of Lines 19 – 20, in which Edward simply says:

> Well Warwicke, let Fortune doe her worst,
> Edward in minde will bear himselfe a King. (F. 3v)

By contrast, Edward's confidence that his mind might 'exceed' the compass of Fortune's wheel in the resilience of its pursuit of earthly aims is a position unavailable before the period of this study. It represents a reconsideration of Fortune's operations, and the correct responses to Fortune, initiated by Premierfait and Lydgate, and carried forward by Baldwin, Ferrers, and other members of the zealous syndicate responsible for the earliest and most excitingly transformative editions of the *Mirror*. By the mid-sixteenth century the writers in this emergent tendency might have known a thing or two about Machiavelli, or at least might have heard his name. Of more significance, however, is the prior development within the *Mirror* tradition of a very persuasive 'pre-Machiavellian' articulation paralleling some of that writer's most influential suppositions and tenets bearing on the conduct of magistrates in the world.

three

Fortescue and Pecock
Two Parcyalle *Men*

THIS REALLY WAS SCOUNDREL TIME. REGARDLESS OF ALLEGIANCE, every major writer of the mid-fifteenth century experienced extreme travails: accusation, harassment, imprisonment, dispossession, and, frequently, forced recantation under threat of figurative, civil, or actual death. Each, this is to say, suffered at the hands of partisans and scoundrels, and each was at one time or another thought to *be* a partisan and scoundrel. Moreover, writers operating in such stressed circumstances could hardly fail to internalize some of the very accusations directed against them. Their texts are riddled with prevarication and self-correction, dogged by self-doubt, marked by evidence of contemplated or actual side-switching, and haunted by fears of *dowblenesse*—together with a dog's dinner of other unwholesome symptoms. Among this group I might have included writers like Sir Thomas Malory and George Ashby (whom I do not discuss here, though both were fully embroiled in political struggle and both were imprisoned in circumstances with at least putative bearing on their allegiances). The writers I discuss are the eminent jurist and sometime chancellor John Fortescue and the controversial bishop and theologian Reginald Pecock. Fortescue was captured, threatened with death, and made to recant his Lancastrian writings as the price of reconciliation with Edward IV. Pecock, having offended against both church and state, was forced to participate in burning his own works, and died in close confinement. This is in some ways an unconventional pairing, since one wrote as jurist and constitutionalist and the other as theologian and soi-disant defender of the clergy, and their lives and expressive registers rarely and barely touch. But the exigencies of the mid-fifteenth century touched them both.

I. FORTESCUE'S *DOWBLENESSE*

Proclaimed traitor for his activities on behalf of the deposed Henry VI (27 April 1471)[1] and captured at Tewkesbury (4 May 1471), Fortescue came close to sharing the fate of the many other highborn captives who lost their heads for treason or were slain outright in the days immediately after that convulsive event. His close scrape is emblematized in one near-contemporary list that includes his name among 'men that were heveded' (that is, beheaded), with the subsequent correction 'on lyffe' as a marginal addition.[2] He received a general pardon for his offenses in October of that year,[3] but his attainder was not to be reversed until 1473 – 75.[4] What he promised in order to save his head, we cannot be sure. But the price he paid for reversal of his attainder and restoration of his estates is explicitly rehearsed in his petition for reversal. Addressing Edward IV, he records his accomplishment of an apparent royal behest:

> Consideryng, Soverayn Lord, that youre seid Suppliant lovith so, and tenderith the good of your moost noble astate, that he late by large and clere writing delyvered unto youre Highnes, hath so declared all the maters which were writen in Scotland and elles where, ayen youre right or title . . . ; and also hath so clerely disproved all the arguments that have be made ayen the same right and title, that nowe there remayneth no colour, or matere of argument to the hurt or infamye of the same right and title, by reason of any such writyng.[5]

He has, in other words, recanted in writing all that he previously asserted about the legitimacy of the Lancastrian claim and has apparently delivered his text to Edward for verification.

In this recantation, generally known as his 'Declaration,' he offers a point-for-point withdrawal of assertions earlier made and remade in such tracts as his 'Replicacion' against the claim of the house of York, together with some other arguments that he never personally made but with which his name was associated.[6] The particular form of this recantation is dialogic, interrogative, coercive, and, ultimately, confessional. In furtherance of these characteristics, he creates an interlocutor, 'a lernid man in the lawe,' who mingles expository, admonitory, and prosecutorial functions. At times, this Lernid Man functions simply as a straw man, setting up easy arguments for Fortescue to knock down. He is also assigned certain painful expository tasks and revelations (such as announcing the extinction of the Lancastrian line 'with oute issue'—a situation which provides essential background to Fortescue's own transfer of loyalty—p. 530). At such moments, he conveniently assumes a share of Fortescue's own revisionary burden, thus enacting his author's self-protective wish that some elements of this humiliating task might be assumed by others whose reputation for consistency 'may haue no hurte be it' (p. 532). At other times, though, the Lernid Man articulates principles and demands from somewhere outside the scope of Fortescue's own expectations and wishes. In these autonomous moments, his is the voice of Yorkist authority, keeping notarial track of the past utterances Fortescue is obliged to withdraw or refute, and making sure that he does so. The rationale is that Fortescue, having flooded England with pamphlets and other writings in support of Lancastrian legitimacy, must now clean up his own mess. The point is made that many of these prior writings remain in private circulation and, unneutralized, might turn to 'the Kinges harme.' The Lernid Man tells him that these remedial measures are now his obligation, 'consyderyng that ye be the Kyngs liege man, and of his councell, and founde in his noble grace also grete clemence and fauoures as euer dyd man' (p. 533). Not only is his obligation to neutralize the effects of his earlier, pro-Lancastrian writings, but also to do so publicly enough that his recantation 'may come to the knowlache of the people also clerely as dyde the sayd writinges sent of Scoteland' (p. 523). At the outer edge of its implication, the Lernid Man's voice contains a note of explicit coercion. Should he not do these things, the Lernid Man suggests, the king might be harmed; adding, in a tone of deadpan menace and implied derision worthy of any mafia drama, 'which I am right sure ye wold not were so' (p. 533).

We might regard this Lernid Man as an out-and-out invention, an epiphenomenon of the expository task Fortescue takes in hand. Yet we must also remember that this was an imposed task, not a voluntary one; and that particular elements of his 'Declaration' were requisite to this task of self-rehabilitation. In this sense, the Lernid Man seems also to be born of a certain objective reality, to be viewable as a composite of the various pressures operating upon Fortescue in his newly vulnerable situation. By one measure, the Lernid Man wants only what is due to Edward, only certain adjustments following logically upon Fortescue's acceptance of his new position. By another measure, he is Fortescue's Mephistopheles, and wants everything in this world and the next: Fortescue's reputation for constancy, the core and coherence of his past beliefs—in effect, his political soul. At such moments, the Lernid Man assumes a reality independent of Fortescue's own mind; or, if he is to be situated within Fortescue's mind, he occupies a problematic part, awash in the self-loathing common to confessing subjects. For a confession is what he seeks. At various points his confessor's role becomes apparent. Consider the terms in which he praises and absolves Fortescue for well-doing: 'ye haue confessed the trouthe and declared the cause why ye wrote so, wherin I cane assigne no defaulte in you' (p. 531). (Except, as always in such cases, 'oone matier' always remains to be addressed; in this case the embarrassment of Fortescue's previously expressed denunciations of succession in the female line.)

The Lernid Man considers Fortescue worth more to the Yorkists as a live confessional subject than a dead traitor. He anticipates that Fortescue's self-critical declarations will convey a form of 'value added,' in the sense that a weak argument, discredited or demolished, is worth more to the king than an argument never made at all. Such refutation, he crows, actually strengthens the king's title: 'the kynges title by occasion of yt, and by reason of this declaracion, is more clere, and shalbe more openly knowen that it shuld haue been if that wrytinge hadd neuer be made' (p. 525). In other words, as noted in the 'Declaration' itself, the apparent misfortune of Fortescue's earlier allegiance turns out to be an occasion of good fortune after all. In his own words, 'the same right and title stonden nowe the more clere and open, by that any such writynges be made ayen them.'[7] By his own reckoning, as well as that of the Yorkists, Fortescue is worth most as a participant in a kind of 'loyalty theatre,' a dramatized conversion process that discovers added value and credibility in a new loyalty with the force to effect conversion. (This process need surprise no reader of Foucault, who demonstrates that the theatrics of such a process have their own value, over and above the mere conversion of a single individual.)[8] Moreover, as the Lernid Man thrice emphasizes, this process operates independently of—or even despite—the convert's original intentions: 'For how so be it that when ye wrote them ye intended that they shuld haue been sore agayne the Kings title by which he tho claymed . . . and so thay sowr dyd, and wer so taken of many men, God knowyth; yet nowe, blyssed be God, thay be turned to a contrarie entent and effecte, for thay have causyd alle your forsayd declaracions' (p. 540). Subject to the Lernid Man's suasions, Fortescue is no longer master of his own intent; his mature lifetime of pro-Lancastrian argument is, in effect, turned against itself, to become its own enemy, its own self-eradication serving as a stimulus for new, Yorkist argumentation.

No wonder that Fortescue should reveal some misgivings, caring not only for the evacuation of his own intent, but for the embarrassment to his own reputation such a series of self-reversals will entail. Wishing that he might transfer part of the argumentative responsibility to others, he complains that 'I haue wryten so much tharin to an other entent, as ye know welle, that yf now I do as ye move me, my worke tharin wyll sown so lyke dowblenesse, that in the oppynyone of the people, and namely of simple men, I may than by fall into infame of dowblenesse' (pp. 531–32). The Lernid Man's robust response to this reasonable cavil is immensely telling, with respect to the decorums of mid-fifteenth-century legal and theological and other argumentative writing, and also to the general conduct of partisan politics in that troubled period. He attempts a distinction between the condition of doubleness, which he concedes implicitly that nobody would or should enjoy, and run-of-the-mill partiality, an inescapable condition of life. 'Your wrytynges,' he declares, 'were but arguments,' and you wrote them as 'a parcyall man, seruant to him for whos fauour ye made the arguments' (p. 532). Furthermore, he observes, with crass reference to the recent deaths of Henry VI and Prince Edward, 'his cause is now expired, and he deed, ye may nowe honestly and commendably with oute eny note of blame argue to the contrary entent of that ye haue doo by fore this tyme' (p. 532). Besides, he adds, such adept side-switching is after all what everybody does. 'Sergeauntes and aduocates that been right worshippful men argue dayly to prove the titles of thayr clyantes, and after that in a lyke case for another clyant may arguen to the contrary entent' (p. 532). Nor is this less true of theologians: 'Thus doth Saynt Thomas in Secunda Secunde, and in all his bokes where as he asketh eny questions, and thus doone all the clarks that determyn eny matir in scholes; for this ordre is no dowblenesse, but argument and proof of conynge and vertue' (p. 532). Apparently reassured, Fortescue goes on to reverse and destroy his own argument against female succession, proving it merely 'an informyle tale, and no kynde of silogisme' (p. 534).

Despite the Lernid Man's best efforts, *dowblenesse* still sounds a bit like partiality, and the reverse. Overt partiality does indeed differ from the more extreme sense of *dowbleness* as willful deception (see, for an example, chap. 1, note 46). But Fortescue has used the word in a simpler way, in reference to division of loyalty or inconsistency or side-switching, and in this sense he remains an implicitly *dowble,* as well as confessedly *parcyalle,* man.

Partial, in its sense of 'biased' or 'interested'—in the sense, that is, of French *partial*—is effectively a fifteenth-century invention. The *MED* cites it in Trevisa, but Lydgate is the first to deploy it extensively, as the opposite of 'indifferent' or disinterested. It enters political discourse in the Rolls of Parliament in 1425 in its sense of inappropriate favor for one side over another; in a quarrel between the duke of Gloucester and the chancellor of England, Parliament undertakes to 'procede and acquite hem self . . . withouten tht thei, or any of hem, shall pryvele or appert, mak or shewe hem self, or be partie or partiall thrinne, noght levyng nor eschewing so to do, for affection, love, doubte or drede of any persone or persones.'[9] The problem for Fortescue is that this line of argument requires that he concede points about himself that his entire previous life had seemed designed to withstand. For, in confessing himself partial—and, worse still, partial in impermanent ways—this previously most resolutely loyal of Lancastrians accepts the revised identity of one who, rather than abide in a conviction, espouses it temporarily or even for hire. His and the Lernid Man's line of argument reserves no ground for loyalty outside the scope of temporary argumentative interest—not for lawyers or judges or theologians or for royal servants, either of the king that was or of the king that is now. Partiality is, as the 'Declaration' describes it, a condition of life. Moreover, in a rapidly and constantly shifting political terrain, the constant exchange of one partiality for another (the condition of 'doubleness') is an inevitability—an inherent and inescapable feature.

We can hardly doubt that this rather disenchanted relation to issues of loyalty and permanence constituted a costly admission for Fortescue, for whom 'indifference'—that is, impartiality or even-handedness—had previously seemed an admirable and attainable ideal. Fortescue himself, previ-

ously on higher ground, treated such partiality as the enemy of good counsel; in his *Governance,* on which he probably worked both before and after
the 'Declaration,' he is scathing about Lords who allow themselves to be
moved 'to parciallite,' or to be made 'ffavorable and parcial' by insinuating
servants.[10] In the same text, he imagines that the king's council might be
staffed by disinterested or 'indifferent' people, able to live on their own and
unswayed by possible reward. In *De Laudibus,* written at a time when Fortescue had not yet been required to reconfigure his loyalties, we encounter
his paean to the jury system, in which decisions are made by witnesses who
are 'neighbours, able to live of their own, sound in repute and fair-minded,
not brought into court by either party, but chosen by a respectable and im-
partial officer ('per officiarium nobilem et indifferentem electi') (chap. 27).
This dream of testimony resting safely beyond *parcyalle* self-interest is recur-
rent in Fortescue's writings.

In a perceptive analysis of the 'Declaration,' James Landman suggests
that Fortescue's admission of his partiality is underpinned by his vocational
identity; that, confessing himself partial, Fortescue chooses the role of lawyer
rather than that of juror or judge.[11] The lawyer chooses hypothetical argumentation, 'colour' in pleading, and the requirements of a new client ahead
of the disinterested evaluation of events. Viewing himself as a lawyer, Fortescue need hardly apologize for so routine a matter as simply changing
'clients'—Edward for Henry, the latter's cause having now expired. Yet, as
Landman also observes, this matter of partiality remains complicated. Fortescue is, as it were, double about doubleness, accepting on the one hand
the pragmatism of the profession to which he belongs, while continuing on
the other hand to believe abstractly or academically in the primacy of more
general principles of natural law.[12] Fortescue's inner division might be regarded as a particular instance of a more general fifteenth-century separation, between an expanding and highly pragmatic legal profession (allied
with the Common Law) and burgeoning university-based studies of natural law and political theory (allied with study of Roman and Canon law).[13]
Yet the emergence of so divided a political consciousness invites multiple
explanations, not only at the level of general intellectual and institutional
history, but also in terms of presenting situations and concrete dilemmas.
Fortescue's own attachment to venerable doctrines of steadfast consistency
was subject to extreme, and I think unusual, pressure by exigencies inherent in his political situation.

2. WOUNDED TEXTS

A tenacious loyalist by the standards of any age, Fortescue was for most of his life a beacon of loyalty by the motile standards of the fifteenth century. Appointed Chief Justice of the King's Bench under the Lancastrians in 1442, and recipient of many honors and preferments, he showed his true colors in adversity, in and after the Lancastrian defeat at Towton.[14] Retreating north with the loyalist forces, he was present at the skirmishes of Ryton and Braun-cepeth,[15] in Scotland for two years where he acted as what might now be called 'shadow chancellor,' endured attainder and forfeiture of his estates, settled with the exiled Lancastrians at St. Mihiel in Barre, 1463–71. From the latter location he wrote and petitioned incessantly, and also engaged in embassies to Paris.[16] He then returned to England in April 1471, expecting to find Henry VI readepted and his tutee the prince back in line for the throne. Upon his arrival he learned of the Yorkist victory at Barnet, and, his hopes collapsing, was captured at or immediately after Tewkesbury.

During his later years of exile in Scotland and, especially, in Barre, he accomplished most of his writings—*De Natura, De Laudibus,* an early draft of *Governance,* the genealogical treatises. Although productive, the period of exile can hardly be regarded as a time of rest and reflection. Fortescue does not, by any standard, seem a likely soldier of fortune or roving propagandist, and he was now in his seventies, whatever our exact calculation of his age. His situation of penury, insecurity, and discomfort is well expressed in a letter to the earl of Ormond, sent from St. Mihiel to the latter's post in Portugal, intended to bolster Ormond's commitment to the cause, but nevertheless laced with certain inevitable cautions and pieces of prudential advice. Cautioning Ormond about uncertain travel and dubious loyalty on the part of Louis king of France, he adds:

> We buthe alle in grete poverte, but yet the queen susteynethe us in mete and drinke, so as we buthe not in extreme necessite. Here highnesse may do no more to us thanne she dothe. Wherfore I counseille you to spend sparely soche money as ye have, for whanne ye come hether ye shulle have need of hit. And also here buthe maney that need, and wolle desire to parte with you of youre aune money; and in all this contray is no manne that wolle or may lene you any money, have ye never so grete nede.[17]

Some of the travails of the Lancastrian exiles in Burgundy are corroboratively described by Commynes, who says that he has seen some of them reduced to such poverty, before the duke recognized their plight, that even beg-
gars are not so poor ('ceulx qui demandent l'aumosne ne sont pas si pouvres').
He says that he has seen a duke of Exeter go on foot without stockings ('sans
chausses'), begging his livelihood from house to house, in anonymity.[18]

Although Fortescue endured the probation of sufficient hardship over
a sufficient period to place his sincerity beyond question, he nevertheless remained hostage to an external situation inherently inimical to settled loyalties of any kind. The conflicts of the midcentury produced a regular series of
crises, involving such celebrated switches and turnabouts as Andrew Trol-
lope's desertion of Warwick and return to Henry at Ludlow in 1459, Clarence's carefully orchestrated defection from Warwick and return to Edward
just prior to the battle of Barnet in 1471, Wenlock's concealed Lancastrian
hand while remaining ostensibly loyal to Edward in the events between 1468
and the battle of Tewkesbury in 1471, and Warwick's own ceaseless and rest-
less machinations.[19] In other words, the troubled externals posed by endless
loyalty clashes and succession disputes functioned as a virtual treason machine, a schematic plan for the production and propagation of disloyalties.
As Commynes observed with characteristic acuity, the disputed succession
in England fostered a situation in which nearly everybody was thought a
traitor by somebody, at one time or another: 'Et tous disoyent qu'ilz estoient
traistres, à cause qu'il y avoit deux maisons qui pretendoient à la couronne.'[20]
Herein, rather than in some new bloodthirsty penchant, lies the explanation for the unprecedented scale on which both sides began routinely to execute noble adversaries captured in battle; for, from the point of view of loyalists on both sides, their enemies were traitors to the crown and deserved the
sanctions customarily reserved for treason. Furthermore, this divisive situation, with all the mistrust it fostered, was replicated across the spectrum of
institutions, from the micro level of conflicted loyalties in the countryside
and among gentry families to the macro level of international politics (as expressed, especially, in the tension between Charles the Bold and Louis XI, itself played out by shifty go-betweens and would-be opportunists like Jacques
de Luxembourg, count of Pol and constable of France).

So relentlessly contestatory a situation produces wounded persons and,
in effect, wounded texts as well. For, with respect to matters of partisanship,
even the most securely situated fifteenth-century texts seem always to end up

doubled back on themselves, convoluted in some unexpected way, or bearing or revealing some sort of wound that cannot be concealed and that shows no disposition to heal. Fortescue's *De Laudibus* is a hopeful and even utopian text, dedicated to the nurture of an eager and aspirant prince whom its author fondly imagines to be on the threshold of kingship, as 'rex futurus.'[21] Yet it sits on a foundation of the most distressing circumstances, articulated from a perspective divided between specific indignation and numbed uncertainty about durations and details. Consider, for example, the shifting temporalities of Fortescue's preliminarily recital of events.

> Seviente dudum in regno Anglie nephandissima rabie illa, qua piisimus ibiden rex H[enricus] sextus, cum Margareta regina consorte sua, filia Regis Ierusalem et Cicilie, ac eorum unigenito Edwardo principe Wallie inde propulsi sunt, sub qua et demum rex ipse H[enricus] a subditis eius deprehensus, carceris diutinum passus est horrorem, dum regina illa cum sobole sua patria sic extorrens, in ducatus Barrenni . . . . Miles quidam grandevus predicti regis Anglie cancellarius, qui eciam ibidem sub eadem hac clade exulebat, principem sic affatur.

> [Not long ago (*dudum*), a savage and most detestable civil war ranged in the kingdom of England, whereby the most pious king Henry the Sixth, with Margaret his queen-consort, daughter of the king of Jerusalem and Sicily, and their only son Edward, prince of Wales, were driven out, and whereby eventually (*demum*) King Henry himself was seized by his subjects, and for a long time (*diutinum*) suffered the horror of imprisonment, whilst the queen herself, thus banished the country with her child, lodged in the duchy of Bar. . . . A certain aged knight, chancellor of the said king of England, who was also in exile there as a result of the same disaster, thus addressed the prince.] (Pp. 2-3)

The most detestable kind of cruel madness, we learn, has manifested itself in England, *dudum*—either recently, *or* some time since, *or* for a long time. As a result of it, King Henry himself has *demum*—finally, at last—been seized by his own subjects and has for a long time, or *diutinum,* suffered the horror of imprisonment. Here choice of the perfect tense (as opposed to the imperfect) implies a kind of hopeful closure, almost as if the imprisonment is as good as over, even as *diutinum* reintroduces a wholly opposed sense of its prolongation. Expelled, the queen and prince were lingering—killing time, practically, in Barre (*morabantur*), and Fortescue portrays himself as also exiled by the same disaster. Presiding over these indeterminacies, the acknowledgment of *clades*—catastrophic defeat or overthrow—frames and haunts the entire text, conditioning and undermining, in the passages which follow, even its moments of rhapsodic effusion.[22]

Even the determinedly upbeat *Governance of England,* conceived in a positive spirit as a 'selling' document for a new model of royal finance and a revamped royal counsel, does not conceal its own sense of political and social upheaval incompletely resolved. In his articles drafted for the Lancastrian prince for transmission to the earl of Warwick, constituting a kind of preliminary draft of the *Governance,* Fortescue interrupts his auspicious thoughts about Henry's readeption to concede the extent to which many have suffered 'in this tyme of the kinges grete trouble.'[23] In the same text he stumbles into an admission—possibly with a nervous side glance to Warwick and then partly effaced in *Governance*—that immoderate grants have been given: 'And trewly ther hath bene gevun in late daies to somme oon lorde temporell much mor lyuelode in yerly value than woll paye the wages of alle the newe counseill' (p. 351). Despite his strong Lancastrian loyalties, he does not forgo mention of the defects of Henry's Council: 'which was mooste of grete lordis that more attended to their owne matieres thanne to the good universall profute' (p. 350). The king himself, although on the brink of readeption, is conceded to be in poor financial circumstances: 'forasmoche as the king is now in grete pouertie' (p. 352). And even in the tidied-up final version of the *Governance,* rebellion lurks as an everpresent possiblity—in this case, via rejection of the proposal that impoverishment of the commons would assure that 'thai wolde not rebelle, as now thai done oftentymes' (chap. 12, p. 137). Latent civil unrest is also signaled in less explicit ways, as when Fortescue mounts an astounding argument in favor of English courage, to the effect that 'It hath ben offten tymes sene in Englande, that iij or iiij theves ffor pouerte haue sett apon vj or vij trewe men, and robbed them all' (p. 141). The French have no heart for such exploits, he says, and brags that 'ther bith therfore mo men hanged in Englande in a yere . . . then ther be hanged in Ffraunce . . . in vij yeres' (p. 141).

This text will accrue its own more personal mark of disloyalty, evidencing the inherent doubleness of its own communicative situation. Undoubtedly composed in the first instance for Henry VI, as indicated by the presence of so many of its passages in the articles communicated to Warwick,[24] this text was redrafted for consideration by Edward IV in the years immediately following his resumption of rule. The trace of this rededication can be read off in several manuscripts of this work. The Laud manuscript, on which Chrimes based his edition, gives us the probable intended reading, when it says at the end of chapter 19, 'I blessed by oure Lord God for that he hath sent King Edward the iiijth to reigne vpon us.' Yet the Yelverton MS 35, 'John Vale's book,' substitutes Henry VI for Edward IV, as does the version of *Governance* in Harley MS 542 (copied by Stow from Vale's book). And, most ambivalently of all, MS Claudius A.viii, while retaining Edward IV, adds that it was 'wrighten to King Henry the Sixt by Sr John Fortescue.'[25] All these manuscripts were written after the fact, and so the mixed dedication cannot be understood precisely as documentation of the moment of Fortescue's loyalty 'transfer'. But it can be read as evidence of a residual uncertainty about the emphasis, direction, and purpose with which and for which it was written at all. Certain of the *Governance*'s purposes may, as I suggest below, be thought to surpass or outlive 'regime change.' But, in other ways, it bears the indelible mark of the mixed and shifting circumstances in which it was composed.

Present within another 'upbeat' contemporaneous presentation is a similar sense of the inescapability of certain consequences and residues of internal division. This is the 1472 tract, possibly delivered as a speech to Parliament, by John Alcock, bishop of Rochester. Although patriotic in intent—offered on the king's behalf and designed to stir the country to war with France—this speech cannot avoid, and in fact predicates itself upon, evidence of trouble in the land. Warning of 'discencion and discorde,' the speaker allows that 'every man of this lande that is of resonable age hath knowen what trouble this reame hath suffred, and it is to suppose that noon hath escaped but att oo tyme or other his part hath be therein.'[26] No man has escaped indeed, and, even in this progressive and jingoistic speech, the imagery of disease intrudes: 'Suche is the condicion of every body that the discrase of oo membre distempereth all the other' (p. 275). The speaker warrants that causes of distemper have been uprooted and are now 'extincte' with 'no colowre or shadowe' left to trouble men's minds, but he is whistling in the graveyard. For, we learn, 'yet is there many a grete sore, many a perilous wounde left unheled' (p. 275). The symptom of this wound is, as in the *Governance,* an unassimilated social remainder: 'the multitude of riotous people which have att all tymes kyndeled the fire of this grete division . . . comytyng extorcions, opperessions, robberies, and other grete myscheves.' There are, he says, too many of them to kill; the 'remedie' is to send them abroad in the king's new wars. But the image of an infected realm lingers, as in so many other texts of the midcentury. One recalls, for instance, the Lancastrian *Somnium Vigilantis,* with its enthusiam for strict enforcement of attainder against the Yorkists in 1459—a text in which Fortescue may have had a hand. There, the Yorkists set a 'contagious example' and their conclusions are found 'infecte with reprefe.'[27] Arguing against pity, the speaker offers a similitude: 'I have a roten tothe in my mouthe that vexieth me nyght and day. Is hit better to pull him oute and so make a gape in my mouthe . . . or elles to plaster him to the confusioun and undoyng of alle the other?' The inflection, he concludes, is untreatably deep: 'Thay bene inextirpable, thay bene incurable' (p. 517). What is more, the infection, even when contained—restricted in this case to Yorkist conspirators—is ever likely to spread. This is pessimistic writing, dubious about the possibilities for healing and regeneration within the body politic, justifiably fearful whether anyone can escape infection, at one or another time.

3. WAS FORTESCUE A 'PROPAGANDIST'?

A critical tendency of the previous century removed the rose-colored 'constitutionalist' glasses through which the Victorians had beheld Fortescue, and discovered him to be a partisan scrambler and a self-interested side-switcher to boot. Stripping away the nostrums of the 'liberal sentimentalists,' S. B. Chrimes first found him a man of his own time, his choices delimited by available theoretical and political options.[28] The Fortescue who emerges from his analysis is something of a pragmatist, operating within a set of received ideas, less devoted to a set of constitutional ideals than to the consolidation of royal power under terms of public assent. This view has been elaborated and extended by Anthony Gross, who has considered Fortescue as a 'skilled careerist,' arguing that his ideas cannot be considered in isolation from the exigencies of his political biography.[29] In its disenchanted form, analysis of Fortescue as an enlivened participant in political struggles of his day has given rise to the suggestion that he was involved in the production of political propaganda. As J. R. Lander has it, '[I]t was always difficult to depict him as a profound political philosopher. He is now much more convincingly seen as a propagandist propping up successive fragile political regimes of his own day.'[30]

This adjusted view of Fortescue possesses considerable explanatory force. For one thing, virtually all of his surviving writings—as well as most of his writings that are lost but known to have existed—are occasional and 'situated' writings, writings in a cause. This is true for all of his major works, including *De Natura Legis Naturae* and *De Laudibus Legum Anglie*, both of which were written in France, or in some combination of Scotland and France, for the nurture of Prince Edward and his formation as future Lancastrian king.[31] His *Governance of England* was probably aimed at Henry VI in the first instance, then presented with reworkings to Edward IV.[32] Most of his other writings are more explicitly political still: the Lancastrian treatises, some now lost, written in Scotland and France, the 'Declaration' itself, the memoranda written to court assistance from Louis XI of France.[33] Moreover, Chrimes and his successors are undoubtedly correct in pointing out that Fortescue's writings are a good deal more hospitable to consolidation of monarchic authority than many of his 'constitutionalist' admirers—from the seventeenth-century parliamentarians through Victorian devotees like Plummer—have supposed. Fortescue himself is completely explicit on the matter: in *De Laudibus,* referring back to *De Natura,* he observes, 'It is sufficiently shown . . . that the king ruling politically is of no less power than he who rules his people regally, as he wishes.'[34] The prince who rules *politice,* in this formulation, cedes nothing when he acknowledges the restraint provided by the laws of his realm, since he and his people will become effectively one, not so much through parliamentary operations as through an identity of purpose registered in nerve, bone, and sinew. But Fortescue's political purposefulness need not cause us to conclude that his writings retain nothing of their own.

The severance of Fortescue's writings from various Stubbsian and wishful narratives about the steady advance of constitutionalism is obviously to be applauded, as is the recontextualization of his work within the exigencies and practical possibilities of his own time. The labeling of Fortescue as a 'propagandist' may be less productive, depending on the sense in which the word is understood. If the term 'propagandist' merely implies that Fortescue was a 'situated' writer, negotiating among and between and on behalf of various arrangements of power, I see no conceptual harm in its use. Writing is always 'situated' in this sense, and an understanding of Fortescue's location within an array of possibilities over which he had little ultimate control can only sharpen our sense of his accomplishment. His writing is certainly, in this respect, always 'occasional,' and always in ways witting and unwitting registers its occasion. But a further, or derivative, sense of the term 'propagandist' causes me some unease. In this sense, the propagandist is seen as a witting self-contractor, a 'pen for hire,' a self-governed and fully self-conscious master of his own political choices—as a person who has made a choice, even if it happens to be an expedient one, to commit to a particular perspective or hew a certain line in the analysis of events. Here I would demur, since I view many aspects of Fortescue's writings as inherent in his location within what Pierre Bourdieu would term a 'productive field'—a set of terms already impressed with prior connotations, and unavoidably implicated in the practical circumstances in relation to which they were employed.[35] By this I do not mean to deny social efficacy to Fortescue's texts, or to deny him a significant role in promulgating and advancing policy under conditions not of his own making. Quite the contrary. In the arguments that follow, I claim that Fortescue's writings accomplished a good deal of important social work. But I find this work a good deal less pointed in its applications, and considerably less serviceable to the interests of any one sponsoring regime, than the word 'propaganda' would seem to imply.

Fortescue composed his texts within a shifting set of enunciative conditions that were, to return momentarily to Bourdieu's terminology, inherent in his situation within a linguistic field. On the one hand, he was the beneficiary of a constituted political discourse, within which he, as Chief Justice of the King's Bench and as effective 'shadow chancellor' in the exiled court of Henry VI, could frame authoritative political pronouncements. On the other hand, his very medium was inherently flawed, its language and concepts insufficient to paper over the discrepancies and contradictions posed by a fractured political situation. I have already suggested that Fortescue was doomed by the stressed representational and linguistic medium in which he wrote to produce 'wounded' texts. These texts straddle and embrace contradiction, irreconcilable postulates and doxa, and invest in irrational prejudices, unexamined hierarchies, and even protonationalist jingoisms. The further, and deeper, contradiction of these texts inheres in their very gesture toward self-stabilization. This is, of course, their attempt to firm up their politics by professing loyalty to a single dynastic philosophy or a particular royal incumbency. Support for a particular monarch turns out to be a lure, in that the very gesture designed to rescue the subject from partisanship actually returns him to a partisan position. In so shifty and untrustworthy a political field, the would-be loyalist is converted into a treacherous survivalist, by the necessity to reconfigure and redirect his own object-choices. Seeking to extricate himself and his reader from the imputation of treachery, Fortescue found himself advocating one, and then another, particular legitimation, and thus yielding to the very situation of *dowbleness* he had sought to avert.

Fortescue's eventual triumph, and his actual claim to emancipation from *dowbleness,* rests on his capacity to see beyond the particular dynastic system that commands his present support.[36] This further horizon arises in Fortescue's insistence that, beyond the details of particular incumbencies or particular successions, the exercise of political power is *itself* discussable. Without denying abstract ideas of unction or divine sanction, he consistently displays himself as more interested in the actual arrangements by which *any* king might govern the land. Moreover, these arrangements are knowable, and even arguable, in cogent and accessible terms. In other words, his actual importance rests less in his support for any particular incumbency, than in a written practice which suggests that the state might be coherently described. Fortescue's state remains a 'natural' one in the fifteenth-century sense of the word, which postulates its divine origins and rationale. But divine sanction does not render it any the less susceptible to discussion and description. In this sense, I agree wholeheartedly with another of Chrimes's formulations, that the fifteenth century found 'the state . . . sacred but . . . not mysterious' (p. 120). This, I believe, captures it exactly: the state might still operate by divine sanction as well as human assent—no fifteenth-century commentator could have thought otherwise—but it is unmysterious in the sense that its terms and processes lie open to reasoned discussion.

Fortescue is a lawyer with a brief and a client, but he interprets these terms in his own way. His brief advances a view of a natural, even rational, state, its processes available for scrutiny and discussion. His client may be the king, but only the king who receives his message. This point may be illustrated with respect to the much-discussed visionary and dedicatory passage occurring near the end of *Governance.* Imagining a new arrangement by which the king will better husband his resources and rule with the advice of his council, he proclaims this arrangement a 'newe ffundacion,' akin to other endowments but with the whole kingdom as beneficiary:

> And, trewly, yff the kyng do thus, he shall do therby dayly more almes, than shall be do be all the ffundacions that euer were made in Englond. . . . The ffundacion of abbeys, of hospitals, and suche other houses, is nothyng in comparisoun herof. For this shalbe a collage, in whiche shul syng and pray for euermore al the men of Ingland spirituel and tem-

porel. And ther song shalbe suche among other antemes: I blissed be oure lord God, for that he hath sent kyng Edward the iiij to reigne vpon vs. He hath don more for vs, than euer dide kyng of Inglond, or myght have done before hym. The harmes that hath fallen in getyng of his Realme, beth now bi hym turned into our altheyr goode and profite. (pp. 155–56)

Rather unaccountably claiming this as an 'overlooked' passage, Lander emphasizes its literal and programmatic aspects.[37] Whereas I would see it as rather ecstatic in tone, and in fact nearly apocalyptic in its view of utter social transformation. But my point lies elsewhere, having to do with the conditional nature of the song to be raised in this chantry. This song will be dedicated to Edward, and thanks will finally be given *in spite of* 'the harmes that hath fallen in getyng of his Realme,' *if* he accepts and implements Fortescue's program. Edward is heaven-sent, but his success is ultimately conditioned upon his adoption of practical recommendations. Fortescue's brief is finally not for Edward's kingship, but for a particular set of fiscal and prudential and consultative arrangements, some of which he previously recommended to Warwick, via the prince, and others, for consideration of Henry VI. Fortescue's obsession is less with gaining royal favor than with advancing a set of ideas about governance. Thus, rather than simply a benefactor, Edward IV must have seemed to him a potential convert in an ongoing effort to secure action on his proposals for betterment of the realm.

4. FORTESCUE AND THE NATURAL STATE

Fortescue is the preeminent English contributor to a fifteenth-century discussion of what might be called the 'natural' state. This discussion had commenced even before the dissemination of Aristotle's *Politics* in the thirteenth-century West, and continued through the Machiavellian 'moment' of seventeenth-century England and beyond.[38] Some care must be taken in the matter of terminology, since, even in the limit case of Machiavelli, we cannot blithely equate the 'natural' state with a 'secular' state. Even the most aggressive medieval exponents of this tradition understand the state to enjoy some kind of divine sanction, at least in the form of some eleventh-hour providential relation to the divine. But, whatever the precise form of the state's relation to divine dispensation, the natural state, like other creations of natural reason, lies open to consideration and description in terms of its own processes and rules. This proposition is less likely to be stated baldly than simply to be placed tacitly into effect, enacting itself in a de facto rather than de jure way. Thus, in the dialogic *De Laudibus,* the precocious prince displays his quick wit but also gets ahead of himself when he observes to Fortescue that 'The law, to a knowledge of which you exhort me, is human, decreed by man, and treats of this world' (chap. 2). Fortescue hastens to remind him that 'all human laws are sacred' ('omnes leges humane sacre sunt'—chap. 3). Nevertheless, having made this pious point, he makes a further distinction that effectively reinstates the prince's perception: God constrained the kings of Israel to the reading of Deuteronomy, not just because its laws are sacred—since all the books of the Bible (and not just Deuteronomy) are sacred—but rather because these are 'the laws by which the king of Israel is obliged to rule his people' (chap. 3). In other words, the laws that found and incorporate the natural state have a distinctive status, related to the practical exigencies of rule, and are amenable to pragmatic study in their own right.

Underpinning all legality and law is, for Fortescue, the concept of natural law or the Law of Nature, a legal authority that is divine in the sense of enjoying divine sanction, but that arises in human nature. It is, as he says in the preface to his *De Natura Legis Naturae,* declared by the canons to be divine ('facri Canones dicunt Legem Nature legem esse Divinam'), but received its first beginning from human nature, and has since persevered immutable ('illa ab exordio humanae naturae originem sumpsit, et immutabilis perseverat').[39] It precedes all other human laws and kingly dignity itself. The consequence of this relationship is that Fortescue's natural law enjoys what might in today's terms be thought of as 'relative autonomy': it functions by the reflected light of divine origin and approval, but nevertheless it possesses singular and unimpeded force and effect within its own sphere. This relationship between divine law and a relatively autonomous human law, mediated by natural law, receives what might be its most resonant exposition in *De Natura* chapters 42–43, in his comparison of divine law to the sunlight that controls the 'day' of our spiritual life, and human law to the moonlight that controls the shadowed realm of our temporal or secular behavior ('quae preest nocti tenebrosae hujus temporalis conversationis'—vol. 1, p. 107). Although the moon and the planets receive their light from the sun, they nevertheless obey their own laws and are omnipotent within their own, limited, sphere of action. As he urges it:

Does any astrologer ever perfectly know the course of those other stars, who only considers the journey of the sun and only knows its rising and setting? Rather, the oblique circle the zodiac teaches us the movement of the sun, but does not completely determine the ebb and flow of the other planetary orbits. For every planet turns within its proper sphere, in which it reveals the powers of its own nature ['quilibet namque planeta in propria versatur sphaera, in qua ipse suae naturae explicat vires'—p. 108], and nevertheless does not evade the powers of the sun in which all the planets participate, without diminishing its brightness.

The sense in which each planet reveals or develops (*explicat*) the powers of its own nature is likewise the sense in which natural and human law govern worldly affairs—not independently, to be sure, and thus not in a strictly 'secular' way, but nevertheless autonomously within their own domain.

Because human or civil law is mediated by natural law, it enjoys some aspects of natural law's autonomy. Recall that the king ruling politically as well as regally (in a 'regimen regale et politicum') does not enjoy sole possession of the law. This situation is signaled by the very title of the ninth chapter of *De Laudibus:* 'Rex politice dominans non potest mutare leges regni sui' ('A king ruling politically is not able to change the laws of his kingdom'). This concept of politics, and the law as a product of consultative process, is hardly peculiar to Fortescue. He famously, even if with a certain element of elasticity, disclaims originality and assigns the inspiration for his 'regimen regale et politicum' to Aquinas and to Giles of Rome. He is, however, as Nicolai Rubinstein has observed, original in applying the concept of 'political' and thus consultative rule not to only to republics but to a particular form of monarchy as well.[40] Although he is the first to take this argumentative step, his logic is implicit at earlier junctures in English political and legal theory, as when the 'Articles of Deposition' condemn Richard II for saying that 'his lawes weren in his mouthe, and other while in his breste.'[41] Fortescue would grant the king's final responsibility for the law. But, as his surrogate the chancellor is at pains to explain, the laws 'are made not only by the monarch's will, but also by the assent of the whole realm' ('Sed non sic Anglie statuta oriri possunt, dum nedum principis voluntate sed et tocius regni assensu ipsa conduntur'—chap. 18). Moreover, they are not to be changed 'without the assent of the commons and nobles of the realm, in the manner in which they first originated' ('sine communitatis et procerum regni illius assensu, quali ipsa primitus emanarunt'—chap. 18).

Belief in the consensual basis of the law stimulates Fortescue's advancement of a cluster of origin-myths standing independent either of God or of the sovereign. In *De Laudibus,* he bends himself to the creation of an originary myth that is wholly natural in its contours. According to this myth, men like Nimrod, Belus, Ninus, and the leaders of the Romans and the Hebrews stepped into an effective vacuum and arrogated power to themselves, instituting regal rule (chap. 12). In rare instances, however, law is the first principle that conjoins the people, and the king is linked to the people by the laws, even as the head is linked to the body by its structure of nerves ('sicut per nervos compago corporis solidature, sic per legem . . . corpus huiusmodi misticum ligatur et servatur in unum, et eiusdem corporis membra ac ossa . . . soliditatem denotant per legem ut corpus naturale per nervos, propria retinent iura'—chap. 12). This is a 'mystical' body, but the particularities of its operation are entirely 'natural' and man-made. By means of a man-made compact England sprang forth as a dominion regal and political out of Brutus's band of Trojans ('regnum Anglie quod ex Bruti comitiva troianorum quam ex Italie et Grecorum finibus perduxit, in dominium politicum et regale prorupit' [with the eruptive near-violence of *prorumpo* implying a new emergence or beginning, within a purely human context]). The law, as Fortescue summarizes it, consists ultimately of three elements: natural principles, human customs, and statutes that codify custom ('omnia iura humana aut sunt lex nature, consuetudines, vel statuta que et constituciones appellantur'— chap. 15)—with constitutions or statutes always informed by the law of nature ('ius naturale'—chap. 16). Hence, although overseen by God, and although 'mystical' in the intangibility of its unifying principles, the law remains 'natural' and—more important for the argument I am presently conducting—subject to natural or rational analysis.[42]

Briefly recapitulating the same subjects in the introduction to his *Governance,* Fortescue rehearses a condensed but similar myth of origins in which God himself serves the people of Israel as king, reigning 'politekily and roialy,' and yet the people of Israel displease God by seeking as king a man who would rule 'only roialy' (chap. 1). Once again he cites Nimrod and Belus as early founders of royal rule, to be modified only later, when mankind became 'more mansuete, and bettir disposed to vertu,' at which point fellowships like those of Brutus 'made a body pollitike.' He adds that 'thai and he vpon this incorperacion, institucion, and onynge of hem self in to a reaume, ordenyd the same reaume to be ruled and justified by suche lawes as thai all wolde assent vnto; wich lawe therefore is called *polliticum,* and bi cause it is ministrid bi a kynge, it is called *regale'* (chap. 2). Fortescue is interested in what might be considered as 'comparative government,' leading to an explanation of how differences arose between different kinds of kingdoms. Yet, in the process, he devises a myth of incorporation or invention, in which God is not personally at all involved. This is not a 'secular' theory, properly speaking, because God is its first cause and ultimate judge; yet the crucial terms and metaphors by which it is expressed are natural, bodily, and lie open to historical and analytical consideration.

Here I might reintroduce Chrimes's suggestion that Fortescue establishes a theory of the state that is 'sacred but not mysterious.' Sacred, of course, in its ultimate sanction; Fortescue could not have thought, or been able to think, otherwise. But, simultaneously, as a natural and manmade creation, subject to analysis and reasoned judgment. This conviction that the contours of a nature state exist and are susceptible to description, and his effective banishment of God from the most significant details of his ensuing exposition, are consistent with a heightened mid-fifteenth-century emphasis on the language of statecraft and with a usable political vocabulary.[43]

Fortescue is very far from declaring his natural, and political, state the abode of the *parcyalle* man. His natural state is a place of reconciliation and concord, in which jurors attain objectivity by relinquishing local prejudice; in which counselors forgo gain in order to represent the interests of the realm; in which originary myths portray the abandonment of separate struggles in favor of mutual interest; in which the whole of the kingdom becomes, as it were, a singing school. Fortescue presumably took no joy in declaring himself, or in being forced to declare himself, *parcyalle,* and his conception of the state as singing school attempts the imaginary rescue of its subjects from partiality. Nevertheless, his imagined state implicitly acknowledges partiality as a precondition of its own existence. The realm both regal and political is, after all, a more amenable setting for the representation and possible reconciliation of divergent interests than is the realm exclusively regal. The very idea that singular interests must be set aside in the composition of such a realm already concedes the existence of such impulses, already proposes the processes of politics as the hoped-for place for the reconciliation their singular claims. Even though his regal and political realm articulates no formal description of treason, its possibility is nevertheless constantly implied. In the downside or negative shadow of Fortescue's ideal realm rests a no-man's land of troubled partiality and potential doubleness. Which is to say that even within Fortescue's idealistic imaginary, a place exists in which a troubled and divided career like his own might nevertheless occur.

5. PECOCK IMAGINES THE NATURAL STATE

Fortescue's *regimen regale et politicum*, founded upon natural law and the sciences proper to the study of the natural state, may be brought into fruitful comparison with the implicit politics of his ecclesiastical contemporary Reginald Pecock. In a series of treatises and books, this self-willed and opinionated bishop conducted an argument—never encouraged and ultimately condemned by his own ecclesiastical associates—for a vigorous lay orthodoxy grounded in the exercise of natural reason. Employing a freewheeling mixture of ecclesiastical, exegetical, and homiletic modalities, Pecock tackles questions of governance less frontally than his politically minded and legally trained contemporary. Yet an outline theory of the natural state is realized by implication in Pecock's voluminous surviving writings. Occasionally his statecraft is on full display. In his *Donet* he argues in terms very consistent with those of Fortescue that the duties of the secular prince include 'making, and ordeyning to be made, lawis, with comoun assent of his peple, for reule of alle his lege men, not oonli in contractis and couenauntis aboute propirte and therto purtenauncis, or in keping pees, but also in alle othire maner of gouernauncis longing to the comoun profite.'[44] At other times, and with at least equal pertinence, his views may be glimpsed, as it were, awry. They may, for example, be recovered through stray or seemingly incidental linguistic choices and images, moments when he lets fall an assumption about governance on his way to some other argumentative destination. Or they may be found in bits and pieces of practical observation strewn almost incidentally through his work for varied purposes of exemplification. When such fragmentary indications are assembled, a surprisingly well articulated view of the later medieval state begins to emerge.

Noticeable throughout Pecock's writings is a kind of syncretism, in which the vocabulary and imagery of governance imbues religious discussion, but with implications that exceed its immediate context and purpose. Consider, as an example, his reflections on traditions of the Sabbath. He notes that the practice of forgoing gainful work one day each week is not based on revelation, but is a 'gouernaunce' which is 'moral in law of kynde' and that it will never be revoked because it is 'grounded in lawe of kynde, that is to seie, in doom of pure resoun' (*Donet*, p. 129). A *gouernaunce*, for Pecock, is something like a practice or rule-governed observance. The *lawe of kynde* is natural law, originally God-given, but susceptible to logical investigation and substantiation.[45] The *doom of pure resoun* is not an intuitive but a rational, logical, and often syllogistic exercise. So understood, Pecock's remark proves consistent with the general trend of his argumentation, which presses constantly towards enlargement of the sphere of natural and rational understanding. So robust is this sphere in Pecock's view that it leaves only a relative handful of matters—such as the arcana of the trinity or the mystery of the eucharist— reliant for their acceptance upon revelation or scriptural authority. This model of government grounded in laws and ruled by reason is, in the first instance, religiously derived, but its implications as a general model for statecraft can hardly be ignored. This discussion of religious *gouernaunce* offers an inextricable fusion of a synodal and a parliamentary process, issuing in something approaching a unified philosophy of rule.

Pecock's faith in rational deliberation over matters of religious faith regularly spills over into declarations of support for collective decision making in civil as well as devotional spheres. The breadth of his thinking on these subjects is often expressed through micro-myths of origin and hypotheses of social contract. In the case of the Sabbath, for example, he imagines that one 'may and oughte hoolde as for a likely trouthe or a likeli opinioun,' that men might have agreed among themselves to set aside a day of prayer, with apostles and fathers consenting to their determination. Thus the determination of the day of the Sabbath becomes a matter of political process, grounded in the exercise of human reason. Consider this remarkable admixture of an overtly political vocabulary in the temporary service of a theological argument:

> bi doom of good pollitik resoun and profitable gouernaunce and good reule, the peple chese of her owne deuocioun, withoute comaunding of the prelatis in tho daies, to be taken to hem oon daie in the weke, at the leest, euen as bi lijk doom of good pollicye thei chese with fre deuocioun . . . placis and housis or templis whidir men schulde come forto therynne to gider in comune. (*Donet*, p. 132)

The analogies of this kind of associational and foundational thinking with various post-Aristotelian theories of the natural state are amply evident.

Equally evident is the easy migration of terms and concepts of *pollitik* reason, profitable *gouernaunce,* good *reule,* and good *pollicye,* across and between the bounds of religious and civil practice.

Pecock's choice of the term *gouernaunce* to describe habits, regulations, and practices is, as I have suggested, somewhat independent of what he might call *reule,* or terms of legal and political association per se. Nevertheless, this informal enlargement of the sphere of *gouernaunce* suggests the existence of an insecurely bounded but enlarged zone in which matters of human, as opposed to divine, choice and value are paramount. Thus the project of his *Repressor* is founded not upon scriptural authority but rather a delimitation of such authority, in favor of the 'doom of natural resoun, which is moral lawe of kinde and moral lawe of God, writun in the book of lawe of kinde in mennis soulis' (p. 18). Natural *resoun* is the taproot of Pecock's philosophy of biblical interpretation, but its fruits and branches are available to all, and for purposes broader than exegesis or scriptural supplementation. Elsewhere, he speaks of 'thilke forest of lawe of kinde which God plauntith in mannis soule,' and he extends the social resonance of his analogy by likening the branches of this forest to those brought by uplandish men to London on Midsummer's Eve, these branches available for harvest both by clerics and by laymen 'for to delyvere hem to citeseins in Londoun that her housis be maad the more honest ther with' (pp. 29–30). The fruits of this forest are open to laypersons as well as clerics, and have a determinative role in the arrangements by which all persons choose to govern themselves, as well as in establishing the conditions of good citizenship. Natural reason alone cannot ground articles of faith, but it is responsible for the greater share of the laws available to mankind. As Pecock ambitiously, or even rather aggressively, puts it, 'The more deel and party of Goddis hool lawe to man in erthe, and that bi an huge gret quantite ouer the remanent parti of the same lawe, is groundid sufficiently . . . in the inward book of lawe of kinde and of moral philosophie, and not in the book of Holi Scripture' (pp. 39–40).[46]

Pecock's views, such as his notorious harangues of the later 1440s in support of episcopal absenteeism and avoidance of responsibilities for preaching, had always excited controversy. During and after his 1457 heresy trial his accusers leaned heavily on his preference for natural reason over the authority of scripture. Gascoigne, inveterate opponent and his most unrelenting critic, retrospectively critiques the contentions of his 1457 sermon for their overreliance on natural reason ('non volunt homines sequi sacrarum scripturarum auctoritatem sed humanae racionis sensum'), and for their illicit use of natural philosophy in their conclusions ('philosophiam naturalem false applicant ad suum intentum').[47] Likewise, according to Gascoigne, he was accused at his 1457 trial of scornfully refusing assent to the Fathers unless their writings were confirmed by natural reason ('dicendo "Vath!" de scriptis eorum sanctorum nisi racione naturali dicta sua probarent'—p. 214). Not that Pecock himself had failed to provide his opponents with ample illustration of his preference for natural reason over scripture. This preference is boldly affirmed throughout his work, as in this declaration from his *Folower:* 'y seie, write and teche . . . bi the largist book of autorite that euer god made, which is the doom of resoun, and also bi the grettist doctour that is a this side god him silf, which is resoun' (pp. 9–10). The actual charges against Pecock, when the time came, tended to be very specific and prosecutorial, in the sense of emphasizing points demonstrably at variance with acceptable doctrines and credal statements. At the top of the list, for example, was his suggestion that one need not believe that Christ actually descended to hell. Nevertheless, in his confession, Pecock insisted on brushing past such cavils to identify his own most central guilt as an overreliance on natural reason and a preference for the judgments of reason over biblical authority. Thus he went to the heart of the matter by indicting himself, as reported in the Englishing of his abjuration, of 'presumeng of myn owne natural witte and preferring the natural iugement of raison before th'Olde Testament and the Newe and th'auctorite and determinacion of oure modre Holy Chirche.'[48]

Kantik Ghosh explains that the 'realm of the natural' dominates Pecock's theology, and leads to his preference for processes of reason over text-based authority.[49] Moreover, once reason has been put in play, its implications are increasingly difficult to contain or control. The realm of the natural is an unbounded one, and leads Pecock finally to what Ghosh calls 'a Utopian rationalist idealism,' offered 'as a solution to all religious ills.' An intended solution to religious ills, indeed, and its utopian vision does not stop at the church door. For Pecock constantly transgresses the boundary between the ecclesiastical and the civil, invariably at the expense of the former and to the augmentation of the latter. One area of such transgression results from an incessant temptation to enrich his writings by analogies and images of the natural state. Under the aegis and sponsorship of medieval exemplarity, illustrative instances and narratives of daily life repeatedly surface in the 'high' matter of his theological and philosophical texts. Mishtooni Bose has recently explained this aspect of Pecock's writing in terms of his departure from the practice of high theology, in favor of a more philosophically based endeavor to influence a lay reading public. Discovering a precedent in Aquinas's suggestion that 'techniques of disputation depend for their success on a disputant's willingness to adapt material and argumentative grounds according to the expectations and assumptions of his interlocutor,' she shows how Pecock grounds his imagistic experiments on his and his audience's shared reliance upon an unwritten 'lawe of kinde.' The principles of this law, she observes, are established by the fruits of his readers' 'own social observation.' In this endeavor to enlist the natural capacities of the reader's 'lay intellect,' she locates the rationale for his evocation of 'the concreteness of the rituals and quotidian practices of the city.'[50]

So prone is Pecock to illustrations from homely examples drawn from the daily life of medieval institutions and systems of economic exchange that a virtually intact rendition of everyday mid-fifteenth-century social arrangements emerges from his texts. Doubting the necessity that truths of moral philosophy be confirmed in the Bible, or that all religious practices are grounded in the Bible, he turns for an illustrative instance to guild organization and practices of consumption. Just as moral philosophy occupies its own sphere, and need not solicit biblical authority for its conclusions, so one might be asked, '"Where findest thou it groundid in tailour craft,' whanne that a point or a treuthe and a conclusion of sadeler craft is affermed.' Or if one were asked, '"Where fyndist thou it groundid in bocheri?" whanne a point or a treuthe and conclusioun of masonrie is affermed' (*Repressor*, p. 49). The crafts, he urges, in agreement with civic practice of the day, are fundamentally distinct, even when they might seem allied. But what, he wonders, if crafts do not keep to their bounds, as when spurriers and cutlers gild their spurs and knives?

> For certis though the sporier and the cuteler be leerned in thilk point of goldsmyth craft which is gilding, . . . yit thilk point of gilding is not of her craft, but oonli of goldsmyth craft: and so the craftis ben vnmedlid, though oon werkman be leerned in hem bothe and vse hem bothe, right as if oon man had lernid the al hool craft of goldsmythi and the al hool craft of cutleri, and wolde holde schoppis of bothe. (p. 50)

Although marshaled for altogether different purposes, this vision of an array of crafts each keeping its 'seueralte in boundis' is simultaneously a vision of civic order. One might argue that Pecock's excursus on crafts is essentially the 'vehicle' or 'ground' for an argument, the 'tenor' of which is a point about the separate provinces of moral law and scripture; yet the metaphorical vehicle cannot be said simply to disappear from consideration. Rather, it lingers, attaching itself to other such images to form an effective social imaginary within Pecock's text.

Again and again Pecock returns to the circumstances of civil life and organization, as in his extensively illustrated contention that many things unaddressed in scripture are no less real for that. In a remarkable passage, he inventories elements of daily life unmentioned in scripture:

> In al Holi Scripture it is not expressid . . . that a lay man not preest schulde were a breche, or that he schulde were a cloke, or that he schulde were a gowne, or that he schulde die wollen clooth into other colour than is the colour of scheep, or that men schulden bake eny fleisch or fisch in an ovyn, or that men schulde make and vse clockis forto knowe the houris of the dai and nyght. . . . Also noughwhere in Holi Scripture is mensioun mad or eny ensaympling doon, that a womman schulde were upon her heer and heed eny couerchief of lynnen threde or of silk. (p. 118)

And so on through such matters as the Englishing of the Bible (suitable, he believes, for laymen); to the shaving of beards; to jesting, running, leaping, shouting, playing at games; to singing, playing, and laughing; to the brewing of beer and ale. The truth, he urges, of none of these practices or 'gouer-naunces' is to be known from scripture alone, or scripture at all. These are man-made practices, developed within the natural world, and susceptible either to lawful or unlawful use.

Pecock is, above all, an enthusiast of his own arguments, and his enthusiasm often carries him beyond his immediate purposes and into deeper water. Starting with the premise that many worthy clerical practices are unfairly condemned by Lollard critics because they lack the warrant of scripture, he moves into the more challenging zone of practices that are neutral in themselves but lawful if done in God's service (singing, playing, and laughing), to practices unlikely to be done for God but nevertheless extant in the world ('Where is it also grondid in Holi Scripture that men myghten allowe-abili or schulden pleie in word bi bourding, or in deede by rennyng or leping or schuting, or bi sitting at the merels, or bi casting of coitis?'—p. 120), and finally into practices which conduce to sin (such as brewing and consuming ale and beer), the vice of which is not condemned in scripture, but that must nevertheless be condemned on more practical grounds, since they are seen to promote sin and shorten life. Carried forward by a law of unintended argumentative consequences, Pecock sets out to defend clerical prerogative, but ends up as an expositor of mundane and worldly practices that elude scriptural authority altogether and that must be evaluated, pragmatically, in their own terms. Given the vigor of his prose, Pecock might fairly be considered an inadvertent celebrant of everyday life. Busily going about its chosen activities, the world as he portrays it is self-governing and self-governed, possessed of engrossing interest not only as a creation of God, but in its own right.

I do not, of course, claim complete exceptionality for the homeliness of Pecock's anecdotage. The world as a source of illustrative incident constantly informs homiletic texts like Robert Manning's *Handling Sin* and John Mirk's *Festial,* and even the most cloistered writings such as Julian of Norwich's *Revelations* rely constantly on the phenomena of daily life to convey elusive spiritual conceptions. So, too, are aggressively worldly behaviors mingled with spiritual intimations in Langland's fair field of folk and among Chaucer's pilgrim band. But even Chaucer's pilgrimage is assigned a spiritual objective, and his surprisingly verbose and doctrinaire Parson, his voice so long postponed, is granted the final word. In other words, these writings, however worldly in inflection, retain a vigorous and nonperfunctory spiritual frame. Within this frame, worldly experience is ultimately assessed according to a celestial repository of values and judgments. Whereas—and rather paradoxically, given his avowedly Christian and aspirationally orthodox intentions—Pecock comes closer than any of these writers to breaking the frame. *Resoun* is his wedge, and he is the advocate of reason's employment—particularly in the religious sphere, but, derivatively, in relation to worldly arrangements as well. No less in his way than Fortescue a natural philosopher, Pecock accords full and virtually independent weight and meaning to the things of this world, regarded steadily and in their own right.

6. *SEDICIOUS* PEACOCK

The diverse series of interrogations, public humiliations, and after-the-fact curtailments that might collectively be labeled 'Pecock's heresy trial' was obviously countenanced by, and was to some extent orchestrated by, Archbishop Bourchier. But, as both Jeremy Catto and Wendy Scase have observed, his time of troubles must be regarded as civil as well as ecclesiastical. Scase flatly, and correctly, declares that 'a major motive behind Pecock's downfall was political'—not necessarily that he was caught in Lancastrian-Yorkist crossfire, but political nonetheless in the sense that his downfall was at least jointly concocted by the civil arm.[51] She agrees with Catto's conclusion that 'proceedings against Pecock only began in response to the complaints of lay councillors and officers of the City of London.'[52]

Pecock seems to have laid himself open to charges of political conniv-ance, and thus to civil as well as ecclesiastical reprisals, by injudicious utter-ances. His archenemy Gascoigne cites an ill-considered 1456 letter to Thomas Canyng, mayor of London. Gascoigne characterizes this letter as extremely suspect, with regard to disturbance of the faith and also to insurrection within the realm of England ('et anno Xti 1456 misit literam suam Majori Londoni-arum, Canyng nomine, qua lecta ut valde suspiciosa perturbacionis fidei, et insurreccionis in regno Angliae').[53] This letter seems, moreover, to have contributed to many of Pecock's subsequent difficulties when the mayor brought it to the attention of royal officials ('idem Major misit illam literam regi Henrico Sexto; quae ipsum et dominos suos in odium ipsius Pecok epis-copi multum excitavit'). Gascoigne, in fact, links it directly to Pecock's pro-bation before Archbishop Bourchier and the twenty-four doctors. The in-surrectionary contents of Pecock's inflammatory letter cannot be known. But it must be said that Pecock's own writings abound in naturalizations and de-mystifications of regality, of a sort that could hardly commend them to a seated king.

In any case, this letter in combination with other affronts seems to have angered Henry VI and the lay lords, and may be credited as partial provo-cation to a letter of John viscount Beaumont to Henry VI on 24 June 1457.[54] In this letter (preserved in the register of Richard Asshton abbot of Peter-borough and thus at least a semipublic document) Beaumont complains of Pecock's transgressions and urges royal action. In these circumstances, the languages and prosecutorial strategies of political sedition and theological heresy are inextricably confused. Himself a lay lord and prominent Lan-castrian, Beaumont couches his assault theologically, in terms of Pecock's 'diuerse conclusions . . . to the most pernicious and next to peruercyoun of our faith . . . sith Makamete was,' and proposes that Pecock's writings be ex-amined ecclesiastically, by 'the best clerkes of bothe vniuersites.'[55] Even so, the proposed advantages to Henry are political as well as spiritual. Beaumont reminds him that the foundation of Henry V's subsequent successes was his persecutory activities, citing the activities of previous princes 'and in speciall

of your owne fadyr of most noble memorie, that first began with mighti pun-
ischyng and suppressing of enemies of the faith and Chirche, and aftir all his
dayes had victoryes of his enemies and did gret thynges.' Moreover, Henry
accomplishing his parallel task, the way will lie open to greater triumphs,
not necessarily limited to the ecclesiastical realm: 'this don and yt be as fame
renneth and myghtly punished, douthtyth not but gretter victories and many
shall shortly folowe.' Evidently, a commission including masters in theology and doctors in canon and civil law, numbering, in Gascoigne's account,
twenty-four in all, examined his writings and declared them erroneous and
heretical.[56] Pecock's ultimate trial appears to have been orchestrated by Archbishop Bourchier. But the very mixed and tantalizing recitals of these events
by contemporary chroniclers suggests a strong civil presence throughout.
Note the mixture of civil and ecclesiastical venues and personnel in Scase's
excellent summary of the matter: 'According to Whethamstede's register,
Pecock was brought before a meeting of the Council at Westminster, was
charged by the archbishop, and expressed his willingness to recant. . . . In
Gascoigne's version Pecock was expelled from the Council which met around
11 November. His expulsion was announced at St Paul's Cross on 13 November 1457 by Dr John Pynchbek who at the same time issued a condemnation
of Pecock's teaching on the creed on behalf of the archbishop and bishops.
On 20 November 1457, and again on 28 November, at Lambeth, where secular lords were also present, Pecock appeared before the archbishop and revoked his heresies' (p. 109).

This admixture of the civil and the ecclesiastical also shows forth in
the language of Pecock's opponents. Accused of perfidious doctrines, Pecock is also described from the outset in terms of civil disorder. According
to Whethamstede, a certain doctor, perfidious of doctrine, 'insurrexit infra
regnum'—rose up in the kingdom—but with 'insurrexit' as the customary
term under which rebellion was identified and prosecuted, already identifying him as a threat to civil as well as religious order. A letter particularly
revealing in its linguistic texture is addressed to Henry VI by Robert Stillington, canon of Wells, and Thomas Lowe, bishop of Asaph, probably in
September 1458, subsequent to Pecock's abjuration, as part of a vehement and
continuing campaign opposing his reinstatement to any ecclesiastical position. There, the terms of their condemnation certainly include Pecock's purported heresies, but also identify him as a 'sedicious persoune' (f. 322r).[57] With
the progressive rhetorical and prosecutorial commingling of heresy and sedition throughout the fifteenth century, this emphasis on the worldly aspect

of Pecock's transgression is no surprise; that heresy constituted a threat to the laws and statutes of the realm and a derogation of the royal prerogative had been assumed and understood since the reign of Henry V.[58] Yet Lowe and Stillington have more to say on this matter: 'the saide Reynold distrueth not oonly the pouair and iurisdiction of regalie and preesthode, and . . . suengly subuertethe all ordre and direction of the lawe positiue and polletique gouuernaunce amonge cristen pouple, as wel in spiritualte as temporalte' (f. 322v). This 'lawe positiue' is not ecclesiastical law, and neither is it Pecock's own natural law, but rather the civil law of the land.[59]

Pecock lays himself open to Lowe and Stillington's rebuke with his written views, including the belief that the civil law of England is superior to ecclesiastical law in its ability to restrain bad practices based on customary claims: 'The reule of the kingis lawe of engelond is more resonable and more pure and more avoiding the seid inconuenientis and myschefis than is the spiritual lawe of the chirche' (*Reule*, p. 333). Pecock in fact comes very close to the key recommendation of Fortescue's *Governance* in his suggestion that the prince's powers of taxation should be limited by legislation and common consent: 'not seching neither taking of hise legis her propir godis without consent of the comunalte and withoute greet neede of the comunaltees profit. . . . [And] that he take no service of hem agens her wil ferther or in eny other wise than in his resonable lawe afore maad bi consent of the same legis' (*Reule*, p. 337).[60] Pecock's views are registering in areas well beyond his own ecclesiastical and theological purview, touching the law of state and the whole matter of 'polletique gouuernaunce.' That Pecock is seen as sponsor of a 'secte' devoted to promulgating his views is consistent enough with the prosecutorial language of the day, but, again, the terms in which his sect is described possess a strong civil coloration; his followers are not simply coreligionists, but are 'faultours and adherentes' (f. 322v)—aligned with him, that is, in the language of treasonous insurrection. A philosophically allied letter from Henry VI to the chancellor and masters of the University of Oxford likewise pursues this matter of adherents, finding that they 'collude' with Pecock and labeling them 'sedicious' in their intent; relying on the language of military repression rather than ecclesiastical inquisition, the king promises to follow in the steps of his progenitors by defending the Church, not just by heresy trials but through armed encounter, 'to th'effusion of our blode and extremite of our lyf.'[61] Equally suggesting Pecock's encroachment upon the secular sphere is a 1458–59 letter from Archbishop Bourchier seeking to unearth books by Pecock in the province of Canterbury

and describing them as riddled with seditions, divisions, and scandals ('cedi-
ciones, seccionesque, et scandala').[62]

One wishes, of course, to know more about the lost letter to Canyng, but
ample explanation exists in his surviving writings for the general consterna-
tion he seems to have caused. Royal accomplices Lowe and Stillington catch
something of the volatility of the moment, and the sense that Pecock's writings were always potentially combustible, in their letter to Henry VI, urging against the Pope's intervention and Pecock's restoration to his see. They
argue that Pecock's restoration would be unwise, owing to 'th'inconstance
and fraille disposicion of the pouple these dayes' (f. 322v)[63]—referring, presumably, not only to the instability of their religious views but also, as Catto
points out, to such civil disturbances as those of 1449–50, a Kentish rising
of 1456, and the possibility of riotous assemblies in London in 1457.[64] Within
the interpretative context provided by such sentiments and such events, Pecock's writings turn out to abound in troublesome excursions into the domain
of worldly circumstances and contingencies.

Consider one line of speculation in his *Repressor,* for its potential to unsettle a reigning monarch and his counselors. No single rule or state of affairs,
he argues, persists for long, or resists the pressure of external events. Before
analyzing a man's deed or *gouernaunce,* weight must be given 'for and bi his
causis, hise motyues, and hise circumstauncis.' And, drawing a conclusion
with considerable reverberation in the changeable world of later Lancastrian
England, he argues that *politik* ordinances do not long persist in the world:
'moral gouernaunces of mennis conuersacioun, namelich suche that ben politik (that is to seie, suche wherbi prelatis of the chirche or othere ouerers gou-
erne othere men vndir hem bi spiritual policie or worldli policie) stonden
neuere thorugh long tymes vndir oon reule, neither vndir oon maner to be
doon, neither stonden in alle placis like wise or vndir lijk reule to be doon'
(*Repressor,* pp. 105–6).[65] This is, of course, a common enough sentiment, but
nevertheless potentially disturbing to settled rule. Pecock first perturbs
the situation for secular governors by refusing to stop at the boundaries of the
spiritual but insisting on the applicability of his point to matters of *worldli
policie.* Then he solicits additional distress by expressing his view of political change 'out of place' by eschewing the comforting generic enclosure of a
'Fall of Princes' or some other textual format in which simple changeability
and political uncertainty are subsumed within a stable providential and homiletic frame.

Writings generated in opposition to Pecock reveal again and again that his choices and procedures are both dangerous in themselves and heightened in their danger by their potential to inflame an unstable external public. His choice of the English vernacular; his eschewal of the sermon in favor of the written word; the unpredictable consequences of manuscript transmission and circulation—all were disturbing to a political/clerical establishment that considered itself to be living in dangerous times.

The vernacular as a language of religious controversy had, of course, been significantly curtailed since the 1407–9 *Constitutions* of Archbishop Arundel,[66] and if Pecock thought his intention of defending the episcopate against his detractors would gain his works a place among the few exceptions he was ultimately to be mistaken. Gascoigne and others had certainly not gotten over complaining about his unseemly choice of English as a language of theological discussion, and this problem is confounded by his additional decision to circulate his work in written form. As Gascoigne has it, he deserves rebuke for various causes, including that he wrote of serious matters in English, and that these writings were more apt to lead readers and hearers astray than to profit them ('quia scripsit tales profundas materias in Anglicis, quae magis aptae errant laedere legentes et audientes quam illis proficere').[67] Pecock retained his faith in writing until the end. He had been an occasional, and controversial, sermonist, including his much-debated sermon devoted to bishops' duties delivered in 1447 at Paul's Cross. Yet, controversy having arisen, Pecock found himself battling shadow opponents. An extant summary statement of his views on this occasion has him insisting that if anyone comes forward with objections to his statements he should have an opportunity to reply in writing, and that, if no such contradictor appears, then-Archbishop Stafford should pronounce that his statements have gone uncontradicted ('peto me ad sibi respondendum in scriptis de die in diem admitti. Quod si nullus huiusmodi contradictor inueniatur, vos auctoritate vestra pronuncietis illas conclusions pro ista vice non habere contradictorem').[68] Here imagined is a different kind of recourse to written argument than that of his vernacular books, since its addressees would probably be found principally amongst the episcopate and other learned controversialists. Yet the move toward writing and written response is paralleled by Pecock's own desire to move his case from *audientes* to *legentes,* and to avail himself of the less finite or temporary means of persuasion that writings afford. The accusations against him refer constantly to the extent to which he not only wrote and taught against the tenets of the Church, but that he also published his views; and not only did he offend with publication ('publicatione') but with other sorts of promulgation too ('propalatione,' suggesting something like 'broadcast' or 'wide diffusion').

Gabby, abstruse, often awkwardly phrased, what demand might they have satisfied and what popularity enjoyed? His adversary Gascoigne observes derisively that his many adherents, slathering him with the oil of adulation, were accustomed to style him the most learned man of his time, or 'maximum scientificum mundi.'[69] Polemical intentions aside, Gascoigne's remarks do seem to concede Pecock's popularity. A number of other indications suggest Pecock's success in gaining wider purchase for his views. One is the campaign against his writings conducted at the time of his trial and after his abjuration, as documented by Bourchier's letter deploring his influence in Canterbury and a letter of Henry VI asking that his books be searched out in Oxford.[70] Despite active attempts at book-burning at the time of his trial and in Oxford and elsewhere,[71] the interesting thing is that—though only in single and isolated copies—so many of his writings survive. A letter of Edward IV to Pope Sixtus IV, written in 1475/6, complains that 'after the death of said Reginald, the writings and treatises composed by him multiplied in such wise that not only the laity but churchmen and scholastic graduates scarcely studied anything else, so that the pestiferous virus circulated in many human breasts.'[72] Even allowing for the inflation and alarmism customary in such cases, this expression of concern, nearly twenty years after Pecock's accusation and abjuration, would seem to argue for continued interest and traffic in his works. Pecock complains in the *Donet* that prior drafts of this work, and other works, have enjoyed an unintended circulation; that they 'ben runne abrood and copied ayens my wil and myn entent,' and that this has occurred 'bi vncurtesie and vndiscredioun of freendis, into whos singuler sight y lousid tho writingis to go' (pp. 6–7). This remark might be interpreted only as immodesty on the one hand or self-protection on the other, except that it is corroborated by less friendly statements.

Underlying all this distress is a sense that Pecock's writings are gaining an illicit hearing by harnessing new technologies of writing and circulation. As Beaumont puts it, 'Yt ys so now that grete noyse rennyth that ther shuyld be diuerse conclusions labored and subtilly entended to be enprented in mennes hertis, by privy, by also vnherd, meenes.'[73] 'Vnherd' is something of a pun here; Pecock's means of circulation, in writing for private reading, are both exceptional and unanticipated, even at this late date, and also silent, in the sense of their potential for transmission in private and unauthorized settings. Compounding all this unease are the continuing fears provoked by the Lollard heresy—a heresy seen to present opportunities for rulers to behave in statesmanlike ways (as in Beaumont's own letter), but also a source of concern with respect to the loyalty and stability of the populace.[74]

So far is Pecock from regarding himself as a spokesman for any sort of laicization that in the *Repressor* and elsewhere he refers to his argumentative opponents as the 'lay peple' and enemies of 'the clergie' (p. 136). Yet, ironically, this aloof defender of clerical privilege seems to have had considerable popular appeal, this antipopulist to have struck a number of rather populist notes. His faith in natural reason and, however incidentally, the appearance in his works of an informal and politically inflected vocabulary for the description of civil existence may have been among its sources of appeal. Certainly, orthodox apologists, like John Bury in his answer to the first book of the *Repressor,* with his dedication to Archbishop Bourchier and its praise of Bishop Lowe, single out his exaltation of natural reason over the authority of scripture as one cause of the need for his condemnation.[75] For these and other reasons, Pecock was brought to heel, in ways not entirely dissimilar from the requirements the Yorkists would impose upon Fortescue some fourteen years later. As previously discussed, Edward would require Fortescue formally, and with attention to specified points, to retract his writings on the legitimacy of Lancastrian succession as a price of survival and with a bribe of possible rehabilitation. Pecock, like Fortescue, seems eager to participate in the revision and redirection of his own previous project. When his books were called in for scrutiny in 1457, he appeared, according to Gascoigne's rather scornful account of the matter, to have made hasty attempts at revisionary correction. He made an initial argument that he should be responsible only for those he translated in the past three years (this notion of translation already injecting a slight note of disavowal) and was able to correct with his own hand: 'voluit inducere coram illo archiepiscopo omnes libros suos quos fecit infra triennium ante illum diem . . . sed non pro aliis libris suis quos ipse episcopus Pecok ante illum triennium tradidit aliis hominibus, quia, ut dixit, illi libri non fuerunt correcti per ipsum Pecok.'[76] When he did submit his books, Gascoigne says, they were found rife with cancellations and erasures and new insertions in his own hand ('inventi tunc fuerunt illi libri ipsius Pecok in pluribus locis cancellati et rasi in

diversis locis, et iterum de novo scripti per eundem episcopum'—p. 211).[77]
This belated and piecemeal attempt reveals Pecock—as constantly in his
career—to be incompletely unaware of the extent of the forces arrayed
against him, and the extent to which his writings, when carefully inspected,
were bound to cause offense. The result was that Pecock was forced not only
to abjure—first in Latin and then, publicly, in English—stipulating that his
own books should not be retained, urging their delivery to the archbishop,
and assenting to their public burning:

> suche bookes . . .deliuere in all goodly haste vnto my saide lord of Can-
> terbury. . . . To thes declaratcion of myn conuersion and repentaunce,
> I haue openly assent that my said bookis, werkis, writingis, for consid-
> eracion and cause aboue reherssed, be deputed to the fier and openly
> brent into example and terrour of all othre.[78]

Whether Pecock was, as imagined by the chroniclers, forced to take a hand
in the burning itself is less clear. But there can be no doubt of the tenor of
the event. Whethamstede says his books were dramatically burnt, upon his
utterance of the foregoing words.[79] Gascoigne supposes that had Pecock, at
the end of his revocation, come any closer to the fire, the irate crowd would
happily have burnt him as well: 'si ipse descendisset ad ignem, in quo libri
sui comburebantur, populus ibi eum projecisset in illum ignem.'[80]

By considering two such different cases within the bounds of a single chapter, I do not mean to elide very substantial differences in the argumentative
traditions of the legalist and the theologian, or in the immediate purposes
of their arguments or in their respective fates. Yet the fact that each of the
two most energetic and creative authors of vernacular argumentative prose
in the mid-fifteenth century was required in the end to disavow his own
writings, and even to participate in their figurative or real destruction, invites reflection upon the difficulties which these unstable times imposed even
upon self-styled defenders of loyalty. In Fortescue's and Pecock's choices,
we reexperience the ever-painful collision between the relatively autonomous world of speculative or utopian discourse and the fractious and insti-
tutionally implicated arrangements with which it was forced to contend. The
fraught circumstances of the mid-fifteenth century overbore each writer's
imaginative attempt to remake the world. Fortescue was required to pro-

duce self-revisionary writing as a condition of reconciliation. Worse still for Pecock, refused the restoration he had sought and forbidden ever to write again. One of the conditions of his last confinement at Thorney Abbey was 'that he haue nothing to write with, ne stuff to write vpon.'[81] For Fortescue, the injunction was to keep writing, although, as it were, against himself. Whereas Pecock was condemned to silence, and also, by condoning the destruction of his books, to relinquish hope of his rehabilitation by subsequent tradition.

four

Waiting for Richard

Yorkist Verse, 1460–1461

JOHN WATTS HAS OBSERVED THAT SUCCESS IN FIFTEENTH-CENTURY
political debate depended upon an ability 'to harness "accepted principles"
of the mid-fifteenth-century polity.'[1] One front in this effort was comprised
by a handful of extremely effective Yorkist poems written in and around the
climactic year 1460. Relying, as they do, on capture and redeployment of
familiar materials, these poems practice a form of what may be called ideological bricolage. Here I introduce the term 'ideology' not as some master determinant of the poem's objectives, but rather in relation to a considerably
more piecemeal and dispersed operation.[2] The ideological impulse, as I am
here describing it, eschews the allure of total explanatory systems, relying instead on the smallest constituent elements of conviction. These are the key-
words, turns of phrase, and implicit structurations that underpin or inspire
belief.[3] Rather than operate under conditions of disguise and disavowal, the
poem's enlistment of ideologically charged materials is fully, even blatantly,
on display.[4] Marked for attention by their enriched symbolic potentiality,
these materials may thus be understood less as practicing than as 'practiced

upon'. Far from determining the contours of the poem in which they appear, they are the objects of the poet's designs. I do not, however, mean to propose the poem as a kind of trophy case for these materials' static display. The poem's claim on them is staked, as it were, on the fly. It demonstrates an ability to claim them *in the act of claiming them:* by building them into a narrative of one's own, or one's party's own, accession to power.[5]

Especially in the transitional years of 1460–61, Yorkist verse is ardently but awkwardly aspirational, committed to the imaginary enactment of an imminent, but long postponed and still elusive, legitimation. The hypothetical and utopian element of these poems predominates to the extent that the precise terms of the legitimation they seek is not always even completely clear: varying from week to week and circumstance to circumstance, it might be the return of Richard duke of York to a seat of unimpeachable influence as a magnate of the realm, his designation as Henry's successor, his coronation, the survival of his son and heir Edward, or Edward's own kingship. In every case, though, the poems themselves are participants in, rather than simply observers of, this process. They not only articulate but also *enact* patterns of movement from exile to arrival, from exclusion to incorporation into sanctioned authority.[6]

In this chapter I concentrate on two poems, in order to illustrate their knack for a particular form of political action, which is to solidify broadly held patterns, expectations, beliefs, yearnings, and opinions in forms favorable to the accomplishment of a Yorkist political agenda. One is the verses posted on the gates of Canterbury, 1460, as incorporated in the Davies chronicle.[7] The other, sharing many impulses and techniques, is an addendum to Holkham archives Deed no. 116, recently edited, with commentary, by Richard Beadle.[8] The former is easily accessible only to those whose libraries possess a set of Camden Society publications, and, as a convenience to the reader, J. S. Davies's original edition is reprinted in full as Appendix 1 to this chapter. The full edition of the latter is more easily accessible in *Medium Aevum,* but, with thanks to Richard Beadle I have reprinted his edited text (without commentary) as Appendix 2 to this chapter.

I. CANTERBURY, 1460: FROM PROPHECY TO ASTROLOGY AND BACK AGAIN

Autumn 1459 found Richard duke of York's forces scattered at Ludlow, with Richard himself fleeing to Ireland while Warwick, Salisbury, and the main party headed for Calais. The Yorkist lords were attainted at a subsequent parliament in Coventry, suffering confiscation of their lands and goods. Resisting Somerset's attempts at Lancastrian recapture, Calais became a center of Yorkist agitation and intrigue. Issuing from Calais was a stream of letters, proclamations, provocateurs, and spies, targeting the entire Southeast, with Canterbury as a particular objective. In June 1460, the Yorkist earls would embark for England, with Canterbury as their first important destination, to be followed in September by Richard's arrival from Ireland. In the meantime—during the Lenten period of March–April 1460—a poem was written, addressed 'To the ryghte Worshypfulle Cyte of Caunterbury,' and, according to the 'Davies' chronicler, who preserved it, was 'sette vppon the yates of the cyte of Caunterbury.'[9]

This poem begins with what might be considered a ground-clearing maneuver. Its outer enclosure has the effect of unsettling the current political state of affairs—the mundane 'given' or political status quo—in favor of a set of possibilities more congenial to the installation of a new regime. I refer to the poem's initial claims for the ascendancy of astrology over prophecy. Astrology, we learn, possesses the power to set aside judgments of the senses and effects of memory:

> The celestialle influence on bodyes transytory
> Set asyde alle prophecyes, and alle commixtione
> Of iujementys sensualle to ofte in memory.

This being a 'state of England' poem, concerned with matters of good rule, the 'iujements sensualle' that dog the speaker's memory presumably involve that inescapable situation attested by direct ('sensualle') observation: the incumbency of Henry VI. For all his weaknesses, the problematic Henry was the sitting king, duly invested and now in the thirty-eighth year of his reign. As the same *Rolls of Parliament* that record Richard's attainder observe in Henry's behalf, the latter has 'for his tyme bee named, taken, and reputed King of Englond.'[10] As Henry would himself elaborate, at a later (and, for him, less happy) time: 'My father was King of England and peaceably possessed the crown of England for the whole of his reign. And his father and my grandfather were kings of the same realm. And I, a child in the cradle, was peaceably and without any protest crowned and approved as king by the whole realm, and wore the crown of England some forty years, and each and all of my lords did me royal homage and plighted me their faith.'[11]

More oppressively still, from the Yorkist point of view, this status quo was bolstered by a good deal of very effective pro-Lancastrian prophecy, dating especially from the first, hopeful years of the infant Henry's accession to the throne. This accession had been greeted with a rush of hopeful prophecy, remaining in circulation into the 1450s. The text of 'Lilium regnans,' in which a king will free the Holy Land; a purported letter from the Sultan of Syria predicting the advent of a hero-ruler; a prophecy that Henry will invent the Holy Cross; Henry as a 'Lion's Cub' under whom the church will prosper; the substantial (though finite) victories of 'Rex Henricus'; the Henrician prophecies gathered by John Shirley in MS Ashmole 59—all represent an auspicious surge during the first decades of Henry's reign.[12] These prophecies were countered in the 1450s by Yorkist alternatives—or at least prophecies left open to the possibility represented by Richard duke of York— such as 'The Cock in the North,' which imagines that the people might choose a new lord.[13] Nonetheless, a substantial body of countervailing Yorkist prophecy would be generated only with the accession of Edward IV. In 1460 existing or established prophecy was still mainly something to be gotten out from under and overthrown.[14] In that spirit our poet opens a second front, asserting the power of 'celestialle influence,' which can 'set aside alle prophecyes,' and alter the imprint of existing arrangements as sealed in people's memories.

An added virtue of celestial influence is its apparent objectivity, reliant not upon mere sense impressions, but upon *motion itself,* as expressed in and through the observable motions of the planets. Based on the Aristotelian idea that motion is the primary cause of change, planetary motions were widely understood to produce sublunar effects. Multiple systems of causality were introduced to explain the actual linkage, but the premise that 'transitory' bodies produced alterations in human affairs was widely embraced, as was its corollary, that worldly effects might in turn be forecasted.[15] Promised within this understanding was a new degree of verifiability and hence a new level of scientific stature.[16] Simultaneously, the astrologers' calculations were themselves gaining progressive refinement, and were accordingly assigned more and more cultural capital. On the growing precision of calculations in the mid-fifteenth century, J. D. North observes that 'One might well deplore the game they were playing for its sheer futility, but the fact remains that there was a growing professionalism in the best academic astrology.'[17] This somewhat equivocal, but definitely growing, repute was in turn available for interested appropriation, and in the situation of the midcentury it was especially adaptable to Yorkist purposes.

Although the Lancastrians themselves had previous recourse to astrological investigations,[18] the most visible astrological scandal of the century militated against dynastic security. This was the celebrated accusation of prognostication against Eleanor of Gloucester, which in turn opened scandalous and disturbing vistas on the life and prospects of Henry VI. To be sure, as North and Carey and others have emphasized, the crime of which Eleanor—and confederates Bolingbroke and Southwell and the Witch of Eye—stood accused is not astrology per se but rather plotting the king's death by necromancy and the black arts. Nevertheless, both Southwell and Bolingbroke were, in the words of North, 'practised astrologers,'[19] with Southwell an Oxford graduate in medicine and Bolingbroke principal of St. Andrews Hall at Oxford. And these confederates were understood to have predicted catastrophe or death for Henry VI. That astrology was consequentially involved is suggested by the royal rejoinder: two of the king's principal servants, John Langton and John Somerset, were charged to go into the matter, and a result of their efforts was an astrological treatise (not necessarily under their authorship but probably as a result of their encouragement) entitled 'Cum rerum motu . . . ' and devoted to the refutation of dire predictions against the king. Such rebuttals notwithstanding, astrology was widely understood to have raised grave questions about Henry VI's continuance in office, and to supersede other discourses bent on maintaining the status quo. In this union of astrology and politics we have an 'inflammable mix,'[20] and the Yorkists must have hoped that the flames would continue to lick Henry's feet.

Thus our poem invokes planetary motion in opposition to settled bets: to trump favorable pro-Lancastrian prophecies surrounding Henry VI's birth and mandate in France, and also to counter three decades' direct experience of Henry as sitting king. All this, in its first stanza. By the time the poem's ending is reached, a different state of affairs will prevail. Imaginatively, the poem's audience will have indulged an experience of welcome to Richard as its presumptive king. Having taken us from the situation of an aspirant king to that of a presumptive one, the poem finds itself with an altered agenda, with a reduced need for astrology's unsettling effects. Prophecy is, by contrast, the preferred medium of settled power. Having dispatched prophecy at its outset, the poem ends by reattaching itself to prophecy at its end.

The poem concludes with an addendum in a different metrical and stanzaic form; an addendum that, if not authorial, may be read as evidence of reception, and as an enthusiastic endorsement of all that has come before.

> The deed man gretethe yow welle,
> That ys iust trew as stelle,
> > With verray good entent,
> Alle the Reame of Englond
> Sone to louse from sorowes bond,
> > Be ryghte indifferent iugement.

But who is this 'deed man' who 'gretethe … welle' the audience of the poem, heralding a new era of justice and a liberation of England from 'sorowes bond'? This reference finds its lodging point in broadly Galfridian prophetic traditions circulating in England in midcentury and familiar to many members of this poem's audience. A crucial collection of such prophecies is BL MS Cotton Rolls ii.23, which may be dated to circa 1450, ten years before our poem, and includes a prophecy of the 'Thomas of Erceldoune' type entitled 'The Cock in the North.'[21] Amidst the varied animal symbolisms and other deliberately ambiguous prophetic elements of this poem, we learn that the flawed realm of England—'troy vntrewe'—will tremble to hear the words of a 'dede man.' This dead man will, however, announce a happy event, upon which all prophecies ('bridlyngton, bede, bokis, and Banaster [fourteenth-century William Banister][,] … Thomas [of Erceldoune], and merlyon') agree. According to the 'The Cock in the North,' this event is the choice of a new lord whose herald and sponsor the dead man will prove to be:

> Then shall saxons chese theym a lord,
> That shall rewle hem rightfully and bryng hem vndere.
> A dede man shall make be-twene hem a-corde,
> And this a ferly and a grete wondere.
>
> He that is ded and buryed in sight,
> Shall ryse agayn, and lyve in lond,
> In confortyng of a yong knyght
> That ffortune hath chosen to be here fere.

The presumed identification of the Saxons' new lord with Richard duke of York is fortified by the nature of MS Cotton Rolls ii.23, possessed of what R. H. Robbins identifies as a 'strongly Yorkist slant' (p. 310). Included in Cotton Rolls ii. 23 are such texts as 'The Prophecy Proffesid and j Pight,' which imagines a 'man of mykill might'—probably Richard—who, released from thralldom, will recover France.[22] Thus the 'deed man' of our 1460 poem merges with the 'dede man' of 'The Cock in the North,' as a herald of Richard's coming and the general release 'from sorowes bond' to attend that arrival. Supplemented by its enthusiastic early reader, the poem completes a circuit: from astrology as the preferred medium of the disempowered, back to prophecy as the preferred vehicle of the newly or prospectively empowered.[23]

2. CANTERBURY, 1460: THE KING'S ARRIVAL AS QUASI-LITURGICAL EVENT

Publicly posted on the gates of a city still nominally loyal to the king and still ruled by his deputies, our poem addresses a divided constituency. True, groundwork had been laid. 'Little Falconbridge,' whose activities are cited in the poem, had been working to build Yorkist consensus in the area. Soldiers loyal to Warwick had skirmished with followers of Somerset in Sandwich. Articles explaining the duke of York's position were sent to the archbishop of Canterbury—who, an early convert, was among those who met the Yorkist earls upon arrival at Sandwich 'wythe hys crosse before hym.'[24] Yet divisions remained. Lancastrian captains were in at least nominal charge of the town.[25] Even as Warwick and the Yorkists approached the city, some Lancastrian diehards counseled resistance: 'They that were nat frendely to the erles, counseyled the mayre and the comynalte for to ley gennes at the brege for to kepe thaym owte, and so a lytelle diuision there was among the citezens, but yt was sone ceased.'[26] And, despite the archbishop's rapid conversion, the priory as a whole continued as a center of Lancastrian sentiment and opposition, well into the reign of Edward IV.[27] Indicated in such a situation would seem to be not more partisanship but less, or at least more attention to consensus building among the potentially variable readership of the poem. Accordingly, the poem addresses its potentially fractured public in terms of the most broadly acknowledged ideas and structures pertaining to kingship—those public rituals and shared liturgies through which monarchy was crucially performed and reperformed, made and remade, within forms conducive to broad assent.

Most likely composed in the Calais propaganda mill while Richard's fortunes remained in eclipse, this poem represents an extraordinarily creative response to a variety of expository demands.[28] Its gift is to respond to these demands in its own terms, *as a poem*. Thus, even as its topicality creates a pressure for the immediate fulfillment of worldly aims, it remains fully possessed of its own 'textual condition,' of a text's equivocal relation to the world. Moreover, rather than conceal this condition of textuality, our poet seems deliberately to cultivate it. Eschewed are such obviously eventful genres as letter, 'excusation,' accusation, article, or proclamation, in favor of the ultra-stylized and 'literary' register of the *balade* tradition, replete with such hyper-textual devices as repetition and refrain, macaronic wordplay, complicated biblical and liturgical allusion. Analytical account must, in other words, be taken of this text's own formal autonomy[29]—an autonomy that, in any case, its hyper-literariness would hardly allow us to forget. For this poem accomplishes a good deal of social and political work precisely by enlisting form *as form* in the service of its extrapoetical objectives. Rather than treat formal precedents as empty or contentless bearers of topical meaning, this poem recruits to its purposes the inexorable dictates of planetary motion, the heightened expectations of prophecy, the rhythms of the liturgical cycle, the formalities of the royal entry, and the repetitive form of the refrain poem itself. More specifically, it employs the external form of the *balade*, with its characteristic emphasis on progression-within-repetition, to propose a number of mimetic circuits: from irresolution to new certainty, from deprivation to plenitude, from sorrow to joy, from expectation to fulfillment.

These mimetic circuits embrace the energies of some widely accepted ritual practices. One of these practices is that ceremony of royal 'entry' or *accessus,* in which the monarch's arrival is hailed as an occasion that alters a previously unacceptable situation of interregnum, travail, or ill-relations. Although the entry is a 'scripted' performance rather than a literary genre per se, entries were often written up after the fact, in poems and prose passages that are effectively 'generic' in a literary sense. Examples of this written genre would be Richard Maidstone's elaborate Latin verse account of Richard II's reconciliation with the City of London (1392); the detailed prose account in the *Gesta Henrici Quinti* of Henry V's triumphal entry into London after his victory at Agincourt; and Lydgate's account of the newly crowned Henry VI's entry into London, 1432.[30] All these texts are, like our present poem, marked by an overall structural 'turn' from deprivation to re-joicing (from Richard's anger to his restoration of London's privileges; from stalemate in France to Henry V's apparent reconquest; from mourning for Henry V and government by council to the hope of an active kingship). All are highly dependent upon supplementary writing, both English and Latin. The author of the *Gesta* approvingly quotes the many mottoes on display, and also suggests that participants were provided with written copies of songs to be sung and other elements of the performance: they perform 'litteram procedentes,' 'following their text.' The heightened availability of written matter to view is emphasized in Lydgate's poem, with its description of a tabernacle of wisdom and arts, in front of which the character of Sapience displays a written gloss: 'a scripture . . . / Able to be redde with-oute a spec-takle,' and other 'scriptures' abound throughout.[31]

I propose that this poem's most salient features—its regal subject mat-ter, and celebratory inclination, its biblical tags, its predictive momentum, its indulgence in quasi-liturgical time-out-of-time—would have summoned its audience's experiences of the 'royal entry' as a frame for its reading ex-perience. The royal entry might be thought of as 'quasi-liturgical,' in that it enlists such liturgical features as Latin tags, scriptural citations, and im-plicitly processional form in the advancement of its monarchic argument. Yet our present poem relies in a still more profound way upon familiar rhythms of the liturgical year. Recall that it initially situates itself at a time 'of faste and spirituelle afflixione'—presumably, the period of Lent, between 4 March and 12 April 1460, during that springtime of York's forced exile in Ireland.[32] This is hardly an adventitious association. Not only were the Lenten weeks of that year already weeks of political expectation, but the poem itself then explicitly invokes Lenten imagery as an element of its appeal. As liturgi-cal scholars have always realized, the climax of the liturgical year occurs in Easter week with that event anticipated since Advent, the conversion of sor-row to joy.[33] The event in question is, of course, the resurrection of Christ, liturgically announced in the celebrated trope of the visit by the three Marys to the sepulcher. Yet this event is heralded by a kind of anticipatory an-nouncement, which is the liturgical celebration of Christ's entry into Jeru-salem, in the services for Palm Sunday. And, as Eamon Duffy has noted, the Palm Sunday procession associated with the Mass of the Sarum rite was utterly focal in the ceremonialization of Holy Week, and 'the most elaborate and eloquent' of the Church's processions.[34] In keeping with the expressive action of the Easter liturgy and the liturgy as a whole, the liturgy of Palm

Sunday crucially depends upon the creation of an expectation and its fulfillment. So, within this poem, is liturgically inflected rhythm and language deployed in order that an expectation may be both created and fulfilled.

The poem begins with a predicament: a nation is trapped in iniquity and unable to hear its prophets. This predicament is epitomized in the refrain of the first seven stanzas, drawn from Isaiah 1.5: 'Omne caput languidum, et omne cor merens' ('Every head faint, and every heart sorrowing'). Its 'peripetie' then occurs in its next three stanzas, when the nation is liberated by the arrival of its redeemer (epitomized by the switch to the triumphal refrain of the next three stanzas, 'Gloria, laus et honor tibi sit, Rex Christe Redemptor': 'Glory, praise, and honor be to you, Christ King, Redeemer.' The latter line may be read less grandiosely, as an expression of thanks to Christ for the redemption of England by the return of his chosen one, Richard duke of York. Or it may be more extravagantly read as a comparison between Christ as heavenly and Richard as earthly, king. Either way, this repeated line's explicit liturgical citation is to the first line of the principal hymn of the Mass for Palm Sunday—also 'Gloria laus et honor tibi sit rex christe redemptor'[35]—responsively sung by boy singers in a high place ('pueri in eminenciori loco') and the choir, as the Palm Sunday procession approachs the church. They then enter the church, and unveil the Crucifix, with the antiphon of welcome, 'Ave rex noster.' Here celebrated, according to the antiphon, is the welcome given to Christ's arrival in Jerusalem: 'Cvm audisset populus quia ihesus uenit ierosolimam acceperunt ramos palmarum et exierunt ei obuiam et clamabant pueri dicentes hic est qui uenturus erat pro salute mundi [var: populi] hic est salus nostra et redemcio israel' ('When the people heard that Jesus was coming to Jerusalem they cut branches of palm and they went to him in the way and the boys cried out, saying here is he who was to have come for the salvation of the world [var: the people] here is our deliverance [health] and redemption, Israel'). Gathered here in this liturgical moment are the relevant themes of expectation, arrival, entry, celebration, and, especially, deliverance ('Eripe me de inimicis meis').[36]

The liturgy is, of course, all about turnarounds, reversals of fortune, upheavals. Here, with respect at least to the temporary 'turnaround' of Christ's entry into Jerusalem, a familiar liturgical experience, widely shared by any and all potential readers of this poem, is harnessed to support and confirm a wished-for Yorkist transition, from illegitimate to legitimate rule. The repetitive form of the refrain poem, the powers of prophecy, the ceremonial welcome of the monarch, the rhythms of the liturgical year—all engage the late-medieval audience at a level deeper and more persuasive than sectional politics or the particular choice of a political incumbent. The poet who arrogates these larger momentums to his purposes gains the right to assign their beneficiaries: to designate the person or persuasion on whose behalf they are presumed to operate. By such means, the Yorkist poem co-opts its audience's 'right to respond,' preemptively assigning to its claimant the symbolic capital of widely held mimetic forms. In the very act of recognizing the royal entry as this poem's absent correlative, its audience already commits itself to a line of interpretation that grants de facto recognition to Richard's aspirations. A noncomplying audience is left to scramble for points of resistance located outside the experience of the poem.

3. TEXT AS POLITICAL INTERTEXT

Implicit thus far in my discussion has been this poem's problem with its audience. In the indeterminate political situation of spring 1460, with Yorkist intrigue well launched but apparent Lancastrian loyalists still in nominal control, our poet could not be certain of the spirit in which his poem would be read. Furthermore, this uncertain interpretative situation was greatly exacerbated by the matter of public display. On the one hand, the 'posted' poem relies upon a cluster of what might be considered articles of faith: in the existence of a politically involved public; in the consequentiality of that public's determinations; in the existence of a common discursive space within which that public might be sought and addressed.[37] On the other hand, this 'public' could in no sense be treated as a unitary phenomenon. There on the Canterbury gates, open to the gaze of any arguably literate passerby, and even to aural/oral promulgation, the poem becomes an object of potentially idiosyncratic interpretation. Faced with unpredictable political loyalties and unknowable literate competencies, this poem has every reason to embrace a carefully considered relation to its audience and that audience's competencies and proclivities.[38] It is consummately shaped to effect several different kinds of capture: first, to attract attention of passersby, and, second, to engage their loyalties on behalf of the Yorkist cause. Pivotal in this act of capture is the deployment of terms, experiences, and beliefs already current in its audience's experience. Especially emphasized and valued are elements likely to be considered pre- or nonpolitical in any 'partial' or political sense: a familiar bit of liturgical or prophetic structure, or, in the examples to follow, a free-floating and familiar keyword, or bit of doxa (or unexamined presumption), or even a piece of dogma (if so widely accepted as not to be noticeable as dogma at all). These elements belong to the public domain, widely broadcast by currents of rumor, maxim, familiar experience, or scandal. They possess accrued value, in the sense that they are already officially or unofficially imbued with strong belief, but not yet securely or irrevocably claimed as the invariable property of any one interest or position. The realization of this value requires mobilization by a party skillful enough to enlist them in the service of its current objectives. Our poem's endeavor is to stake its own successful claim upon them, and to deploy them in the Yorkist cause. Among them are the following.

Tainted lineage. Any competitor for a hereditary position can clear the ground fastest by leveling an accusation of genealogical impropriety against a rival. This is a widely accepted, and proven, means of disturbing the claims of an incumbency. Thus, for example, the troubled atmosphere of succession at the time of Edward III's dotage sponsored rumors of John of Gaunt's status as an illegitimate changeling, substituted in the cradle for a smothered daughter by an anxious queen.[39] The Lancastrians, seeking to disqualify Richard II from rule, likewise encouraged rumors of his illegimate birth. According to Adam of Usk, 'many unsavoury things were commonly said, namely that he was not born of a father of a royal line, but of a mother given to slippery ways ['lubrice uite dedita']—to say nothing of many other things I have heard.'[40] Bolingbroke is even said by Froissart to have directly accused Richard of bastardy: 'of you, whose manners and conditions are visibly so different from the valiance and prowess of the prince, it is said . . . that you are son of a clerk or canon—since at the time that you were engendered and born in Bordeaux there were many very beautiful and young ones in the household of the prince.'[41] The success of these allegations is confirmed by a French chronicler's reports that London crowds denounced the captive monarch with cries of 'petit bastard' and 'mauuais bastart.'[42] Records of treason allegations also suggest that such talk had worked its way down to the level of domestic gossip. The indictment of Thomas Austin has it that his wife railed against Richard, saying that 'the kynge was neuere the prynses sone and . . . that his moder was neuere but a strong hore.'[43] Nor was Bolingbroke himself exempt from such accusation; one John Sparrowhawk reported that a tailor's wife had told him that Henry was not John of Gaunt's son at all but was son to a butcher of Ghent ('niesque il feust fitz a vn bocher de Gaunt').[44]

Thus, lamenting that the 'regnum Dei' has now become the 'regnum Sathane,' our poem treads a proven track in its opening allegation that

> This preuethe fals wedlock and periury expresse,
> Fals heryres fostred, as knowethe experyence.

Its reference is somewhat unclear. The falsity is to be traced to Henry's great-grandfather, or to the taint of usurpation clinging to his line, or some more particular allegation bearing on his mother's conduct, or, as is most likely, the matter of his own marriage and the succession of his son Edward. As the chronicler who records this poem has already observed of the troubled thirty-eighth year (1459–60) of Henry's reign, 'The offices of the reme . . . peled the pore peple, and disheryted ryghtefuylle eyres, and dede many wronges. The quene was defamed and desclaundered, that he that was called Prince, was nat hir sone, but a bastard goten in avoutry' (p. 79).

Nor were the Yorkists to remain unscathed by such allegations. Fortescue, writing in the service of the Lancastrian cause against the Yorkists early in the 1460s, notes that their claims involve descent through Lionell's daughter Philippa, but that—beyond the weakness of a line in the female line—'The whiche Edward hathe no righte to the seide crowne bi thaboveseid dame Philip, for it is playnely founde in the cronicles of France and of Seelande, that the seide dame Philip was consayved in advoutrye.'[45]

In this discourse of inheritance/disinheritance and legitimacy/illegimacy, the important thing is less that evidence be given than that the allegation be made at all, and allowed to do its work.

Perjury. Notice that our poem links 'fals wedlock' with 'periury': 'this preuethe fals wedlock and periury expresse.' The point being, I should think, that a false dynasty must always and inevitably perjure itself, about the foundation of its own right to rule. Indeed, the Lancastrian dynasty was thought by its opponents to have been involved in perjury from its barest beginnings. Henry Percy and others accused Bolingbroke of breaking the solemn oath he took at Doncaster, in which he pledged himself to seek only restitution of his ducal inheritance, and he was widely understood to have tricked Richard out of his safe haven in Conwy Castle with a false oath not to harm his person.[46] This perspective on the Lancastrian usurpation—swamped and buried by successes of Henry V—reasserted itself during the reign of Henry VI and became an element of 'Yorkist' historical understanding. Although the Yorkist presentation at Edward IV's first parliament of November 1461 soft-pedals Northumberland's (and, by implication, Henry's) perjured oath on the sacraments at Conway Castle, it nevertheless takes pains to point out that Bolingbroke acted 'ayenst Godds Lawe, Mannes Liegeaunce, and oth of fidelite.'[47] A poem of Yorkist political retrospect, composed after the accession of Edward IV, puts it more explicitly:

> Than cam henry of derby, by force & myght,
> & undir the colour of false periury . . .[48]

That the latter-day Lancastrian regime was not particularly active on the perjury front would have seemed a technicality, for it was, by the nature of its founding, inherently built on a foundation of falsity.

Of course, an aspiring dynasty has its own uses for perjury. Given his frequent oaths of loyalty to Henry VI, and his cynical participation in the 'Loveday' of 1458, Richard duke of York must be considered one of the leading perjurers of all time. John Vale's book mentions 'Thoothe by the duc of Yorke in Paulis and in semblable wisee sworen oones at Westminster and another tyme at Coventrie at several tymes in sundre yeres' (p. 193), and also his 1452 declaration of loyalty at Ludlow (p. 195); in each case, Richard swore fealty upon the sacrament: 'And to the verray prefe that it is so I offer my selfe to swer that on the blessed Sacrament and receive it, the whiche I hope shalbe my salvacion at the day of doome' (p. 195).[49] Naturally, the Lancastrians made much of these oaths in their Attainder of York in the parliament of November 1459. Of the oath at Paul's, we are told, with a remarkable insistence on the details of York's undertaking, that he 'was sworne, of his fre motion and desire, in the Cathedrall Chirche of Seint Poule in youre Citee of London, upon the blessed Sacrament and used it, and upon the holy Crosse, and also upon the holy Evangelies by hym touched . . . which Othe by hym sworn as followeth, was subscribed with his owen hande with his signe manuell, and also sealed by hym with the Seale of his armes, and so doon by his handes delyvered to You [to Henry] in fourme as foloweth' (followed by a full transcription of York's oath, in which he swears to bear Henry 'feith and trouth . . . all the dayes unto my lyves ende').[50] This promiscuity naturally enough laid him open to contemporary critique; in her letter to the City of London in 1461, Queen Margaret observes that York acted 'contrary to his liegaunce and divers solempne othes of his owne offer made uncompelled or constraigned.'[51] Even the loyalist annalist Whethamstede was perturbed by York's 1460 claim, believing it opened him to a charge of perjury since he had previously sworn loyalty to the king.[52] In this respect, Edward IV's perjury on the sacraments at the city of York in 1471 may be seen to honor something of a 'family tradition.'[53]

The Yorkist accusation against the Lancastrians prompts the observation that 'it takes one to know one.' The more important point, though, is that neither side had clean hands in this respect. The side with its hands on the mechanisms of publicity, and thus able to jump out front with an accusation, is the one most likely to conceal its own wrongdoing and by turning this accusation to its own account.

Oppression. In a manifesto promulgated on the way to Ludlow in 1459, the earl of Warwick accuses the Lancastrians of many things, including 'perjuries and extortions.'[54] 'Extortions' are in turn normally linked with their dark twin, 'oppressions.' Richard II, resuming the throne upon his majority in 1390, launched a law-and-order campaign, one aspect of which was an assault on oppressions and extortions of the people. He must have been pleased when Chaucer wrote a complicit poem, 'Lack of Steadfastness,' in which he complained that the countryside was rife with 'oppressioun' and urged his prince to 'hate extorcioun.' (One of the key maneuvers for the would-be ideologue is to urge strenuously that the prince undertake a course of action to which he has already committed himself.)[55] An aversion to extortion is not, of course, the prerogative of any single political party. *Nobody* likes oppression; the point is to represent one's party as the one that dislikes oppression most of all. Although his law-and-order campaign lapsed once he regained sole rule, Richard would refurbish the claim at another time of need when, in 1397, he accused Gloucester and the other senior appellants of 'extorsiones' and 'oppressiones.' And then, Henry having come to power in 1399, some of Richard's co-conspirators against Gloucester were stripped of their gains because of 'extorsions, wronges, and oppressions' done to the people. Closer to our period, the Lancastrian *Somnium Vigilantis* defended the proscription of the Yorkists at the Coventry Parliament of 1459 on the basis of 'what extorcions, what injuries and oppressions, what partie makynge and division they did and caused to be done.'[56]

The point is, of course, that opposition to oppression belonged not just to the Lancastrians but to any regime that could claim it. To some, such opposition was the defining characteristic of any successful ruler. According to the English version of the *Book of Fayttes of Armes*, 'Prynces soverayne ... for none other thyng were establlysshed but for to doo right to everyche of their subgettis that shold be oppressid for any extorcion and for to deffende and kepe them.' [57] No wonder that, as reported in the Davies Chronicle, the Yorkist manifesto addressed to the archbishop of Canterbury turned the king's followers into the oppressors, practicing 'oppressyone, extorsion' and other wrongs against 'Goddys churche' (p. 86) and also against his people and cast Richard as the remedy for this situation. In short: our poem could suppose a good deal of uptake for itself when it argues in its second stanza that England was suffering 'Vnryghtewys dysherytyng with false oppresse.'

Exile. The argument of 'exile' could, again, count either way. As discussed in chapter 1, Bolingbroke made effective use of this motif when he returned to England, from exile, in 1399. Now, a structurally similar argument is arrogated to the Yorkist cause. Richard duke of York was popularly viewed through the lens of exile as early as 1450, when Cade as 'Captain of Kent' complained about 'the highe and mighti prince the duc of Yorke, late exiled from our seid soveraigne lordes presence by the mocion and stering of the traytours and fals disposed the duc of Suffolke and his affinite.'[58] The joint statement of 1460 likewise complains that oppressions and extortions have caused justice and righteousness to be '*exyled* of the sayde londe' (p. 86), and here the Yorkist lords tap into a powerful stream of biblical and political imagery. The tangible correlative of exile is, of course, that York had himself been in exile in Ireland since the 1459 debacle at Ludlow, and Warwick and others had taken refuge in Calais — all having been attainted in the Coventry Parliament of the same year. The adaptability of exile to Yorkist purposes is additionally suggested by the fact that in an entry for 1450 Gregory's Chronicle reconfigures York's 1447–50 lieutenancy of Ireland as a form of banishment from which he has now returned: 'Ande in the ende of the sayde same yere Rycharde, the Duke of Yorke, come to the sayde Parlymeantt, for the sayde Duke was before banyshyd for certayne yerys.' [59] Thus our poem evokes a strong image when it observes, sarcastically, that

Harry, oure souerayne and most Crystyne kyng,
His trew bloode hathe flemed bothe be swerde and exyle.

'Trew bloode' references, of course, the Yorkist genealogical claim, which was at least as strong as Henry's (coming through Gaunt's younger brother Edmund, first duke of York in the male line, and through Lionel, Gaunt's elder brother, via Anne Mortimer, in the female line). And it is this true blood that has been put to flight or driven out, into a condition of exile. Yet part of the power of the imagery of exile lies in its derivative implications: if 'exile' is the *fort* in Freud's anxious child's narrative game, then 'return' is the *da;* or, to put it less grandly, if 'exile' is the 'tick,' then 'return' is the 'tock.' Referencing exile in a poem of imagined return is a way of enlisting a powerful narrative expectation in its own right. Naturally enough, the fulfilled expectation is also well represented in Yorkist poetry; following upon Edward IV's success in the battle of Northampton, a poem of celebration informs us,

> . . . I take witnesse
> Of certeyn persones that late exiled were,
> Whos sorow is turned into ioyfulnesse.[60]

So does our poem imagine exile's end. Exhorting Christ to restore York and his associates 'to thayre honoure as they had before,' it indulges a reverie of celebration and rejoicing:

> And euer shalle we syng to thyyn Hyghe Excellence,
> Gloria, laus et honor Tibi sit Rex Christe Redemptor!

Treason. The discourse of treason is so widely distributed and prevalent in the later Middle Ages as to defy compact summary. Yet new circumstances, arising first in the years after 1381, were leading to an enlargement and diversification of the treason claim, with articles and prosecutions making increasingly opportunistic use of the hitherto restricted language of treasonous accusation in order to rally support and obtain convictions.[61] Before 1450, however, treason accusations tended to be mounted strategically, by an enstated authority, against persons rather emphatically out of power. Thus, when Henry IV employed the full gamut of treason terminologies against Blount and his associates in the rebellion of the earls in 1401, or when Henry V launched treason accusations against the Lollards after the so-called Oldcastle Rebellion of 1415, these monarchs were in secure possession of the mechanisms of the household judiciary and the King's Bench and other established institutions. After 1450, with the institutions of monarchical authority in more severe contestation, and division among and between King, Council, and even Richard duke of York as sometime Protector, treason accusations tended to fly both ways, with each party arrogating the language of treason in its accusation of the other. Thus we read in Jack Cade's Proclamation of 1450 that 'It is a hevy thynge that the good Duke of Gloucester was apechid of treson by o fals traytour alone . . . ; but the fals traytur Pole was apechyd by all the holl comyns of Ingelond.'[62] Or of York's and Somerset's simultaneous and mutual treason accusations at the skirmish at St. Albans, 1455: '[The duke of York replied that] he absolutely intended to lay hands on the traitors who were with the king ['les traytres qu'ilz estoient entours lui'] so they could be punished. . . . [The duke of Somerset replied that] he had no traitors near him except the duke of York, who had risen against his crown' ('il n'entendoit point avoir aulcuns traytres empres lui se n'estoit le duc d'Yorc mesmes qui contre sa couronne c'estoit leve').[63] Or, in the Paston letters, that 'Lord Rivers was brought to Calais and . . . my Lord of Salisbury berated him, calling him knave's son, that he should be so rude as to call him and [his fellow] lords traitors, for they shall be found the king's true liegemen when he should be found a traitor.'[64]

The crucial point about such taunting exchanges is that 'treason' had itself become a mobile signifier, available for application and use by either party. (Thus, by this discursive avenue, may we understand the most grisly innovation of mid-fifteenth-century warfare, which was the summary quasi-judicial execution, usually by beheading or occasionally by hanging, of opposing lords and gentry by each battle's winning party. Underwriting this unchivalrous conduct was the mobility and prevalence of the treason accusation.) Given that York had already been found formally guilty of treason in proceedings of attainder in the Coventry Parliament of 1459, a retort within the body of our poem seems inevitable. Finding the entire corporate body of England guilty from the soles of its feet ('the pore tyler of the lond') to its head (its 'ennoynted crown'), it hurls back the charge, arguing that England's treasonous state is widely known: 'Euery reame cryethe owte of Engelondes treson.'

Heresy. The arch-accusation of the fifteenth century enters our poem imagistically, when we read that 'Tempus [is come] eradicandi the wedes fro the corne.' Biblical in its origins, this figurative language of eradication goes back to Matthew 13:38: 'The good seed are the children of the kingdom.

And the cockle are the children of the wicked one.' Christ in Matthew is referring to the end of time ('the harvest is the end of the world ... Even as the cockle therefore is gathered up and burnt with fire; so shall it be at the end of the world'—13:39–40). But this passage was invaluable throughout the Middle Ages for enjoining the present-time destruction of the wicked, heretics in particular. As early as 1179, Peter of Blois, hearing of a heresy in York, reminded the archbishop that it was important to watch lest the shoots of the vines 'degenerent ... in labruscam, frumenta in lollium.'[65] This image of cockles and weeds among the good corn was pervasive. A network of associations widely represented in art and sermon literature in and after the twelfth century portrayed Christ as good grain, as the 'mill of the host.' The corruption of good grain by heresy thus had an added implication, disastrous in the late medieval centuries when the status of the eucharistic host become an object of such active contention. In polluting the symbolic body of Christendom with its weedy growth, heresy threatened the purity of the host itself. Accusing Chaucer's Parson of Lollardy, Harry Bailly complains that 'He wolde sowen som difficulte, / Or springen cokkel in our clene corn' (ll. 1183–84). In compromising the purity of the 'clene corn' that issues in the eucharistic host, the heretic attacked the very foundation of Christian community. The follow-on implication is clear enough: the heretic must, like any weed, be uprooted, extirpated.[66]

But who are the heretics here? The suggestion that the pious Henry and his followers might in any way have been heretical is, of course, utterly unfounded. To be sure, the Yorkists were not above hinting at such a thing; the Davies chronicler includes the Articles addressed by Richard to Archbishop Bourchier, his eventual follower, according to which oppression, extortion, and other harms are said to have been done to God's church and his ministers. Certainly no heretics, the Lancastrians were thought at least to lie open to an imputation of insufficiently strenuous action against corrupting heresies. In any case, little enough warrant is required to do what this poem does: to liken Henry's advisors to heretics, with the added imputation that they deserve no better treatment. Thus, these bad tares are not heretics per se, but Henry's evil counselors, who must be rooted out and destroyed. The virtues of this imputation in the undecided year 1460 are multiple: it can provide an argument either for retaining Henry as figurehead, with a new body of apt counselors including Richard duke of York, or for his supplantation, now or later, by a Yorkist successor; additionally, it can both indict Henry's followers for being 'soft on heresy' and inimical to the interests of the church, even as it casts them metaphorically as bad and corrupting advice givers in the political sphere.

Community and true commons. By appealing to buzzwords, familiar structurations, and other shared elements, the Canterbury verses aim to bridge possible differences among and between members of their own audience. Thus, their ultimate aspiration is not only to convert individuals one by one, but to create a hoped-for solidarity, modeled by the collective audience response to their appeal. Drawing on the deepest rhythms of the liturgical year, as well as scraps of things already known and believed, they re-create their audience as an expectant community, united by its experience of deprivation, hope of redemption, and all the other, more incidental views it holds in common. The poem's very first lines began with a fleeting nod to the *chanson d'aventure,* in which the narrator is an 'I' who, in solitude, reflects on the parlous state of the times and seeks solace in biblical precedent. It progresses to the possibility that a like-minded community of Yorkist supporters — the 'we' of the poem's midsection — will share in the sorrows of Richard's exile. And it ends with a vision of an enlarged and regenerated community that will embrace the poem's reader — the 'thow' individually and familiarly addressed in its last stanza:

> And thow shalt syng wythe vs thys verrey trew sens,
> Gloria laus et honor Tibi sit Rex Christe Redemptor!

'Thow shalt syng with vs' — an enlarged community of the realm joining with a core of more permanent supporters, their union signaling a new solidarity, a process of conversion now complete.

This appeal to community is hardly restricted to Yorkist verse,[67] but is one of its cornerstones, and may be found in numerous Yorkist poems. The Yorkist poem on the battle of Northampton rather ingeniously makes the captured Henry himself its spokesman, declaring his relief to be freed from his pack of 'curre-dogges' and returned to his loyal (Yorkist) following. Truth, he says, has replaced falsehood, and returned from exile:

> . . . now the trewe comynerys of kent
> Be comyn with you, falsehed to destrewe,
> And truthe long exiled now to renewe.

These 'trewe comynerys of kent' have a deep historical lineage, traceable at least to the reported 'wache worde' of the rebels of 1381, including many from Kent, who expressed solidarity 'Wyth kynge Richarde and with the trew communes.'[68] So is their voice heard in Jack Cade's predominantly Kentish rising in 1450, which launched its program of complaints on behalf of 'symple and pore peopull' within Kent as well as, more broadly, the 'pore people and commones of the reaume.'[69] Some of its concerns are quite local, involving such matters as possible blame resting on Kent for the death of Suffolk or the jurisdiction of the court of Dover, and others are national in scope, involving the loss of lands in France and the composition of the royal Council. Its information base is, however, described as that which is known by common people, 'noised by comun voyses.' The more proximate point of reference to these true commoners of Kent may be found in the swell of Yorkist support for Edward, Salisbury, and Warwick upon their disembarkation from Calais, and the number of recruits who followed them to London and thence to Northampton. These Kentishmen copied and circulated another of Cade's manifestos in 1460, under the subsequent rubric 'Tharticle of the commones of Kente at the coming of therls of Marche Warrewic and Salisbury with the lordes Faconbrigge and Wenlok from Cales to the batell at Northampton anno 1460.' Still current, such matters as the earlier death of Gloucester continued to rankle, and are produced on behalf of 'the kinges trewe liegemen of Kente,' speaking for 'alle the pouer communes of Englande.'[70]

Similarly, the 1461 Holkham verses—the poem next considered in this chapter—will develop a sense of loyalist community. The poet imagines, correctly, that the triumph at Towton was based on the successes enjoyed by a core of Yorkist lords who fled overseas after the defeat at Ludlow, and who returned to England in June 1460: the rose (Edward), the ragged staff (Warwick), Falconbridge (the fishhook), augmented by long-standing supporter the white lion (duke of Norfolk). This group in turn attracted adherents, and these adherents become a 'community':

> Yett, serys, prey we
> For the good comunité
>   That wyth thes lordys er went.
> Cryst, that neuer dedyst ovtrage,
> Send thes lordys good passage,
>   In ryte to hem her tent.

The 'good comunité' of these lords and their followers is a growing band, and, given the poem's expressed concern about the rose's continuing vulnerability to 'treturys' still abroad in the land, recruits are obviously welcome. The form of such recruitment is figured in the enlarged band of well-wishers who 'prey' for the community of lords, and for their 'good passage,' to their rightful intention ('In ryte to hem her tent').

These fitful imaginings of community and the political possibilities vested in its allegiances advance and recede based on incident and occasion. They may hardly be considered a formal theory of the state, and certainly not a Stubbsian way-station on an orderly itinerary to constitutional rule. Nevertheless, their occasional nature and their informality of utterance notwithstanding, they may participate in an idea of the political realm and public political space—'politik,' as Fortescue put it more formally and rigorously, in his theory of lordship 'roiall and politik,' rather than simply 'roiall' alone.[71] Like theories of community itself, Fortescue's theory lay open to varied appropriation, belonging neither to Yorkists nor Lancastrians, but to whomever was able successfully to claim it, or to whom it was successfully assigned. Complexities attending upon Fortescue's own manuscript tradition—in which God has variously sent 'king Henry the vjthe' and 'Edward the ivthe' to rule over us—bear out the suggestion that theory, whether in the form of street-level opinion or of high political polemic, is available to the leader, and his followers, who can claim it.[72]

4. IMAGINATION AND IMPASSE: THE 1461 HOLKHAM VERSES

As we have seen in the 1460 verses, the real world will not always supply correlatives to the ardent or utopian imagination. Richard duke of York can be *sought* as king, but the world of events and contingencies must nevertheless deliver him up in that capacity. The 1460 verses celebrate an arrival yet to occur, and one that would in some respects never occur. Yet it nevertheless fully indulges this action at an imaginative level, employing the 'as-if' register of the subjunctive to suppose Richard duke of York to be—depending on how we translate 'in principibus'—either seated among princes or settled in the enjoyment of princely honors: 'Sette hym ut sedeat in principibus.' Shifting, in its final stanza, to the celebratory refrain 'Gloria laus et honor,' it offers a mimetic fulfillment of expectation, that proposes to its audience the

experience of attendance at a royal entry, even though that entry is still anticipated and unachieved. In other words, this poem proposes a premature celebration, praising God for delivering Richard without the corroborative event
of his actual arrival. This is, in consequence, a poem that anxiously brushes
past its own central event, substituting the momentum of quasi-liturgical
energy and ecstatic assertion for any more apt or tangible kind of political
eventfulness.

A similar substitution occurs in another previously written poem, written to celebrate the Yorkist victory at the battle of Northampton. This poem
first celebrates the new joyfulness of persons lately exiled—Richard duke
of York ('the rose'), Edward earl of March, Richard earl of Salisbury, and
Richard earl of Warwick. Then, having described the exploits of the latter
three in capturing and parading king Henry, it offers a previously withheld
detail: their leader, Richard duke of York, has not been present for any of
this, having failed thus far to return home:

> Now god, that madest both nyght & day,
>   Bryng home the mayster of this game,
> The duke of yorke, for hym we pray,
>   That noble prynce, Richard be name . . .[73]

Here an ideological wish or figment encounters a historical actuality. Obviously, this poem works best with Richard on the scene, and its initial mention of 'the rose' has allowed its reader to think that his return from exile
has been one of the fruits of God's providential intervention. This small deception is consistent with poetry's hospitality to imagined objects of desire.
Nevertheless, when a poem's desired objectives are historically specific, then a
time might always arise when external reality is invited to supply them. Here,
a gap opens between an ideologically infused imaginary, in which Richard
returns to claim the kingship, and a recalcitrant state of historical affairs.[74]
Many medieval poems contain such a gap, and some of them even adopt its
presence as their founding premise; hence, the ubiquity of that poetic form
we call the 'complaint.' Yet the author of this celebratory poem has no apparent wish to be a complaint writer; he would rather celebrate an accomplished
fact, and that fact seems rather awkwardly to elude him. Consequently, an
element of embarrassment shadows this poem, as well as others under consideration here. This embarrassment expresses itself as an uneasy obscuran-
tism around the moment of kingship's reclamation and reconsecration. In

fact, these poems set for themselves a hard double task: they seem intent not only on eliding the moment of the throne's successful recapture but also on concealing the fact of the elision. They jump back and forth in time, from pre- to post-, in a fashion that denies the centrality of the very moment they are intended to celebrate. Because Richard's own hesitant, duplicitous, and forsworn path to the throne does not encourage unblemished celebration—because, that is, the reality of Richard's ambitions could not be consistently or completely subordinated to an imaginary design[75]—these poems are forced into a zone of legerdemain and evasion.

A similar reticence is evident in a situation where we would not expect to encounter it: in a 1461 Norfolk poem, here called the 'Holkham verses,' written to celebrate the accession of Edward IV. (For the full text, see Appendix 2 to this chapter.) The difference is that, unlike the 1460 Canterbury verses and the poem written after Northampton, the altered circumstances of autumn 1461 have now made a crowned king available for representation. Even so, this poem still seems unable fully to embrace him. These verses may be described as possessed of a brooding beginning and a hopeful end, but still no 'middle.' They open in broad address to a general public, in ballad meter and claiming association with 'jestovrys . . . talys.' Their burden is to express an ominous climate of treachery, in the death of Humfrey duke of Gloucester and the loss of France, and still abroad in the land. Then occurs a sudden switch—in midpoem and, in fact, in midstanza—to a more optimistic set of announcements, involving 'the rose,' Edward IV:

> But yet, sorys, mak we no bost,
> Henglond was al-most lost,
>   Tretourys so fayre gon glose.
> Of all the flourys that heuer wer sett—
> Lely, premerroll or viholett—
>   I perey Cryst saue the rose.

Just when the traitors, or *tretourys,* seemed likely to prevail, the possibility of the rose comes into view. Its existence is precarious, it requires Christ's attentive intervention, but it offers a counterfoil to the treacherous and deceptive circumstances that have previously prevailed. Groundwork for this alteration has, we learn, been laid by a band of companions—Edward, Warwick, Falconbridge, and (a matter of local pride) John Mowbray duke of Norfolk—who have labored for a year to set the kingdom right. Were it not for their activities, 'we had be chente' or 'shent.' In their midst, the rose shows himself—'the rose hem schewys.' In reference both to their journey from Calais to England in spring 1460 and to their exertions since, it wishes them 'good passage.' False shrews and traitors are still abroad, and the poem celebrates their infliction of 'mech sweme,' or much sorrow, on their ranks at the unnamed, but clearly indicated, battle of Towton.

Remarkably, unmentioned in this poem's sudden transition from 'wol' to weal—or at least to a state of qualified hopefulness—is the fact that, between the miseries of 1447–50 with which it begins and the battle of Towton at the end of March 1461, Edward IV had been crowned king of England, having been proclaimed in London on 4 March of that year. We are told only that the band of companions has labored for the prevous year—an eventful and topsy-turvy year encompassing Richard duke of York's exile, the victory at Northampton, Richard's return and rash death at Wakefield, and Edward's victories at Mortimer's Cross and finally Towton. Interesting itself in ten-year-old grievances, and then in a single, cataclysmic battle (the like of which even the partisan author hopes never to see again), the poem skips the apparently most pertinent occurrences, including the termination of a sixty-two-year waiting period with a Yorkist claimant's ascent to the throne. The poem's editor, Richard Beadle, aptly poses the altogether pertinent question of why it is structured around old grievances on the one hand and a subsequent victory, on the other, with so little reference 'to the complex events of the intervening period' (p. 110). His answer is that precedent for this structure is to be found in other texts of the period; he observes, for example, that Vale's rendition of the 1460 article of the commons of Kent upon the coming of the earls likewise reiterates such long-festering grievances as the murder of Duke Humfrey and the loss of France, similarly presuming them fully relevant to the present time. Citing C. D. Ross, Beadle suggests that 'in 1460 the causes of widespread disillusionment with the Lancastrian regime were much the same as they had been ten years before' (p. 111). Granting such structural precedents, however, they do not resolve all the questions we might have about what Beadle agrees is a 'sudden temporal shift' at the center of the Holkham text. The Canterbury verses and the poem on Northampton were unable to produce an event that remained in abeyance, the crowning of a Yorkist king. The Holkham poem, by contrast, actually has that event *at its disposal*, but nevertheless partially elides it (excepting only the most muffled reference to a year of labors), and partially displaces it (onto the battle that temporarily secured Edward's throne).

How is it that, even with a crowned Yorkist king abroad in the world, this loyalist poem continues to find him unrepresentable? I believe that the materials for a partial answer lie in the external situation: the encumbering previous history of Richard duke of York's forsworn oaths and evasions; the fact that an anointed king was alive, in refuge with his entourage intact in Scotland; the expedient haste with which Edward had been proclaimed by his own Yorkist captains in London; and the telltale four-month gap between Edward's secular acclamation and installation (1–4 March 1461) and his actual Westminster coronation with full regalia (28 June 1461).[76] Whatever new 'facts on the ground' were established at Towton, this remained a moment in English history when an awkward and ambiguous and decidedly nonunanimous change of regimes militated against representation of an unblemished succession or a liturgically unclouded coronation. In this respect, a small crisis of representation within a Yorkish poem exists in concert with a larger crisis of succession in the nation as a whole. Lucien Goldmann would have called this relationship a 'homology'—a repetition of the terms and conditions of an event in one register (in this case, the macro-register of a kingdom) in those of another register (in the limited compass of a hastily composed and casually disseminated little poem).[77] This poem's inability to represent Edward as crowned king suggests the persistent nature of the English succession crisis, even at a moment when the Yorkists might have wished to consider it fully resolved.

The Canterbury verses, the poem on Northampton, and the Holkham verses all circle around a consummation that must, because of recalcitrant external realities or residual scruples, be postponed or withheld. Each must nevertheless be considered provisionally successful in bringing consolations of literary art to the unappeasable demands of political desire. Each poem effectively arrays or garlands its claimant with the most current predictive technologies, the deepest and most persuasive liturgical rhythms, the most evocative available political language. If these poems conjoin 'art' and 'propaganda,' they do so in a way that respects art's deeper propensity, which is not to rest easy within its own bounds, to probe the conditions of its own existence, to sponsor imaginative sallies into or across unclaimed or unsettled ground. Finally, these poems display art's elasticity, allowing somewhere near their own emotional center the kinds of disturbing and unreconciled details (such as the death of 'xxx.m.' at Towton) from which countersuppositions might be formed.[78]

APPENDIX I.
BALAT SET UPPONNE THE YATES OF CAUNTERBURY

From *An English Chronicle of the Reigns of Richard II, Henry IV, Henry V, and Henry VI*, ed. J. S. Davies, Camden Society, 1st ser., no. 64 (London, 1856), pp. 92–93.

Whan the erles knew the trew hertes of the peple, they dysposed theyme dayly for to com in to thys londe. And nat longe before theyre commyng, thys balat that folowethe was sette vppon the yates of the cyte of Caunterbury.

> In the day of faste and spirituelle afflixione,
>   The celestialle influence of bodyes transytory,
> Set asyde alle prophecyes, and alle commixtione
>   Of iujementys sensualle to ofte in memory,
> I reduced to mynde the prophete Isay,
>   Consideryng Englond to God in greuous offence, with
>   wepyng ye;
> This text I fonde in his story:—
>   "Omne caput languidum, et omne cor merens!"
>
> Regnum Anglorum regnum Dei est,
>   As the Aungelle to seynt Edward dede wyttenesse;
> Now regnum Sathane, it semethe, reputat best,
>   For filii scelerati haue broughte it in dystresse.
>
> This preuethe fals wedlock and periury expresse,
>   Fals heryres fostred, as knowethe experyence,
> Vnryghtewys dysherytyng with false oppresse,
>   Sic "omne caput languidum, et omne cor merens!"
>
> A plantâ pedis, fro the pore tylyer of the lond
>   Ad verticem of spiritualle eke temperalle ennoynted crown
> Grace ys withdrawe and Goddys mercyfulle hand,
>   Exalted ys falsehod, trowthe ys layde adoune;
> Euery reame cryethe owte on Engelondes treson.
>   O falshod with thy colored presence!

Euer shulle we syng duryng thy season,
  "Omne caput languidum, et omne cor merens!"

"Omne regnum in se divisum," sayethe dyuyne Scrypture,
  "Shall be desolate," than folewethe translacione
Into the handes of theyre enemyes, Jewes arn figure;
  And now ys Englond in lyk reputacione,
In wey to be conquered; truste it for sewre!
  Jhesu, for thy mercy and thy noble reuerens,
Reforme vs to goodnesse and condicione pure,
  For, "omne caput languidum, et omne cor merens!"

Harry oure souerayne and most Crystyne kyng
  His trew bloode hathe flemed bothe be swerde and exyle;
What prynce by thys rewle may haue long enduryng,
  That also in moste pouert hath be long whyle?
Tho bestys that thys wroughte to mydsomer haue but a myle—
  But euer mornethe Engelond for ham that be hens
Wythe languysshyng of herte rehersyng my style,
  "Omne caput languidum, et omne cor merens!"

Jonathas ys ded that Dauid shuld restore
  To the presence of the kyng, vnyte to make
Murum pro domo Israel, presthode dar no more
  Put hymself forthe, his fat benefyce he shuld forsake.
Mercyfulle God! it ys tyme thow for vs awake.
  Mercenarius fugit, ne wylle make resistence,
He ferethe the wolf that wolde hys bonys crake,
  "Omne caput languidum, et omne cor merens!"

Tempus ys come falshede to dystroy,
  Tempus eradicandi the wedes fro the corne,
Tempus cremandi the breres that trees noye,
  Tempus evellendi the fals hunter with his horne,
Tempus miserendi on por alle to torne,
  Tempus ponendi falsnes in perpetuelle absence,
Thoroughe whom we syngyng both euyne and morne,
  "Omne caput languidum, et omne cor merens!"

Send hom, most gracious Lord Jhesu most benygne,
    Sende hoom thy trew blode vn to his propre veyne,
Richard duk of York, Job thy seruaunt insygne,
    Whom Sathan not cesethe to sette at care and dysdeyne,
But by The preserued he may nat be slayne;
    Sette hym ut sedeat in principibus, as he dyd before,
And so to oure newe songe, Lorde, thyn erys inclyne,
    Gloria, laus et honor Tibi sit Rex Christe Redemptor!

Edwarde Erle of Marche, whos fame the erthe shalle sprede,
    Richard Erle of Salisbury named prudence,
Wythe that noble knyghte and floure of manhode
    Richard erle of Warrewyk sheelde of oure defence,
Also lytelle Fauconbrege, a knyghte of grete reuerence;
    Jhesu ham restore to thayre honoure as thay had before,
And euer shalle we syng to thyn Hyghe Excellence,
    Gloria, laus et honor Tibi sit Rex Christe Redemptor!

No prynce, alle thyng consydered, wythe honoure
    In alle thyng requysyte to a kynges excellence
Better may lyue, serche any worthy predecessoure;
    Yet hastow souuerayne lord in these lordes absence
Of alle thaym to a kyng ryghte resonable expens;
    Thay shalle come agayne and rekene for the scoore,
And thow shalt syng wythe vs thys verrey trew sens,
    Gloria laus et honor Tibi sit Rex Christe Redemptor!

        The deed man gretethe yow welle,
        That ys iust trew as steele,
            With verray good entent,
        Alle the Reame of Englond
        Sone to louse from sorowes bond,
            Be ryghte indifferent iugement.
To the ryghte Worshypfulle Cyte of Caunterbury.

APPENDIX 2.
THE HOLKHAM VERSES

This text is derived from that presented by Richard Beadle, 'Fifteenth-Century Political Verses from the Holkham Archives,' *Medium Aevum* 71 (2002), 101–21. Spelling is modernized (thorn to "th" and yogh to "y") and Beadle's more ample glosses are reduced. See his essay for well-developed explanatory materials.

Cryst th*a*t deyid vp-on the rod,
Graunt vs y-torne to good;
   This werd is b*u*t a quyle.
Karp I wyll a m*er*lous spell:
5   To chrewys in this lond dwell—   [shrews]
   Thei werk many a wyle.

Covetyse is on of thoo,
I-wys a may not go th*er*-fro,
   Fol wyl ye may aspye.
10   I chall tell of the tother,
That is the fals chreve-is brothe[r],
   Is nam is isserie.   [usury]

B*u*t now wyl I prefe be resu*n*
That covetys hath brovt tresu*n*,
15   Thus ses many a man.
Jestovr*ys* tell in her talys,
W*y*t*h* gens of australys
   This tresu*n* be-gan.

This tresu*n* was so strong,
20   It went to fer in this lond,
   Tys nat for to layn.   [hide]
In a tovne me*n* call Beri—
Syth was Hengelond neu*er* meri—
   Th*er* was a good duk slayn.

25 Tretourys in this lond wer to or thre;
To that deth consendydyn he,
   And mad mech stryfe.
Hevyl yyrster cum on her pate!
He-feyth, sorys, itt was to late
30   That thei lost her lyffe.

Sorys, *and* ye wyl vnderstonde,
Ther wer mo tretevrys in Engelond,
   But I know nott all.
But, thore tretourys gouernans, [through]
35 We han lost all we had in Fraunce,
   And all-most mad tharle. [thrall]

I tel yov sum, but not ilke-a dell:
The Bechop of Chychester bar the previ sell,
   A-nother the hakenay—this was a merlous chanse. [hireling]

40 Her-ken, sorys, sekerly,
They rennyn thorow all Normondy,
   In-to the hey rem of France.

They sparyd neyther for hot nen cold,
Tyl Normandy was bovth *and* sold,
45   *And* Hangoy [and] Mayne. [Anjou]
Herken, sorys, a tale fol trew:
Many a man chal chonge is hew
   Or is be gett agey[n].

Thes Frense men mak gret boste
50 That Normandy is thus loste,
   Bothin vp *and* down.
Ther dede thes treturys grett hovt-rage;
It is vr gyngys heritage,
   And longyn to the crovn.

55   B*u*t yet, sor*ys,* mak we no bost,
      Henglond was al-most lost,
           T*r*etour*ys* so fayr*e* gon glose.
      Of all the flour*ys* th*at* heu*er* wer sett—
      Lely, prem*er*roll or viholett—
60   I perey Cryst saue the rose.

      Sor*ys,* all a[nd] som,
      Prey for the qvyt lyon,
           Tys a best fol gente.
      Herky*n,* sor*ys,* all in fere,
65   *And* thei had not l[a]bord the last yere,
           I-feyth, we had be chente.

      For the feyth th*at* God yov gaffe,
      Preyth for the raggyd staffe,
           Also for Fakyn*n*bryge.

70   Q*ua*n thes iiij knyt*ys* hem be-thowte
      That Hengelond th*us* chuld cu*m* to nowte,
           And heu*er* mad thrall,
      Thei rememb*er* hem in er mend;
      To-ward borialys gon thei wend,
75   Thei went for lyfe *and* all.

      In May fodomyng,   [blossoming]
      All messom*er* fayr*e* spryngyng,
           Th*us* the rose hem schewys.
      Cryst for is peté,
80   Kepe hym, yf is wyl be,
           From all false chrevys.

      Cryst th*at* deyed on Good Friday,
      Late neu*er* no tr*e*tur*ys* hy*m* be-tr*a*y,
           In no maner kend.
85   Lo sor*ys,* for charité,
      Th*us* all pray we,
           Wyt*h* stedfast hert *and* mend.

Cryst of hevyn, as he may best,
Send vr qvyte lyon good rest,
90   Qwer-so-heuer he fare.
Lady Mari, that blysful flore,
Be thes knytys sokoure,
    And kepe hem fro care.

The ragged staff and the fysch hoke,
95   Qvyther thei wend be strem or broke,
    Ryte wel mote hem spede.
Fader and Son and Holy Goste,
Soth-fast God of mytys moste,
    Help hem att her nede.

100 Yett, serys, prey we
For the good comunité
    That wyth thes lordys er went.
Cryst, that neuer dedyst ovtrage,
Send thes lordys good pasage,
105   In ryte to hem her tent.

Now hustralys of tresun hath lest is hold,
Borialys is wax ryte bold;
    This tresun hath do tene.
Herken, sorys, all in fay,
110 Tys nott yet many a day
    Tornyd hem to mech sweme.

Sorys, it is novt to leyne,
xxxᵛ.m. on a feld wer slayne.
    It is the more peté.
115 Cryst that bovth-ist man so dere,
Graunt vs grace oure lyf dayes here,
    Neuer swech a-nother to se.
                    Amen.

five

'Royal Christology' and
York's Paper Crown

DESPITE THEIR SPARING USE OF THE SIMPLIFYING TERM 'SECULAR,' several chapters in this book might seem to imply that political language is always forged at the expense of the religious. The idea of a zero-sum game, in which worldly, and especially political, description occurs only as a subtraction from the language of the sacred, does not serve us well—not in the general case and certainly not in the complex situation of those centuries which bridge the late medieval and the early modern. Whatever the efforts at purification of the languages of politics and religion, the reconvergence of their domains seems always imminent, or always to be happening. Furthermore, certain subject matters and certain sites or registers seem particularly hospitable to this reconvergence. The conditions and possibilities of the theatrical are, I argue here, particularly encouraging to the rediscovery of the sacred, and to the union of religious imagery with more resolutely secular concerns. Here I may seem to approach Stephen Greenblatt's suggestion that medieval sacramentalism is converted to, and recycled as, renaissance theatre.[1] Yet my argument differs in proposing an affinity between sacramentalism and the theatrical that does not simply await discovery within the art of Shakespeare but is evident *throughout* the 'late medieval' and 'early modern' periods. Failure to appreciate this continuity has resulted in a severe underestimation of the aesthetic preworking of eventually Shakespearean materials by his late-medieval and early-Tudor precedessors.

To gain purchase on this complicated subject, I isolate a single example in which the languages and motives of politics and religion vie for predominance: the death of Richard duke of York. In addition, I focus on a single, contested symbol around which secular and sacred motives converge, seeming sometimes contradictory and sometimes complementary in their effects. This symbol consists in the crown itself, as introduced in the derisive crowning thought to have occurred either just after or just before York's 1460 decapitation at Wakefield.

I. POLITICAL STRUGGLE, MERE LIFE, AND THE POSSIBILITY OF SACRIFICE

York's death exemplifies a barbarity at once atavistic and new that occurs with increasing frequency in the course of the fifteenth century. The barbarity is that of extrajudicial murder, especially directed against aristocratic prisoners after battles and skirmishes of the midcentury 'Rose' wars. Telltale anticipations of a new climate may be seen in such events as the quasi-judicial execution of Humfrey duke of Gloucester, the clandestine execution of Suffolk, the repressive 'harvyste of hedys' taken in Kent after the Cade rising,[2] and the strong-arm thuggery resulting in the effective murders of Somerset, Northumberland, Clifford, and others at St. Albans in 1455. Even beyond such instances, though, the specifically new practice of which I speak involves the routine execution of aristocratic prisoners taken in battle in the aftermath of the fray. The practice of medieval warfare according to its continental model involved the slaughter of common soldiers at will, but preservation of noble prisoners, who were often kept with amity and comfort, for prospective ransom settlements. Although exceptions may of course be noted,[3] the English seem normally to have subscribed to this model until the fifteenth century, when wholesale, and eventually even routine, departures may be observed.

Edward IV was probably the first to promulgate the new practice as a matter of policy. One index of its novelty is the response of contemporary observers, who find it worthy of special notice. Commynes reports that Edward described his habit after battle as mounting on horseback and crying out that common soldiers should be saved and gentlemen put to the sword, with few or none escaping.[4] This account is corroborated by the Davies Chronicle (or *English Chronicle*), which reports that, on the eve of the battle of Northampton, 'the sayde erles of Marche and Warrewyk lete crye thoroughe the felde, that no man shuld laye hand vpponne the kyng ne on the commune peple, but onely on the lordes, knyghtes and squyers.'[5] In any event, and from either side, or any corner, of any disputed field, an open season on noble adversaries was effectively declared. Prior to any formal edict, Richard duke of York, the earl of Salisbury, and others were beheaded by the Lancastrians after the battle of Wakefield (we are told that they were 'take a slayne'—taken and slain).[6] Owen Tudor and others were beheaded in the Hereford marketplace after the battle of Mortimer's Cross.[7] The earls of Devon and Wiltshire were taken and executed in the aftermath of Towton in 1461.[8] Edward's mop-up of resistance in 1461–62 involved numerous beheadings, climaxing in 1462 with the drawing and beheading of the earl of Oxford and his son 'with other knyghtes and the kynges rebelles, traytors and adversaryes with oute the londe.'[9] After the Lincolnshire rising of 1470, captured adherents of Warwick were treated with exceptional violence: some were 'takene and beheddede' after the initial battle, and then, while seeking escape at Southampton, 'xx. Persones of gentylmen and yomenne were hangede, drawne, and quartered, and hedede; and after that thei hanged uppe by the leggys, and a stake made scharpe at bothe endes, whereof one ende was putt in att bottokys, and the other ende ther heddes were putt uppe one.'[10] After the battle of Tewkesbury in 1471, a number of prominent Lancastrian noblemen taking sanctuary in the abbey church were first apparently pardoned by Edward but were then taken and beheaded.[11] ('Taken but not slain was 'Sere Jhon Fortescu.' This was the occasion of Fortescue's initial appearance on a list of those 'hevede.')[12] Some reports had it that Prince Edward was not slain on the battlefield, but 'afterwards, by the avenging hands of certain persons.'[13] As a footnote to this battle, we read in the *Arrivall* that, following the death of Prince Edward, 'sonne aftar, wer taken, and slayne, and at the Kyngs wylle, all the noblemen [of his entourage] that came from beyond the see with the sayde Edward . . . and other also theyr parte-takers as many as were of eny might or puissance.'[14]

A dynast always has good reason to wish the elimination of a rival claimant, but a larger momentum and new rationale may be observed in these events. Underlying these executions is the presumption by each of the shifting sides in the conflict that its adversaries were engaged in actively treasonous behavior and deserved no better. Commynes points out that the disputed succession in England fostered a situation in which partisans of each side considered themselves justified in regarding their adversaries as traitors: 'Et tous disoient qu'ilz estoient traistres, à cause qu'il y avoit deux maisons qui pretendoient à la couronne.'[15] Having, in effect, already openly and notoriously demonstrated their treasonous intentions by taking the field against the occupant, or claimant, of the throne, those taken on the field were thought not to deserve or require the formalities of judicial procedure.

The prevalence of such extrajudicial violence contributed to the view, solidified in the eighteenth and nineteenth centuries, that the dynastic broils of the fifteenth century were a nadir of English civilization, a moment of domestic paralysis witnessing the blind self-extinction of the later medieval English aristocracy. Corrective accounts of the twentieth century have greatly modified such exaggerated claims of impact, first of all with respect to the scale of the events. The first battle of St. Albans, for example, may have involved no more than 5,000 men, and other crucial engagements such as Barnet and Tewkesbury probably no more than 10,000.[16] One skeptical commentator has argued that the total period in which troops were in arms 'amounted to little more than twelve or thirteen weeks in thirty-two years.'[17] Moreover, the continuities of English daily life were scarcely interrupted; as A. J. Pollard has commented, 'The arts of peace flourished, because society as a whole was for the most part untouched by the horrors of war.'[18]

Granting that the deaths of some dozens of noblemen were statistically insignificant relative to the population as a whole, the fact remains that these same deaths were nevertheless both conspicuous and urgent, in the sense that they seemed to contemporary chroniclers and commentators to demand commentary and analysis. They represented a possible wound to the common weal and in fact to the whole concept of the common weal—one that invited consideration and, if possible, some form of reclamation. This reclamation could occur through the reknitting of a fabric of continuous meaning by means of the relocation of an apparently gratuitous death within a meaning-making system.

The interest of the party perpetrating a summary execution is likely to be rather rudimentary—simply to sweep a rival or an adversary from the board with as little stir as possible, or to demean him with the suggestion that he deserved no better. When most symbolically ambitious, such executions might be intended to exemplify a rightful exercise of sovereign power— a consolidation of that power or a celebration of its victory. The aims of the contestatory party might be more complex, especially as they involve an invocation of the language and imagery of victimage or even of potentially meaningful sacrifice. In either case, the situation of a death that awaits an imposition of meaning puts me in mind of Walter Benjamin's discussion of the suffering subject at the mercy of sovereign power. I speak here of his concept of the lowest ebb to which the suffering subject can be reduced prior to death, the minimum or null-point of his humanity, described by Benjamin as the revelation of his *bloße Leben:* 'mere' life or 'bare' life, life stripped to its essence and undefended against whatever rebuke the state or temporary sovereign chooses to administer.[19] Bare life is, as it were, life stripped down and prepared for the imposition of symbolic meaning: either to become an object lesson in the sovereign's assertion of power or to unsettle sovereign power through that primary 'weapon of the weak' known as martyrdom.[20] The sovereign's goal is, in effect, to present the rival's death as ignominiously as possible, and hence as subject to his or her decree. No less is it the goal of the rival's supporters to suggest that his death has a significance that exceeds sovereign control, that it possesses an implicit dignity commensurate with the language and imagery of martyrdom.[21]

This symbolic contest is at once political (in its objectives, the gains it seeks to realize) and religious (to the extent of its reliance on the medieval heritage of religious symbolization). Its occasions are many. The second and third parts of Shakepeare's *Henry VI,* alone, represent the lonely (and usually isolate) deaths of Suffolk, York, Rutland, Clifford, Warwick, Somerset, Edward prince of Wales, and ultimately king Henry himself. Furthermore, this contest immediately summoned the utmost of representational ingenuity. Unaware of any imperative to restrain their creativity prior to Shakespeare's coming, the fifteenth-century chroniclers tackled their subjects with zest, enlisting the richest representational traditions at their command: elements of visible display, gesture, spectatorship and empathetic participation, high affect, symbolic vestment, strategic alternation of silence and vigorous verbal exchange, and the full panoply of what might generally be called 'the theatrical.' All these resources are employed at one time or another in fifteenth- and early-sixteenth-century accounts of the death of Richard duke of York.

2. YORK'S PAPER CROWN: AS MOCK-CORONATION

Little enough is actually known about Richard duke of York's death at Wake-field, except that he rashly engaged a superior Lancastrian force, and that Richard and his youngest son, Rutland, were either slain in battle or captured and beheaded after. York's head was placed on display probably on the gates of the city of York, and it was possibly mockingly adorned with a paper crown. The detail of the paper crown appears in an anonymous set of fifteenth-century *Annales* mistakenly assigned to William of Worcester.[22] In this account Richard, somewhat ignominiously foraging for food, is drawn into battle and killed on the field. His body is taken to York and, the next day, beheaded and a paper crown placed despitefully upon his severed head: 'Caput quoque ducis Eboraci in despectu coronaverunt carta.' Whether historical or invented, the notion of placing a paper crown on Richard's head begs for some consideration here, as does the fact that this action was performed despitefully ('in despectu').[23]

This 'crowning' (*cornaverunt*) depends for its meaning upon a tradition of mock-coronation, and it references a series of mock-crownings of unrightful, or at least unsuccessful, pretenders to the throne. At the end of the thirteenth century, for example, the head of the Welsh rebel Llewelyn, who had cited prophecies of Merlin in support of his claim to the crown of Britain, was mounted on a stake and brought to London for display on the Tower, crowned with a derisive garland of ivy: 'caput ejusdem Leolini amputatum, et apud civitatem Londoniensem, ubi Brutus solebat coronari, deportatumque, paloque superpositum et hedera, id est 'yvi,' coronatum, super Turrim Londoniensem fuit erectum, ipsius Merlini exponens prophetiam.'[24] Similarly, in 1305 the Scottish rebel Wallace was brought to trial in Westminster Hall, and enstated on a dais and crowned with laurel (with the dais, or *scamnum*, standing in for enthronement in the coronation ritual), the explanation being the popular report that he had previously said he should wear the crown in that very hall: 'cum lauri coronatus; pro eo quod ipse asseruit, tempore praeteriot, coronam in eadem auala portare deberet, sicut vulgariter dicebatur.'[25]

The point of crownings in this tradition revolves around the claimant's immodest presumption—an implication to which Richard was uncommonly vulnerable. Activated by this crowning is the fact of Richard's aspiration to secular kingship, his very worldly aspiration to wear an earthly crown. Mocked here is his desire for the ceremony of coronation, the wished-for consequence of his late-career decision to put aside decades of prevarication and to go all-out in pursuit of the throne. As manifested in his actions upon his return from Ireland in 1460, this was—or at least seemed to skittish contemporaries—so blatant as not only to affront the Lancastrians but also to embarrass his most loyal supporters. Thus even the mainly Yorkist Whethamstede has him, upon his recent return from Ireland, clutching at the cushion on the king's throne, and looking eagerly to those assembled for their (unforthcoming) acclamation.[26] The Crowland Continuator has him make for the throne, claiming the sole right of sitting upon it, spouting genealogy all the while; and then, offensively, moving into the king's apartments.[27] York's paper crown may thus associate him with Llewelyn and Wallace: in all these cases, the point of the derision is an ironical inversion, in which the claimant is given something he sought, but not in the form in which he sought it.

Derision is a hard thing to control. Although the paper crowning is presumably assignable to York's Lancastrian adversaries, even a mock-coronation could already be said, backhandedly or under a sign of negation, to grant some of his claims. Though Richard is mocked, and even though the readership of this passage is at least provisionally invited to join in the mockery, the effect of this ridicule is to reclothe him in at least some of his ambitions and attributes. Even if proferred with derision, the paper crown reconstitutes him, not just as a suffering body or a gory head with a severed trunk, but as a claimant of the throne, a man of ambition, a dynast who has just suffered the death of his youngest son. Meaning to dispatch his claims, his adversaries run the risk of relaunching some of them, in a backhanded concession of the very meanings they had meant not to acknowledge. In consequence of its potential symbolic density, the tradition of the paper crown was not soon to disappear.

The effective canonization of the tradition of the paper crown was its adoption into Hall's *Union of the Two Noble Houses*. Hall departs from the *Annales* in portraying Richard entering into battle as a chivalric hothead, rather than a mere forager for food. And he finds his own vivid language for the description of Richard's ill-fortuned sally into the hands of Clifford, which left him 'enuironed on euery side, like a fishe in a net or a deere in a buckestall,' and 'within halfe an houre slain and ded.'[28] But then, although somewhat condensing the *Annales'* chronology, Hall adopts its ascribed motive of mockery, agreeing that the crown was placed for purposes of amusement on York's decapitated head:

And [cruell Clifforde] came to the place wher the dead corps of the duke of Yorke lay, and caused his head to be stryken of, and set on it a croune of paper, and so fixed it on a pole, & presented it to the Quene . . . in grete despite and much derision, saiyng: Madame, your warre done, here is your kynges raunsome, at which present, was much ioy, and great re-ioysing. (1548, f. 183v)

Appropriately to his more detached vantage point, Hall deftly balances his perspectives here. On the one hand, 'cruell' Clifforde is the perpetrator, and with the violation of York's corpse and the elaborately courteous 'presenta-tion' of the severed head as a gift to Margaret is likely to cause recoil. On the other hand, the head as 'ransome' reminds the audience that York has held Henry as his captive,[29] and held the crown itself captive to his ultimate suc-cession; in the brief apparent respite between York's death and the rise of his son Edward, Henry will be 'ransomed' or freed and Prince Edward re-sume his previous place in the royal succession.

Confirming the centrality of the 'paper crown' tradition in the sixteenth century is, by the way, its adoption in the first (1559) edition of the *Mirror for Magistrates*[30]—most likely, since the Mirror authors claim him as a frequent source—from Hall. In the monologue of Richard duke of York, the order of events and spirit of Hall are carried forward, with Richard as example of 'over rash boldnes.' Speaking with 'shrekyng voyce out of the weasande pipe of the headles bodye,' Richard explains that, once his son was dead, Clifford

> . . . came to the campe where I lay dead,
> Displyde my corps, and cut away my head.
> And whan he had put a paper crowne theron,
> As a gawring stocke he sent it to the Queen. (ll. 139–42)

Adorned with the crown, York's head becomes a 'gawring stocke' or object of display; a spectacular object, in the literal sense of the word. In the fif-teenth century, response to this display might have divided along party lines, with Lancastrians joining in the derision and with Yorkists sourly contem-plating the inadvertent ironies of incompletely acknowledged kingship. Now, the mid-sixteenth-century audience of Hall's *Union* or the writings of the *Mirror* syndicate would have found less cause for either allegiance, but would presumably have found in Margaret's and Clifford's actions an effect of misplaced (and short-lived) triumphalism. York's original and apparently sense-less death has, in other words, already begun to accumulate meaning, and, more important, meaning over which even its impresario Clifford could have enjoyed little ultimate control.

3. YORK'S PAPER CROWN: AS POLITICAL MARTYRDOM[31]

If the paper crown participates in a tradition of mock-coronations, it par-ticipates at least equally in an even more powerful symbolic tradition, that of the mock-crucifixion. In this tradition, the victim is rescued from oppro-brium and the humiliation of *bloße Leben* via association with Christ's de-spiteful crowning by his tormentors in the Gospels. As we shall see, this is an extremely volatile comparison. One would suppose that a persecutor with any sense would act urgently to foreclose any possibility of comparing his victim's sufferings to those of the crucified Christ, since any sharing-out of Christ's sufferings implies an ultimate possibility of sharing in Christ's final glory. But misguided attempts to wield one or another element of Christo-logical imagery for demeaning purposes do seem sporadically to have been made. A point of reference for the later medieval period was the martyr-dom of Jan Hus, subjected in his final hours to what Foxe describes as 'con-teumelious obprobries.'[32] As Foxe tells his story, commencing immediately after his degradation, 'there remayned another knacke of reproche, for thei caused to be made a certaine crowne of paper, almoste a cubite deepe, in the whiche were paynted thre deuils of wonderfull uglye shape, and this title set ouer their heades, Heresiarcha.' His cap falling to the ground when he keels to pray, the 'souldiours' guarding him replace it, saying 'let vs put it agayne vpon his head that he may bee burned with his maisters the deuyls whome he hath serued.' Reasonably enough, the door to so favorable a comparison hav-ing been opened, Hus turns it promptly to symbolic account: 'The which whan he sawe, he sayd, my lorde Jesus Christ for my sake did weare a crowne of thorne: why should not I then for his sake agaum were this light crowne, be it neuer so ignominius: truly I will do it and that willingly.' Then the tormentors—who like all tormentors in such cases seem unable to learn from their own errors—open the door to an additional, Christological turn: 'When it was set vpon his head the bishops sayde, nowe we commit thy soule vnto the deuyl.' To which Hus replies, 'But I, saide John Hus (lifting his eyes vp towards the heauens) do commit my spiritie into thy hands.'

IOHN HVS.

John Hus. From John Foxe, *Actes and Monuments* (1563), Magdalen College Arch. B.I.4. Courtesy of the President and Fellows of Magdalen College Oxford.

Such despiteful crownings evidently become standard fare in the Spanish Inquisitions of the following century, with mitres called 'corocas' placed upon the heads of burnt martyrs.[33] This is, of course, a highly unstable representational stratagem, since, as Hus's attributed response well demonstrates, the deep tradition of Christ's abjection immediately allows an inversion in which the intended symbol of degradation is converted to a marker of spiritual glory. In this vein, martyrs themselves often adopt one or another form of 'crowning' in direct emulation of Christ. In Foxe's account of yet another martyrdom, 'Anthony Person, pullyng the straw vnto him, layd a good deale therof vpon the top of his head, saying: this is Gods hat: now am I dressed like a true souldiour of Christ.'[34] Person thus pits himself against the 'souldiours' of the civil arm, who torment him as did the tormentors of Christ, even as he asserts a form of respectful emulation (at the distance prescribed by sixteenth-century Protestant decorums) of Christ. The mistake of these would-be mockers is to suppose that one derision can be isolated from another; that the derision directed against Christ by his tormentors can be safely quarantined from the derision *they* mean to direct against Christ as an unlikely epigone of their God. Person's genius—and the genius of all these heretics—is to assert a common denominator with Christ, by suggesting that, precisely *as* objects of derision, they have more in common with Christ than their tormentors have supposed.

Whether manipulated by resourceful victims or introduced by sympathetic viewers or commentators, the elements of mock-crowning can hardly resist assimilation to the ubiquitous and more powerful imagery surrounding the sacrifice of Christ. Sometimes deliberately, sometimes with apparent inadvertence, this imagery is marshaled in defense of York's disparaged claims. One such marshalling—the earliest that I know—occurs in Abbot John Whethamstede's mid-fifteenth-century *Register*.[35] In this account York, together with the earl of Salisbury, was taken alive at Wakefield ('ceperunt in bello vivos'), as a consequence of which he was not only decapitated but also subjected to verbal and other symbolic mistreatment before his death. As the *Register* has it, York, especially among the captured lords, was mockingly mistreated, treated *multum ludibriose,* in the following fashion:

Nam statuentes eum super unum parvum formicarium colliculum, et quoddam sertum vile, ex palustri gramine confectum, imponentes per modum coronae super caput suum, non aliter quam Judaei coram Domino, incurvaverunt genua sua coram ipso, dicentes illusorie,—"Ave, rex, sine regimine. Ave, rex, absque haeriditate. Ave, dux et princeps, absque omni populo penitus, et possessione." Et hiis, una cum aliis variis, in eum probose opprobrioseque dictis, coegerunt ipsum demum, per capitis abscissionem, clameum relinquere suae justitiae vendicationis. (p. 382)

[For, standing him on a little anthill, and, placing on his head in the manner of a crown a sort of lowly chaplet, woven of marsh-grass, they bent their knees before him like the Jews before the Lord, saying, feigningly, 'Hail, king, without kingdom. Hail, king, without inheritance. Hail, duke and prince, without a following, or possessions.' And with such shameful and opprobrious utterances, together with other variations, at last, by decapitation, they ended his pursuit of his rightful claim.]

To treat someone *ludobriose* is to treat them in game or play, with implied mockery; not necessarily to cast them in a literal 'play,' but to treat them with a mixture of festivity/trickery/mockery/theatricality which goes all the way back to the Plautine *ludus,* and still holds here. This 'playful' near-pun is sustained by the fact that the torturers address Richard *illuso-rie:* 'mockingly,' in Classical Latin, a sense still present here, but also, in the later medieval lexicon, in a spirit of invention, of feigning or illusion—a hypothetical state that may be likened to a 'playlet' or deliberately composed spectacle. Centralizing York as an object of regard, casting themselves as mock-subjects, they turn him into the effective subject of a 'play,' and the effect of a play is to create a zone of free or hypothetical meanings, within which new meanings are invented and new associations formed. Here, the meanings mainly involve analogies between York's sufferings and those of Christ—right up to the final decapitation, the final terminus of the traitor and the saint, typically the last step in a process preceding the figurative crowning and the canonizing of the martyred saint. Once this kind of imagery begins to flow, York's tormentors have already in effect lost their representational game. But I would like to pause a while, to see how they lost it.

What, we must ask, is here being played *with,* and to what effect? Much demands exploration here, including the rather prepossessing—and, in Lancastrian terms, unfortunate—comparison of Richard with the crucified Christ. This passage is, of course, a conflation of several familiar Gospel passages, its chaplet of marsh grass embracing the crown of thorns, the garment with which Christ is bedecked, and the reed with which he is beaten. These elements are to be found in the Gospels, already couched in the theatrical language of ludic play or 'playful' mockery:

And, platting a crown of thorns, they put it upon his head, and a reed in his right hand. And, bowing the knee before him, they mocked him [Vulgate: *illudebant ei*], saying, 'Hail, King of the Jews.' [*Ave rex iudae-orum*]. (Matt. 27:29)

And they clothed him with purple; and, platting a crown of thorns, they put it upon him. And they began to salute him: Hail, king of the Jews. [*Ave rex iudaeorum*] And they struck his head with a reed [*arundine*]. (Mk. 15:17–19)

All these suggestions are woven in, but our passage also shows the productive influence of concurrent vernacular elaborations. Consider, for example, its exploration of the ironies of Richard's situation as aspirant to the throne, well known for his royal ambitions, but currently possessed of nothing more solid than his negotiated status as Henry's heir. Imagining himself king, he enjoys none of that office's appurtenances: 'Hail, king, without kingdom. Hail, king, without inheritance. Hail, duke and prince, completely without a people, or possessions.' A parallel situation is attributed, in the nearly contemporary York mystery plays, to Christ, when his tormentors, unable to grasp the nature of his claims, mistake his heavenly pretensions for earthly ones and deride the unfounded nature of his rule. Crowning him with 'brere,' placing a purple cape upon his shoulders, and fetching a reed for a sceptre, they seat him upon a throne and show mock reverence, in order to 'gudly hym grete on this grounde.'

> Ave! riall roy and rex judeorum!
> Hayle! Comely kyng, that no kyngdom has kende,
> Hayll! Vndughty duke, thi dedis ere dom,
> Hayll! Man, vnmyghty thi menye to mende.
> Hayll! lord with-oute lande for to lende.[36]

The 'ground' is itself a kind a *platea,* centre of a performance that toys with the audience's sense of unsought (but, ultimately and ironically, earned) reverence. *Our* 'duke without possessions' cannot avoid—nor is his representation in Whethamstede intended to avoid—association with his precursor, the divine but 'Vndughty duke . . . vnmyghty (his) menye to mende.'

In fact, although Whethamstede finds York suffering from *probose opprobrioseque*—shameful and opprobrious—utterances, he remains an extreme symbolic beneficiary of this exchange. What he has to give it is, in effect, nothing—his destitution, his separation from any possibility of succor, his silence. Yet silence is the 'language' that marks his separation from the community, as embodied in the verbose torturers, and its denial of his achievements. His silence is discovered, in turn, to possess a proclivity for the sacred, as revealed in the imagery of Christ's sacrifice, including Christ's own silence at the hands of the torturers. In consequence, we are left looking at a monumental collapse of Lancastrian 'spin,' in which Whethamstede, with his intermittent but persistent Yorkism, glimpses quasi-divine stature at the moment of this presumptuous and hotheaded claimant's lonely death. Here the languages and trajectories of religion and secular politics enjoy a brief but potent convergence, as the imagery of Christ's sacrifice is arrogated to the enhancement of the Yorkist cause.

4. EQUIVOCAL SHAKESPEARE

Christological imagery comes a bit harder in the sixteenth and seventeenth centuries, or must at least be claimed on slightly altered terms. Setting aside for a moment the reservations of fifteenth-century Lollards and some others about iconographic representations, the hallmark of Christ's sacrifice in the later Middle Ages is its extreme availability for all sorts of reiterative representation, reevocation, meditation, comparison. By contrast, a prevalent sixteenth-century view—especially among Protestants but with some influence even among Catholics—discovers the sacrifice of Christ to occur uniquely, distinctively, and nonrepeatably.

The shift I want to signal is conveniently epitomized by Euan Cameron, who describes a late medieval consensus about a 'sacrificial mass' which 'repeated' Christ's original sacrifice every time the Mass was celebrated. Whereas he describes the sixteenth-century Protestant view (anticipated, of course, in earlier centuries) as antirepetitive, in the sense that 'the communion service . . . should be the sign of Christ's passion, not the repetition of it to the point of redundancy.'[37] As a consequence of this shift in outlook, the sixteenth century exhibits an added reticence with respect to the unchecked and unimpeded reiteration of Christ's sacrifice. Not only Protestant but also Catholic martyrology may be seen as at least touched by a new deference to the singularity of Christ's sacrifice.[38] In the mid-sixteenth century, Foxe's Protestant hagiography and its various Catholic counterparts are likely to agree in discovery of certain qualities of fortitude, quiet resolve, good cheer, and purposeful exemplarity on the part of their martyrs. If an external warrant for martyrdom is to be sought, it is most likely found in the martyr's testimony to consistent belief in a true (vs. of course false) church, and to certain consistencies of practice and belief to be discovered by Catholics and Protestants alike—in the recent church by the former, and in the early church by the latter.[39]

Thus we might assume that any approach by Shakespeare to what Kantorowicz called 'Royal Christology' would be a halting one.[40] Indeed, a good deal of equivocation and turbulence attend the stubborn and embarrassing eruptions of such sacred imagery into the late-sixteenth-century textual world of realpolitik. Understandably enough, modern commentators have tried to corral Shakespeare's rampant and erratic sacral symbolism by one or another oversimplification: either by taking it too 'straight' on the one hand or by subsuming and neutralizing it as part of an argument for outright and unproblematic 'secularization' on the other. A mainly superseded scholarly tradition (in which I was trained) found Shakespeare wielding medieval sacrality and theocentric world order on behalf of Tudor teleology.[41] This satisfying synthesis has been under constant revisionary attack, first by modernist critics like Ribner and Ornstein who asserted Shakespeare's intellectual subtlety and independence, and later by New Historicist and postmodernist critics who found the Tudor belief system (even in the generally orthodox strivings of Hall and the 'Holinshed' compilers) to be more fissured and internally at odds than Tillyard's orderly account could possibly have credited.[42] For good enough reasons, our own view is to find more wrinkles and contradictions, and less capacity for totalization, than Tillyard presumed in the construction of his 'world picture.'

Nevertheless, the Tudors and Stuarts were of no mind to relinquish what might be thought of as different 'strategic sacralities.' They are often to be found, for example, in different sorts of nervous or fitful embrace of what might have been thought medieval ideas of sacral kingship. I take note, in this respect, of Richard McCoy's judicious conclusion that 'Shakespeare thus affirms some of the mysterious force of sacred kingship not through propagation of its claims but through an ambiguous equivocation.'[43] The apparatus of sacral kingship and the traditional supports of sacred order are always present in the plays (both positively asserted by spokespersons like 'good duke Humphrey,' and negatively implied by their conspicuous absence), albeit in desuetude, in a ruined and ineffective condition, preserved incidentally as the rubble out of which a new symbolic edifice can be made.[44] In my reading, Shakespeare's history plays usually treat medieval sacral traditions—of prophecy and divination, divine right, trial by battle, the sacerdotal function—as windfall symbolic capital. As windfall capital, they are available to be transferred, expropriated, reused, and squandered, without apparent regard to their maintenance and even in derision about their continued viability. Yet powerful sacral imagery gains provisional advantage just by 'staying around,' by lurking on the fringes, or at the interstices, of discourse, ever eligible for reappropriation on revived or altered grounds.

Nor did the external context of drama in the 1590s foreclose such acts of appropriation. Later sixteenth- and earlier seventeenth-century political culture provided a new and fertile ground for Christological imagery, at exactly the point at which it might have seemed likely to be withdrawn from such usage and confined more strictly to Christ's own person. This is the ground of political symbolization, which ransacked earlier religious tradition for usable materials, even as monastic properties were looted and redistributed a half century before. John Phillips has written about the arrogation of (Christological) symbols by Protestant rulers of various persuasions following in the wake of Henry VIII's attack upon the institutions of Catholicism. Flourishing during the reign of Elizabeth was 'a civil-religious ambience whereby Englishmen could be loyal to God and king, and with clear conscience circumvent the loyalty to Rome and the institutions of Roman Catholicism. . . . The divine right of kingship was not renounced. Instead it was defined outside the context of Roman and Catholic defense and authority.'[45] And Richard C. McCoy argues that 'Under the Tudor Reformation, this immanent royal presence became an animating and redemptive real presence, binding ruler and ruled together in a communion stronger than any proffered by an alien papal authority.'[46]

If this later period was more cautious in its Christology, the symbols of Christ's passion were nevertheless available to be resummoned, particularly in relation to charged episodes or moments in the course of kingship, or to certain vital symbols such as the royal crown. Some of the symbolic urgency of York's crown was evident in the fifteenth century, whether in the *Annales* with its mock-coronation or the *Register* with its mock-crucifixion. And the crown, as vital symbol, certainly made the passage from late-medieval to early-modern political culture. The crown was, initially and irrevocably, divided, as both the symbol of a particular incumbency (the sign that, through coronation and unction, a particular person has been chosen as rightful king of the realm) and also a more general symbol, unattached to any incumbency, of the realm itself. In the former capacity, it is a possession, it belongs to a single, anointed individual, and is the sign that he holds the kingdom in fee. In the latter capacity, it eludes any singular gesture of control, possessed by no one person and passing from incumbency to incumbency depending on inheritance, conquest, acclamation, or other circumstance. In this respect, the crown's multiplicity conforms to Kantorowicz's terminology; it represents the 'natural' body of the individual and historical 'crowned king,' and it also represents the 'mystical body' that is no one man's possession, but figures the realm itself, upon which no individual can lay more than temporary claim.[47] The attempt to secure or possess the crown is thus inherently futile; it constitutes an object of aspiration, but one that defies 'ownership' in any ordinary sense of the term.

To the extent of its attachment to a single, 'natural' body, the crown was subject to a host of vicissitudes, vexed questions of ownership, and even downright degradation. One can hardly view otherwise those occasions when it was placed in pawn as security for a £2000 loan to Richard II in 1382,[48] and, even more remarkably, was divided into sections—a fleur de lys and three pinacles—and pledged to finance the French wars of Henry V, not to be redeemed until 1430–31.[49] In this respect, it may be seen as mobile, moving from claimant to claimant, place to place, task to task—still a symbol, but a motile or moving symbol, in every sense of the word. At the same time, to the extent that it represented the king's mystical body, and was thus immortal, the crown possessed a sublime meaning beyond issues of ownership. In this guise, it not only stood for the whole of the kingdom, but also the quasi-sacramental process by which God elects a vicar or sacerdotal representative to rule the land.[50] The symbolic motility of the crown could only be enhanced by such Christological associations. If the king was vicar of Christ[51] and Christ's representative on earth, then any derogation of his status might be epitomized through evocation of Christ's martyr's crown of thorns. This comparison draws upon both strands of the crown's meaning. The crown was seen as as hyper-'natural' (natural with, as it were, a vengeance), even as Christ possessed a natural body and was subject to physical torment on earth. It was also seen as mystical and holy, even as Christ's own divine body was ever-separable from the torments of the world. The instability, and ambivalence, surrounding York's crown or any crown opened a wide range of highly nuanced associations and meanings.

Before returning to York's crown, I would like to enrich the context of consideration by looking briefly at two other texts of the late sixteenth and seventeenth century in which 'royal Christology' saturates an intense meditation on the king's crown. First, another and slightly later Shakespeare play in which crown imagery is ubiquitous, his *Richard II*. Perhaps the retrospective medievalism of this play allowed Shakespeare to indulge some previous or anachronistic beliefs about sacral kingship. But the *true* anachronism of this play—as observed by Kantorowicz, who draws his most trenchant examples of the medieval doctrine of the king's two bodies precisely from this play— is the fidelity of its views on kingship to an emergent late-sixteenth-century political and juridical theory of the crown. The crown, and ideas about the crown, are vital constituents of this play. The subject is introduced early on by Gaunt, when he chides Richard for his susceptibility to flattery with its attendant costs to his reputation:

> Thy deathbed is no lesser than thy land,
> Wherein thou liest in reputation sick. . . .
> A thousand flatterers sit within thy crown,
> Whose compass is not bigger than thy head,
> And yet, encagèd in so small a verge,
> The waste is no whit lesser than thy land. (2.1.95–96; 100–103)

Invoked here is what Peter Brown would have called an effect of '"inverted magnitudes," by which the object around which boundless associations clustered should be so tiny and compact.'[52] So is the crown at once compact—no larger than the circuit of Richard's brow—and infinitely large—encompassing the entire kingdom. This is the respect to which Kantorowicz has so persuasively drawn our attention, with the crown both pertaining to Richard's natural body as it sits upon his brow and referent in its mystical aspect to the entirety of the kingdom. The duality of this symbol is registered in the concept of the 'verge,' which in English law was a patch of land immediately occupied by the king, its boundaries moving as he moved, over which he enjoyed absolute suzerainty and complete legal control. Richard's 'verge' has shrunken to the limit of his corrupt perceptions, the brow encircled by the crown, even as his mystical domain, the entirety of the kingdom, is corrupted by his ill judgment and susceptibility to flattery. His is a 'blemished crown,' a crown that Henry's supporters expect him to 'Redeem from broking pawn' (2.2.295).

Imagining his anointment irreversible, Richard delusively supposes his crown not gilt but 'golden' (3.2.55). But harsh political tidings propel Richard into his falls-of-princes meditation ('let us sit upon the ground, / And tell sad stories of the death of kings'—3.2.150–51), and thence to this reflection on his crown's sacral emptiness:

> . . . For within the hollow crown
> That rounds the mortal temples of a king
> Keeps Death his court; and there the antic sits,
> Scoffing his state and grinning at his pomp.' (3.2.156–59)

In another miracle of scale, the crown here becomes an amphitheater, or at least a theater-in-the-round, in which an anticourt constitutes its own irreverent spectacle, mocking Richard's pretensions.

Infinitely adaptable, this shape-shifting, will-o'-the-wisp crown seems to possess a mobility all its own, like those motile and mobile objects of medieval romance, such as Balin's sword which jumps in the river and swims downsteam to Winchester to arrange its own destined meeting with Galahad (and its ultimate progress to Lancelot, who will use it to slay Gawain). Here, people strive variously to retain and possess it, and it is both an object and an arena of contention. At the climactic moment, Richard stages his struggle with Bolingbroke precisely as a tug-of-war over the crown, dramatizing that recurring moment of embarrassment in which a kingdom is discovered to have too many claimants and too few crowns. (This moment is parallel with that of Georges Franju's *Les yeux sans visage*, a horror film that pivots on what Carol Clover has described as the dilemma of 'too many faces and not enough skin.')[53] As Richard says,

> . . . Here, cousin, seize the crown.
> Here, cousin. On this side my hand, on that side thine.
> Now is this golden crown like a deep well
> That owes two buckets filling one another,
> The emptier ever dancing in the air. (4.1.172–76)

Not simply a passive object of contention, the crown itself turns out once again to possess significant interior resources within which a more complete visualization of the situation is made available. The crown in effect becomes a well of desire where desire's extent can be estimated and understood. Not fully quoted here is a lengthy exchange (4.1.181–94) in which the griefs that attend the crown, and those that accompany it, and those that remain, are canvassed. Then Richard, ever chief impressario of his own theatrics, presides over his own ceremony of degradation, commencing with:

> Now mark me how I will undo myself.
> I give this heavy weight from off my head. (4.1.193–94)

But of course Richard already knows that the crown can be lost, or alienated, but cannot be securely conferred—since, at least in the absence of appropriate unction, it cannot really be possessed. As he has said about Bolingbroke to Northumberland,

> But ere the crown he looks for live in peace
> Ten thousand bloody crowns of mothers' sons
> Shall ill become the flower of England's face. (3.3.94–96)

Shakespeare could, of course, enter this prophetic mode with confidence, since he knew what would come to pass and what he had already written about it. But the relevant point is that in Shakespeare's history plays many aspirants 'look' for the crown, but the crown looks out for itself. The crown knows its own terms and its own conditions of peace, and—in the slightly uncanny way in which objects can know things—knows that those conditions will remain elusive for Bolingbroke and for his successors.

Shakespeare thus views the crown in the ambivalent way in which his contemporaries—whether Protestant or Catholic—viewed many elements of their medieval, sacral inheritance. The Elizabethans wanted the crown, as a quasi-sacramental object, as part of the panoply of their own late-blooming concept of sacerdotal kingship. But they were only intermittently aware of its elusiveness, its difficulty of possession, its power to mislead or betray. The fantastical imagination that the crown might be possessed can inspire a form of mistaken self-regard. This is the frame of mind in which the crown's aspirants and temporary possessors are so liable to misplaced or fantastical Christological associations. Even though Richard mounts no imagistic attempt on Christ's crown of thorns, he does resort—in the very scene of the crown's resignation—to the imagery of Christ's Passion. Thus, of his false followers:

> . . . Were they not mine?
> Did they not sometime cry 'All hail!' to me?
> So Judas did to Christ. . . .
> God save the King! Will no man say 'Amen'?
> Am I both priest and clerk? Well then, Amen.
> God save the King, although I be not he.
> And yet Amen, if heaven do think him me. (4.1.159–61, 163–66)

Analogizing himself to Christ, he recovers a sense of his sacerdotal function; acknowledging the loss of his earthly or natural right to the crown, he imagines that heaven might persist in recognizing his symbolic or spiritual right to the crown by virtue of anointment. On the strength of this imagination, he thinks himself betrayed by his own followers, in the manner of Christ. Likewise, he imagines himself the victim of a sort of Passion, in his own right:

> Though some of you, with Pilate, wash your hands,
> Showing an outward pity, yet you Pilates
> Have here delivered me to my sour cross. (4.1.229–31)

Richard here participates in the ambivalent—or perhaps one might say opportunistic—Tudor view of the symbolic capital still available within partially debased elements of late-medieval sacramentality.

Outliving the Tudors, 'royal Christology' would experience a belated resurgence in and around the case of Charles I. Charles I, as ventriloquized in the apologetic royal portraiture of *Eikon Basilike*, demonstrates facility in this discourse in his assertion that 'I will rather choose to wear a crown of thorns with my Saviour than to exchange that of gold, which is due to me, for one of lead.'[54] In this case, Charles rejects a proposed exchange—of the emblem of his sacred or theocratic kingship for the baser and more mutable substitute proposed to him by Parliament—in favor of a different symbolic trajectory, with its transit from an earthly crown to a martyr's crown and a direct participation in the symbolic aura of Christ's sacrifice. Charles himself then made a similar, but modified, claim on the scaffold, proposing to 'go from a corruptible to an incorruptible Crown'[55]—in this case, from an earthly crown now acknowledged to lack imagined qualities of transcendence to the martyr's Crown of salvation. The explicit association with Christ is omitted from this final speech, but is amply present in Charles's self-representations, and those of his followers, and those of his subsequent cult.[56] In a prayer constructed for Charles by the author of the *Eikon Basilike*, he regrets having briefly forgotten 'to imitate my crucified Redeemer . . . and in my dying extremities to pray to Thee, O Father, to forgive them, for they knew not what they did' (p. 157). A closer conjunction still is embraced in his meditation upon his own death, which explicitly associates his sufferings and those of Christ: 'If I must suffer a violent death with my Saviour, it is but mortality crowned with martyrdom' (p. 179). These hints and suggestions are furthered in a flood of writings, some before and especially after, the death of Charles, including works such as Symmons, *A Vindication of King Charles* (1648), which offered fourteen parallels between Charles and Christ.

5. YORK'S PAPER CROWN AGAIN

Elements of the medieval belief system that seem to be present mainly as 'consumables'—as disposable items to be manipulated for temporary advantage—turn out to possess residual power, available to be resummoned under new conditions of possibility. Skepticism, and even overt resistance, can in the right set of circumstances turn out only to be what they so often were in medieval drama and homiletics: as necessary preludes to the miraculous. Some of the circumstances to which I refer include the presence of an unusually durable belief; the availability of a medium within which that belief can reinstantiate itself; and a set of new historical circumstances in which that belief may be activated and reengaged. The belief in question is that version of sacred kingship in which the king is found to possess attributes of the divine, and compared to Christ, and most crucially is found in martyrdom to possess elements of Christ's own sacrifice. The medium is the Shakespearean stage. The historical circumstances are those of late Tudor and early Jacobean monarchy, the divine propensities of which were enjoying a cautious and hesitant amplification.

Shakespeare is in accord with the spirit of his time when he offers us an account of York's death in which Christological associations are held somewhat at bay. Its structuration is less Passion-derived than that of the Whethamstede tradition, and more evidently reliant upon the secularity of the *Annales*-Hall tradition. York's death is predominantly viewed through the lens, not of martyrdom, but of ironic anti-coronation. But I use the word 'predominantly' with deliberation. Even under conditions of resistance—including its theological and cultural discouragement—the imagery of Christ's sacrifice retains certain limited, but very persistent, powers of repropagation.

Shakespeare acquires his source by a virtual accident. Whethamstede's analysis might have been a kind of 'sport,' likely to have died on the vine, and indeed it languished for a hundred years before the Holinshed compilers restored it to view. In his first edition (1577), Holinshed prints the Hall account, with its emphasis on mock-coronation, more or less verbatim, as the now-standard sixteenth-century version. No sooner is it done, though, than, in their 1586 edition, Abraham Fleming and his collaborators reinstate the alternate tradition, by turning to Whethamstede (whom they marginally credit) as an add-on. Describing the decapitation of the dead York and his head's presentation, fixed on a pole and crowned with paper, to Queen Margaret, they add:

> Some write that the duke was taken alive, and in dereision caused to stand on a molehill, on whose head they put a garland in steed of a crowne, which they had fashioned and made of sedges or bulrushes; and having so crowned him with that garland, they kneeled downe afore him (as the Jewes did unto Christ) in scorne, saieng to him; Haile king without rule, haile king without heritage, haile duke and prince without people or possessions.[57]

They retain Worcester's molehill in preference to Whethamstede's anthill, but carry most of the latter's other materials into this addendum.

The recovery of Whethamsted is abetted by the nature of Holinshed's text, which, although experienced as an apparent unity, actually carries forward a congeries of writings by earlier chroniclers and historians. These earlier writers are not, by the way, anonymous; in fact, their names are placed on ostentatious display as Holinshed marginalia: Strabo, Higden, Froissart, Walsingham, Harding, Enguerrand de Monstrelet, Titus Livius, the Croyland Continuator, 'the Arrivall of Edward IV' credited to Fleetwood, John Whethamstede, Polydore Vergil. Yet even as these writers' appearance 'in the margins' constitutes a form of recognition, such citations also mark the place of an effective disappearance. For the passages attributable to these named sources effectively fade without other demarcation into the collectivity we call 'Holinshed.'[58]

In cases like this one, given an incentive to look around and behind Holinshed as a unitary 'source,' we restore an element of internal difference and variance to view. One aspect of this difference is the unexpected pertinacity of these constituent texts' adherence to their original aims, even in their new locations and even new extensive alteration by intermediate hands. Rather than cede their difference, they assert their claims by a stubborn adherence to their original purposes and a surprising knack for re-propagating themselves in their new location. One might say that they retain some of their own DNA, like that murderer's hand grafted to the arm of an honest citizen in movies like *Mad Love* (1935) or *Hands of Orloc* (1961); it wants to go on doing what it always did, which in that case was to throw knives at people. So do these prior and disguised sources indefatigably (and atavistically) go on doing some of their original work. Our Whethamstede account, restored to Shakespeare's view, will not prove docile, will in effect prove unwilling to act as inert matter or passive clay simply awaiting the shaping hand of Shakespeare's genius. Like the hands of Orlac, it will want to do some of what it used to do. And, behaving in this unruly way, it will be the occasion of a partial recovery of the sacred within the new ambit of the Shakespeare play.

Certainly, as far as a dramatic intention can be derived from the scene of York's death in *The True Tragedie of Richarde Duke of Yorke and the death of the Good King Henrie the Sixt*,[59] it remains a secular event, conceived within the tradition of the mock-coronation.[60] Although Shakespeare's scene possesses a certain cousinship to accounts of Christ's taunting by his torturers (since that taunting relies upon his pretensions to kingship), its symbolic ambit less obviously relies upon the gospels than upon orthodox medieval coronation behaviors. 'Dogged York,' as Gloucester calls him (*Contention*, 3.1.158) has repeatedly and promiscuously sought the trappings of kingship, and the reality of office which they portray—the sceptre (*Contention*, 5.1.9), the throne (*Tragedie*, 1.1.51), and, of course, the crown (*Tragedie*, 1.1.114, 166, etc.). This is the ambition to which Margaret speaks, in the mock-crowning as she devises it:

> York cannot speak unless he wear a crown.
> A crown for York, and, lords, bow low to him.
> Hold you his hands whilst I do set it on.
> Ay, marry, sir, now looks he like a king,
> Ay, this is he that took King Henry's chair,
> And this is he was his adopted heir.
> But how is it that great Plantagenet
> Is crowned so soon and broke his solemn [quarto: 'holy'] oath?
> (*Tragedie*, 1.4.94–101)

Following the Worcester-Hall tradition, Margaret evidently places a paper crown (rather than a garment of rushes) on York's head.[61]

The referents here seem mainly to York's earthly ambitions, evoked by Margaret's reference to the parliamentary maneuvering through which York supplanted Prince Edward as Henry's heir; and by her citation of his now-violated oath that Henry should reign undisturbed until death; and her later (l. 105) reference to Richard's intent to rob Henry's 'temples of the diadem.'

Assuming for herself the role of archbishop and presiding cleric, she constitutes her followers as beholders and participants in a coronation ceremony, and when she suggests that they 'bow low to him' the object of her irony is his failure to attain an earthly, rather than a heavenly, crown.

Yet here Margaret stages a play . . . and, as in Whethamstede's fifteenth-century rendition of Richard's death, the play-within-a-play is a privileged area with respect to reaccommodation of the sacred, a propitious circuit for a return of the sacral repressed. The premise of this much-altered and augmented playlet remains the same as that of Whethamstede: the reduction of Richard to a state of abjection, coupled with the kinds of *probose opprobrioseque* taunts with which we have become familiar. At least at this momentary juncture, Margaret possesses a sovereign's rights with respect to York's ultimate fate. Once York falls into the hands of the Lancastrians, he becomes, in effect, Margaret's subject, and is already as good as dead, has *already* died a symbolic death at her hands, awaiting only the completion of the process by his literal death, his murder: his decapitation and his head's display. Thus abandoned to an external will, a will that expresses itself playfully and mockingly by prolonging his torment, Richard awaits, and then receives, his death. And the prepossessing fact about Richard's death is this: even in a Shakespearean form, held rather consciously distant from traditions of martyrdom, and even when treated by Margaret as a murder pure and simple, it cannot finally resist or withstand reattachment to the Christian vocabulary and imagery of sacrifice.

As with the Lancastrian torturers in the Whethamstede account, Margaret's taunts are no doubt intended ironically, pointing to the gap between York's inflated regal ambitions on the one hand and his human vulnerability on the other. But a veneer of irony is a very weak control, over so powerful a body of imagery as this. For the imagery of Christ's sacrifice is liable to assert itself in unpremediated ways; it becomes, almost inevitably, imagery out of control, imagery at odds with the apparent purposes of the act. Mocking Richard's destitution, Margaret's ironic pretense inadvertently opens a 'side door' through which the sacred can reenter this play. Any kind of 'play' with the elements of the sacred is 'dangerous' play for monarchs who would consolidate their authority by denying their subjects the dignity of sacrifice. In the York mystery cycle, Christ's torturers became, by ironic inversion, his unwitting prophets, testifying to the elements of his majesty for a biblical or dramatic audience that knows how to interpret the signs. Similarly, these secular torturers risk giving York, not just his

death, but the gift of a sacrificial death. Where these torturers go wrong
is not just in attempting to construct irony from such powerful and potentially 'runaway' elements, but in accepting these elements within an imaginative form of symbolic play, in which fusion, or perhaps I should say 'fission,'
can occur in the presence of any Christological imagery at all.

Margaret's 'staging' of her little play may thus be said to escape its apparent purpose:

> Come make him stand upon this molehill here,
> That wrought at mountains with outstretchèd arms
> Yet parted but the shadow with his hand.
> What—was it you that would be England's king? (1.4.68–71)
> [var: Was it you that reuelde in our Parliament,
> And made a preachment of your high descent?—quarto, B.3.verso]

She clearly intends reference to York's earthly claims. Kingship was certainly
York's objective, and notoriously so, and the quarto variant is even more
'worldly' in its recognition of the stir York made in Parliament and the genealogical terms in which he cast his actual claim. The 'molehill' is no longer
Calvary in her figure, but rather a diminished equivalent of his inflated or
'mountainous' objectives, diminished first by being worldly rather than spiritual and second by York's present defeat. Nevertheless, Shakespeare presumably knew the canceled Whethamstede-Holinshed alternative, and his
depiction of the living Richard, atop his molehill, readmits some of Whethamstede's canceled sacrificial imagery to this scene. Does he stand on his
molehill with 'with outstretchèd arms'? Margaret's taunt refers to his former
ambitions rather than his present degradation. Yet her reference also would
seem to constitute an implied stage direction, with Richard's arms *now* 'outstretchèd' not in a 'power grab' but in an enforced repetition of the crucifixion of Christ.

This playlet thus becomes an arena for the unintended rediscovery of
York's potential for redemption. York, destitute on the stage, first alone and
stripped of his followers, and then in the hands of his enemies, joins the procession of characters in the *Contention* and the *Tragedie* who are stripped
down to 'bare life,' to life without meaning or possible redemption. But then
the imagery of sacrifice, eluding Margaret's stage-managerial control, awards
him the possibility of an escape from the conditions of bare life, even when
such an escape is least to be expected. So, too, does Margaret, engaging in

a kind of frenzy of self-defeating symbolizations, redouble this sacrificial aura by presenting York with a devotional object or relic for his cult of secular martyrdom:

> Look, York, I stained this napkin with the blood
> That valiant Clifford with his rapier's point
> Made issue from the bosom of thy boy.
> And if thine eyes can water for his death,
> I give thee this to dry thy cheeks withal. (I.4. 80–84)

Once again, within the imaginatively favorable compass of the play-within-a-play, imagery breaks through the constraints of its original purpose. Rutland here becomes martyr, his suffering metonymically emblematized in his own blood like a Christian saint.

Furthering this imagery of martyrdom is, of course, York's paper crown, already introduced by Margaret in her mock-coronation of lines 93 ff. This play has, of course, been saturated with discussion of the crown, crowns, and the strife over their getting and having, their wanting and refusal, their possession, dispossession, and spoilage. A bare hint of the crown's ubiquity is the fact that it is mentioned some sixteen times in Act 1, scene i alone. Crownings and seizures of the crown are vividly and repeatedly imagined, epitomizing York's political imaginary and that of his sons:

> RICHARD: Father, tear the crown from the usurper's head.
> EDWARD: Sweet father, do so—set it on your head. (1.1, 113–14)

Now finding himself with a crown indeed, but not the one he had sought, York sets out to rework its symbolism. The unwanted crown, the derisive paper crown, is returned to Margaret with his curse:

> There, take the crown—and with the crown, my curse:
> And in thy need such comfort come to thee
> As now I reap at thy too cruel hand. (165–67)

But the implicitly sacred imagery of this play-within-a-play has opened the way to the revalorization of this crown as a symbol of martyrdom. Renouncing the worldly crown, York is quick to announce the symbolic gain he has accomplished:

Hard-hearted Clifford, take me from the world.
My soul to heaven, my blood upon your heads. (168–69)

And then, stabbed by Clifford and Margaret:

Open thy gate of mercy, gracious God—
My soul flies through these wounds to seek out thee. (179–80)
[var: My soule flies foorth to meet with thee.—quarto, B5, recto]

York is not wrong in concluding that his treatment at the hands of his tormentors has given him that right so often accorded to solitary sufferers in Shakespearean drama: the right of victimage. As Michael O'Connell has perceptively observed, 'in Shakespeare . . . bodies in pain, bodies that have suffered violence and death, achieve a kind of authority and power over those who have inflicted their suffering.'[62] For this authority to be realized, however, the presence of an external, and stabilizing, vocabulary of sacrifice is required. That is what Clifford and Margaret concede to York by virtue of their rather heedless plunge into the symbolic vocabulary of martyrdom. Granting him the imagery of sacrifice, alluding—even in a displaced way—to outstretched arms, displaying a de facto relic, these tormentors who would delimit and seal up the meaning of his death by mockery actually allow their victim to claim a sacrificial view of his own demise. Conceiving himself as a martyr, York imagines his soul's immediate access to heaven. His martyrdom is, of course, implicitly Christological—a reading strengthened in the later folio, in which York's soul not only issues to meet God, but issues from his wounds. York might be said, rhetorically, to overplay his hand here, in this evocation of Christ's wounds and his own soul's rapturous ascent to God; but the point is that, in their reckless deployment of imagery and charged language, Margaret and Clifford have given him a hand to play.

At the same time, so histrionic and so blatantly self-serving is York's response that we find ourselves more aware of his penchant for grandiose self-staging than of any more properly theological insight. Actually, York's haste to cloak himself in Christological symbolism covers a more problematic act of presumption on his part. Kantorowicz has pointed out a possible flaw in the 'two bodies' analogy, when moving between king and Christ.[63] Although the 'two bodies of Christ'—mortal and divine—would seem to present an analogy to the king's two bodies, the analogy does not hold. The king's natural body remains mortal in a sense in which the body of Christ, who always possessed an eternal part, does not. In this sense, it is possible for a king to overpresume in the matter of his sacerdotal identification with Christ—as one may argue that Richard II and Charles I and York all do. What Richard tries to do in Shakespeare and what Charles tries to do in *Eikon* is to rescue and redeem their own natural bodies by employing the figure of the martyr's crown, and the accumulated symbolic identification of martyrdom as *imitatio Christi* to elide the divide between mortal man and immortal Christ. So, too, does York, but (he not having yet been anointed king) with even more extreme presumption. Arrogating this potent imagery to his own situation, York must finally be seen as the overreacher he always was. His rapturous depiction of his soul's flight to God's embrace must finally be put down to an act of prideful self-deception. However symbolically potent his self-glorification, its very extremity finally invites an implicit critique that may be read as the final marker of an ultimate Shakespearean reserve.

7. A CONCLUDING NOTE ON THE 'HORIZONS' OF TUDOR RESPONSE

Everything has now been restored to the Whethamstede passage. Or, to put it differently, this passage has now provoked Shakespeare into an exploration and representation of its full range of endangered meanings. These include its aesthetic assertion of the play as inventive space; its historical depiction of York as a political martyr; its spiritual assertion of a connection with the sacrifice of Christ. I do not mean that any of these elements has been achieved without some modification to its new circumstance. Neither the sacredness of Richard's sacrifice nor, for that matter, its politics have retained Whethamstede's original inflection.

Conditions for the emergence and celebration of the sacred, especially in its sacramental aspects, have shifted between the mid-fifteenth and late sixteenth century. As Christ's sacrifice ceased to seem infinitely iterable and came to be seen as unique and unrepeatable, a certain reticence is associated with its reappearance, a higher threshhold to be overcome. But the point is less that the theater offers a sanitized or secularized arena for its reappearance, and more that—as always with 'the theatrical'—it offers a propitious place for its rediscovery as sacred and sacramental experience. Doubly propitious, in fact. First, since the Elizabeth theater offers in abundance that place of ludic 'play' with sign and meaning that I have already assigned to medieval theatrics. Second, because it is, in terms I have already borrowed from O'Connell, an 'embodied' art, an art fully reliant on real 'presence,' and thus a place particularly propitious for rediscovery of the spiritual significance of the mundane. Shakespeare does not move easily or glibly to the sacrificial analogy. It is, as in the case of Richard duke of York, discovered only in the most extreme conditions of symbolic destitution. Even then, it appears less as an infinitely repeatable experience than a fleeting singularity—glimpsed only, as it were, fleetingly and awry. But even under these altered presuppositions, the 'early modern' play-within-a-play continues to provide an arena for a refreshed consideration of the sacred, and its potential for use and abuse, within the elemental condition of the human life.

Nor is a heightened interest in 'royal Christology' a matter of pure spirituality, never touching the practical political ground. We have already seen the use of Christological imagery in the service of Yorkist interests, and Elizabethan interests, and Carolingian interests. Although we are dealing with matters of imagination and spirit that do not lend themselves to purely functional analysis, the fact remains that associations of rulers—whether living or dead—with Christ paid vital symbolic dividends at each of these different historical moments, each in its own way. Each of these was a charged moment, with political capital up for grabs or in the process of being newly assigned. The resort to Christological imagery at such moments registers the high stakes of the game being played.

six

Postscript
Tudor Faction

IN WHETHAMSTEDE AND OTHER TEXTS CONSIDERED IN THE PREVIOUS chapter, political and dynastic struggle is presented as the crucible within which striving and circumstance are given meaning. Yet for the contemporary audience of Shakespeare's Henry VI plays—so well settled within its own contemporary 'horizon'[1] and only minimally possessed of a historicizing interest in the past—what point of interest or attachment was to be found within this mayhem? One line of analysis might suggest that, as in our own contemporary artworks such as Kon Ichikawa's *Burmese Harp* (1956) or Miklós Jancsó's *Red and the White* (1967), the very pointlessness of superseded struggles may in effect have *been* the point. For Hall and Holinshed, the particular nuances of dynastic preference have receded, with the conflict now represented mainly as a rather indiscriminate historical nightmare which set the stage for (in Hall's title) *The Vnion of the Two Noble and Illustre Famelies* . . . Seen in the broadest perspective, a goal of Tudor historiography, from Polydore Vergil through Holinshed, was, after all, to establish the marriage of Henry Tudor and Elizabeth of York as the terminus of major domestic dissent, after which amity was presumed to rule. Thus, as Hall has it in his dedication to Edward VI, 'as kyng henry the fourthe was the beginnyng and rote of the great discord and deuision: so was the godly matrimony, the final ende of all discencions, titles and debates.'[2] Nor does Shakespeare, in accord with this emphasis in his chosen materials, exactly 'take sides' in his portrayal of the rivalry of the two houses, or associated squabbles of the day. When he displays a preference, it is for the occasional transdynastic moment, as exemplified by Henry V's conquests on behalf of the whole nation, or the historically surprising imputation of generous statesmanship to Humfrey duke of Gloucester.

My aim is not so much to dispute this analysis as to couple it with a supplementary suggestion, aimed at the discovery of an additional point of contact for the sixteenth-century audience of fifteenth-century English events. Rather than simply wishing to see fifteenth-century disturbances overcome by Tudor statecraft, the Elizabethan audience might have discovered an intrinsic interest in the representation of an earlier and highly fragmented political situation. Of course, this new audience would have approached the subject in its own way—and, with respect to my own emphasis in the present study, in its own distinctive terms. The particular interest, or one might even say absorption, of the Tudor audience in matters of political partiality and contention may be epitomized in its coinage and deployment of the term 'faction.' Not only did this term take hold quickly after its introduction into English early in the sixteenth century, but it virtually saturated ensuing political discussion.[3] In turn, Tudor interest in the politics of *faction* allowed and underwrote an interest in the broils of preceding centuries. Possessed only of minor interest in their own right, these broils became more important when viewed through the lens of a new term with a distinctive and freshly pertinent range of implication.

Not that the Middle Ages had lacked its own vernacular vocabulary of sectionalism and centrifugal attachment. The fourteenth century had, for example, been particularly well endowed with such terms. Consider in this respect a civic proclamation from the turbulent 1380s, with Mayor Nicholas Brembre allowing neither 'alliances, confederacies, conspiracies, ne oblicacions for to bynde men to-gidre' and forbidding 'congregaciouns or couynes, in gaderyng or ygadred.'[4] This is, of course, a mixed list, tumbling together inherently 'medieval' terms of obligation and sworn association (*alliances, confederacies*), hints of treasonous colluson (*conspiracies*), simple crowd control (*congregaciouns, gaderyng[s]*), and proto–party politics (or *covynes*). But it is certainly an ample, and adaptable list, especially when supplemented by other easily available terms. Drawn originally from the vocabulary of vassalage, *allegiance* could be adopted either in its original sense of obligation to a liege-lord or in a broader application to horizontal 'ties' among social equals. Prominent in heated religious discussion of the late fourteenth century, but not limited to those discussions, were *co(n)venticle* or illicit gathering for mutual reading or self-instruction, and *secte* with its commingled partisan and heretical overtones. Barely available, but emergent and ready for transmission to the fifteenth and sixteenth centuries was *parti(e)*—first simply meaning a 'part' or 'segment' of a whole, but already occasionally referring to a shared political alignment. Such a precocious usage is to be found in Chaucer's 'Melibee,' in which a surgeon who heals all patients without respect to the affiliations, says, 'unto oure art it is nat pertinent to norice were ne parties to support' (VII, l. 1014).

As we have already seen, many of these terms continued into active use in the fifteenth century. The new sense of *partie* is, for example, confirmed in use. In his *Serpent of Division*, Lydgate does not rely solely on the perils of divison itself, but suggests that such fragmentation can be confirmed by more persistent political alignments. Thus we find both Caesar and Pompey at the heads of respective *parties*: 'And all this while the Romeyns stondynge in dowte to whiche partie thei shulde enclyne, other the partie of Sesar or of Pompey,' and their members' shared fortunes are conveyed in the consequence that 'in this mortale bataile all the partie of Pompey was put to flight and slawen.'[5] This usage coexists in Lydgate with the older sense of partie as a 'part' or 'segment.' But by the midcentury it has become prevalent. In the *Somnium Vigilantis*, for example, the Orator Regius argues that 'reconciliation is possible 'whann both parties bene reconsileable'[6]—employing the term in a sense midway between 'both participants' and something more like a modern sense of 'both political alignments.' This latter sense is, in turn, extended in a particularly rich passage in which the Orator argues of Richard duke of York's following that 'All the contres aboute knowen well what extorcions, what injuries and oppressions, what partie makyng and division thay did and caused to be doon. How many prive conventicles under thaire tuicion and support have ben made to the subversion and misdrawynge of many men.' And then, ironically, 'Thes ben notable poyntes of perservynge of the common welth' (p. 519).[7]

Nevertheless, the common property of all these terms of *covyne* and *partie* as employed in the fourteenth and fifteenth centuries is that they are regarded as aberrations, as emergent and inherently evanescent threats to civil order. The adherent of Richard duke of York in the *Somnium Vigilantis* acknowledges the ideal of a unified kingdom, arguing that Richard and his followers seek pardon 'from the kynge and the royame' (p. 515). York's grouping represents itself to 'entende the commen welthe of alle the royame' and in no sense to be a breakaway faction. Their task, as they understand it, is one of 'reformacion' rather than 'rebellyoun' (p. 515). The Orator has a different perspective, arguing that their presence is inconsistent with a robust regime, and that they should be extirpated or destroyed like a rotten tooth in a healthy mouth, for the good of all. Different as these two perspectives might be, neither supposes that a party pursuing policies and agendas contrary to the preservation of the 'common welth' should be expected to survive. The Yorkist argues for the consistency of his party's proposals with a program of reform; the Lancastrian would exterminate them. Neither, that is, imagines this divided situation as a new kind of status quo.

In the area of Tudor usage and thought surrounding the introduction of the term 'faction,' a slight but telling adjustment occurs. Although the word might have entered English at almost any time, in translation of or by analogy with L. *factio,* the year of its actual appearance was 1509, in a funeral sermon delivered by then-Bishop John Fisher for the countess of Richmond, mother of Henry VII. The context of this appearance is less concerned with matters of high statecraft than with domestic polity, addressing the countess's adroit handling of cabals within her household. Yet the immediate verbal context is nevertheless telling: 'Yf ony faccyons or bendes were made secretly amongst her hede Officers, she with grete polycye dyde boulte it oute.'[8] Already in this first appearance, the phenomenon of *faccyon* summons those countermeasures available within the ambit of *polycye.* Faction is, in other words, a civil problem or challenge to good governance, addressed by the range of strategic countermeasures that the well-schooled practice of governance affords.

Reliance upon *faction* expands rapidly throughout the century, in translated works like Norton's Calvin and Nicolls' Thucydides, and also in original works of statecraft and policy. Among them I might cite a single example, chosen for its resonances with earlier themes of this study. The year 1572 saw the appearance of *A treatise of treasons against Q. Elizabeth and the croune of England,* a controversial pamphlet attributed to Catholic loyalist John Leslie and arguing that the queen has been duped and misled by a power-seeking Protestant *faction.*[9] Assailed in the preface to this pamphlet is a 'lawlesse

Faction of Machiauellian Libertines,' whose members only pretend to a new religion but whose actual commitment is 'to execute, what so euer should be committed vnto them, by those that haue created and set vp the Faction' (p. 5). Realizing that he may be introducing a term new to his readers, Leslie helpfully defines it: 'I cal a Machiauellian State & Regime that where R[e]-ligion is put behind in the second & la[s]t place: wher the ciuil Policie, I meane, is preferred before it, & not limited by any rules of Religion, but the Religion framed to ser[u]e the time and policy: wher both by word & ex-ample of the Rulers, th[e] ruled are t[a]ught with euery change of Prince to change also the face of their faith' (p. 7). As here imagined, the Machiavel-lian state advances the civil realm, proceeds by *policie,* and treats religion as a screen for the new system that supplants it. Faction is the abode, or even architect of this new civil arrangement, and one does not imagine faction, cloaked with religious trappings and bent on long-term domination, pass-ing soon from the scene. Faction here seems a long-term, if not permanent, feature of civil polity.

In this, sixteenth-century *faction* differs from the more provisional and opportunistic arrangements going by other names in earlier centuries. Ar-rayed in this new and formidable understanding, it enters many arenas of discussion, including those chronicle traditions leading to Shakespeare. Ed-ward Hall, for example, looking retrospectively at the broils of the fifteenth century, finds them not only to consist of shifting arrangements involving power-hungry dynasts and opportunistic aristocrats, but to bear the earmark of *faction.* Hall tells us in his *Vnion* that, following the death of his father, Edward earl of March turned to 'the erle of Warwyche, inwhome rested the chefe trust of that faction.'[10] On the other side, Edward gathering his forces, King Henry retreats to the north: 'king Henry and his faction nesteled and strengthened hym and his alyes, in the North regions and boreal plage' (p. 185). Later, Edward having become king and Warwick having deserted to the cause of Henry, this new opposition concludes that, 'as long as kyng Edward lyued, . . . kyng Henryes faction should neuer prosper' (p. 203).

Through such channels we come to Shakespeare, whose dramatic pur-poses as well as his desire to remake English history for Tudor audiences are well served by the terminology and accompanying assumptions of *faction.* We need hardly be surprised to learn that, in the Henry VI plays, Richard earl of Gloucester is most adept among the leading characters in the lan-guage of faction. In the *True Tragedie,* for example, it is Richard who styles *all* of them factionalists. Speaking of Margaret's growing strength, he warns that 'If she have time to breathe, be well assured / Her faction will be full as strong as ours' (5.3, ll. 14–17). Aside from such incidentals, Shakespeare's larger revision of fifteenth-century politics along the lines of faction is what interests me here. I speak, in particular, of the 'Temple-Garden Scene' of *1 Henry 6*, a scene generally supposed to have been written by Shakespeare and, more important, a scene without an identified chronicle source. This is the scene in which Somerset and Plantagenet (Richard duke of York) respectively adopt the red and white roses of Lancaster and York. As Plantagenet says, plucking his rose,

> . . . by my soul, this pale and angry rose,
> As cognizance of my blood-drinking hate,
> Will I forever, and my faction wear. (2.4, ll. 107–9)

At this moment we witness the solidification of the Tudor view, in which the shifting alignments of the mid-fifteenth century are regarded as a long-term contest of two antagonistic factions, headed by the 'houses' of Lancaster and York.

Vergil, Hall, and their successors commit themselves to the idea that strife effectively ends with the Tudors, although they, and certainly Shakespeare, knew well enough that this was not so. Far from ending with the Tudors, the politics of faction were a virtual invention of their reigns. Despite ambitiously promulgated myths of stability, an aspect of Elizabeth's rule is that, in J. A. Sharpe's summary, 'a fair number of her loyal subjects seem to have been more or less constantly afraid and insecure.'[11] An element of this insecurity was the factional underpinning of Elizabethan society, and the extent to which any semblance of stability required a constant factional balancing act. One of the earliest analyses of the period is contained in the late-life retrospect of Sir Robert Naunton, secretary of state to James I, composed ca. 1640. As he describes the trajectory of his analysis, 'The principall note of her raigne will be, that she ruled much by faction and parties, which she herselfe both made, upheld, and weakned, as her owne great judgement advised.'[12] Modern historians have not doubted the centrality of faction to later sixteenth-century rule, although they have been a good deal less sanguine about Elizabeth's control of the situation. In the course of his account of the weaning of the English aristocracy from violence, Laurence Stone found little positive to report before 1603. Describing the ubiquity of aristocratic and factional violence, he says that 'In the fact of such open threats of

violence so close to her person Elizabeth could only temporize and procras-
tinate, keeping the balance of force sufficiently even to prevent a major ex-
plosion.[13] He goes on to describe, corroboratively, such crises as the Percy
rebellion of 1569 and the Essex turmoils of the 1590s. That persons who experienced the faction-ridden 1590s were able to jump the gap and to link their
own horizon of experience to that of the middle ages is evident from Essex
supporters' sponsorship of a production of *Richard II* on the eve of his af-
fray, and from Elizabeth's own celebrated response to that event.[14] Especially
when recast in the new language of faction, the perils and enticements of
fifteenth-century political division had not lost their power to address and
agitate the late Tudor imaginary.

n o t e s

INTRODUCTION

1. This view was, to some extent, anticipated by S. B. Chrimes, when he commented of Fortescue's mid-fifteenth-century *De Laudibus*, 'He, first of mediaeval writers, brought political philosophy from the clouds to earth by basing his theoretical analysis upon observation of existing conditions, and was thus at once reverting to the Aristotelian outlook, and in some degree anticipating the standpoint of Machiavelli' (*De Laudibus Legum Anglie* [Cambridge: Cambridge University Press, 1942], p. ci). My own interpretation seeks to avoid some of the implications of an unfolding *récit,* or long arc stretching from Aristotle to Machiavelli. In claiming for the fifteenth century an expansion of descriptive political language and an attitude of relative candor about political affairs, I mean to suggest less about that moment's contribution to an overarching discussion than its exceptionality and its adherence to its own very particular terms and conditions. I also view this moment as highly vulnerable to interruption, especially, in the years after 1485, by a surge of early Tudor providentialism. Nevertheless, I mean to suggest that, muting Chrimes's unnecessary claims about Fortescue's prescience, he has it essentially right.

2. *Capitoli,* ed. Giorgio Inglese (Rome: Bulzoni Editore, 1981), p. 119, ll. 115–17.

3. Howard Patch, *The Goddess Fortuna in Mediaeval Literature* (Cambridge, Mass.: Harvard University Press, 1927), esp. pp. 8–18.

4. I am guided in this observation by the brief but perceptive remarks of Anne Sutton and Livia Visser-Fuchs, *Richard III's Books* (Gloucester: Sutton, 1997), p. 209.

5. Alexander Murray, *Reason and Society in the Middle Ages* (Oxford: Oxford University Press, 1978), pp. 98–101.

6. The salty afterthought—'or that which we *call* fortune'—is not present in all manuscripts. Contamine here follows MS Bibliothèque Nationale Nouvelles

Acquisitions françaises 20960. On alternate readings, some omitting this phrase, see the edition of Joseph Calmette (Paris: Honoré Champion, 1924), vol. 1, textual note to p. 79.

7. *Calendar of State Papers and Manuscripts . . . in the Archives . . . of Milan,* ed. Allen B. Hinds, vol. 1 (London: Stationery Office, 1912), p. 76.

8. The idea that Fortune's wheel might be arrested in its course by exercise of human calculation is hardly unique to Edward IV's propagandists. Some forty years later, the young Hernán Cortés would have a dream in which a revolving wheel with buckets—some full, some being emptied, some empty—could be arrested at its moment of plenitude with a nail. Later, in Mexico, he would adopt as his device a wheel of fortune and a silver figure of a man with a hammer in one hand and a nail in the other. See J. H. Elliott, 'The Mental World of Hernán Cortés,' in *Spain and Its World, 1500–1700* (New Haven: Yale University Press, 1989), pp. 27–41, at p. 34. I am indebted for this reference to Margaret Meserve of the University of Notre Dame.

9. Jacob Burckhardt, *The Civilization of the Renaissance in Italy,* trans. S. G. C. Middlemore (London: Phaidon, 1950), p. 2.

10. I am more inclined to think that fifteenth-century language was what it was, than that it 'prefigured' anything. Nevertheless, I consider Starkey's call for a reconsideration of fifteenth-century political language an entirely welcome one. See *Revolution Reassessed: Revision in the History of Tudor Government and Administration,* ed. C. Coleman and D. Starkey (Oxford: Clarendon Press, 1986), p. 8.

11. *Revolution Reassessed,* pp. 13–27; quotation at p. 24. Regrettably, given his revisionary aims, Starkey neglects the extensive prehistory of *commonweal* in fourteenth-century discussions of *common profit* and *common spede.* Moving from a fourteenth-century association of *common profit* and a fifteenth-century association of *common weale* with actions taken in the interest of the common good, sixteenth-century *commonwealth* came to be associated with a polity constituted around consensual ideas of providential election. See A. N. McLaren, *Political Culture in the Reign of Elizabeth I* (Cambridge: Cambridge Univerity Press, 1999), pp. 80–90. Viewed in their widest perspective, the implications of these terms may be traced in precursor texts all the way back to Aristotle; see Kempshall, n. 33, below.

12. Quentin Skinner, *The Foundations of Modern Political Thought,* vol. 1 (Cambridge: Cambridge University Press, 1978), p. x.

13. Quentin Skinner, 'Language and Social Change,' in *The State of the Language,* ed. L. Michaels and C. Ricks (Berkeley: University of California Press, California, 1980), rpt. in *Meaning and Context: Quentin Skinner and His Critics,* ed. James Tully (London: Polity Press, 1988), pp. 119–32; quotation at p. 132.

14. For a trenchant critique of Skinner's supposition that authorial intention can delimit the meaning of a text, see Joseph V. Femia, 'An Historicist Critique of "Revisionist" Methods for Studying the History of Ideas,' *History and Theory* 20

(1981). Rpt. in *Meaning and Context: Quentin Skinner and His Critics*, pp. 156–75; esp. pp. 171–75.

15. My own view is that we can know things about an author that are not exhausted by his or her own conscious purposes, and that we can know things about a text that it cannot know about itself (Paul Strohm, 'What Can We Know about Chaucer That He Didn't Know about Himself?' in *Theory and the Premodern Text* [Minneapolis: University of Minnesota Press, 2000], pp. 165–81). This is not to deny that authors have purposes, or that their purposes are interesting. For example, I relate some innovations in the writing of Laurent de Premierfait and John Lydgate to a desire to please their respective patrons. But I am unwilling to claim that conscious purpose exhausts the reservoirs of meaning in either text, and I cannot imagine that most critics would want to do so either.

16. *The Languages of Political Theory in Early-Modern Europe*, ed. Anthony Pagden (Cambridge: Cambridge University Press, 1987), pp. 19–38.

17. Pocock strikes what seems to me a fair balance between individual initiative on the one hand and the constraints of the language system of the other. Interestingly, Pocock's own reading of Skinner discovers a similar balance in his contemporary's recent work, predicated on a shift in Skinner's writings from an insistence on authorial intention to an acknowledgment of unintended implications within verbal performance. For Pocock's discussion of Skinner, including judicious remarks on the extent to which an individual can be said to own the words he or she employs, see 'Introduction to the State of the Art,' in *Virtue, Commerce, and History* (Cambridge: Cambridge University Press, 1985), esp. pp. 4–7.

18. John Watts, '*The Policie in Christen Remes*: Bishop Russell's Parliamentary Sermons of 1483–84,' in *Authority and Consent in Tudor England: Essays Presented to C. S. L. Davies*, ed. G. W. Bernard and S. J. Gunn (Aldershot: Ashgate, 2002), p. 43.

19. On the concept of the action-seeking text, see Danilo Marcondes de Souza Filho, *Language and Action* (Amsterdam: Benjamins, 1984).

20. On the thin line between 'performative' language on the one hand and 'symbolic' events on the other, see Paul Strohm, 'Walking Fire: Symbolization, Action, and Lollard Burning,' in *Theory and the Premodern Text*, pp. 20–32.

21. Especially as delineated in Pierre Bourdieu, *Outline of a Theory of Practice* (Cambridge: Cambridge University Press, 1977), and Anthony Giddens, *Central Problems in Social Theory* (Berkeley: University of California Press, 1979).

22. On this subject I defer to the recent, and stimulating (though occasionally eccentric), work by Jonathan Hughes, *Arthurian Myths and Alchemy: The Kingship of Edward IV* (Gloucester: Sutton, 2002), which treats a number of illustrated rolls of Edward IV and evidence of their use for public display.

23. *The Great Chronicle of London*, ed. A. H. Thomas and I. D. Thornley (London: G. W. Jones, 1938), p. 215.

24. All the different sorts of muddle and overlap we embrace along with such convenient but oversimplified terminologies are explicated by S. B. Chrimes, *Lancastrians, Yorkists and Henry VII* (London: Macmillan, 1964).

25. As urged by R. L. Storey, *The End of the House of Lancaster* (Gloucester: Sutton, 1986).

26. In correspondence, February 2003.

27. J. L. Austin, *How to Do Things with Words* (Cambridge, Mass.: Harvard University Press, 1962), esp. pp. 4–11.

28. Also pertinently expressed as cases when 'different authors carried out variant acts in the same language' (p. 27) and as 'a game recognized as open to more than one player' (p. 28). For no reason that is clear, or sufficient, to me, Pocock wants common political languages always to be made available in the first instance by 'ruling groups' (p. 24). Although this 'top-down' theory gains some support in a common-sense understanding of the exercise of social power, I would nevertheless doubt this generalization—unless the 'ruling group' of England be construed as something so general as the 'community of the literate.' Provision should be made, in my view, for important and even durable linguistic contributions to be made by contestants effectively 'out of power.'

29. 'A Defense of the Proscription of the Yorkists in 1459,' *English Historical Review*, 26 (1911): 512–25. Editor J. P. Gilson suggests that this title, given in a seventeenth-century catalogue, 'may have been taken from the lost beginning, or from an old cover' (p. 513); may, that is, have a degree of authority.

30. Paul Strohm, *Social Chaucer* (Cambridge, Mass.: Harvard University Press, 1989).

31. E. P. Thompson, *The Poverty of Theory* (London: Merlin Press, 1978), esp. pp. 287–90.

32. Janet Coleman, 'The Science of Politics and Late Medieval Academic Debate,' in *Criticism and Dissent in the Middle Ages*, ed. Rita Copeland (Cambridge: Cambridge University Press, 1996), pp. 181–214. I draw Rundle's phrase from his idiosyncratic, but provocative, essay, 'Was There a Renaissance Style of Politics in Fifteenth-Century England?' in Bernard and Gunn, eds., *Authority and Consent in Tudor England*, pp. 15–32. Rundle's answer to his own question is, effectively, no; but that political discourse in fifteenth-century England was nevertheless marked by a proliferation of native, together with some Classical and especially Ciceronian styles (see esp. p. 24).

33. This vastly important tradition is well summarized by Nicholai Rubinstein, 'The History of the Word *Politicus* in Early-Modern Europe,' in Pagden, ed., *The Languages of Political Theory*, pp. 41–56. My only demurral would be with respect to Rubinstein's conclusion that the emergent sense of 'politic' as connoting duplicity or cunning awaited Machiavelli, whereas I argue in ensuing chapters that this sense of the word was abroad, and in fact flourished, in fifteenth-century England. For a

convenient summary of the dissemination of Aristotle's *Politics,* see D. E. Luscombe and G. R. Evans, 'The Twelfth-Century Renaissance,' in *The Cambridge History of Medieval Political Thought, c. 350 – c. 1450,* ed. J. H. Burns (Cambridge: Cambridge University Press, 1988), esp. pp. 334–38. Also see Coleman, 'The Science of Politics,' esp. pp. 201–4. On the vernacular promulgation of the *Secretum Secretorum,* see A. H. Gilbert, 'Notes on the Influence of the *Secretum Secretorum,' Speculum* 3 (1928): 84–98.

34. *Li Livres dou Tresor,* ed. Francis Carmody (Berkeley: University of California Press, 1948), p. 21. Claiming centrality for the Ciceronian/Senecan tradition in discussions of civic virtue is Quentin Skinner, 'Ambrogio Lorenzetti: The Artist as Political Philosopher,' *Proceedings of the British Academy* 72 (1986): 1–56. Although expressive of the complexity of this inheritance is Latini's own precocious use of Aristotle's *Ethics* in proposing the centrality of *la politique.* On Latini's sources, see also the fine discussion of Maurizio Viroli, *From Politics to Reason of State: The Acquisition and Transformation of the Language of Politics, 1250–1600* (Cambridge: Cambridge University Press, 1992), pp. 25–30.

35. *Tresor,* pp. 231 ff. See Carmody's introduction, pp. xxix–xxx; Viroli, *From Politics to Reason of State,* pp. 14–25. The tradition of the Cardinal, or secular, virtues and the language of virtue, from its Aristotelian origins, is definitively surveyed by M. S. Kempshall, *The Common Good in Late Medieval Political Thought* (Oxford: Clarendon Press, 1999).

36. A particularly apt discussion of Gower's interweaving of different strands (including the *Secretum Secretorum* and the digest of the Nichomachean Ethics transmitted within Brunetto Latini's vernacular *Tresor*) is M. A. Manzalaoui, '"Noght in the Registre of Venus": Gower's English Mirror for Princes,' *Medieval Studies for J. A. W. Bennett,* ed. P. L. Heyworth (Oxford: Oxford University Press, 1981), pp. 159–83.

37. Appendix to John H. Fisher, *John Gower: Moral Philosopher and Friend of Chaucer* (New York: New York University Press, 1964), p. 312.

38. Although I might here note that Gower's discussion of *policie* is more traditional, in its emphasis on good, and public-spirited, practice than some of the applications discussed in this study, and thus belongs more to their antecedence than to their more immediate context. (See chap. 2, p. 124).

39. Second ed. (Oxford: Blackwell, 1957).

40. Important corrective remarks on the *De Re Publica* of Titus Livius Frulovisi, and its importance as a link in the chain of reasoning on the secular state stretching from Marsilius of Padua to Machiavelli, are, for example, offered by Grady Smith, *Travel Abroad: Frulovisi's 'Peregrinatio'* (Tempe: Arizona Center for Medieval and Renaissance Studies, 2003), esp. pp. 19–23.

41. Ph.D. dissertation, Cambridge University, 2002.

42. (Oxford: Oxford University Press, 2004–5).

ONE. *POLITIQUE* PERJURY IN THE *ARRIVALL* OF EDWARD IV

1. A comment by Susan Crane on an early lecture version of this chapter.

2. *The Chronicle of Adam of Usk, 1377–1421,* ed. C. Given-Wilson (Oxford: Oxford University Press, 1997), pp. 64–65.

3. *Dispatches . . . of Milanese Ambassadors in France and Burgundy, 1450–83,* ed. Paul M. Kendall and Vincent Ilardi (Athens: Ohio University Press, 1970), pp. 44–45.

4. 'I am Richard II, know ye not that?' Reported by John Nichols in *The Progresses and Public Processions of Queen Elizabeth,* 2nd ed. (1823), iii, p. 552.

5. Thomas Walsingham, *Historia Anglicana,* Rolls series, no. 28, pt. 1, vol. 2 (1864), p. 232.

6. Edited from Stow's transcript (BL MS Harley 543, ff. 32–49), by John Bruce, Camden Society, 1st ser., no. 1 (London, 1838). The title 'the Arrivall,' prefixed to Stow's transcript, is of dubious authority but may reflect a lost precursor. At the head of Stow's transcript is an alternate title, 'Edward the fowrthe and the bastard Fawlconbridge,' which alludes to the concluding sections of the narrative in which Falconbridge is offered as an inept foil to Edward's more timely and strategically sound machinations. I have, however, retained the *The Arrivall* for reasons of familiarity. Quotations from this text represent my own transcriptions, and thus differ slightly from the full version attached to this chapter. Except in some very minute particulars, the printed version is sufficiently authoritative to provide a working text.

7. This Ravenspur was the location of a town, Ravenser, extinguished by the shifting sands of that 'spur' (fifteenth-century *sporne* or *spurn*) which came ultimately to be known as 'Spurn Head' or 'Spurn Point' (A. H. Smith, *The Place-Names of the East Riding of Yorkshire and York* [Cambridge: Cambridge University Press, 1937], pp. 17, 19). It was a place of possible shipwreck (in 1427 a hermit, Richard Reedbarowe, petitioned for funds to build a beacon there: see *Victoria County History: Yorkshire East Riding,* vol. 1 [London: Institute of Historical Research, 1969], p. 49) but also, with its deserted character and its shifting sandy beaches, a good place for purposeful clandestine disembarcation.

8. As John Watts put it in a recent communication, 'Edward's move wasn't necessarily a quotation.'

9. *The Eighteenth Brumaire of Louis Bonaparte* (New York: International Publishers, 1963), p. 15.

10. This is, of course, why the lords in Parliament went through such contortions in their designation of Richard duke of York as Henry VI's successor rather than his substitute in 1460; whatever their view of the merits of the Lancastrian succession, they had experienced Henry VI as an anointed king. *Rolls of Paliament* (*RP*), vol. 5, pp. 376–77.

11. *Historia Anglicana,* Rolls series, no. 28, pt. 1, vol. 2 (London, 1863), pp. 232–38.

12. 'Chronicle of Dieulacres Abbey, 1381–1403,' ed., trans., and introd. M. V. Clarke and V. H. Galbraith, 'The Deposition of Richard II,' *Bulletin of the John Rylands Library* 28 (1930): 125–81; at p. 173. This and an associated Cistercian chronicle, unusual among surviving English texts for their sympathy to Richard, have been highlighted and discussed by Chris Given-Wilson. Given-Wilson, ed., *Chronicles of the Revolution* (Manchester: University of Manchester Press, 1993), pp. 153–56.

13. Thomas Usk, in his *Testament* of ca. 1386, is exceptional in his early use of ME *perjury*, accompanying the term with a definition: 'Every othe . . . muste have these lawes, that is trewe jugement and rightwysenesse, in whiche thynge, if any these lacke, the othe is ytourned into the name of perjury.' See Thomas Usk, *The Testament of Love*, ed. R. A. Shoaf; originally published Kalamazoo, Michigan, for TEAMS Texts, 1998; cited from Internet edition, www.lib.rochester.edu/camelot/teams/ uskprol.htm, bk. 1, chap. 7, p. 16. The more common Middle English usage was to find a false oath-taker to be *forswore* or *forsworn*. See, in this regard, MS Julius B II, the Middle English rendition of the articles of Richard II's deposition, as published in *The Chronicles of London*, ed. C. L. Kingsford (Oxford: Clarendon Press, 1905), passim. Yet in this case the term *periurie* was also available for use; see Kingsford, *Chronicles of London*, p. 32.

14. Jean Creton, *Histoire du Roy d'Angleterre Richard*, ed. J. Webb, *Archaeologia* 20 (1824): 1–423.

15. Oxford Bodleian Library MS Arch. Selden B.x, f. 154b. See also *The Chronicle of Iohn Hardyng*, ed. Henry Ellis (London, 1812), p. 350.

16. See also *The Chronicle of Iohn Hardyng*, p. 352. A continuing grudge resulting from such a missworn oath is offered by the Dieulacres Chronicler as an explanation for Henry Percy's dissatisfaction with Bolingbroke's election as king, saying that a sign of Percy's dissatisfaction was his refusal to attend the coronation since Bolingbroke had previously sworn to the two Henrys (Percy and the earl of Northumberland) upon the relics of Bridlington that he had never sought the crown, saying that the dukedom of Lancaster was plenty for him ('quia Henricus dux iuravit aliis duobus Henricis super reliquias de Bridlynton quod coronam nunquam affectaret . . . ; ducatum Lancastrie sibi sufficere fatebatur') (p. 179). Interestingly, this comes from the section of the chronicle identified by Clarke and Gailbraith as being continued by a second writer of more Lancastrian susceptibility; might this account for the substitution of an oath on the Bridlington relics, rather than (presumably more gravely) on the sacrament?

17. James Sherborne argues, in 'Perjury and the Lancastrian Revolution of 1399,' that Henry's motives might still have been unfixed when he took the oath—or made his promise—at Doncaster. See *Welsh History Review* 14 (1988–89): 217–41.

18. *RP*, 5, p. 346. The Act notes that he was 'sworne . . . upon the blissed Sacrament and used it.'

19. Nor need the list of Richard's perjuries have ended where it did. Note might have been taken of the less than wholehearted ceremonial following the first battle of St. Albans, in which Henry was recrowned by Richard's own hands, or on the celebrated 'Loveday' of 1458 in which Richard walked in procession and universal amity proclaimed. Yet another 'solempne Othe' was broken immediately after the succession settlement of 1460, in which Richard swore to God on a Bible not to take any actions contrary to Henry's reign or royal dignity (*RP,* 5, p. 378). For related instances see below, chapter 4, pp. 183–85.

20. As a fissured text the *Arrivall* contains at least some perspectives on Edward that are not strictly partisan or propagandistic in intent. The *Arrivall* is a composite work, described by its own author as having been 'compiled' from his observations and 'true relations' of others who were present at the events described. At least one of his sources is known: a newsletter or *une memoire en papier* composed in French by a follower of Edward's named Nicholas Harpisfeld, to inform Charles duke of Burgundy and other continental supporters of his successes at Barnet and Tewkesbury. First thought a spinoff of the much longer and more narratively sophisticated *Arrivall,* this *memoire* or newsletter has been shown by the successive analyses of several excellent scholars in fact to be its precursor text and partial source. See J. A. F. Thompson, '"The Arrival of Edward IV"—The Development of the Text,' *Speculum* 46 (1971): 84–93; Richard F. Green, 'The Short Version of *The Arrival of Edward IV,*' *Speculum* 56 (1981): 324–36 (including the text of an English variant of the newsletter); Livia Visser-Fuchs, 'Edward IV's "Memoir on Paper" to Charles, Duke of Burgundy: The So-called "Short Version of the Arrivall,"' *Nottingham Medieval Studies* 36 (1992): 167–227 (including editions of Edward's letter to the duke of Burgundy and the text of the memoir). The *Arrivall* author does indeed embrace materials from a version of the *memoire,* and in his concluding paragraph quotes from it; the surprising candor about Edward's motives and deceptions throughout the *Arrivall* may in fact have something to do with the existence of this newsletter, with its own generic bias toward pragmatic explanations, somewhere in its genetic past. Nevertheless, the *Arrivall* is ten times longer than its precursor, and draws from many additional sources, some oral and undoubtedly some written. Such additional sources, unknown and probably now unknowable, undergird Edward's deceit of the citizens of York about his long-term aims; an account of an auspicious Palm Sunday 'miracle'; more detailed descriptions of tactics at the battles of Barnet and Tewkesbury; and a plethora of smaller amplifications and observations. These different sources, in turn, serve as conduits for a range of differently inflected attitudes, and sometimes awkwardly inconvenient details, into this aspirationally Yorkist account. To put it differently: if even the most integral text tends to be, as we now say, 'fissured,' then this amalgamated text greatly multiplies its own internal occasions of difference and divergence. Because the earliest version of this text is the one transcribed by Stow from a copy in the possession of William Fleetwood, recorder of the

city of London (see note 48, below), a further element of amalgamation exists in the possibility that this text has been additionally influenced by sixteenth-century usages and perspectives. As will become clear at the end of this chapter, however, I doubt the presence of much sixteenth-century material, precisely because the later decades of that century became more, rather than less, conservative with respect to forms of behavior condoned or even applauded in the *Arrivall.*

21. Although the source for these additions is lost, an analogue exists in Wavrin's *Recueil des Croniques d'Engleterre.* It is by no means an anti-Yorkist account. It was originally prepared for Edward's ally and brother-in-law Philip of Burgundy, and sumptuous presentation copies of at least the three earliest volumes (stopping well short of the events in question) were given to Edward IV himself—vols. 1 and 3 now extant as BL MS Royal 15 E IV and BL MS Royal 14 IV. Wavrin is nevertheless a somewhat more inclusive text than the *Arrivall,* and expands upon certain omissions and puzzles in the *Arrivall's* rendition, allowing us to view in higher contrast an analysis only adumbrated in the English text. Rather than simply appear as a hapless dupe, Martin de la Mer now reappears among other citizens who doubt Edward's professions. Admitted to the city with fifteen men-at-arms and twelve archers, Edward is led to an assembly of the commons who greet him with shouts of 'Vive le roy Henry!' Edward then gives them his set speech about aiming only to recover his dukedom—re-created by Wavrin according to good chronicle convention—and converts them to this limited cause. Martin is unappeased, however, and demands that Edward proceed to the Minster where he take a solemn oath in the presence of the whole people, never to pretend to claim the crown of England ('serment sollempnel, present tout le peuple, de non jamais pretendre droit a la couronne d'Angleterre'—p. 647). Edward temporizes, Gloucester recommends killing the recorder and Martin de la Mer, and Edward then beats an orderly but somewhat inglorious retreat from the city. Emphatically visible in the Wavrin account, and still partly visible in the *Arrivall,* is Edward's deliberate concealment of his true objective. We also learn from Wavrin that his ruse was penetrated by astute observers and was viewed as what, if subjected to the test of a sworn oath, would have amounted to undeniable perjury. See Jehan de Waurin, *Recueil des Croniques,* ed. William Hardy, Rolls series, no. 39, vols. 1 (Introduction) and 5 (text) (London, 1864), p. 91.

22. For a revealing countercase, see below, n. 46.

23. Anne Sutton and Livia Visser-Fuchs, *Richard III's Books* (Gloucester: Sutton, 1997), p. 220.

24. Stow's copy-text routinely substitutes *w* for *u,* as in 'Edward the fowrthe.' *Polyqwe* is thus equivalent to *polique.* The condensation of *politique* to *polique* is evidently, according to A. S. G. Edwards who has kindly given his advice on the matter, a straightforward matter of internal scribal eye-skip over the anticipated *ty* or *ti.* (Edwards adds that for Stow such eye-skips are not uncommon.) Usually an adjective in English, *polyqwe* is here, as often in French, employed as a noun.

25. The same Palm Sunday that imaginatively undergirded the poem posted on the gates of Canterbury in 1460. See chapter 4, pp. 179–80.

26. Wendy Scase, 'Writing and the "Poetics of Spectacle": Political Epiphanies in *The Arrivall of Edward IV* and Some Contemporary Lancastrian and Yorkist Texts,' in *Images, Idolatry, and Iconoclasm in Late Medieval England*, ed. J. Dimmick, J. Simpson, and N. Zeeman (Oxford: Oxford University Press, 2002), pp. 172–84.

27. On the conscription of St. Anne to Edward's political program, see Miri Rubin, 'Religious Symbols and Political Culture in Fifteenth-Century England,' in *Fifteenth Century IV,* ed. L. Clark (Woodbridge, Suffolk, Boydell: forthcoming), pp. 11–12.

28. Michel de Certeau, *The Writing of History* (New York: Columbia University Press, 1988), p. 157.

29. Eamon Duffy, *The Stripping of the Altars: Traditional Religion in England, c. 1400–c. 1580* (New Haven: Yale University Press, 1992), pp. 22–27.

30. Writing of Commynes, Joël Blanchard describes the influence of Italian ambassadorial *relazioni*, with their precision, commitment to rapid and clear-eyed description of cross-currents and motives, evaluation of influential individuals, and analysis 'des rapports de force': *Commynes l' Européen: L'invention du politique* (Geneva: Droz, 1996), pp. 88–89. These *relazioni* may be regarded as broadly prototypical of the varieties of writing assessed in this chapter. On English counterparts of such dispatches, see C. A. J. Armstrong, 'Some Examples of the Distribution and Speed of News in England at the Time of the Wars of the Roses,' in *Studies in Medieval History Presented to Frederick Maurice Powicke*, ed. R. W. Hunt et al. (Oxford: Clarendon Press, 1948), pp. 429–34. Armstrong's valuable study emphasizes the respect in which such transmissions served the needs of rival magnates. Nevertheless, implicit in the quest for rapid and reliable news is the presence of a concerned populace, itself eager for information and liable to rapid shifts of allegiance on the basis of what it has learned or thinks it knows.

31. Citing several examples of tactically sophisticated fifteenth-century writing, Felix Raab argues for the existence of a bifurcated situation or tension between faith in divine ordinance on the one hand and political facts on the ground on the other, a tension 'which remained below the surface of political consciousness and was not made overt by any attempts at theorization': *The English Face of Machiavelli* (London: Routledge, 1964), pp. 22–25. Without contesting his point about theorization, I would nevertheless counterargue that the fault line ran less between two ways of seeing the world and more between different genres of writing, some of which (such as the newsletter and the diplomatic dispatch) possessed an inherently worldly bias, as a result of their raison d'être and their location within a productive field.

32. *Dispatches . . . of Milanese Ambassadors*, vol. 1, pp. 33–34.

33. Philippe de Commynes, *Mémoires*, ed. Philippe Contamine (n.p.: Imprimerie Nationale Éditions, 1994), II, chap. 2, p. 119.

34. *Mémoires*, III, chap. 4, p. 187. My interest is in Commynes's analysis of machination and treachery as general states of human affairs. But for an analysis of Commynes's particular views of the instability and treachery of the English, see Jean Dufornet, *Philippe de Commynes: Un historien á l'aube des temps modernes* (Brussells: De Boeck Université, 1994), pp. 112–28.

35. Expressed most recently and thoroughly by Blanchard, *Commynes l'Européen*.

36. As it happens, Commynes will assign to God a bit more scope than this, but only a bit. Speaking of the ruin that fell upon England after its loss of its French possessions, he offers what might be considered a qualified theory of God's action in the world:

> Still some say, 'God does not punish people as he was accustomed to do in the time of the children of Israel, tolerating bad princes and bad people.' I believe that he no longer speaks to people as he once did. . . . But, as for bad princes, you may see that none or few live unpunished; but their punishment may not occur on the particular day nor hour which those who suffer might desire ['mais ce n'est pas tousjours à jour nommé, ne à heure que ceulx qui souffrent desirent"]. (III, chap. 4, p. 185)

God is still at work, but in less scrutable ways: all will be accomplished, but as unpredictable and unintended consequences. The question is, does this view of God impinge upon Commynes' world of practical calculation?

Commynes gives this question an interesting answer when he explains the ultimate failure of the duke of Burgundy. Noting Burgundy's many good qualities, he nevertheless finds the duke lacking in good sense, and believes that when sense is lacking none of the rest counts for much. And sense, he believes, comes from the grace of God ('Si le tres grand sens n'y est, tout le demeurent n'est riens: et croy qu'il fault que cela viengne de grace de Dieu'—III, chap. 3, p. 183). In other words, the duke's failure is the decision of God, because God could have chosen to give him more brains! But is this not, finally, a circular assertion? Burgundy's lack of sense was his downfall, and the final admonition is less to obey God than simply to show sense; to live intelligently, or, more important, shrewdly, in the world.

37. So apposite was his analysis in the view of the French that Louis offered him a large reward, were he to defect to the service of Louis, and others able to appreciate his urbanity.

38. See above, introduction, nn. 32–35.

39. *Li Livres dou Tresor,* ed. Carmody, I, 4, p. 21.

40. Richard duke of York himself used the word in something like this sense in his articles of 1455, projecting as benefits of the protectorate 'the politique and restfull rule and governance of this his [the king's] lande' (*RP,* vol. 5, p. 286). On 'restful governance' see the commendation of Richard duke of York by the speaker of the

1461 parliament as committed to 'restfull governaunce' and 'pollicie' (*RP,* vol. 5, p. 465). (Richard, having moved from outside to inside the succession via his designation as Henry's rightful successor is here successful in gaining assent to his claim to the better or more accepted sort of *politique.*)

41. David Scott Kastan, '"Proud Majesty Made a Subject,"' in *Shakespeare after Theory* (London: Routledge, 1999), p. 22.

42. Note that the most telling illustrations in Ernst Kantorowicz's *The King's Two Bodies* (Princeton: Princeton University Press, 1957) come, not from the Middle Ages, but from the Elizabethan period, including special attention to Shakespeare's *Richard II.* See below, chap. 5, pp. 221-22.

43. Also discussed in chap. 5, below.

44. Kastan, "Proud Majesty Made a Subject," p. 127.

45. *The Great Chronicle of London,* ed. A. H. Thomas and I. D. Thornley (London: G. Jones, 1938), p. 215.

46. I do not, of course, mean to suggest that this kind of highly risky self-exposure is the invariable vector of Edwardian display. The nearly contemporary *Remembrance* of the 1470 rebellion in Lincolnshire, possibly written by the *Arrivall* author and certainly by someone in his circle, takes another tack entirely. Whereas the *Arrivall* shows Edward temporarily deposed and struggling by any available means to regain his crown, the *Remembrance* records a two-week period in the previous year when he was still crowned king and was seeking to counter Warwick's and Clarence's maneuvers in the North. This densely circumstantial account, with constant reference to letters sent and received and other sources of written and oral testimony and documentation, must have been written for circulation among the king's supporters and possible waverers. Its representational strategy, entirely different from that of the *Arrivall,* is now to present Warwick and Clarence, not only as rebels, but also as the 'subtle' ones, the architects of a 'subtle and fals conspiracie.' The king is open and trusting, frankly and spontaneously replying with 'a letre of thanke of hys own hande' in response to a shifty missive from Clarence, even when 'whiche message so sent by the duc was fals dissimulacion, as by the warkez aftre it appered. Nevertheles the king, not undrestanding no suche doublenesse, but trusting tht they ment truly as thay shewed [sent commissions to the duke and earl]' (*Chronicle of the Rebellion in Lincolnshire, 1470,* ed. J. G. Nichols, Camden Society, orig. ser., vol. 39 [1847], pp. 1-28; rpt. in *Three Chronicles of the Reign of Edward IV,* ed. K. Dockray [Gloucester: Alan Sutton, 1988]). Here the author takes a different kind of representational risk on Edward's behalf, portraying him as a trusting innocent, unable even to grasp the possibility of 'suche doublenesse.' The *doublenesse* is that of divided loyalty, in which Clarence feigns continuing fealty to Edward, even as he pursues a separate course on behalf of his own and Warwick's interests. As represented in the *Arrivall,* Edward will shortly prove himself well capable of such *doublenesse* by pretending loyalty to Henry VI even as he pursues his own interests—

although, of course, not named as such and presented under the mask of astute policy formation. But for now he is an innocent victim, his trust abused as the duke and earl 'dissimiled falsly' with him (p. 7), in their conduct and especially in their subversive letters. To the king, they sent many a 'plesaunt letre' to set him at his ease, even as 'undre this they sent theire messages daily to the kinges rebelles' (p. 8). In this divided conduct, 'theire unnaturelle and fals double treason apperethe.' The king, 'not undrestonding theez fals dissimulacions' (p. 9), continues to conduct himself as a simple man of bluff courage, only gradually allowing his suspicions to arise, when a casket is taken, 'wherinne were founden many mervelous billez, conteining matter of the grete seduccion, and the verrey subversion of the king and the common wele of alle this lande' (p. 10). Subtlety and connivance, now viewed negatively, are shifted to the conspirators, even as Edward is now presented as a guileless man of action.

47. 'Language and Social Change,' p. 127.

48. He must have valued it, because the copy now extant (BL MS Harley 542) was copied by Stow in his own hand, from a now-lost version in the possession of William Fleetwood, recorder of London, and found among Stow's papers. Yet whether or not he had his copy in hand when composing his *Annales*, he ignores it in that work. See *Arrivall*, pp. xiii–xiv; Gransden, vol. 2, p. 481.

49. *Chronicle of . . . King Edward the Fourth,* ed. J. O. Halliwell, Camden Society, 1st ser., vol. 10 (London, 1839), p. 14.

50. *Annales* (London: Th. Adams, 1615), p. 423.

51. Here, and in other background matters, I rely upon Denys Hay, *Polydore Vergil: Renaissance Historian and Man of Letters* (Oxford: Clarendon Press, 1952).

52. *Three Books of Polydore Vergil's English History,* ed. Henry Ellis, Camden Society, 1st ser. 1, vol. 29 (London, 1844), p. 137.

53. *The Prince,* trans., Harvey Mansfield, 2d ed. (Chicago: University of Chicago Press, 1998), p. 70.

54. London, 1550 edition, printed by R. Grafton, fol. xxv, verso.

55. Verbal parallels would establish the influence of the *Arrivall* in any case, but the 1587 edition confirms its source by citing 'W. Fleetwood' as a marginal authority. (See n. 38.) The 1587 edition is reprinted as Holinshed, *Chronicles,* vol. 3 (London: J. Johnson, 1808), pp. 303–5.

56. The absence of the final moralization may be noted in Holinshed, *The Chronicle of England . . . ,* vol. 2 (F. J. Hunne, 1577), Pollard-Redgrave 1897:8.

57. An early comment on this phenomenon is offered by John Bruce, the nineteenth-century editor of the *Arrivall*, who observed, 'In these various ways the red rose was blanched" (p. xiii).

58. *The True Tragedie of Richarde Duke of Yorke, and the death of the good King Henrie the Sixt,* printed in facsimile as *The True Tragedy of Richard, Duke of York, 1600* (Tudor Facsimile Texts, 1913).

59. *Richard Duke of York,* in *The Oxford Shakespeare,* ed. Stanley Wells and Gary Taylor (Oxford: Clarendon Press, 1988). I have cited the modernized text for convenience, except to note telling differences between the quarto (note 58) and folio (note 59) versions. One such difference, as it happens, involves this very line. In the earlier quarto version Machiavelli does not appear. We encounter Cataline in his stead, in 'set the aspiring Catalin to school' (E3.1, recto). This may simply be a case in which the quarto has a weaker or ill-remembered version; but it may also stand as an indication of the novelty of the Machiavellian reference, with it appearing only in the later, folio version.

60. Weaker still in the *True Tragedie:* 'But I onely claime my Dukedome, / Vntill it please God to send thee rest' (G1, recto).

TWO. LYDGATE AND THE RISE OF *POLLECIE* IN THE *MIRROR* TRADITION

1. 'Baldwin to the Reader,' in *The Mirror for Magistrates,* ed. Lily B. Campbell (Cambridge: Cambridge University Press, 1938), p. 69.

2. See 'The Suppressed Edition of *A Mirror for Magistrates,' Huntington Library Bulletin,* no. 6 (1934): 1–16; and the introduction to *The Mirror for Magistrates,* ed. Lily B. Campbell, pp. 4–7. See also W. A. Jackson, 'Wayland's Edition of the Mirror of Magistrates,' *The Library,* 4th ser., 13 (1932–33): 155–57.

3. Bibliothèque Nationale Paris MS fonds anglais 39. See Paul Strohm, 'Jean of Angoulême: A Fifteenth Century Reader of Chaucer,' *Neuphilologische Mitteilungen* 72 (1971): 69–76.

4. Renate Haas, 'Chaucer's *Monk's Tale:* An Ingenious Criticism of Early Humanist Conceptions of Tragedy,' *Humanistica Lovaniensia* 37 (1987): 44–70. Haas locates the tale's critique in its exposure of the early humanist's uneasy linkage of divine providence on the one hand and an inherently incommensurate and effectively secular conception of Fortune's aimless operations on the other. As will become clear in my argument below, I regard this apparent inequivalence as the form's greatest asset, and as a key to its unflagging dynamism.

5. Manuscript tradition supports a close identification of Chaucer's *Monk's Tale* with the tone and spirit of Boccaccio's work, in the frequent headnote 'Heere bigynneth the Monkes Tale De Casibus Virorum Illustrium,' here cited from the Ellesmere manuscript, as reproduced in the *Riverside Chaucer,* p. 241. Although not necessarily (in fact probably not) authorial, these headnotes embody a perception of similitude, an early 'reader's response.' Criseyde's speech likewise has its counterpart in Boccaccio's *Filostrato,* IV, ll. 133 f.

6. Henry Ansgar Kelly, *Chaucerian Tragedy* (Woodbridge, Suffolk: D. S. Brewer, 1997), p. 26.

7. The Paris edition of 1520, in facsimile, ed. Louis Brewer Hall (Gainesville, Fla.: Scholars' Facsimiles & Reprints, 1962), 1a.

8. David Wallace, *Chaucerian Polity: Absolutist Lineages and Associational Forms in England and Italy* (Stanford: Stanford University Press, 1997), pp. 300–307.

9. As Kelly aptly observes, 'Any prince, vicious or otherwise, who did take up Boccaccio's Prefaces with a humble will to be directed along the right path stood in danger of being seriously misled' (*Chaucerican Tragedy*, p. 29).

10. *Inferno*, ed. and trans. Mark Musa (Bloomington: Indiana University Press, 1996), canto VII, l. 78.

11. On Machiavelli's reliance on Fortune's sway in the affairs of men, and the corrective scope he allows to human enterprise, see Allan H. Gilbert, *Machiavelli's 'Prince' and Its Forerunners* (Durham: Duke University Press, 1938), pp. 216–21. Of course, this counterdiscourse was always latently present. Consider Gilbert's citation of Giraldus Cambrensis, writing in the early thirteenth century: 'Cum autem audaces fortuna juvet et provehat, quem magis animositas et audacia quam magnos et fortunatos decet?'

12. Thomas G. Bergin, *Boccaccio* (New York: Viking Press, 1981), p. 270.

13. As argued in Paul Strohm, *Social Chaucer* (Cambridge, Mass.: Harvard University Press, 1989), chaps. 1, 2.

14. See Richard F. Green, *Poets and Princepleasers: Literature and the English Court in the Late Middle Ages* (Toronto: University of Toronto Press, 1980), pp. 155–56. On Humfrey's patronage and its effect on Lydgate's orientation, see Wallace, *Chaucerian Polity*, pp. 332–33. As Wallace wryly observes, 'Lydgate plainly falls victim to the contradiction of the heart of his enterprise: that of trying to write of past *viri illustres* while a contemporary "mighty man" wields a pen and scraper at his side' (p. 333).

15. BL MS Royal 18 D.vii, f.2v. See also *Lydgate's Fall of Princes*, ed. Henry Bergen, EETS, ES, vols. 121–24 (Oxford: Oxford University Press, 1924–27), vol. 1, p. lv.

16. F. 5r; see also Bergen, *Fall*, vol. 1, p. lxiv.

17. As presented by R. J. Lyall, 'Letter and Spirit in the Chaucerian Humanism of James I of Scotland,' plenary paper delivered at the New Chaucer Society, Glasgow, July 2004.

18. *De fato et fortuna*, ed. Concetta Bianca (Florence: Olschki, 1985), p. 213.

19. Germane here is James Simpson's discussion of the 'political' virtues in Alan of Lille's *Anticlaudianus*. His point is that Alan separates the 'political' virtues from the 'catholic' virtues that exist within the institution of the church: 'One of the derivations given for this name "political" virtue concerns its relevance, unsurprisingly, to the practice of civic government, since, as Alan says, the word *politica* derives from *polis*, or city, and pagans as much as Christians practiced civic virtues' (p. 45). He adds that many of Alan's virtues 'are species of the Cardinal virtues. The virtues Risus, Pudor and Modestia in particular are closely derived from accounts

of Temperance in the Ciceronian/Stoic tradition; Ratio derives from Prudence, while Pietas, Fides and Largitas are derived from accounts of Justice' (p. 48). Simpson, *Sciences and the Self in Medieval Poetry* (Cambridge: Cambridge University Press, 1995), pp. 42–54.

20. F. 3r; see also Bergen, *Fall*, vol. 1, p. lvii.

21. For a pertinent discussion of the dissemination of Aristotle's *Ethics* and the availability in the *Ethics* of an ideal of Prudence as an acquired disposition of the soul that forms practical opinions 'with regard to the sphere of possibles or variables where something can be or cannot be, can be done or not be done,' see Janet Coleman, 'The Science of Politics and Late Medieval Academic Debate,' in *Criticism and Dissent in the Middle Ages*, ed. Rita Copeland (Cambridge: Cambridge University Press, 1996), pp. 181–214; at p. 197. On the exploration of the active life prior to full-blown humanism—based on the thirteenth- and fourteenth-century dissemination of Aristotle's *Poetics* and *Ethics*—see Alastair Minnis, '"I speke of folk in secular estaat": Secularity and Vernacularity in the Ages of Chaucer,' Biennial Chaucer Lecture, delivered at the New Chaucer Society meeting in Glasgow, July 2004.

22. See, for example, Kempshall, *The Common Good in Late Medieval Political Thought*, esp. chap. 1, 'Albertus Magnus: Aristotle and the Common Good.'

23. Macrobius, *Commentariorum in Somnium Scipionis Libri Duo*, ed. Luigi Scarpa (Padua: Liviana, 1981), bk. 1, sec. 6, p. 136.

24. 'Et est politici prudentiae ad rationis normam quae cogitat quaeque agit universa dirigere ac nihil praeter rectum velle vel facere humanisque actibus tamquam divinis arbitris' (bk. 1, sec. 7, p. 136).

25. Vincent of Beauvais, *Speculum Doctrinale* (Venice: Harmann Lichtenstein, 1494), bk. 4, sec. 9.

26. Brunetto Latini, *Li Livres dou Tresor*, ed. F. J. Carmody (Berkeley: University of California Press, 1948), pp. 231–75.

27. *Das Moralium Dogma Philosophorum des Guillaume de Conches*, ed. John Holmberg (Uppsala, 1929), throughout, but quotation at p. 79. Crucial for the dissemination of the Ciceronian/Senecan tradition of the Virtues in civil politics is Quentin Skinner, 'Ambrogio Lorenzetti: The Artist as Political Philosopher,' *Proceedings of the British Academy* 72 (1986): 1–56. Skinner finds Lorenzetti's murals at the Palazzo Pubblico in Sienna consistently influenced by, among others, Latini, especially in their representations of Magnanimity, Temperance, and Fortitude—and overall to stand in an effectively pre-Aristotelian/Aquinian tradition. Closer to home, see J. D. Burnley, *Chaucer's Language and the Philosophers' Tradition* (Cambridge: D. S. Brewer, 1979), esp. pp. 134–50. For a discussion of the virtues in fifteenth-century English political life, see John Watts, *Henry VI and the Politics of Kingship* (Cambridge: Cambridge University Press, 1996), pp. 23–25; for another fifteenth-century instance in which the Virtues are placed in the service of secular statecraft, see John

Watts, '*De Consulatu Stiliconis:* Texts and Politics in the Reign of Henry VI,' *Journal of Medieval History* 16 (1990): 251–66; esp. 254–55.

28. Ed. F. J. Furnivall, EETS, ES, 72 (London, 1897): 'Prudence, attemperance, strengthe, and right, / Tho foure ben virtues principal; / Prudence gooth by-fore and yeueth light / Of counseil, what tho other thre do shal' (ll. 4754–57).

29. *Three Prose Versions of the Secreta Secretorum,* ed. Robert Steele, EETS, ES, no. 74 (London, 1898), pp. 145–208; quotation at p. 146.

30. Such generic hybridity is not, of course, uncommon. In his short but definitive discussion of the *Miroir au Prince,* J.-P. Genet finds relatively few 'pure' instances of the genre, as exemplified by Aquinas and Giles of Rome, but cites a wide range of less generically exclusive 'political literature of the court,' mainly designed to be more easily understood by the laity, including works by Gower, Chaucer, Hoccleve, and Lydgate. Jean-Philippe Genet, *Four English Political Tracts of the Later Middle Ages,* Camden Society, ser. 4, vol. 18 (London: Royal Historical Society, 1977), pp. ix–xix.

31. Kempshall, *The Common Good,* pp. 45–46.

32. On the virtue of Prudence and its tilt towards the secular, see Alexander Murray, *Reason and Society in the Middle Ages* (Oxford: Oxford University Press, 1978), pp. 33–37; and James Simpson, *Sciences and the Self in Medieval Poetry* (Cambridge: Cambridge University Press, 1995), pp. 53–55. On the early-fifteenth-century Italian humanist revival and application of the Cardinal Virtues, and especially *fortitudo,* to civic life, see Hans Baron, *In Search of Florentine Civic Humanism,* vol. 1 (Princeton: Princeton University Press, 1988), pp. 94–157. A pertinent essay by Colin Fewer, 'John Lydgate's *Troy Book* and the Ideology of Prudence,' observes, in essential agreement with the position expressed here, that 'a significant part of Lydgate's project is to demystify the operation of Fortune, locating the origins of historical processes in the contingent sphere of human action and motivation—in the conduct both of great men and of relatively minor characters, and in the context both of parliaments and of entirely mundane, routine moments in the narrative' (*Chaucer Review* 38 [2004]: 229–45; at 231. A cautionary note on my valorization of Prudence in Lydgate's *Fall* is provided by Robert R. Edwards, who argues for Prudence as a late-medieval ideal, but also an ideal subject to repeated frustration elsewhere in the Lydgate canon. See 'Lydgate's *Troy Book* and the Confusion of Prudence,' in *The North Sea World in the Middle Ages,* ed. Thomas R. Liszka and Eorna E. M. Walker (Dublin: Four Courts Press, 2001), pp. 52–69. Other works centralizing Prudence include Hoccleve's *Regiment* and Yonge's *Gouernaunce;* see nn. 28–29, above. Having already noted the instability of vernacular English, Yonge proposes a surprising but indicative pairing with his discussion, 'Of Prudencia and cunnynge.' For another fifteenth-century English treatment of Prudence, see the 'Boke of Noblesse,' with its discussion of 'how a prince and a ledar of peple shulde use prudence and

justice by example of the noble senatoure called fabricius,' and its conclusion that the leader of a city must above all else 'be a prudent man' (BL Royal 18 B. xxii, f. 28).

33. Maura Nolan makes a very compatible point about the status of Fortune in Lydgate's early 'Serpent of Division.' Distinguishing between traditions that insist upon static exemplarity and those that allow for historical contingency, she points out that they represent 'fundamentally incompatible visions of historical causation and the role of human agency in history.' Lydgate attempts to overcome this incompatibility by demanding appropriate attention to the contradictory claims of each: '"Wise governours" are given an impossible task: to accept the inevitability of the "sodeyne change of this false worlde" while simultaneously behaving as if such change could be prudently foreseen and prevented.' See 'The Art of History Writing: Lydgate's *Serpent of Division*,' *Speculum* 78 (2003): 99–127; quotation at p. 127. I embrace this perception wholeheartedly, believing such a contradiction inherent in the tradition, and brought to a point of heightened visibility by Lydgate, whose *Fall* alternates between an insistence on the unavoidability of Fortune's snares, even as he extends the argument I am noticing here, according to which the prince can arm himself by prudential foresight.

34. On the relation of *Ratio* to Prudence, and on the central role that Alan of Lille assigns to *ratio*, see Simpson, *Sciences and the Self,* p. 48.

35. *Mirour* in *The Complete Works of John Gower,* ed. G. C. Macaulay (Oxford: Clarendon Press, 1901), vol. 1, p. 144, ll. 12409–11.

36. *Siege of Thebes,* ed. A. Erdmann, EETS, ES 108 (1911), l. 843.

37. *The Minor Poems of John Lydgate,* part 2, ed. Henry N. MacCracken, EETS, OS, vol. 192 (London, 1934), pp. 682–91.

38. Henry V is instanced as an exemplar of force, prudence, and righteousness, and—now evidently removed to the sphere of legend—considered as fit companion to the storied nine worthies.

39. Caroline Barron, 'The Political Culture of Medieval London,' in *The Fifteenth Century IV,* ed. L. Clark (forthcoming, Boydell Press), pp. 1–22; quotation at p. 10.

40. John Stow, *A Survey of London,* ed. C. L. Kingsford, vol. 1 (Oxford: Clarendon Press, 1908), p. 272.

41. The French book is no doubt by Christine de Pisan, for which see below, p. 124. For the Senecan attribution, see Quentin Skinner, who provides evidence that the treatise in question was probably the *Formula vitae honestae:* 'a treatise of remarkably wide circulation generally believed to be by Seneca himself' but 'correctly attributed to Bishop Martin of Braga'. 'Ambrogio Loenzetti: The Artist as Political Philosopher,' *Proceedings of the British Academy* 72 (1986): 5.

42. MS Bodley 263, f. 448.

43. This analysis of Lydgate's attempts at 'fortune-proofing' his prince aligns interestingly with James Simpson's discussion of Lydgate's politics in his *Siege of*

Thebes. Simpson describes the concern of Middle English writers 'to define a secular ethics appropriate to political action,' noting Lydgate's interest in the ethical nexus provided by the Virtues, including Truth and, especially, Prudence, as expressed in the virtues of 'prudential foresight.' His view of the *Siege* as framed by this concern is quite congruent with the present analysis of the *Fall*. Yet at this juncture we diverge, not so much in concept as in our reading of the evidence provided by two very different poems, as Simpson finds in the *Siege* a profoundly pessimistic limitation of 'the space for rational, politically prudent action.' In this instance, the destruction of human designs is accomplished not so much by Fortune as by 'the irresistible backward pull of history.' See '"Dysemol daies and fatal houres": Lydgate's *Destruction of Thebes* and Chaucer's *Knight's Tale*,' in *The Long Fifteenth Century*, ed. Helen Cooper and Sally Mapstone (Oxford: Clarendon Press, 1997), pp. 16–33.

44. A. S. G. Edwards, 'The Influence of Lydgate's *Fall of Princes* c. 1440–1559: A Survey,' *Mediaeval Studies* 39 (1977): 424–39.

45. Printed by Pynson (1494 and 1527), Tottel (1554), and Wayland (1554/5). Evidence provided to me by Alexandra Gillespie suggests that the 1494 edition enjoyed what was for the fifteenth century an unusually large print run of 600 copies. This is known from a lawsuit in which Pynson sued one John Russhe over his debt for '[600] of bocas off the falle of prynces,' along with 'divers other bokys to a great value' that Pynson delivered to Russhe to 'sende them into the counter to sell.' Of course, Pynson's interests might have been advanced by some exaggeration in the total number of copies. See Alexandra Gillespie, *Chaucer and Lydgate in Print: The Medieval Author and the History of the Book, 1476–1579* (Oxford: Oxford University Press, 2005).

46. Edwards observes that 'It would seem that in certain respects Boccaccio's original historical materials were of subordinate importance to English readers. . . . It is rather Lydgate's own sententious generalities that seem to have struck a sympathetic note with his readers' ('Influence,' p. 431). This observation is not, of course, in necessary conflict with my emphasis on Lydgate's turn to the world; for it is in the nonhistorical, non-narrative segments of the poem that many of the terminologies potentially applicable to contemporary circumstances are most extensively mooted.

47. See Lydgate, *Fall*, vol. 121, bk. I, ll. 372–85, p. 331; Calverley, *A dialogue bitwene the playntife and the Defendaunt Compyled by Wylliam Caluerley whyles he was prisoner in the towre of London* (Bodleian Facsimile, c.3), ll. 483–505. Calverley's reliance upon Lydgate was pointed out by Julia Boffey in a paper given at King's College, London, June 2002.

48. George Cavendish, *Metrical Visions*, ed. A. S. G. Edwards (Columbia: University of South Carolina Press, 1980). Edwards demonstrates Lydgate's influence on pp. 9–11. I am reliant on the text of this fine edition.

49. This God is inexplicit with respect to the emergent Protestant-Catholic divide, with Cavendish presenting himself as mourning equally the deaths of Edward VI and Mary.

50. Gillespie, *Chaucer and Lydgate in Print*; John Thompson, 'Reading Lydgate in Post Reformation England,' in *Middle English Poetry: Texts and Traditions*, ed. A. J. Minnis, York Manuscripts Conferences Proceedings (York: York Medieval Press, 2001), pp. 181–209. Thompson describes Baldwin's project as being 'to further "politicise" Lydgate's poem in line with the temper of the times.' His analysis, however, concerns itself more with what might be considered 'the politics of printing history' than with the body of Lydgate's text. He offers particularly apt illustration of the way in which Wayland and Tottel generated simultaneous traditional and progressive signals for their republications of Lydgate in his discussion of Wayland's reuse in his edition of the *Fall* of the title pages originally intended for the suppressed 'protestant' edition: 'The choice of decorative device for the Wayland print may have been a simple printer's convenience, but may also reflect at some level William Baldwin's desire to maintain an Edwardian and reformist theme for his collaborative Lydgatian project. The various Wayland titles deploy a folio compartment that had already been used by the Stationer and protestant printer John Day.... Day had first used the compartment in 1551 for the title page of his third Bible, comprising Becke's revision of the Taverner version combined with the Tyndale New Testament.' He describes a similar background for the folio compartment of Tottel's *Fall* in the same year (pp. 202–3). With respect to Wayland as a 'Catholic' printer, I have had a very informative correspondence with T. S. Freeman, who observes that 'In 1556, John Wayland turned one of his apprentices, Thomas Green, over to the authorities, when he discovered that Green possessed a copy of John Olde's translation of Rudolph Gualter's treatise, Antichrist (Acts and Monuments, 1563 edition, p. 1685). Green was whipped for possessing the book. In his first edition, Foxe called Wayland a 'promoter' (i.e., informer) but he removed this epithet—although not the story—in subsequent editions' (correspondence, 5 June 2004). On Whitchurch's protestantism, see Norton's preface to his translation of Calvin's *Institutes,* in which he is described as 'an auncient zealous Gospeller' (London: H. Middleton, 1587, p. i).

51. That Lydgate was not simply a passive or precedental presence, but served as an important influence upon individual writers, is suggested by the case of Sackville's *Induction* and Henry duke of Buckingham's *Complaint*. In addition to possible local influences (for which see the annotations to Marguerite Hearsey, ed., *The Complaint of Henry Duke of Buckingham* [New Haven: Yale University Press, 1936]), Sackville cites Lydgate in canceled lines from his own manuscript, including:

Loke in the prologue of Bochas fol. Lxiiii. . . .
I haue no fresh licour out of the conduictes of Calliope.
I haue no flowers of rethoricke through Clio.

To which may be compared the following lines in Lydgate:

I mean as thus, I haue no freshe lycour
Out of the conduits of Calliope,
Nor through Clyo in rethoryke no floure (See Hearsey, pp. 91, 124).

52. The printer in question must have been, in effect, a wholesaler. Contemporary records generally distinguish between the 'printing house,' where books are actually manufactured, and a 'shop,' where books are sold, although Peter Blayney has detailed instances parallel to this one, in which a printer would have had books available for sale. See Peter W. M. Blayney, *The Bookshops in Paul's Cross Churchyard*, Occasional Papers 5 (London: Bibliographical Society, 1990), esp. pp. 10 – 11, where the distinction between 'shop' and 'printing house' is made. Blayney describes modest shops, consisting only of a hinged board projecting from the front of a building; but the shop in this case must have been of the more substantial, 'walk-in' variety. Also see Blayney, 'John Day and the Bookshop That Never Was,' in *Material London, ca. 1600*, ed. Lena Cowen Orlin (Philadelphia: University of Pennsylvania Press, 2000), pp. 322 – 43.

53. Frank Freeman Foster, *The Politics of Stability: A Portrait of the Rulers in Elizabethan London* (London: Royal Historical Society, 1977), pp. 12 – 13. Recall, in this regard, Thomas Elyot's address of his *Book Named the Governour*, to 'inferior governours called magistrates' (London: Everyman, 1907), p. 48.

54. Annabel Patterson, *Reading Holinshed's 'Chronicles'* (Chicago: University of Chicago Press, 1994): 'Crucial to the project as I am redefining it was the construction and education of a new kind of *readership . . .* that would itself be composed of literate individuals spanning a fairly wide cross section of socioeconomic groups, but predominantly, like the members of the "syndicate" themselves, middle-class citizens' (pp. 15 – 16; original emphasis). Like Patterson, I discover an affinity between writers and their intended readers.

55. *Mirror for Magistrates*, ed. Campbell, pp. 20 – 50.

56. Arnold Hauser, *Philosophy of Art History* (New York: Meridian Books, 1963), p. 230.

57. David Cressy observes that prior to the second half of the seventeenth century, 1,500 copies or less constituted an average print run, and that a relatively small social elite could have absorbed most of the titles produced; certainly, by such a measure, the politically interested middle strata of London-Westminster could have amply supported this publishing endeavor. See David Cressy, *Literacy and the Social Order: Reading and Writing in Tudor and Stuart England* (Cambridge: Cambridge University Press, 1980), p. 47.

58. W. F. Trench, *A Mirror for Magistrates: Its Origin and influence* (Edinburgh: privately printed, 1898).

59. 'Humphrey Duke of Gloucester & Elianor Cobham His Wife in *A Mirror for Magistrates, Huntington Library Bulletin*, no. 5 (1934): 121.

60. See *Tudor and Stuart Proclamations, 1485–1714,* ed. Robert Steele (Oxford: Clarendon Press, 1910), vol. 1, p. 48.

61. Calvin, *The Institution of Christian Religion, bk. 4, chap. 20* (London: R. Harrison, 1562, 492r). The whole of this concluding book, 'Of Ciuile gouernement,' abounds in terminologies pertinent to this study. Calvin addresses at some length the responsibilities of *magistrates,* and considers matters of *policie, lawe, iudgement,* proper constrains on *rigorousnesse,* and more. Arguing that 'the spiritual kingdom of Christ, & the ciuile gouernement are thynges far a sonder' (f. 491r), he proposes a distinction congenial to many of the theorists under consideration here.

62. Boccaccio's 'Preface' to *De Casibus,* cited from Lydgate, *Fall,* vol. 1, p. xlvii.

63. James Simpson has observed, in correspondence, that some elements of a more rational view of Fortune's operations may be discovered in the previous later fourteenth-century writings of John Gower. Gower observes that 'man is overall / His oghne cause of wel and wo. / That we fortune clepe so / Out of the man himself it groweth.' *Confessio Amantis, The Complete Works of John Gower,* vol. 2, ll. 546–49.

64. On the availability of Machiavelli's views, and especially the political pragmatism of *Il Principe,* in England in the early 1550s, see Felix Raab, *The English Face of Machiavelli: A Changing Interpretation, 1500–1700* (Toronto: University of Toronto Press, 1964). Raab cites evidence of knowledge about Machiavelli as early as 1539 (the likely date of Reginald Pole's animadversions against *Il Principe,* and also emphasizes the more receptive responses of Richard Morrison and William Thomas. See esp. pp. 30–51. Also see, for the suggestion that Edward VI was receptive to Machiavellian thinking in mediated form, E. R. Adair, 'William Thomas,' in *Tudor Studies,* ed. R. W. Seton-Watson (London: Longmans, 1924), pp. 133–60. Adair cites Thomas's reply to an apparent request by the king that he elaborate some of the topics of his proposed discourses for the king's edification: 'Mr Throgmerton declared yor Mats pleasre vnto me, and deliuered me wthall the notes of certain discourses, which according to yor highness commaundement I shall most gladly applie; to sende you one everie weeke if it be possible for me in so little tyme to compasse it' (BL MS Cotton Vespasian D.18, ff. 28–29; at p. 142. See Catherine Shrank's account of William Thomas's adaptations of Machiavelli for the education of the young Edward VI in *Writing the Nation in Reformation England,* (Oxford: Oxford University Press, 2004). As she observes, a parallel interest in, and knowledge of, Machiavelli is shown in Stephen Gardiner's 1555 treatise written for Philip of Spain.

65. This encouraging speculation arises in Machiavelli's *Capitoli,* when he imagines the abode of Fortune as comprising many different spinning wheels, and proposes that one might leap between them: 'sarebbe un sempere felice e beato / che potessi saltar di rota in rota' ('a man who could leap from wheel to wheel would always be happy and fortunate . . .'). *Capitoli,* ed Giorgio Inglese (Rome: Bulzoni

Editore, 1981), p. 119, ll. 115–17); trans. *Chief Works,* ed. A. Gilbert (Durham: Duke University Press, 1965), vol. 2, p. 747. His proposal is, however, overtly subjunctive and wishful, and he shifts to an acknowledgment that this possibility is ultimately denied.

66. Allan H. Gilbert, *Machiavelli's 'Prince' and Its Forerunners* (Durham: Duke University Press, 1938), pp. 204–21.

67. Hugh G. Dick, 'Thomas Blundeville's *The true order and Methode of wryting and reding Hystories* (1574),' *Huntington Library Quarterly,* no. 2 (1940): 149–70.

68. Bodin, *Method for the Easy Comprehension of History (La methode de l'histoire),* trans. Beatrice Reynolds (New York: Columbia University Press, 1945), p. 15.

69. Farnham is perceptive in his delineation of a tension between tragedies of inevitable 'retribution' which exploit a popular Tudor taste for tragic justice and those alternate moments which 'allow that an ambitious prince, by studying the lessons of tragical stories, may avoid tragedy.' But Farnham's disposition is to propose a teleological development, with retribution winning out in the end. My own, somewhat different, analysis proposes an 'early Tudor' moment in which these two perspectives coexist, in fact seem frequently to require each other, with formal deference to God's providential scheme as a concomitant to the delineation of a sphere of practical political action. See the classic study of Willard Farnham, *The Medieval Heritage of Elizabethan Tragedy* (Berkeley: University of Cailfornia Press, 1936), esp. pp. 271–303.

70. *Romaunt of the Rose, Riverside Chaucer,* ll. 1455–1705.

71. The audience of the *Mirror* is placed in a spectatorial vantage point of relative security, but one that always acknowledges implicit dangers. Thomas duke of Gloucester tells us, revealingly, that he was hoisted on Fortune's wheel, even

> As one on a stage attending a playe,
> Seeth not on whiche side the scaffolde doth reele,
> Tyll tymber and poales, and all flee awaye. (ll. 65–67, p. 94).

Even as Thomas was placed in a position of insecure spectatorship with regard to his own experiences, so is the reader of his narration similarly situated. One is, as it were, onstage, having entered into the fiction on the basis of a propensity for political 'vice,' yet insecurely so: a participant-observer, separated from the story by the frail scaffolding of genre, consciousness of fiction, temporal removal, and all the rest, but ever liable to be plunged into a more intimate and experiential relation with the matters at hand.

72. *Renaissance Conceptions of History in 'The Mirror for Magistrates'* (Berkeley: University of California Press, 1935).

73. *The Middle English Translation of Christine de Pisan's 'Livre du Corps de Policie,'* ed. Diane Bornstein (Heidelberg: Carl Winter, 1977).

74. *Governance,* ed. Plummer, chap. 15, p. 148.

75. John Watts, '*The Policie in Christen Remes:* Bishop Russell's Parliamentary Sermons of 1483–84,' in *Authority and Consent in Tudor England: Essays Presented to C. S. L. Davies,* ed. G. W. Bernard and S. J. Gunn (Aldershot: Ashgate, 2002), pp. 50–51.

76. 'Active Policy of a Prince,' *George Ashby's Poems,* ed. Mary Bateson, EETS, ES 76 (1899), title at l. 85.

77. *Chronicles of London,* ed. C. L. Kingsford (Oxford: Clarendon Press, 1905), p. 164.

78. *Paston Letters and Papers,* ed. Norman Davis, vol. 1 (Oxford: Clarendon Press, 1971), p. 503.

79. One aspect of these terms' close association is etymological, bearing on the simultaneous knowledge of English and French by many of England's politically involved classes. In French, the single word *politique* normally (though not invariably) embraces both English *policie* and English (adj.) *politique.* As we have already seen in chapter 1 of this study, English *politique* could mean 'public spirited' but also something more like 'astute' or 'calculating.' For English speakers encountering difficulty in converting *politique* to a noun, and employing *policie* in its place, some 'bleeding' of meaning is inevitable. Whatever the etymological explanation, however, the adjectival *politique* came in English to be the usual term for policy's artful implementation. I am indebted for this observation to Michelle Warren, Department of Romance Languages, University of Miami. She adds, in correspondence (17 April 2004), that if English writers who know French 'can distinguish between "politics" and "policy" in English, but must use "politique" for both in French, then even the English "politic(s)" cannot be entirely free of the double connotation of "politique."' She adds the qualification that French writers, like Christine de Pisan, sometimes use 'policie' with a sense like ModE 'politics.' A related point was made (on the occasion of a 26 March 2004 lecture at the University of Miami) by Rebecca Biron, also of Romance Languages: in the literature of the Spanish Conquest, *politica* was at once the policy of Isabela la Católica (in its prudential or public-spirited sense) and the connivance of pirates (seeking private gain).

80. Rubinstein, 'The History of the Word *Politicus*,' in *The Languages of Political Theory in Early-Modern Europe,* pp. 41–56; quotation at p. 54.

81. See chapter 1, above, p. 33.

82. See chapter 3.

83. Thoroughly aired in Geoffrey Bullough, ed., *Narrative and Dramatic Sources of Shakespeare,* 4 vols. (London: Routledge, 1957–75).

84. *The Chronicle of Adam of Usk,* ed. C. Given-Wilson (Oxford: Clarendon Press, 1997), pp. 64–65.

85. *Henry the Sixth,* ed. and trans. M. R. James (Cambridge: Cambridge University Press, 1919).

86. *Petrarch's Remedies for Fortune Fair and Foul,* trans. Conrad H. Rawski (Indiana University Press, 1991), vol. 1, p. 4.

87. Victoria Kahn, *Machiavellian Rhetoric from the Counter-Reformation to Milton* (Princeton: Princeton University Press, 1994), pp. 3–43, esp. pp. 249–51, nn. 1–8.

88. On telling differences between the folio and the quarto versions, see chap. 1, n. 59.

89. These comments were developed in conversation with Sandra Prior and Sealy Gilles in the encouraging environment of a New York MEDS meeting.

THREE. FORTESCUE AND PECOCK: TWO *PARCYALLE* MEN

1. Rymer, *Foedera,* XI, 709–11.

2. MS Phillipps 9735, f. 279. Printed in *The Paston Letters,* ed. James Gairdner, vol. 5 (London, 1904), p. 104. He is listed as a member of 'Harrys party' but not listed as 'slayne in the felde' although not excluded from those 'xlij knyghtys that were slayne aftyr' in *Gregory's Chronicle,* ed. James Gairdner, Camden Society, 2d ser., 17 (1876): 217. A mistaken attribution in an attachment to Leland's *Collectanea* has one 'Fosterus,' marginally corrected to 'Fortescue,' as 'primus Justitiarius Angliae,' on a list of those 'Donati vita ab Eduardo rege.' See *The Itinerary of John Leland,* ed. Lucy Toulmin Smith, vol. 4 (London: Bell and Sons, 1909), Appendix I(b), p. 163.

3. CPR, 1467–77, p. 296. See also Leland, *Collectanea,* ed. Th. Hearne (1712), vol. 2, p. 505.

4. Petition for reversal of attainder, 6 October 1473 (*Rolls of Parliament* [*RP*], 6, p. 69); Exemplified, 14 February 1475. See also Clermont, ed., *The Works of Sir John Fortescue,* vol. 1 (hereafter, *Works,* 1869) (London: Private distribution, 1869), p. 41.

5. *RP,* vol. 6, p. 69.

6. In this category would fall the old story, apparently promulgated in the fourteenth century by John of Gaunt, about the weakening of the Lancastrian claim by unjust exclusion of Henry III's son Edward Crouchback from the line of succession. *Works,* 1869, p. 524.

7. *RP,* vol. 6, p. 69.

8. Michel Foucault, 'The Spectacle of the Scaffold,' in *Discipline and Punish* (New York: Vintage Books, 1979), pp. 32–72.

9. *RP,* 4, p. 296.

10. *The Governance of England,* ed. Charles Plummer (Oxford: Clarendon Press, 1885), chap. 15, p. 145.

11. James H. Landman, 'Pleading, Pragmatism, and Permissible Hypocrisy: The "Colours" of Legal Discourse in Late Medieval England,' *New Medieval Literatures* 4 (2001): 139–170, esp. pp. 140–48, 165–70.

12. Landman acutely demonstrates the presence of this ambivalence even within what might appear Fortescue's more serenely high-minded works, discovering aspects of the 'partial' Fortescue even in the 'principled' *De Laudibus Legum Anglie*,' p. 165.

13. On the growth of a 'science' of politics in a university setting, see Janet Coleman, 'The Sciences of Politics and Late Medieval Academic Debate,' in *Criticism and Dissent in the Middle Ages*, ed. Rita Copeland (Cambridge: Cambridge University Press, 1996), pp. 206–9.

14. The best and most authoritative short account of Fortescue's life is that of S. B. Chrimes, in his introduction to *De Laudibus Legum Anglie* (Cambridge: Cambridge University Press, 1942), pp. lix–lxvii.

15. *RP,* 5, p. 477.

16. These biographical details are sustained by the life records printed in Clermont, *Works,* 1880, pp. 57–90. With respect to his 'shadow chancellorship,' Henry's official correspondence refers to him as 'Jehan Fortescu, chevalier, chancellier du Roy Henry Dangleterre' (p. 76) and as 'nostre amie et loial chancellier Jehan Fortescu, chivalier' (p. 78). The prince, in *De Laudibus,* refers to him as 'cancellarius.' Fortescue refers to himself, more modestly, as 'miles quidam grandevus,' but adds, 'predicti Regis Anglie cancellarius' (p. 2). Details of his possible investiture are uncertain, but the position was at least tactically, imaginatively, and aspirationally assigned to him. See Chrimes, *De Laudibus,* pp. 145–46.

17. *Works,* 1869, pp. 24–25.

18. Commynes, *Mémoires,* bk. 3, chap. 4, p. 184.

19. For convenient references to the first three instances, see James Ramsay, *Lancaster and York,* vol. 2 (Oxford: Clarendon Press, 1892), pp. 215–16, 368–72, 332. On Wenlock, see also my own discussion in chapter 1. On Warwick, see Paul Murray Kendall, *Warwick the Kingmaker* (London: Allen & Unwin, 1957).

20. *Mémoires,* bk. 2, chap. 2, p. 100.

21. Text and translation from S. B. Chrimes, ed., *De Laudibus,* p. 2.

22. The sense of dislocation and even confusion that penetrates the text as a whole emerges in a telling disturbance of sense arising in relation to the prince's sojourn in Barre. Extolling the jury system and the reliability of neighbors, the prince says, 'I myself know more certainly what is now done in England than what has been done here in Barre where I at present reside.' But Fortescue speaks to him in a placatory way, explaining, 'You were a youth when you left England, prince, so that the nature and quality of that land are unknown to you.' Clearly, the main sense of this passage (p. 67) is that the prince could be expected to know little of his native land; that, leaving it as a child, he is forgetful of its practices, with those of Barre necessarily seeming more real to him. Later printed editions correct the prince's statement by inverting its sense, but, as Chrimes points out, all the manuscripts support the original confusion. Fortescue himself, suffering nearly a decade of exile from a na-

tive land which he remembers with both distress and idealization, seems essentially confused about matters of residence, experience, and affiliation.

23. Plummer, *Governance*, Appendix B, p. 349.

24. See the discussion in Colin Richmond and Margaret Kekewich, 'The Search for Stability,' *The Politics of Fifteenth-Century England: John Vale's Book*, ed. M. Kekewich et al. (Stroud: Alan Sutton, Yorkist History Trust, 1995), pp. 43–66.

25. For a discussion of these matters see Chrimes, pp. 87–96. For a more recent and more fully developed discussion, see Richmond and Kekewich, *John Vale's Book*, pp. 53–57. These ambiguities are further multiplied by the suggestion of John Watts, in correspondence, that 'Edward IV could presumably be a reference to Edward of Lancaster [that is, Prince Edward, son and heir to Henry VI] as well of Edward of York.'

26. Printed in *Literae Cantuarienses*, ed. J. B. Sheppard, Rolls series, no. 85, vol. 3 (London, 1889), pp. 274–85; at p. 275.

27. S. B. Chrimes, 'A Defence of the Proscription of the Yorkists in 1459,' *English Historical Review*, 26 (1911): 512–25; at pp. 519, 520.

28. S. B. Chrimes, 'Sir John Fortescue and His Theory of Dominion,' *Transactions of the Royal Historical Society*, 4th ser., vol. 17 (London, 1934), 117–47. Substantially reproduced in *English Constitutional Ideas in the Fifteenth Century* (Cambridge: Cambridge University Press, 1936), pp. 307–24.

29. See Anthony Gross, *The Dissolution of the Lancastrian Kingship: Sir John Fortescue and the Crisis of Monarchy in Fifteenth-Century England* (Stamford: Paul Watkins, 1996), esp. pp. 67, 89–90.

30. 'Dissolution,' p. xviii. Fortescue is also seen (rather woodenly) as an author of 'legitimist propaganda' in Paul E. Gill, 'Politics and Propaganda in Fifteenth-Century England: The Polemical Writings of Sir John Fortescue,' *Speculum* 46 (1971): 333–47. Although not specifically writing about Fortescue, Charles Ross has domesticated the term in relation to fifteenth-century writings in his 'Rumour, Propaganda and Popular Opinion during the Wars of the Roses,' in *Patronage the Crown and the Provinces in Later Medieval England*, ed. Ralph A. Griffiths (Gloucester: Alan Sutton, 1981), pp. 5–29. See also J. R. Lander's 'Propaganda, Compensations, and the State of the Country,' in *The Limitations of English Monarchy in the Later Middle Ages* (Toronto: University of Toronto Press, 1989), pp. 41–55.

31. The opening chapters of *De Laudibus* identify the prince as addressee, and in fact as interlocutor in this text; in chapter ix, Fortescue refers to the contents of *De Natura* as 'in Opusculo quod tui contemplacione . . . exaravi,' 'in a small work which I wrote for your consideration' (pp. 26–27).

32. *John Vale's Book*, pp. 53–66.

33. For a list and discussion of Fortescue's surviving and lost works see Chrimes, *De Laudibus*, pp. lxxvi–ix. Several pro-Lancastrian works including 'A Genealogy of

the House of Lancaster' were evidently destroyed in the Cottonian fire. For a résumé of Fortescue's varied and extensive Lancastrian arguments, now lost—one 'en forme de livre' and one described as 'ung autre memoire assez longue' to Louis of France— see the nearly contemporaneous résumé printed in *Works*, 1869, pp. 34–35.

34. Chrimes, *De Laudibus*, pp. 26–27. Also see J. H. Burns, 'Fortescue and the Political Theory of *Dominium*,' *Historical Journal* 28 (1985): 782.

35. See Pierre Bourdieu, *Language and Symbolic Power* (Cambridge, Mass.: Harvard University Press, 1991), passim., but especially 'The Production and Reproduction of Legitimate Language,' pp. 43–65. For Bourdieu, the right to act as a participant and contestant for authority within a constituted field entails, at least in part, a certain nonacknowledgment of, or even obliviousness to, some of the rules of the very game which is being played. According to his analysis, Fortescue could not be an entirely competent player, if all the stakes of play were apparent to him at all times. Some of the volition in his choices must be assigned to the constitution of the total expressive field, with its own evasions and suppressions, within which his texts were produced.

36. For a differently argued but conceptually compatible account of Fortescue's political vision see John Watts, 'A Newe Ffundacion of is Crowne': Monarchy in the Age of Henry VII,' in *The Reign of Henry VII*, ed. Benjamin Thompson (Stamford: Watkins, 1995), pp. 31–53.

37. *Limitations*, p. 13.

38. See the introduction above, nn. 32–35.

39. *De Natura*, in *Works*, 1869, p. 63.

40. *De Natura*, c. xvi; *De Laudibus*, chap. xi; *Governance*, chap. 2. Rubinstein observes that he borrows his concept of the distinction between *regimen regale* and *regimen politicum* from Aquinas and Giles of Rome, but applies that distinction not, as they do, to monarchies and republics, but to two different kinds of monarchy. See 'The History of the Word *Politicus*,' in *The Languages of Political Theory*, pp. 50–51.

41. MS Julius B II, f. 30r; printed in *Chronicles of London*, ed. C. L. Kingsford (Oxford: Clarendon Press, 1905), p. 31. Fortescue would obviously have concurred in the Lancastrian estimation of Richard's offense, and probably alludes to Richard's transgression when he tells the prince: 'You have already heard how among the civil laws there is a famous sentence . . . which runs like this, "What pleased the prince has the force of law." The laws of England do not sanction any such maxim, since the king of that land rules his people not only regally but also politically, and so he is bound by oath at his coronation to the observance of his law' (*De Laudibus*, pp. 78–79).

42. David Wallace suggests that this particular form of the state's emergence as an object of analysis 'may be aligned with developments in theology: the shift from Aristotelian scholasticism to nominalism. As theology finds it less and less possible to "describe" God, there is an increasing tendency to turn to analysis of what CAN be described—including such phenomena as the state. Later, of course, Augustinian theology comes in to support the claims and methods of absolutism. But

this fifteenth-century moment seems to puddle interestingly in this middle, evolving ground' (correspondence, 20 March 2004).

43. Speaking of Fortescue's departure from the fourteenth-century theories of FitzRalph and Wyclif, J. H. Burns takes note of 'the total absence, in Fortescue, of the theological context of that kind of theory.' His view is that FitzRalph and other predecessors within traditions of theological writings on the state have political implications, but that it would be misleading to call their constructs political theories as such. By contrast, 'the dominium with which Fortescue is concerned . . . is almost always, in one sense or another, political' ('Fortescue and the Political Theory of *Dominium*,' p. 797).

44. Works cited include *The Donet*, ed. E. V. Hitchcock, EETS, OS, no. 156 (London, 1921), here, p. 75; *The Folewer to the Donet*, ed. E. V. Hitchcock, EETS, OS, no. 164 (London, 1924); *The Reule of Crysten Religioun* (hereafter *Reule*), ed. W. C. Greet, EETS, OS, no. 171 (London, 1927); *The Repressor of Over Much Blaming of the Clergy* (hereafter *Repressor*), ed. C. Babington, Rolls series, no. 19, vols. 1–2 (London, 1860).

45. On the sense in which natural law is a law of God, see *Repressor*, p. 6.

46. Pecock is here, to be sure, arguing with one eye on the Lollards and their insistence on biblical grounding of religious practices and truths; part of his aim is to lay a foundation for pilgrimages and other encouraged practices that have developed without scriptual sanction. Nevertheless, the *effect* of his anti-Lollard strategy is greatly to bolster the law of nature within his system, and to invite condemnation by orthodox clerics like John Bury who would base natural law on scriptural authority. See *Gladius Salomonis*, published in *Repressor*, esp. p. 591.

47. Gascoigne, *Loci e Libro Veritatum*, selected and edited from Oxford Lincoln College MS Lat. 117, 118 by J. E. Thorold Rogers (Oxford: Clarendon Press, 1881), p. 28.

48. Wendy Scase, 'Reginald Pecock,' in *English Writers of the Middle Ages*, vol. 8 (Aldershot: Variorum, 1996), p. 133.

49. Kantik Ghosh, 'Bishop Reginald Pecock and the Idea of "Lollardy,"' in *Text and Controversy from Wyclif to Bale: Essays in Honour of Anne Hudson*, ed. Anne Hutchison and Helen Barr (forthcoming, Brepols).

50. Mishtooni Bose, 'Reginald Pecock's Vernacular Voice,' in *Lollards and Their Influence in Late Medieval England*, ed. Fiona Somerset et al. (Woodbridge: Boydell, 2003), pp. 217–36; quotations from pp. 222, 218, 217. I have only slightly hinted at the rich analysis of this fine essay, with its suggestive analysis of the instabilities inherent in Pecock's expository stance.

51. Scase, 'Reginald Pecock,' pp. 103–11.

52. Jeremy Catto, 'The King's Government and the Fall of Pecock, 1457–58,' in *Rulers and Ruled in Late Medieval England*, ed. Rowena Archer and Simon Walker (London: Hambledon Press, 1995), pp. 201–22; quotation at p. 202.

53. Gascoigne, *Loci*, p. 212.

54. Catto, observing that Pecock probably intended his letter to be private, accepts Gascoigne's assertion that it proved something of a 'trigger' in this case ('The King's Government,' pp. 202–3).

55. Scase, 'Reginald Pecock,' pp. 120–22.

56. Attested in a papal mandate (printed by Scase, 'Reginald Pecock,' pp. 127–28); Gascoigne, *Loci*, pp. 211–12.

57. Oxford, Bodleian Library, MS Ashmole 789, ff. 322r-23r.; Scase, 'Reginald Pecock,' pp. 134–37. In all but a few minor respects I have followed Scase's superb transcriptions.

58. A crucial study of the progressive breakdown of the discursive barriers between civil sedition and ecclesiastical heresy is Margaret Aston, 'Lollardy and Sedition, 1381–1431,' *Past and Present* 17 1960): 1–44.

59. A gloss on this matter is to be found in a parliamentary text of 7–8 Edward IV, in which the state of the realm is surveyed, preliminary to a request for a subsidy for a new invasion of France. This text discovers in Justice 'grounde well and rote of all prosperite, peas and pollityke ruyle,' and finds that Justice resides in Law, which is threefold: 'the Lawe of God, Lawe of nature, and posityfe Lawe.' *RP,* 5, p. 622.

60. On the duties of the secular prince see also *Donet*, pp. 74–79.

61. Scase, 'Reginald Pecock,' pp. 138–39.

62. Scase, 'Reginald Pecock,' p. 124.

63. Scase, 'Reginald Pecock,' p. 136.

64. Catto, 'The King's Government,' pp. 208–9. This list of disturbances can be extended, especially for London in the years 1456–58. See the pertinent survey of Ralph A. Griffiths, including the observation that Pecock's abjuration 'made its own distinctive contribution to the tense atmosphere in the city.' *The Reign of Henry VI* (Berkeley: University of California Press, 1981), pp. 790–97.

65. See also Pecock's very pertinent remarks on old and new forms of 'politik gouernaunce,' *Repressor,* vol. 2, pp. 436–37.

66. Nicholas Watson, 'Censorship and Cultural Change in Late-Medieval England: Vernacular Theology, the Oxford Translation Debate, and Arundel's Constitutions of 1409,' *Speculum* 70 (1995): 821–64.

67. For example, *Loci*, p. 213.

68. Scase, 'Reginald Pecock,' p. 130.

69. Gascoigne, *Loci*, p. 215.

70. Scase, 'Reginald Pecock,' pp. 124, 138–39. For a more widely broadcast mandate, see ibid., pp. 123–24.

71. Gascoigne, *Loci*, p. 216.

72. Trans. I. D. Thornley, *England under the Yorkists, 1460–1485* (London: Longmans, Green, 1920), pp. 196–97; from *Calendar of State Papers, Venice,* I, no. 451.

73. Scase, 'Reginald Pecock,' p. 121.

74. As in Lowe and Stillington's previously cited reference to 'th'inconstance and fraille disposicion of the pouple these dayes' (Scase, 'Reginald Pecock,' p. 136).

75. MS Bodleian Oxon. 108; printed as appendix to *Repressor*, vol. 1, p. 572 passim.

76. Gascoigne, *Loci*, p. 211.

77. On Pecock's propensity to insert corrections in his own hand, see Bury's *Epistle*, in *Repressor*, vol. 1, p. 573: Bury comments that he was working from a manuscript 'quae propriis annotavit digitis.'

78. Scase, 'Reginald Pecock,' pp. 132–43.

79. This and subsequent references to his trial and abjuration are taken from *Registrum Abbatiae Johannis Whethamstede*, ed. H. T. Riley, Rolls series, no. 28, vol. 6, pt. 1 (London, 1872), pp. 279–83.

80. Gascoigne, *Loci*, p. 216.

81. Scase, 'Reginald Pecock,' pp. 139–40.

FOUR.   WAITING FOR RICHARD: YORKIST VERSE, 1460–1461

1. John Watts, 'Polemic and Politics in the 1450s,' in *The Politics of Fifteenth-Century England: John Vale's Book*, ed. M. Kekewich et al. (Stroud: Alan Sutton, Yorkist History Trust, 1995) (hereafter *John Vale's Book*), p. 6. The phrase 'accepted principles' is, in turn, borrowed from Quentin Skinner.

2. Equally to be avoided are the claim that ideology 'determines' everything and the counterclaim that ideology is fully at the disposal of free and purposeful subjects who occupy a prior and preideological position. Even in a shattered or dispersed state, the elements of ideology possess sufficient power to affect the outlook of those who deploy, as well as those who consume it. Nonetheless, a sense remains in which the ideologue is not simply a passive servitor of hegemony, but rather retains some elements of choice at the point of ideological production, in the selection and deployment of ideological elements in the elaboration of a system.

3. See John Watts on 'soundbites, buzz-words, strings of interrelated terms and pre-packaged sections of argument' ('*The Policie of Christen Remes*: Bishop Russell's Parliamentary Sermons of 1483–84,' in *Authority and Consent in Tudor English: Essays Presented to C. S. L. Davies*, ed G. W. Bernard and S. J. Gunn [Aldershot: Ashgate, 2000], p. 43). Those wishing to pursue the foundations of such an argument might consult Fredric Jameson on the 'ideologeme,' which he defines as 'the smallest intelligible unit of the essentially antagonistic collective discourses of social classes' (*The Political Unconscious: Narrative as a Socially Symbolic Act* [Ithaca: Cornell University Press, 1983], p. 76).

4. Here my interests diverge from those of Watts, in my greater emphasis on the procedures by which a sectional interest or party *lays claim* to a charged political

utterance. Watts imagines a process of public political discussion that enriches 'the discursive fields in which politics is conducted' ('Bishop Russell's Parliamentary Sermons,' p. 43). Although I would not disagree with this analysis, my own interest rests in a related sector of activity, that process of self-enhancement by which a sectional political interest expresses its activities in generally admired or broadly evocative language.

5. 'A group asserts its claim to possession of an ideological structure by using it effectively. By producing arguments, representations, and enactments through the apt deployment of ideological materials, the group . . . demonstrates its right to them by disclosing their rightful place in the narrative of that group's ascendancy' (Paul Strohm, *Hochon's Arrow*, [Princeton: Princeton University Press, 1992], p. 73).

6. In terms of speech-act philosophy, these poems may be said to possess a certain perlocutionary force, in that they achieve their ends by effecting a formal capture and enlistment of key terms and formal structures, securing their implicit power for a particular cause and imagined outcome.

7. *An English Chronicle of the Reigns of Richard II, Henry IV, Henry V, and Henry VI*, ed. J. S. Davies, Camden Society, 1st ser., no. 64 (London, 1856), pp. 91–94.

8. Richard Beadle, 'Fifteenth-Century Political Verses from the Holkham Archives,' *Medium Aevum* 71 (2002): 101–21.

9. See Appendix 1 to this chapter.

10. *Rolls of Parliament*, (hereafter *RP*), 4, p. 378.

11. John Blacman, *Henry the Sixth*, ed. and trans. M. R. James (Cambridge: Cambridge University Press, 1919), p. 44.

12. Surveyed in Lesley A. Coote, *Prophecy and Public Affairs in Later Medieval England* (Woodbridge: York Medieval Press, 2000), pp. 178–94.

13. Coote, *Prophecy and Public Affairs*, pp. 195–216. On the predominance of Lancastrian prophecy before 1450, and the rise of competing prophecies of Edward of Lancaster after 1453 and Richard of York after 1450, see Jonathan Hughes, *Arthurian Myths and Alchemy: The Kingship of Edward IV* (Gloucestershire: Sutton, 2002), pp. 117–20.

14. On the rise of specifically Yorkist prophecy in 1461, and especially in the months between Edward's accession in March and his coronation in June, see Hughes, *Arthurian Myths and Alchemy*, pp. 140–55. Hughes dates the prophecies of BL MS Cotton Cleopatra C.iv to this period (although conceding the possibility of a date in the mid–50s), and also emphasizes the prophetic content of 'The Illustrated Life of Edward IV,' BL MS Harley 7353. Although his main interest is in genealogy and, especially, alchemy, he takes note of prophetic materials in Edward's Coronation Roll and other prophetic and genealogical histories focused on his reign.

15. See J. D. North, 'Medieval Concepts of Celestial Influence: A Survey,' in *Astrology, Science and Society: Historical Essays*, ed. Patrick Curry (Woodbridge, Suffolk: Boydell Press, 1987), pp. 5–17; also, North, 'Celestial Influence: The Major

Premiss of Astrology,' in *Astrologi Hallucinati*, ed. P. Zambelli (Berlin: W. de Gruyter, 1986).

16. Hilary M. Carey, *Courting Disaster: Astrology at the English Court and University in the Later Middle Ages* (London: Macmillan, 1992), esp. pp. 152–63.

17. J. D. North, *Horoscopes and History* (London: Warburg Institute, 1986), p. 147.

18. Carey, *Courting Disaster,* esp. p. 152.

19. Carey, *Courting Disaster,* p. 143.

20. Carey, *Courting Disaster,* p. 152.

21. *Historical Poems of the Fourteenth and Fifteenth Centuries,* ed. Rossell Hope Robbins (New York: Columbia University Press, 1959), no. 44, pp. 115–17 (hereafter *Historical Poems*).

22. Coote, *Prophecy and Public Affairs,* pp. 195–96.

23. Much can happen in a year. Written in March–April 1460, the verses posted on the gates of Canterbury anticipate Richard's return. By December 1460 he would have returned, been declared heir to the throne, overreached at Wakefield, been slain, and his head displayed on the walls of York. A second poem, of Trinity College Dublin MS 432, written in or soon after July of that year, celebrates an apparent high-water mark of Yorkist fortunes (*Historical Poems*, no. 89. pp. 211–15). Its subject is the battle of Northampton, where Richard's followers routed the Lancastrians and captured King Henry himself, paying him mock-deference but bringing him under their effective control. Like two companion poems in the same manuscript, this one was either written by the poet of the 1460 verses, or else the Yorkists had a truly exceptional array of talent at their disposal. At any rate, I mention it here because it redeploys a number of concepts and figures from the Canterbury verses, this time in a provisionally triumphalist mode. The body of this poem constitutes an allegorical celebration of the deeds of Edward earl of March, Warwick, and Salisbury—as fetterlock, eagle, and ragged staff—and portrays King Henry as a somewhat befuddled hound whom they liberate from a pack of bad dogs' company. But the frame of the poem reworks familiar elements to signal this auspicious development. Once again, we are told that, in occasional moments of grace, 'sorow is turned into gladnesse.' In the Canterbury verses, the agency of this transition is 'celestialle influence on bodyes transitory.' Here it is, once again, 'bodyes celestiall' working their influence on 'the Erthely body.' The beneficent effect is to improve the fortunes 'of certeyn persons that late exiled were,' turning their sorrow to joy. Yet here a somewhat bolder claim is introduced, parallel to the Canterbury verses' vindication of Richard in the alternate register of prophecy, but even more prepossessing. Now, we learn that the celestial influence is itself given 'infleweinz of myrthe' by God himself, acting out of special grace. Not merely supported by prophecy, the Yorkists' preeminence is seen to issue directly 'thorough godes ovne prouysioun'—to be, in a word, Providential in nature. The poem ends with Richard still awaited, still at least nominally 'obedient to his souereigne,' but it remains alert to every opportunity to track his ascendant fortunes.

24. Davies, *An English Chronicle*, p. 94.

25. Charles Ross, *Edward IV* (London: Yale University Press, 1974), p. 26.

26. Davies, *An English Chronicle*, p. 94.

27. Conversation with Mereal Connor, based on her interpretation of incidents in the *Chronicle of John Stone*, which she is currently editing for publication.

28. Readable as a response to demands, it should not, however, be read simply as their product or inevitable consequence. To be avoided is the tempting function-alist argument that a textual composition issues from the circumstances of its inscription in a straight-line or unequivocal way. To be sure, as a purpose-written poem, it displays its worldly affiliations more conspicuously than might otherwise be the case. Yet the analytical issues attending a discussion of its worldliness are no different in kind from those presented by any text. More blatant, less avoidable ... but not different, and no less complex.

29. On the 'autonomy' of the literary text, relative to its larger ideological and material environments, see M. M. Bakhtin and P. M. Medvedev, *The Formal Method in Literary Scholarship*, trans. Albert Wehrle (Cambridge, Mass.: Harvard University Press, 1985), pp. 26–30.

30. Richard Maidstone, *Concordia*, ed. Charles Roger Smith (Ann Arbor: University Microfilms, 1972); *Gesta Henrici Quinti*, ed. F. Taylor and J. Roskell (Oxford: Oxford Medieval Texts, 1975); 'King Henry VI's Triumphal Entry in London, 1432,' in *The Minor Poems of John Lydgate*, ed. H. McCracken, EETS, OS, no. 192 (London, 1934), pp. 630–48.

31. Each of Lydgate's quoted 'scriptures' is, moreover, associated with a marginal Latin gloss; the latter, presumably, taken from Latin text available at the ceremony, or at least in the ceremony as originally scripted.

32. Arguing from the Davies chronicler's statement that the poem was posted 'nat longe before theyre [the earls'] commyng,' Robbins concludes that the period in question is 'Not Lent, since the poem was written shortly before the invasion of June 28,' arguing instead for Whitsun Eve. Robbins, *Historical Poems*, p. 369. Yet the poem might have been written at any time between York's exile in 1459 and the earls' actual appearance at Canterbury at the end of June 1460. For this, and other reasons relating to the prominence of Palm Sunday imagery within the poem, I find Robbins's suggestion unpersuasive.

33. Influentially described by Hennig Brinkmann as the 'Peripetie von Trauer zu Jubel'—'Zum Ursprung des liturgischen Spieles,' in *Xenia Bonnensia: Festschrift zum fünfundsiebzigjährigen Bestehen des Philologischen Vereins und Bonner Kreises* (Bonn, 1929), p. 140.

34. Eamon Duffy, *The Stripping of the Altars: Traditional Religion in England, c. 1400–c. 1580* (New Haven: Yale University Press, 1992), p. 23. Duffy evocatively describes the procession and other observances of Palm Sunday, pp. 22–27.

35. J. Wickham Legg, ed., *The Sarum Missal* (Oxford: Clarendon Press, 1916), pp. 92–98.

36. Wendy Scase argues persuasively for the liturgy of Palm Sunday (as over against Advent) as a crucial point of reference for the royal entry in general, observing that 'The events of Palm Sunday provided the earthly prototype of the advent of Christ to which the royal entry devisers compared the reception of the earthly monarch.' See Scase, 'Writing and the "Poetics of Spectacle": Political Epiphanies in *The Arrivall of Edward IV* and some contemporary Lancastrian and Yorkist Texts,' in *Images, Idolatry and Iconoclasm*, ed. J. Dimmick, J. Simpson, and N. Zeeman, (Cambridge: Cambridge University Press, 2002), pp. 172–84. She goes on to describe an occasion in the *Arrivall* in which Edward IV was said to have created political capital from a miracle alleged to have occurred in relation to a Palm Sunday procession. Perhaps in the annals of royal propaganda, Palm Sunday was on its way to becoming a kind of floating signifier; the poem 'The Recovery of the Throne by Edward IV' notes that his crucial victory at Towton occurred on that date ('On Palme Sonday he wan the palme of glorye, / And put hys enemyes to endelez langour'). See 'A Political Retrospect,' in *Political Songs and Poems*, ed. Thomas Wright, Rolls series (London, 1861), no. 14, pt. 2, p. 269.

37. A recent, and particularly suggestive, discussion of the late-medieval public is to be found in John Watts, 'The Pressure of the Public on Later Medieval Politics,' in *Fifteenth Century IV*, ed. L. Clark (Woodbridge, Suffolk: Boydell, forthcoming). Watts speaks, relevantly, of 'the sense of a common discursive space; an implicitly national forum to be addressed, but also a treasury—or perhaps an emporium—of acceptable language. To speak, or to write to, or for, or even in, this public was to make a political assertion comparable to that implied in claiming membership of the community; and authority within it was thus distributed very differently, to preachers, poets, prophets and writers of all kinds, rather than to kings and notables.'

38. For an admirable survey and discussion of fourteenth- and fifteenth-century public posting of bills and poems, see Wendy Scase, 'Bill-Casting in Late Medieval England,' *New Medieval Literatures* 2 (1998): 225–47. Allowance must, moreover, be made for the variable literate competencies of its possible readers. This latter problem may, in part, be addressed by more flexible understanding on our part of the nature of late-medieval literacies. Our main advance in the understanding of literacy over the past few decades is in awareness of multiple litera*cies*. That is, the sense that a society enjoys many kinds of functioning literacies: professional, cultivated, and, especially, pragmatic (as influentially first described by M. B. Parkes, 'The Literacy of the Laity,' in *The Medieval World*, ed. D. Daiches and A. Thorlby [London: Aldus Books, 1973], pp. 555–78). Another way of putting this point is that people's literacies were highly eclectic, and even the technically nonlettered would have had surprising areas of recognition, especially of liturgical language. Paralleling this awareness

is the useful concept of the 'textual community'—a more bounded and securely defined grouping than the ephemeral audience of this poem, but still possessed of relevance to it. Such a community (of a sort which the poem, after all, aspires however temporarily to create) need not consist entirely of the literate; in Brian Stock's influential formulation, all that is indispensable to a 'textual community' is *a* reader, one who can read aloud, or explain, or assist in the orientation of a nonreading community to a text. ('Textual communities were not entirely composed of literates. The minimal requirement was just one literate, the *interpres,* who understood a set of texts and was able to pass his message on verbally to others.' See 'History, Literature, Textuality,' in *Listening for the Text* [Baltimore: Johns Hopkins University Press, 1990], p. 23.) Bearing in mind both conceptual points, and also the intensive, Palm Sunday–focused, oral/aural devotional experiences of this poem's likely audience, I should say that a phrasing so familiar as 'Gloria, laus et honor tibi sit, Rex Christe Redemptor' would hardly have been beyond an audience that could read at all, or even a nonliterate audience that could seek to inform itself about the contents of a provocatively posted piece of text.

39. *Chronicon Angliae,* ed. E. M. Thompson, Rolls series, no. 44B (London, 1874), pp. 107, 398.

40. *The Chronicle of Adam Usk, 1377–1421,* ed. C. Given-Wilson (Oxford: Clarendon Press, 1997), pp. 62–63.

41. *Oeuvres de Froissant,* ed. Kervyn de Lettenhove, 25 vols. (Brussels, 1870–72), vol. 16, p. 200.

42. *Chronicque de la Traïson en Mort,* ed. Benjamin Williams (London: English Historical Society, 1846), p. 64.

43. 'The Accusations against Thomas Austin,' ed. A. J. Prescott, in Strohm, *Hochon's Arrow,* p. 175.

44. *Select Cases in the Court of King's Bench under Richard II, Henry IV and Henry V,* ed. G. O. Sayles, Selden Society, vol. 88 (London, 1971), p. 123.

45. *John Vale's Book,* pp. 202–3.

46. James Sherborne, 'Perjury and the Lancastrian Revolution of 1399,' *Welsh History Review* 14 (1988–89): 217–41.

47. *RP,* 5, pp. 463–64.

48. Robbins, *Historical Poems,* no. 93, p. 223.

49. For a poem on Loveday and accompanying notes see Robbins, *Historical Poems,* pp. 194–95.

50. *RP,* 5, p. 346.

51. *John Vale's Book,* p. 142. On the 'political resonance' of 'the many oaths of allegiance to Henry VI sworn by Edward and his father,' with reference to Fortescue, see Watts, *John Vale's Book,* p. 38.

52. *Registrum Abbatiae Johannis Whethamstede,* ed. H. T. Riley, Rolls series, no. 28, vol. 6, pt. 1 (London, 1872), pp. 376–81.

53. *Arrivall,* p. 5. See the more extended discussion of perjury, chap. 1, pp. 26–32. Regarding the 'perjured' steps essential to their own progress to the throne, Richard and his son Edward inclined towards a nonstrenuous view. When the lords at the Parliament of October 1460 mulled over York's claim and expressed concern about 'the grete Othes the which they have made to the Kyng, oure Soverayn Lord, the which may be leyde to the seid Duc of York,' York replied that 'Wherfore sith it is soo, that the mater of the title and clayme of the seid Richard Plantaginet, is openly true and lawfull, and grounded upon evident trouth and justice, it foloweth that man shuld have rather consideration to trouth . . . then to any promise or ooth made by hym into the contrarie' (*RP,* 5, p. 377).

54. *John Vale's Book,* p. 209.

55. See Strohm, *Hochon's Arrow,* p. 71; full references are also given here for the accusations of 1397 and 1399.

56. J. P. Gilson, ed., 'A Defence of the Proscription of the Yorkists in 1459,' *English Historical Review,* 26 (1911): 519 [pp. 512–25].

57. EETS, OS, no. 189 (London, 1937), p. 11.

58. *John Vale's Book,* p. 206.

59. *The Historical Recollections of a Citizen of London,* ed. James Gairdner, Camden Society, 2d ser., 17 (Westminster, 1876–77), p. 195. For his appointment, 9 December 1447, see *Calendar of Patent Rolls,* 1446–52, pp. 185, 401. John Watts has observed in correspondence that this may be a subsequent additional to Gregory's Chronicle, dating from the period 1460–61—thus rendering it additionally significant for the period under present consideration.

60. *Historical Poems,* no. 89, p. 210.

61. On the general subject of treason law in the English Middle Ages, see J. G. Bellamy, *The Law of Treason in England in the Later Middle Ages* (Cambridge: Cambridge University Press, 1970). On the broadening application of the language of treason in the last decades of the fourteenth century, and its enthusiastic appropriation by the Lancastrians in the first decades of the fifteenth, I note Andrew Prescott's unpublished '"The Hand of God": The Suppression of the Peasants' Revolt of 1381.'

62. Stow's 'Historical Memoranda,' in *Three Fifteenth-Century Chronicles,* ed. James Gairdner, Camden Society, n.s. 28 (London, 1880), p. 95.

63. 'The Dijon Recital,' printed by C. A. J. Armstrong, *Bulletin of the Institute of Historical Research,* 33 (1960): p. 63.

64. William Paston to John Paston, 28 January 1460, *Paston Letters,* ed. James Gairdner, vol. 3 (London: Chatto & Windus, 1904), p. 204.

65. Epistle 113 (*Patrologia Latina,* ed. J.-P. Migne, vol. 207).

66. This imagery of cockles and good grain is more fully explored in Miri Rubin, *Corpus Christi: The Eucharist in Late Medieval Culture* (Cambridge: Cambridge University Press, 1991), pp. 312–16. See also Paul Strohm, *Theory and the Premodern Text* (Minneapolis: University of Minnesota Press, 2000), pp. 21–23.

67. On 'community, see Watts, 'The Pressure of the Public.'

68. From the *Anonimalle Chroncile;* see Strohm, *Hochon's Arrow,* pp. 41–42.

69. *John Vale's Book,* pp. 204–5.

70. *John Vale's Book,* pp. 210–12.

71. *Governance of England,* in *John Vale's Book,* pp. 226–27.

72. See Colin Richmond and Margaret Lucille Kekewich, 'The Search for Stability, 1461–1483,' in *John Vale's Book,* pp. 53–55.

73. *Historical Poems,* no. 89, p. 210.

74. On the imaginary aspect of ideology, consider Althusser's influential dictum: 'What is represented in ideology is . . . not the system of the real relations which govern the existence of individuals, but the imaginary relation of those individuals to the real relations in which they live.' *Essays on Ideology* (London: Verso, 1984), p. 39.

75. On the general impression of Richard's overly ardent pursuit of the throne, see chapter 5 of the present study, pp. 210–11.

76. This distinction is documented with considerable elegance in C. A. J. Armstrong, 'The Inauguration Ceremonies of the Yorkist Kings and their Title to the Throne.' Distinguishing between Edward's earlier acclamation and his subsequent coronation, Armstrong observes that 'Perceiving properly that the one was a political act, the other a matter beyond politics, Edward IV or his council dissociated the ceremony of possession from that of coronation.' My own inclination would rather be to regard each as a matter of political deliberation, but to see the former as informed by an interest in expedience, the latter as determined by other considerations of timing and tact. See *Trans. Royal Hist. Soc.,* 4th ser., vol. 30 (1948): 51–73; quotation at p. 68.

77. *Pour une Sociologie du Roman* (Paris: Gallimard, 1964).

78. My final thought about the loyalist Holkham poet is informed by the epigraph, from Hannah Arendt, of a book I recently read, Ron Susskind's *The Price of Loyalty* (New York: Simon & Schuster, 2004), about the current political administration's betrayal of a hopeful servitor, Treasury Secretary Paul O'Neill: 'Total loyalty is possible only when fidelity is emptied of all concrete content, from which changes of mind might naturally arise.'

FIVE. 'ROYAL CHRISTOLOGY' AND YORK'S PAPER CROWN

1. Stephen Greenblatt, *Hamlet in Purgatory* (Princeton: Princeton University Press, 2001), esp. pp. 248–54. Greenblatt argues that the years intervening between the end of the fifteenth and the end of the sixteenth century detached the materials of Catholic sacramentality from their cultural basis, opening them to an afterlife of theatrical reappropriation. While accepting the overall contour of this argument,

I would like to adjust its application in at least two imporant respects. First of all, with respect to the medieval period, I would say that Greenblatt rather unaccountably loses hold of his own starting point as well as its corollary. As he himself so spectacularly demonstrates at the outset, medieval theology always and inevitably possesses its own theatrical component. The corollary is that the meta-theater of both periods *always* provided a privileged site for such reconsideration and renewal of the terms and conditions of sacredness. Second, as I have meant to suggest throughout, I do not think that the line between a 'spiritual' Middle Ages and a 'secular' early modern period can ever satisfactorily be drawn. For a view consistent with mine, and perhaps a bit more adamant, see Sarah Beckwith: 'Greenblatt fails to see the centrality of performance to medieval and Reformation religiosity in both its theological and theatrical senses. This is ultimately why he can see theater as replacing purgatory/religion. . . . Shakespeare's theater does not represent the supercession and succession of religion, purgatory, and ritual action by a disenchanted theater, but the persistence of its historical concerns in the incarnation of performance.' 'Stephen Greenblatt's *Hamlet* and the Forms of Oblivion,' *Journal of Medieval and Early Modern Studies* 33 (2003): 272, 275.

2. *Gregory's Chronicle,* ed. James Gairdner, Camden Society, 2d ser., 17 (1876): p. 197.

3. Apparent precedents might be found in the abusive dismemberment of Simon de Montfort's body after the battle of Evesham in 1265 and the execution of the captive Thomas earl of Lancaster by Edward II at Pontefract in 1322. But Simon de Montfort had previously been slain in battle, and Lancaster died by public execution following a formal proclamation of treason and a subsequent judicial procedure. On Simon de Montfort, see Charles Bémont, *Simon de Montfort,* trans. E. F. Jacob (Oxford: Clarendon Press, 1930), pp. 242–43. On the death of Thomas duke of Lancaster see T. F. T. Plucknett, 'The Origin of Impeachment,' *Transactions of the Royal Historical Society,* 4th ser., 24 (1942): 57; see also *RP,* 2, p. 3.

4. Philippe de Commynes, *Mémoires,* ed. Contamine (n.p.: Imprimerie Nationale, 1994), III, chap. 5, p.192: 'il montoit à cheval et crioit qu'on sauvast le peuple et que on tuast les seigneurs; car de ceulx n'eschapoient nul ou bien peu.' Commynes adds that, upon his departure from Flanders in 1471, Edward had resolved no longer to spare the common soldiers, because of his anger at the commons for their support of the earl of Warwick, and for other causes (III, chap. 7).

5. *English Chronicle,* ed. J. S. Davies, Camden Society, orig. ser., 64 (1856): p. 97. See also, in this same regard, 'Chronicle of the Rebellion in Lincolnshire,' *Camden Miscellany,* no. 1, Camden Society, orig. ser., 39 (1847): 10.

6. *Gregory's Chronicle,* p. 210.

7. *Gregory's Chronicle,* p. 211. This is the astonishing account in which 'a madde woman kembyd hys here and wysche a way the blode of hys face, and she gate candellys and sette a-boute hym brennynge, moo then a c.'

8. *Gregory's Chronicle*, p. 211.

9. Lambeth MS 306, printed in *Three Fifteenth-Century Chronicles*, ed. James Gairdner, Camden Society, 2d ser. 28 (1880): 77–78.

10. Warkworth, *Chronicle*, ed. J. O. Halliwell, Camden Society, orig. ser., (1839): 8–9.

11. Warkworth, *Chronicle*, p. 19. See also the *Arrivall*, ed. John Bruce, Camden Society, orig. ser., (1838), in which a tribunal headed by Richard duke of Gloucester, as Constable of England, passed the sentences. The author comments that the prisoners were, 'upon a scaffolde therefore made, behedyd evereche one, and without eny other dismembringe, or setting up, licensyd to be buryed' (p. 177)—treated, that is, respectfully. On a similar massacre of Lancastrian fugitives who had taken refuge in the parish church at Didbrook, see P. W. Hammond, *The Battles of Barnet and Tewkesbury* (New York: St. Martins, 1990), p. 14 and note. For an interpretation more favorable to Edward IV, insisting that he exercised relative clemency after Tewkesbury and that the men slain had all abused his past generosity, see Charles Ross, *Edward IV* (New Haven: Yale University Press, 1974), p. 172.

12. Warkworth, *Chronicle*, p. 19. On Fortescue's initial appearance on a list of those slain, see MS Phillipps 9735, f. 279. Printed in *The Paston Letters*, ed. James Gairdner, vol. 5 (London, 1904), p. 104.

13. *Crowland Chronicle Continuations 1459–1486*, ed. N. Pronay and J. Cox (Gloucester: Alan Sutton, 1986), pp. 122–23. *Gregory's Chronicle* has him slain, in the field, but nevertheless says that he 'cryede for socoure to his brother-in-lawe the Duke of Clarence' (p. 18).

14. *Arrivall*, p. 38.

15. *Mémoires*, II, chap. 2, p. 117.

16. Charles Ross, *The Wars of the Roses: A Concise History* (London: Thames and Hudson, 1976), pp. 135–40; A. J. Pollard, *The Wars of the Roses*, 2d ed. (Basingstoke: Palgrave, 2001), pp. 68–72.

17. J. R. Lander, *Crown and Nobility, 1450–1509* (London: Edward Arnold, 1976), p. 62.

18. A. J. Pollard, ed., *The Wars of the Roses* (Basingstoke: Macmillan, 1995), p. 18. For a similar comment, see Ross, *Wars of the Roses*, p. 173.

19. 'Zur Kritik der Gewalt,' *Gesammelte Schriften*, vol. 2:1 (Frankfort: Suhrkamp Verlag, 1972), esp. pp. 199–203; for translation, see 'Critique of Violence,' *Reflections* (New York: Schocken Books, 1978), pp. 296–300.

20. I borrow this phrase from James C. Scott, *Weapons of the Weak: Everyday Forms of Peasant Resistance* (New Haven: Yale University Press, 1985).

21. My fuller discussion of these materials in the light of Benjamin's notion of *bloße Leben*, supplemented by additional perspectives of Georgio Agamben, is scheduled for separate appearance in a special issue of *Journal of Medieval and Early Modern Studies*, winter 2005.

22. *Wilhelmi Wyrcester Annales* (Heralds' College MS 48), in *Letters and Papers Illustrative of the Wars of the English in France . . .*, ed. Joseph Stevenson, Rolls series, no. 22, vol. 2, pt. 2 (London, 1864), p. 775. That Worcester was not actually the author of the anonymous (and multiply authored) *Annales* attributed to him was established by K. B. McFarlane, 'William Worcester: A Preliminary Survey,' *England in the Fifteenth Century* (London: Hambledon Press, 1981), pp. 209–10.

23. Another chronicle source that does not mention the paper crown does imply its presence by saying that York's head was displayed 'obprobiose' on the walls of York, together with those of others slain. College of Arms MS Arundel 5, in *Three Fifteenth-Century Chronicles*, pp. 171–72.

24. *Chronicles of the Reigns of Edward I and Edward II*, ed. William Stubbs, Rolls series, no. 76, vol. 1 (London, 1882), p. 90.

25. Stubbs, *Chronicles*, p. 139.

26. *Register*, p. 377.

27. *Crowland Chronicle Continuations 1459–86*, p. 111.

28. Hall, *The Vnion of the Two Noble and Illustre Famelies of Lancastre & Yorke*, 1548, f. 183r.

29. *Gregory's Chronicle* describes his confinement in the bishop's palace in London, and the duke's mocking 'torchelyght' visit, p. 208.

30. *The Mirror for Magistrates*, ed. Lily B. Campbell (Cambridge: Cambridge University Press, 1938), pp. 181–90.

31. For a recent overview of the intersections of fifteenth-century political and religious language and symbolism, see Miri Rubin, 'Religious Symbols and Political Culture in Fifteenth-Century England,' in *Fifteenth Century IV*, ed. L. Clark (Woodbridge, Suffolk: Boydell, forthcoming), pp. 1–12.

32. *Actes and Monuments* (1563), Magdalen College Arch. B. I. 4, p. 240b.

33. A subsequent addition. Printed as *The Acts and Monuments of John Foxe*, 4th ed., ed. J. Pratt (London: Religious Tract Society, n.d.), vol. 4, p. 453. With respect to typicality, we read of the martyrdom of Frances San Romane, 'As he was led to the place of suffering, they put vpon him a Miter of paper, paynted full of deuils, after the Spanish guise' (from the 1583 edition, vol. 2, p. 930). The variety of my Foxe references is a consequence of the numerous changes and augmentations of that volume in the course of its early printing history.

34. *Ecclesiastical History*, publ. John Day (Magdalen Authors, Magd. T. 136), vol. 2, p. 1398.

35. *Registrum Abbatiae Johannis Whethamstede*, ed. H. T. Riley, Rolls series, no. 28, vol. 6, pt. 1 (London, 1872). The account in question occurs at pp. 382–83.

36. *York Mystery Plays*, ed. Lucy Toulmin Smith (New York: Russell and Russell, 1963), p. 334.

37. Euan Cameron, *The European Reformation* (Oxford: Clarendon Press, 1991), pp. 90, 120. Cameron, of course, is here summarizing a highly complex and

multiplicitous theological discussion, which in sixteenth-century England found the sacrifice of Christ to be iterable only as symbol (in what might be called the 'Zwinglian' analysis); to be at once commemorative and to involve Christ's actual presence (in the theology of Cranmer, expressed in language of the Book of Common Prayer); and actually to be iterable in the traditional sense (in Lutheran theology).

38. I should say that my first expectation was to discover a gulf between sixteenth-century 'catholic' and 'protestant' martyrdoms, and in this respect I was somewhat confounded by a phenomenon we all recognize within our fields of actual specialization: that certain tendencies, beliefs, and forms of expression are widely shared out within an entire society, bypassing artificial distinctions of 'high' and 'low,' 'orthodox' and 'heterodox,' 'loyal' and 'traitorous.' By this rule, a certain reserve about the repeatability of Christ's sacrifice may be discovered within 'catholic' as well as 'protestant' hagiography. All parties show increased deference to the unique status of Christ's original sacrifice and a hesitance to conclude that each and every martyr presents an image or a true copy of the crucifixion itself.

39. On the sixteenth-century reluctance, even of Catholic martyrdoms, to presume upon Christological parallels, see Brad S. Gregory, *Salvation at Stake: Christian Martyrdom in Early Modern Europe* (Cambridge, Mass.: Harvard University Press, 1999), pp. 285-87.

40. I borrow the phrase 'royal Christology' from Ernst H. Kantorowicz, *The King's Two Bodies: A Study in Medieval Political Theology* (Princeton: Princeton University Press, 1957), p. 16.

41. This is, especially, Tillyard's view in *Shakespeare's History Plays* (London: Chatto and Windus, 1944), supplemented by his persuasive account of philosophical and cultural unity in his *Elizabethan World Picture* (London: Chatto and Windus, 1943).

42. For a general account of these developments, see Graham Holderness's introduction to *Shakespeare's History Plays: Richard II to Henry V* (New York: St. Martin's Press, 1992), pp. 1-61.

43. Richard C. McCoy, *Alterations of State: Sacred Kingship in the English Reformation* (New York: Columbia University Press, 2002), p. 69.

44. Consider, in this respect, David Kastan's argument that, despite arguments to the contrary, little evidence of 'providential pattern' informs these plays; that theirs is the 'fallen' world of politics and contingent, rather than providential, action. See Kastan, 'The Shape of Time: Form and Value in the Shakespearean History Play,' *Comparative Drama* 7 (1973-74): 259-78.

45. John Phillips, *The Reformation of Images: Destruction of Art in England, 1535-1660* (Berkeley: University of California Press, 1973), pp. 204-5.

46. McCoy, *Alterations of State*, p. 15.

47. Kantorowicz, *The King's Two Bodies*, esp. pp. 7-41.

48. May McKisack, *The Fourteenth Century, 1307–1399* (Oxford: Oxford University Press, 1959), p. 429.

49. James Hamilton Wylie, *The Reign of Henry V,* vol. 1 (1914; New York: Greenwood, 1968), pp. 470–71.

50. This transcendent dimension was figured in the French crown which, as Kantorowicz has reminded us, was dual, containing a thorn from the crown of thorns—therefore at once both crown and relic (*The King's Two Bodies,* p. 339).

51. Kantorowicz observes that, by the end of the Middle Ages, images of the king as image and vicar of God had somewhat supplanted those of vicar of Christ (*The King's Two Bodies,* see pp. 93, 159). But, as the materials of this study will suggest, the Christological imagery never dropped completely from view.

52. Peter Brown, *The Cult of the Saints* (Chicago: University of Chicago Press, 1982), p. 78.

53. Lecture, Pacific Film Archive, 1994. The endlessly resourceful Kantorowicz has noted the same phenomenon, pointing out that an act of 1495 absolved followers of both Lancaster and York of attainder, erasing legal difficulties resulting from 'the former coexistence of two anti-kings or, say we may say, two "Bodies natural," but the existence of only one Crown, one "Body politic"' (*The King's Two Bodies,* p. 372).

54. *Eikon Basilike,* ed. Philip A Knachel (Ithaca: Cornell University Press, 1966), p. 28.

55. C. V. Wedgwood, *A Coffin for King Charles* (New York: Macmillan, 1964), p. 222.

56. Andrew Lacey, *The Cult of King Charles the Martyr* (Woodbridge: Boydell Press, 2003), esp. pp. 18–48.

57. Holinshed, *The Third Volume of Chronicles . . . now augmented . . . to the Year 1586* (n.p.), p. 659.

58. I cannot speculate on Abraham Fleming's motivation in restoring this passage. Another element of textual memory somewhat underplayed by traditional 'source studies' is the sheer adventitiousness of some developments, the sway of the accidental in matters of textual preservation. My impression of his modus operandi is that restoration of the Whethamstede account is less a matter of dogma than some combination of antiquarianism and dutiful pedantry, hand-in-hand with the venerable chronicle habit of comparing sources ('Some say . . . others said') in the service of the chroniclers' own reputation for even-handed veracity. Whethamstede, in keeping with this 'comparative' approach to sources, receives marginal credit for his contribution, as does Hall for his preceding account. However bland the reasoning behind its inclusion, the coupling of the Whethamstede material to the *Annales*-Hall account assures the continued, though subordinated, availability of several threatened fifteenth-century possibilities. I want to suggest that Shakespeare's account takes a

certain implicit advantage of its availability. I would suppose that Shakespeare himself was attracted to this account for *his* own reasons; for its inherent theatricality, rather than for any points of dogma involved. But once revived, and reinstituted, the text displays its vitality by stimulating a repropagation of its own effaced assumptions. On multiple authorship and multivocality, see Annabel Patterson, *Reading Holinshed's Chronicles* (Chicago: University of Chicago Press, 1994), esp. pp. 22-31.

59. Quarto edition. Printed as *The True Tragedy of Richard, Duke of York, 1600* (Tudor Facsimile Texts, 1913). Principal quotations will be taken, for convenience, from Shakespeare, *Complete Works,* ed. Wells and Taylor (Oxford: Clarendon Press, 1988). Selective citations from the quarto will be cited for comparative purposes, in cases of significant deviation.

60. As argued in David M. Bergeron, 'The Play-within-a-Play in *3 Henry VI,*' *Tennessee Studies in Literature* 22 (1977): 37-45.

61. Modern editorial tradition accepts this supposition, inserting a stage direction after l. 96, dictating the placing of a 'paper crown' on York's head, in place of Whethamstede's marsh grass or Holinshed's bulrushes. Authority for this editorial gesture includes the reprise of this situation we are given in *Richard III,* when Richard taunts Margaret with recollection of the time 'When thou didst crown his warlike brows with paper' (1.3.172). See *William Shakespeare: A Textual Commentary,* ed. Stanley Wells and Gary Taylor (New York: Norton, 1997), p. 201.

62. Michael O'Connell, *The Idolatrous Eye: Iconoclasm & Theater in Early-Modern England* (New York: Oxford University Press, 2000), p. 88.

63. Kantorowicz, *The King's Two Bodies,* pp. 271-72.

SIX. POSTSCRIPT: TUDOR *FACTION*

1. I borrow this term from Hans Robert Jauss, *Toward an Aesthetic of Reception* (Minneapolis: University of Minnesota Press, 1982), pp. 29-30.

2. Hall, *Vnion* (1548), p. vi.

3. Simon Adams comments that '"Faction", either as a noun or in its adjectival form "factious", was one of the most over-used words in the Elizabethan political vocabulary.' See 'Faction, Clientage and Party: English Politics, 1550-1603,' in *Leicester and the Court: Essays in Elizabethan Politics* (Manchester: Manchester University Press, 2002), pp. 13-23; quotation at p. 13.

4. *A Book of London English, 1384-1425,* ed. R. W. Chambers and M. Daunt (Oxford: Clarendon Press, 1931), pp. 31-32.

5. *The Serpent of Division,* ed. H. N. MacCracken (Oxford: Oxford University Press, 1911), pp. 58, 62.

6. 'A Defense of the Proscription of the Yorkists in 1459,' *English Historical Review,* 26 (1911): 516.

7. For other midcentury appearances of *partie* as a temporary coalition for unscrupulous advantage, see Falconbridge's 1471 Letter to London ('the paretie of the usurper of our . . . liege lordes Crownne') and the *Arrivall* ('to fortefye theyr partye'—p. 16). The Falcolnbridge letter is transcribed and printed in Reginald R. Sharpe, *London and the Kingdom*, vol. 3 (London: Longmans, 1894), pp. 387–88.

8. John Fisher, *The Funeral Sermon of Margaret Countess of Richmond and Derby*, ed. J. Hymers (Cambridge: Cambridge Univerity Press, 1840), p. 116.

9. Louvain: J. Fowler, 1572.

10. *Vnion*, (1548), p. 184.

11. J. A. Sharpe, *Early Modern England: A Social History, 1550–1760* (London: Edward Arnold, 1987), p. 11.

12. Robert Naunton, *Fragmenta Regalia* (1642; rpt. London: Charles Baldwyn, 1824), p. 8.

13. He adds that 'By blowing alternately hot and cold upon the rival factions, by promoting members of each to positions where they could act as checks upon the other, she managed to stave off the constant threat of serious aristocratic disorder.' *The Crisis of the Aristocracy, 1558–1641* (Oxford: Clarendon Press, 1965), p. 233. Useful reviews of the extent of factional dissention during Elizabeth's reign are to be found in David Loades, *The Tudor Court* (London: Batsford, 1986), 'Faction and Political Strife,' esp. pp. 163–66; and David Loades, *Politics and the Nation, 1450–1660* (Fontana/Collins, 1973), esp. pp. 275–300. In this chapter, rather oddly entitled 'The Years of Stability,' he observes, 'Elizabeth herself was surprisingly supine in her attitude, even after the rising of 1569 had demonstrated once again the political threat latent in such unruliness. She was more concerned to keep the quarreling groups in a state of equilibrium than to put an end to their anti-social behaviour' (p. 297). More recent discussions of Tudor factionalism include David Starkey, 'From Feud to Faction,' *History Today* 32 (November 1982): 16–22; and Simon Adams, 'Favourites and Factions at the Elizabethan Court,' in *Leicester and the Court*, pp. 46–67. Adams is especially valuable, although his own choice is to use the word 'faction' in a more limited sense than that in which it was employed by the Elizabethans themselves.

14. '"I am Richard II, know ye not that?"' Reported by John Nichols in *The Progresses and Public Processions of Queen Elizabeth*, 2d ed., (1823), iii, p. 552.

glossarial index

Vernacular Political Terminology, c. 1395–1559

[Bold type indicates pages on which a term is defined or extensively discussed]

general index

[the appendices to chapters 1 and 4 are unindexed]

PAUL STROHM

is William B. Ransford Professor of Medieval Literature
at Columbia University.